Rev. Mark D. Lottis

Notre Dame

1992

THE MAKING OF MODERN THEOLOGY

19TH AND 20TH CENTURY THEOLOGICAL TEXTS

This series of theological texts is designed to introduce a new generation of readers — theological students, students of religion, ordained ministers and the interested general reader — to the writings of some of those Christian theologians who, since the beginning of the 19th century, have had a formative influence on the development of Christian theology. Each volume in the series is intended to introduce the theologian, to trace the emergence of key or seminal ideas and insights, particularly within their social and historical context, and to show how they have contributed to the making of modern theology. The primary way in which this is done is by allowing the theologians chosen to address us in their own words.

There are three sections to each volume. The Introduction includes a short biography of the theologian, and an overview of his or her theology in relation to the texts which have been selected for study. The Selected Texts, the bulk of each volume, consist largely of substantial edited selections from the theologian's writings. Each text is also introduced with information about its origin and its significance. The guiding rule in making the selection of texts has been the question: in what way has this particular theologian contributed to the shaping of contemporary theology? A Select Bibliography provides guidance for those who wish to read further both in the primary literature and in secondary sources.

Available in this series

1 Friedrich Schleiermacher: Pioneer of modern theology
2 Rudolf Bultmann: Interpreting faith for the modern era
3 Paul Tillich: Theologian of the boundaries
4 Dietrich Bonhoeffer: Witness to Jesus Christ
5 Karl Barth: Theologian of Freedom

Karl Barth 1886-1968

THE MAKING OF MODERN THEOLOGY

19th and 20th Century Theological Texts
General Editor: John de Gruchy

KARL BARTH

Theologian of Freedom

CLIFFORD GREEN

COLLINS

Collins Liturgical Publications
8 Grafton Street, London W1X 3LA

Harper & Row
Icehouse One — 401
151 Union Street, San Francisco, CA 94111-1299

Collins Liturgical in Canada
c/o Novalis, Box 9700, Terminal,
375 Rideau St, Ottawa, Ontario K1G 4B4

Collins Dove
PO Box 316, Blackburn, Victoria 3130

Collins Liturgical New Zealand
PO Box 1, Auckland

ISBN 0-00-599129-3 (cased)
ISBN 0-00-599128-5 (paperback)

First published 1989

Typographical design Colin Reed
Typeset by Swains (Glasgow) Limited
Printed in Glasgow

CONTENTS

CONTENTS

ABBREVIATIONS

———

Barth is the author unless another is indicated. For complete titles and publication details, see the Select Bibliography.

A *Anselm: Fides Quaerens Intellectum*
AS *Against the Stream*
CD *Church Dogmatics;* the reference is given in the form: volume/part, page
HG "The Humanity of God"
KB *Karl Barth,* by Eberhard Busch
M *Wolfgang Amadeus Mozart*
N "No! Answer to Emil Brunner"
R *The Epistle to the Romans*
RP *Karl Barth and Radical Politics,* ed. George Hunsinger

ON TRANSLATIONS AND NOTES

Changes in translations have been made where accuracy or consistency required them, but these are not indicated by notes unless an important question of meaning is involved. Orthography has been changed to be consistent throughout.

The most consistent change in translations concerns the German generic *Mensch*, *Menschen* and their compounds, virtually always rendered in English by the sexist "man" and its variants. Such translations do not even attempt to express in English the inclusiveness (imperfect though it may be) of the German language. Barth always used *Mensch* and *Menschen* for the generic, never *Mann* or *Männer*. He believed that the political restriction of women, especially, was "an arbitrary convention which does not deserve to be preserved any longer" (below, 285); and he at least tried to develop a theology of genuine sexual equality and reciprocity (cf. CD III/4, 116ff.). Hence, the German generic nouns have been variously rendered here by human being, humanity, person, people, men and women, etc. This is to read Barth *in optimam partem*, as he urged his students to treat even those theologians they strongly disagreed with. But, in the interest of historical accuracy, I have resisted my desire to make other changes, particularly in the male pronouns referring to God; they are the historical warts for all to see.

In reprinting the selections from Barth, his citations and footnotes have usually been omitted unless necessary for the meaning; the reader may always consult them in the original publications as indicated at the individual texts. Where notes to the selections are not from Barth himself, they are indicated as from a translator or editor who is identified by initials.

ACKNOWLEDGEMENTS

The publishers acknowledge with thanks permission to reproduce the following copyright texts from works by Karl Barth:

by permission of Scottish Academic Press:
    pp. 31-52 from *God Grace and Gospel* trans. James Strathearn McNab. Copyright © 1959 by Scottish Academic Press

by permission of SCM Press Ltd:
    pp. 534-40 from *Protestant Theology in the 19th Century*. Copyright © 1959 by SCM Press Ltd
    pp. 8f, 13f, 73-78 from *Anselm: Fides Quaerens Intellectum*. Copyright © 1960 by SCM Press Ltd
    pp. 15-50, 113-118, 127-146 from *Against the Stream*. Copyright © 1954 by SCM Press Ltd

by permission of Oxford University Press:
    pp. 42-51, 91-107 from *The Epistle to the Romans*, trans. Edwyn C. Hoskins. Copyright © 1933 by Oxford University Press

by permission of Wm Eerdmans Publishing Co:
    pp. 264-71 from *Fiat Justitia* from *The Christian Life. Church Dogmatics IV/4. Lecture Fragments*. Copyright © 1981 by Wm Eerdmans Publishing Co
    pp. 55-56 from *Wolfgang Amadeus Mozart*. Copyright © 1986 by Wm Eerdmans Publishing Co

by permission of Theologischer Verlag Zurich:
    pp. 67-69, 74-76, 78-94 from *Natural Theology*. Copyright © 1934 by Theologischer Verlag Zurich

by permission of Westminster Press:
    pp. 19-37 from *Jesus Christ and the Movement for Social Justice*, from *Karl Barth and Radical Politics*, edited and trans. by George Hunsinger. Copyright © 1976 by Westminster Press

by permission of T & T Clark Ltd:
    Church Dogmatics, I/1, 390-91; II/1, 172-78; II/2, 52-55, 58-59; III/1,

ACKNOWLEDGEMENTS

91-97, 230-232; III/2, 132-139; III/3, 239-43, 297-99; III/4, 479-80; IV/1, 3-20, 183, 186-88, 244-48, 330-32, 650-56, 674-76; IV/2, 50-51, 614-21, 651-57

by permission of Sciences Religieuses/Studies in Religion:
pp. 117-135 from Sciences Religieuses/Studies in Religion 7/2, Spring 1978. Trans. George Hunsinger

by permission of the Journal of Theology for Southern Africa:
Barmen Declaration, from Journal of Theology for Southern Africa, vol 47, June 1984. Trans. Douglas S. Bax

by permission of John Howard Yoder:
pp. 134-37, Petition of the Bruderschaften on Atomic Weapons (1958) from *Karl Barth and the Problem of War*. Nashville, Abingdon, 1970

by permission of John D. Godsey
pp. 100-101, "Outline of Karl Barth's *Church Dogmatics*" from *Karl Barth's Table Talk*

The editor also wishes to thank the following colleagues for their suggestions and their help in obtaining several texts: Dr Hinrich Stoevesandt, Karl Barth-Archiv, Basel; Professor George Hunsinger, Bangor Theological Seminary; Professor John de Gruchy, University of Cape Town; Professor John Howard Yoder, University of Notre Dame; Professor Martin Rumscheidt, Atlantic School of Theology; Professor John Godsey, Wesley Theological Seminary; Professor James Buckley, Loyola College; Dr Paul Santmire, Hartford; special thanks also to Teri Vaughn of Hartford Seminary for her work on the indexes.

INTRODUCTION
KARL BARTH'S LIFE AND THEOLOGY

Karl Barth's favorite theological painting, which hung over his desk, was Grünewald's Crucifixion from the Isenheim Altar. In it John the Baptist points with elongated index finger to the figure of Jesus on the Cross. Also hanging in the study — level with Calvin, as Barth delighted to point out — was a picture of his favorite composer, Wolfgang Amadeus Mozart. Mozart, Barth said in one of his essays on the composer, "was remarkably free from the mania for self-expression" (CD III/3, 298), and his music likewise invited the listeners "to venture just a little out of the snail's shell" of their own subjectivity (M, 50).[1]*

These paintings are parables; they point to God's free grace and goodness rather than to the human believer. They point to the central theme of Barth's theology: the God who encounters us in Jesus Christ is "the One who loves in freedom" (CD II/1, 257).

When Barth made his first and only trip to the United States in 1962 he urged American theologians to develop a theology of freedom. Even the Statue of Liberty, he said, when properly demythologized, could be a symbol of a true theology of freedom. In its cultural and political expressions such a theology of freedom would liberate Americans from inferiority complexes vis-à-vis Europe and superiority complexes vis-à-vis Asia and Africa. It would also be

> marked by freedom from fear of communism, Russia, inevitable nuclear warfare and . . . all the aforementioned principalities and powers. Freedom *for* which you stand would be the freedom *for* — I like to say a single word — humanity. . . . It would be necessarily a theology of freedom, of that freedom to which the Son frees us, and which, as his gift, is the one real human freedom.[2]

These spontaneous remarks, like the paintings in his study, disclose the same point to be found throughout the *Church Dogmatics*: the center of Barth's theology is the freedom of God acting in love toward humanity in Jesus Christ, which sets us free in all spheres of life — politics, art, economics, science, and especially theology and church — for a life of co-humanity and the praise of God.

---

* Footnotes indicated by figures are on pp. 329ff.

To be sure, we must say at once that Barth's doctrine of freedom is not the libertarian, laissez-faire notion that popular culture has adapted from John Locke, John Stuart Mill, Adam Smith and others. Rather, in the tradition of the Bible, Augustine and classical theology, genuine freedom has content; it is not merely the power to choose without any regard for *what* one chooses. Hence freedom is both a freedom *from* evils and oppressions — in a word, sin — and above all a freedom *for* an authentically human life with God and with our human companions — in a word, humanity. That is the import of Barth's reference to John 8.36: "If the Son makes you free, you will be free indeed."[3]

What sort of man was Karl Barth, this theologian who some have compared to the great classical theologians — Augustine, St. Thomas, Luther and Calvin? The best witness to that is his own writing, but here to introduce him are three vignettes by Dietrich Bonhoeffer, a younger contemporary; Eberhard Busch, for a time Barth's assistant and then his biographer; and John Updike, the novelist whom Barth's writings once helped in a quite personal way. First Bonhoeffer:

> Barth is even better than his books. There is an openness, a willingness to listen to relevant criticism, and at the same time such an intensity of concentration on and impetus pressing for the subject which can be discussed proudly or with modesty, dogmatically or with tentativeness, and it is certainly not meant primarily to serve his own theology.[4]

Eberhard Busch said that when all Barth's writings are published, especially all his letters,

> a rather unique figure will become visible there, someone in whom tenderness and harshness, merriment and a readiness to do battle, openness and reserve, attentiveness and withdrawal, boyish flippancy and adult charm, painful questioning and unbounded confidence, modesty and a full-blown self-consciousness were closely side by side, rubbing one against the other.[5]

John Updike, who tends to focus on the early Barth, was somewhat surprised that a theologian, of all people, could so obviously enjoy living in the world.

> Karl Barth's insistence on the otherness of God seemed to free him to be exceptionally ... appreciative and indulgent of this world, the world at hand. His humor and love of combat, his capacity for friendship even with his ideological opponents, his fondness for his tobacco and other physical comforts, his tastes in art and entertainment were heartily worldly, worldly not in the fashion of those who

accept this life as a way-station and testing ground but of those who embrace it as a piece of Creation.[6]

BARTH'S THEOLOGICAL EXISTENCE

Karl Barth was born on 10 May, 1886 in the city of Basel where he was to spend most of his life.[7] Theology ran in the family; both Barth's grandfathers were pastors in Basel. His parents, Johann Friedrich Barth and Anna Katharina Sartorius were also natives of Basel. Fritz, as the father was known, had recently moved from a pastorate to a teaching position at the College of Preachers, a new institution to train preachers in biblical theology over against the prevailing liberal theology. The photo of Fritz above Barth's desk hints that the father's theological pilgrimage was in a real way a model for the son. In 1888 Fritz was called to succeed Adolf Schlatter in Berne, and here Karl spent his youth.

Barth studied theology in Berne, Berlin, Tübingen and Marburg. He began in 1904 at Berne where, along with student politics and "living it up," he learned the ruling methodology of modern Protestant theology, the historical-critical method. In the semester at Berlin he studied intensely with Harnack, "*the* theologian of the day" (KB, 39), and read Kant thoroughly. He drank deeply at the well of liberal theology, becoming a devotee of Schleiermacher (later to be his chief antagonist) and Wilhelm Herrmann. Barth completed his theological examinations in 1908 and was ordained by his father in the Berne cathedral. He summarized his theological education this way:

I had made myself a committed disciple of the "modern" school, which was still dominant up to the time of the First World War, and was regarded as the only school worth belonging to. In it, according to the teaching of Schleiermacher and Ritschl, Christianity was interpreted on the one hand as an historical phenomenon to be subjected to critical examination, and on the other hand as a matter of inner experience, of a predominantly moral nature. So I was not badly equipped in the autumn of 1906 for taking up a post as editorial assistant on the *Christliche Welt*, a leading journal of the school, which was published in Marburg under the editorship of Professor Martin Rade (KB, 46).

In 1909 Barth left the academic world for the pastorate, serving first as assistant pastor in a German Reformed congregation in Geneva. Here his encounter with the industrial proletariat prepared him for service from 1911 to 1921 in the parish of Safenwil, Canton Aargau. It was a village of less than 2,000 people in a region changing from agriculture to industry; three quarters of the employees worked in factories, mostly producing textiles.

His biographer describes Barth's role in Safenwil as "Comrade Pastor," and this period is certainly the time of his most overt action and teaching as a socialist. He looked back in 1927 and wrote of the "class warfare, which was going on in my parish, before my very eyes, [which] introduced me almost for the first time to the real problems of real life" (KB, 69). In 1911 he gave the lecture on "Jesus Christ and the Movement for Social Justice" reprinted below (pp. 98-114). Another lecture in 1914 discussed "Gospel and Socialism," and his sermons that summer linked God and socialism. Belief in God is revolutionary, he argued. In one published sermon he said that "'the evil' of capitalism was the consequence of a world without God [and] he contrasted this with the Christian hope of a new world brought into being by the 'living God.'" "We should expect more of God," he wrote in another article, and look for something better "beyond war and capitalism."[8] "Socialism," he proclaimed in one sermon, "is a very important and necessary application of the gospel" (KB, 80).[9] In a 1916 essay on "The Righteousness of God" he said that "the capitalistic order and . . . the war" were "the two greatest atrocities of life."[10] And in the first edition of his *Romans* we find perhaps the strongest statement of all: a time will come "when the now-dying embers of Marxist dogma will flare up anew as world truth, when the socialist church will rise from the dead in a world become socialist."[11]

Barth not only preached, lectured and wrote about socialism. He was also a practical activist, helping to organize three trade unions. He gave courses for workers on issues like "working hours, banking [and] women's work" (KB, 88), and interpreted events like the general strike, national and international socialist conferences, and the Russian revolution. He studied factory legislation and insurance, and read the Swiss *Trade Union Journal* and the *Textile Worker*. Despite his bitter disappointment with the involvement of socialists in World War I, in 1915 he joined the Social Democratic Party[12] and was active in party politics, attending the party conference as an official delegate. He was an open partisan in public disputes with capitalists and factory owners in Safenwil,[13] consistently taking the side of the workers even where this led to serious conflict in his congregation.

While such partisanship was necessary, Barth was characteristically independent. In a still unpublished sketch from 1915 on the future of socialism, Barth did not interpret socialism simply in terms of class struggle. Rather, as Jüngel reports, Barth held that "the content of socialism must be identified as justice for humanity, not merely as improvement of the lot of the working class. . . . The innermost essence of socialism should surely be a passion for justice for each and every person. . . ."[14] Later in the Introduction we must discuss further the relation of Barth's theology and socialism. For the present we may observe that his biographer quotes Barth to sum up the Safenwil period as follows: "above all he devoted himself, 'alongside of ministry, especially to socialism. . . .'"[15]

Barth regarded preaching as the chief task of his ministry, and he began with the Marburg gospel of religious experience. In retrospect he felt that he had failed the people of Safenwil. Why? Looking back many years later in his lecture on "The Humanity of God" (see below), Barth summarized the ruling neo-Protestant[16] theology and his own at the time as "*religionistic, anthropocentric,* and in this sense *humanistic.*" For this theology,

> to think about God meant . . ., with scarcely any attempt to hide the fact, to think of human experience, particularly of the Christian religious experience. To speak about God meant to speak about humanity, no doubt in elevated tone, but once more and now more than ever about human revelations and miracles, about human faith and human works. What did it know and what had it still to say about God's divinity? (HG, below 48.)

A theology whose theme was the religion, morality and "secret divinity" of humankind was not, Barth discovered, the theme of the Bible. A theology whose God was a "pious notion," a symbol of the heights and depths of the human psyche, really could not bring a true word of challenge and comfort, a genuinely freeing Word of the Lord. Such religious solipsism and self-justification which imprisoned humanity in itself was most decisively exposed for Barth at the outbreak of World War I.

On 1 August, 1914, the day Germany declared war, ninety-three German intellectuals published a manifesto in support of the war policy of Kaiser Wilhelm II. Among them were most of Barth's theology professors, including Harnack and Herrmann; Harnack even wrote a speech for the Kaiser supporting the war.[17] This theological support for the war finally signalled for Barth the bankruptcy of the liberal theology he had learned. Looking back to see where theology went astray, he came to fix on Schleiermacher. He was similarly dismayed with European socialists who, after recently vowing to offer international resistance to war, predictably rallied around the nationalistic flags of their nations. Barth, for whom there was always an intimate relationship between theology and politics, made a typical double response: he abandoned liberal theology and, in protest, joined the Social Democratic Party!

The years of the war were a time of theological and political unrest for Barth. Preaching became increasingly difficult. Disillusioned with the ruling theology, the basic question was how to speak of God. The unrest was not about doubt or unbelief, so much as *who God really is*, as distinct from our pious notions of God, our wishful illusions and patriotic manipulations; the issue was how to speak properly of God, in distinction from speaking about our own religious feelings. Barth was to wrestle with this theological issue for two decades, making various experiments and advances until, in the early 1930's, he outlined the approach he was to work with for the rest of his life in his multi-volume *Church Dogmatics*. Here we cannot trace all the steps in detail, but must focus on the major developments. (Two excellent detailed treatments are provided by Eberhard Jüngel, and by George Hunsinger who builds independently on the work of Hans Frei and Friedrich-Wilhelm Marquardt.[18])

Barth immersed himself in study of "the strange, new world of the Bible."[19] Above all, beginning in June 1916, he focused on *Romans*, publishing the first edition of his commentary in 1919. However, it was the second thoroughly revised edition of 1922 which sounded like a trumpet throughout the theological world to friend and foe alike.[20]

Barth's *Romans* was an event in the history of twentieth century theology. Karl Adam, the Catholic theologian, said that "it fell like a bomb on the playground of the theologians."[21] Barth himself drew on one of his own experiences and said it was like a man climbing up the church belltower in the dark who, reaching for the handrail, grasped the bell rope instead, and sounded the alarm throughout the whole town. It was this novel commentary that gave the names "theology of crisis" and "dialectical theology" to Barth's work of this period. In two main ways it marks a bold new departure in modern protestant theology.

First, while Barth draws on modern historical-critical studies, the commentary is not a series of critical notes reconstructing the original text, giving precise translations of the original language, adducing philological and archeological data, debating its true authorship, discussing the historical context of its original readers, and so on. Rather Barth revives the Reformation understanding of Scripture and treats it as "Word of God." The Preface to the first edition began as follows: Paul, as a child of his age, addressed his contemporaries. It is, however, *far more* important that, as Prophet and Apostle of the Kingdom of God, he veritably speaks to all people of every age. . . . The historical-critical method of Biblical investigation has its rightful place. . . . But were I driven to choose between it and the venerable doctrine of inspiration, I should without hesitation adopt the latter, which has a broader, deeper, *more important* justification. . . . Fortunately, I am not compelled to choose between the two. Nevertheless, my whole energy of interpreting has been expended in an endeavor to see *through and beyond* history into the spirit of the Bible, which is the Eternal Spirit (R, 1).

Barth states emphatically: "The Word ought to be exposed in the words" (R, 8).

Second, Barth's *Romans* commentary represents the birth-pangs of a new theology, chiefly by its polemic against the ruling liberal theology in which he had been schooled. The essence of this polemic is to assert the *deity* of God over against human religiosity. In a famous phrase Barth describes God as "Wholly Other," as totally different from human expectations and desires. Revelation is said to come "perpendicularly from above," rather than emerging from human religious consciousness. "If I have a system," Barth said, "it is limited to a recognition of what Kierkegaard called the 'infinite qualitative distinction' between time and eternity, and to my regarding this as possessing negative as well as positive significance: 'God is in heaven, and thou art on earth'" (R, 10). Paul was primarily concerned with "the permanent *Krisis* of the relation of time and eternity" (R, 10f.).

These phrases vividly convey the method of dialectical theology which Barth employed in the second edition of his *Romans*; this involved posing an antithesis to every thesis and never resolving them in a synthesis. God and humanity are not on a continuum but only related obliquely like a tangent striking a circle. God's revelation to humanity is not the response to humanity's religious quest for God, but the judgment on it as idolatry. "There is no point of contact in experience or history with the content of eschatological hope. Experience is the absence of hope. Hope is the contradiction of history. . . . God's revolution is the absolute limit to all human revolutions and the judgment which discloses their sin" (RP, 213). While this type of statement included, among other things, a critique of the degeneration of the Russian revolution into a police state, it was not a sanction for the status quo or political passivity. The intent of all this negation, however, was positive. Barth wanted to stress the freedom and primacy of God, and *God's* initiative and grace toward humanity in Jesus Christ. At the same time, as he later admitted himself, the danger here was in merely reversing liberal theology, rather than creating something really new, "making Schleiermacher, for a change, stand on his head, that is, making God, for a change, great at the expense of human beings" (HG, below 51).

Here a pause for perspective is necessary. It is common to read Barth as the theologian who re-asserted the transcendence and primacy of God over against liberal, anthropocentric theology. But this is at best a problematic half-truth. Barth's protest was not only against anthropocentric theology, it was *equally* against its *subjectivism* and *individualism*. In other words, anthropocentrism and privatism are for Barth two sides of the one problem. Positively stated, Barth was as much concerned to develop a *social* and *public* theology as a *theocentric* (christocentric and trinitarian!) theology. From first to last his was a communal theology, and the relation of theology and politics was always intimate in his thinking. His leadership of church resistance to Nazism, his socialist writings and activities, his travels and writings on East-West relations and peace — all these are signs and expressions of the public orientation of his theology. As we continue to review the development of Barth's theology and career, we must not look at him, as it were, through a one-lens telescope, but through a pair of binoculars where God and public life are seen simultaneously and together as one picture.

Barth's *Romans* commentary — actually the first edition, not the more famous second edition — led to his invitation to the chair of Reformed Theology at Göttingen, where he began lecturing in October, 1921. His first task was to digest the literature of his discipline, and especially to train himself in Reformed theology, a tradition which, not without some radical reconstructions, became his theological home. In Göttingen, Barth discovered the theology of the Reformation. He continued his intellectual and personal friendship with Eduard Thurneysen and found theological allies, (at least in sharing the break from liberalism) in Friedrich Gogarten and Rudolf Bultmann.[22] With them he founded the journal *Zwischen den Zeiten* (Between the Times), to which Emil Brunner also contributed. Another theologian with whom Barth had some affinity at this time, and who was also a Religious Socialist, was Paul Tillich; later Barth described their relationship as one of human closeness and theological distance.[23]

Along with lectures on historical and systematic theology, Barth also gave exegetical courses on New Testament books. So it was not surprising that he was invited as Professor of Dogmatics and New Testament Exegesis to the Protestant faculty of theology at Münster, where he taught from 1925 to 1930. Here he gave his first seminar (the subject was Calvin's *Institutes*), and also had an important exposure to Catholic theology through colleagues in the Catholic faculty of theology. At Göttingen Barth had begun to give lectures on dogmatics, and while at Münster he published in 1927 his first attempt at a comprehensive theological statement: an introduction to Christian theology as "The Doctrine of the Word of God."[24] Here he was attempting, he said later, to go beyond the "*diastasis* between God and humanity . . . of *Romans*. . . . I had to understand Jesus Christ and bring him from the periphery of my thought into the center" (KB, 173). But that did not happen in this work: he is still employing the dialectical method and still giving some the impression — against his own wishes — that theology had a basis in existential philosophy (cf. CD I/1, ix). Barth had yet to find his full, authentic voice and method. In Münster, Barth also gave his first course of lectures on ethics,[25] which already united dogmatics and ethics in a trinitarian form as would later be found in the *Church Dogmatics*.

It was also during the Münster period that Charlotte von Kirschbaum ("Lollo") came to work with Barth, indeed, to become a member of his household. She was for decades, he wrote, his "faithful fellowworker. She stayed by my side, and was indispensable in every way" (KB, 185; cf. CD III/3, xiii); it is difficult to read the section on "Man and Woman" in the *Church Dogmatics* — ahead of its time in 1951 — without concluding that her partnership and influence helped to shape what is written there.[26]

By the time Barth took up his third university position at Bonn in March, 1930, the always loose "school" of "dialectical theology" had virtually broken up. But he himself had become something of a star, attracting large numbers of students, even from overseas, and participating in a brilliant but brief flowering of the theology faculty there. His new work focused on Anselm and it had, as the selection below indicates, a profound influence on his theological thinking. In working on his Anselm book Barth felt that he had freed his thinking "from the last remnants of a philosophical i.e. anthropological . . . foundation and exposition of Christian doctrine."[27] Anselm taught him how to move from a dialectical to an analogical method.[28] After a decade of preparation and experimentation, Barth had found his mature voice and began to speak through his *magnum opus*, the magisterial *Church Dogmatics*.

The positive factor in the new development was this: in these years I had to learn that Christian doctrine, if it is to merit its name, and if it is to build up the Christian church in the world as it needs to be built up, has to be exclusively and conclusively the doctrine of Jesus Christ. . . . My new task was to take all that has been said before and to think it through once more and freshly to articulate it anew as a theology of the grace of God in Jesus Christ.[29]

From the standpoint of this "Christological concentration" the volumes of "church theology" poured forth for three decades. (Barth once playfully wondered what the angels thought of his *Dogmatics.* Paul Lehmann replied that he didn't know, but surely "the angels are alone among God's creatures in having the time to read it."[30])

In 1933 the sinister clouds of National Socialism rolled over the springtime of theological renewal. For Barth, Nazism was a resurgent pagan religion, which neo-Protestant theology was ill-equipped to resist. By May, 1934, Barth was a leader in drafting the Barmen Declaration (text below, 148ff.) which called the church to make a clear choice between Christ and Hitler: "Jesus Christ, as he is attested to us in Holy Scripture, is the one Word of God whom we have to hear, and whom we have to trust and obey in life and in death."[31] Barth's one regret about Barmen was that he had not made solidarity with the Jews "a decisive feature" of his draft text (KB, 247f.). Because he refused to take the oath of loyalty to the Führer unless he could add his own qualifications to it, Barth himself was suspended from teaching in November, 1934 and, the following March, forbidden by the Gestapo to speak in public. He returned to Switzerland in May and soon received an appointment at the University of Basel. There he taught and wrote his *Church Dogmatics* and other works until his retirement in March, 1962 at the age of 76.

Barth's years in Basel were rich and included many activities alongside his research and teaching. During the war he was an adamant opponent of Nazism, urging churches and governments to resistance and helping victims who fled to Switzerland. Immediately after the war he was as vigorous an advocate for German reconstruction as he had been an opponent of Hitler. He was active in the peace movement, opposing the re-armament of Germany and the development of atomic weapons, and in particular he tried to lead Western churches to a constructive alternative to the Cold War. He travelled extensively through Europe and Britain, and eventually the United States, giving numerous occasional lectures; and through visits and correspondence he tried to support friends and churches in Hungary, Czechoslovakia and the

German Democratic Republic. The burgeoning ecumenical movement enlisted his interest and help, particularly for the assemblies of the World Council of Churches in Amsterdam (1948) and Evanston (1954); he took a lively and hopeful interest in the Second Vatican Council, studying all its documents, and visited the Vatican in 1966. In 1956 the Mozart bicentennial was celebrated by Barth with special pleasure; he wrote essays, attended many concerts and spent a great deal of money on new Mozart records. And he preached regularly to the prisoners in the Basel gaol.[32]

But Barth's main activity, of course, was working on his *Church Dogmatics*. Even though he never wrote any of the planned fifth "volume" on the Holy Spirit and eschatology, the *magnum opus* eventually comprised 9185 pages in fourteen volumes, "nine times as long as Calvin's *Institutes* and almost twice as long as the *Summa* of Thomas Aquinas" (KB, 486). At the same time Barth was disturbed by the influence and prominence of the theology of Rudolf Bultmann in the 1950's and 1960's, fearing, as we can read in his late Schleiermacher essay (see below, 75ff.), that theology was regressing to the anthropocentric mode of the nineteenth century — against which he had spent a lifetime creating an alternative.[33]

As he aged, slowed down, and suffered various illnesses he nevertheless wrote that he was "thankful to God and to everybody that I am still alive and can read, carry on conversations, smoke, sing psalms and chorales, listen to Mozart, enjoy my fourteen grandchildren and exist from day to day in this positive kind of way" (KB, 472). At the age of 82, Karl Barth died on 10 December, 1968, leaving on his desk a lecture on ecumenical theology broken off in mid-sentence.

BARTH'S MATURE THEOLOGY

The selections from Barth's writings below are each introduced by comments about their main themes and historical contexts. The opening essay, "The Humanity of God," can be read as Barth's own introduction to his theology, first of all reviewing his early critique of liberal theology and the response of his *Romans*, and then sketching some central themes of his mature work. The following selections fall into two main groups. Those in Sections 1 and 2 include some important early writings, and some mostly polemical analyses of nineteenth century authors which are crucial for Barth's alternate understanding of theological work. The Anselm book is a transition to the other main group, Sections 3 to 5, which we can call Barth's mature theology: its fundamental themes are developed in the *Church Dogmatics*, and these are also articulated in the occasional essays on political ethics. The remainder of this Introduction will be devoted to sketching some of Barth's central theological doctrines to provide the context for the texts from the mature theology.

Theology, a word comprised of *theos*, God, and *logos*, word, is concerned with language, talk about God. Everybody talks about God, whether they be Christians, Jews, Moslems, liberals, fundamentalists, Protestants, Catholics, Orthodox, humanists, TV evangelists, superpatriots, atheists, pietists, cultists, capitalists, unionists, feminists, Marxists, politicians, journalists — the air waves are saturated, even polluted, with talk about God. Barth defines dogmatics as that theological discipline in which the Christian community tests itself concerning its own proper and distinctive language about God. It is not free-floating speculation, but a discipline of committed freedom — it is a venture of the church, committed and accountable to that community, even as it calls the community to account; and it is freely committed to a text, the Word of biblical witness to the gospel, even as it questions the text in seeking the "Word within the words." The communal nature of theology explains Barth's change of title from "Christian" dogmatics in 1927 to "church" dogmatics in 1932.

By "dogmatics" Barth does not mean, then, authoritarian teaching imposed by a dictatorial church hierarchy. In no sense are God's nature and will, God's deeds and history, delivered into human hands to be codified into "dogmas"; the prohibition of the first commandment applies to theology, too. Theology for Barth is a pilgrim venture, always open to revision, a self-critical discipline, ever seeking to give a better account of its subject matter. Granted, in the history of the church, ecumenical councils such as the Council of Nicaea and the Council of Chalcedon have formulated doctrines and creeds which successive generations have treated with authority. But in Barth's definition dogma is an "eschatological concept" because a dogma consists of agreement between "church proclamation" and God's revelation attested in Scripture, and this is something the church strives towards, rather than something it possesses (CD I/1, 304ff.). Contrary to the normal association with the English word "dogmatic," dogmatics is a critical task, not an authoritarian imposition.

Barth's theology is built on the foundation of *revelation*, above all

God's revelation in Jesus Christ as witnessed to in Scripture. Hence the title of the first "volume" of the *Church Dogmatics*, "The Doctrine of the Word of God."[34] By founding theology on revelation Barth wishes to stress the utter priority of God, the fact that all knowledge of God depends on God, as indeed does all knowledge of humanity as God's creation. This is a methodological implication of a theology of *grace*, for grace is entirely a matter of God's freedom, God's initiative, God's unmerited love for humanity. Just as the Reformers argued that no human effort could contribute to salvation, but that salvation was receiving in trust God's loving gift of forgiveness and acceptance, so Barth is making the same point in theological epistemology: God is known from and through God. And since God graciously acts in personal self-disclosure, it is a matter of gratitude and faithfulness to respond to that gift, rather than trying to supplement it or substitute for it by some other humanly devised route.

What is at stake here for Barth is certainly not some abstract notion of God's honor, as if human efforts to know God could detract from God's glory; nor is it a biblical fundamentalism which makes unhistorical claims for Scripture and denigrates human reason. Rather, it is precisely salvation, the humanization of humanity, the recovery by God's creatures of their true being in relation to God and to each other. For Barth agrees with Luther that the human mind is a perpetual factory of idols, and that idolatry is dehumanizing: any idol worth its salt ultimately demands human sacrifices. Idolatry and *self*-justification go together, and these are precisely the motivations of human religion no less.[35] God's revealing presence, by clearing out idolatry, simultaneously frees humanity from bondage. This will be illustrated in the discussion below of Barmen versus Nazism.

What is revelation? Not in the first instance the Bible, as though it were a deposit of divinity, an encyclopedia of heavenly oracles — though Barth regards the Bible as an essential form of the Word of God. Nor is revelation "divine truths" taught by the church, such as the incarnation of God in Christ or the doctrine of the Trinity — though the church's witness is also an essential form of the Word of God. Nor is revelation some immediate subjective apprehension of divinity, as in mystical experience or religious emotions. Revelation cannot be reified, turned into an object which can be detached from God and brought under human control. Indeed, if the very term "revelation" is an abstract noun which suggests an object, albeit divine, then we should drop it altogether in favor of the verbal form: God is the *self-revealing*

God; *revealing* is an activity of God as active and gracious agent who communicates with us.

Some have misread Barth's Christocentric doctrine of revelation as if he meant that nowhere else in all history and all the world was God revealed except in Jesus. This misreading would mean that God was imprisoned by the earthly life of Jesus, and that God's grace and Spirit were confined to a brief time and a narrow space — or, at best, that God was confined to the church as the extension of the earthly life of Jesus. But Barth's focus of revelation in Jesus Christ does not deny that God speaks and acts in other people and other times than Jesus of Nazareth. Rather, it sets the terms by which we can recognize God's revelation in all times and places. The Christological concentration is not an exclusiveness which shuts out those who have not encountered Jesus directly; it rather defines the nature of the universal *inclusiveness* of God's grace in Jesus Christ. Barth once made this point very graphically. "God may speak to us through Russian communism, through a flute concerto, through a blossoming shrub or through a dead dog. We shall do well to listen to him if he really does so" (CD I/1, 60). But how do we know that what we may hear in those ways, even from "a pagan or an atheist" (*ibid.*), is truly God speaking and not our own fantasies? The center which defines the circle, the norm by which we "test the spirits," is given in Jesus Christ as known in the witness of prophets and apostles. And that is the revelation which the church is commissioned and commanded to proclaim.

Barth once interpreted his doctrine of revelation by commenting on the Barmen Declaration, and we do well to follow his lead. Both the text of the Declaration and the commentary from the *Church Dogmatics* are printed below (148ff., 173ff.).

The first words of the first article of Barmen are the name of Jesus Christ, who is the Word of God. Of course, Nazis and German Christians also talked about God and talked about Christ: "We see in race, folk and nation, orders of existence granted and entrusted to us by God. God's law for us is that we look to the preservation of these orders."[36] "Christ has come to us through Adolf Hitler. . . . Hitler struck out for us, and through his power, his honesty, his faith and his idealism, the Redeemer found us."[37] "The whole German movement for freedom with its leader, our Chancellor, is for us a present from God."[38] "The life and death of Jesus teaches us that the way of struggle (*Kampf*[39]) is also the way of love and the way of life."[40] Given such co-option, Christian talk about God must be more precise so that it cannot be used to legitimate Nazi racism, nationalism and militarism. Hence Jesus Christ is not a Christ who exemplifies and legitimates Hitler's "struggle," nor is God the source of anti-Semitic doctrines of the *Volk*. The Jesus Christ the church follows and preaches is not created in the image of National Socialism but the one who "is attested to us in Holy Scripture."

What we have here is Barth's teaching of "the threefold form of the Word of God." God is revealed in, God speaks and acts in, Jesus Christ. The human Jesus of Nazareth is the first "form" of God's self-revealing presence, word and action. But the Jesus of the church is not the product of human wishes or the desire for ideological legitimation; the Jesus whom the church confesses and follows is the Jesus of the Bible. Hence the Bible, as witness to Jesus, is the second form of the Word of God; and it is no less Word of God because it is simultaneously a human document. The third form of the Word of God is the witness of the church to this biblical Jesus; when the church speaks of God in a *Christian* way it speaks of this Jesus. Again, Barth does not deny the all too human character of the church's speaking about God; the witness of the church is on the same level, so to speak, as the human Jesus and the Bible as a human text.[41] Yet the miracle of the incarnation is the miracle of God's gracious self-revealing: human being is not a barrier to God's dealing with humanity, but precisely the form which God chooses to act and speak in the world.

There is a definite priority and sequence here, of course: Jesus, Scripture, church witness. And yet Barth is bold to say that when the church speaks faithfully in this way, what occurs is nothing less than the very speaking of God to the world. Is it guaranteed, automatic, that when the church speaks thus of God that God also speaks? Of course not. God's speech remains *God's* speech in the Holy Spirit. But this threefold *form* is the earthen vessel of faithful witness which God may freely choose to make a very word of revelation.

Since God's self-revealing is the action of God as living subject, then this always has an *event*ful and living character. Barth holds that revelation happens "from time to time." Indeed, as he put it in 1927: "The Word of God still happens today in the Bible; and apart from this happening the Bible is not the Word of God, but a book like other books."[42] So revelation is happening, event; it is not, so to speak, a recorded announcement but a living Word spoken into a particular historical situation. Barmen was such a situation and what happened there was, in Barth's judgment, nothing less than an event of God's revelation.

The church now saw itself pulled back and guarded by the Word of

God in contemporaneous self-attestation.... The Confessing Church was, so to speak, only the witness of a situation in which simultaneously there took place a remarkable revelation, as there had not been for a long time, of the beast out of the abyss, and a fresh confirmation of the one old revelation of God in Jesus Christ (CD II/1, 176f.; below 179).

That is why Barth calls the confession at Barmen "a miracle."[43] Barth also documented his belief that Barmen was an event of revelation by changing the text of the first article to read: "Jesus Christ, as he *is being attested for us* in Holy Scripture...."[44]

When God is revealed this means that God is really present to human beings. But it does not mean that we can find manifest deity, raw divinity so to speak, in the world. "Revelation means the giving of signs" (CD II/1, 52; cf. II/1, 17ff.). God is unveiled by being present in forms, veiling forms, which are different from God. Most notably these signs and forms are human language and speech, as in the witness and proclamation of the church; the human witness to the acts of God by prophets and apostles in the Bible; and the true human being, Jesus of Nazareth. Like the elongated finger of John the Baptist, these signs, which do not lose their human, earthly character, point beyond themselves; "along with what they are and mean within the world, in themselves, ... they have another nature and meaning from the side of the objective reality of revelation, i.e., from the side of the incarnation of the Word" (CD I/2, 223).[45]

If God's Word and action and presence does not leave a deposit of raw divinity in the world, but witnessing signs, this means that "knowledge of God in faith is always indirect knowledge of God.... What distinguishes faith from unbelief, erroneous faith and superstition is that it is content with this indirect knowledge of God" (CD II/1, 17). Those who are not content with knowing the works of God through the signs of revelation, those who want direct and unmediated relation to God, will usually end up with idolatry, that is, divinizing part of the world — and that can range all the way from the Bible and religious teachings and figures to economic systems and political ideologies. And idolatry is as much a dehumanizing of humanity as it is a falsifying of God.

If faith is an indirect knowledge of God through signs of God's revealing works, this means that our knowledge of and speech about God is *analogical.* By analogy Barth understands a "correspondence of the thing known with the knowing, of the object with the thought, of the Word of God with the human word in thought and in speech" (CD I/1,

279). Correspondence means similarity in difference. But the crucial issue for Barth is how the terms of the analogy are set. Clearly he rules out taking human experience as the norm and reasoning from that to God as if, when the Bible speaks of the love of God, we would first define love from human relations and then magnify and project this to a transcendent level. Indeed, it was precisely such an anthropocentric and projecting methodology that Barth diagnosed as the deepest ill of modern theology, and of which he found Schleiermacher the formative protagonist and Feuerbach the shrewdest "spy" (see below, 67ff., 91ff.). This procedure is ruled out not only because of the difference between God and humanity, but also because human sin invariably distorts all human experience and all "natural" human thought about God. This means that all such projection is inevitably self-justifying, reflecting and serving the special interests of particular social groups and individual psyches. Racist and sexist ideas of God are sharp and telling examples.

The alternative in Barth's view, adopting a phrase from Romans 12.6, is the "analogy of faith," *analogia fidei*. This is his alternative to the classical Catholic notion of the *analogia entis*, analogy of being, which Barth summarizes as follows. "Everything that is exists as mere creature in greatest dissimilarity to the Creator, yet by having *being* it exists in greatest similarity to the Creator." "*Analogia entis* means that every existing being and we as human beings participate in the *similitudo Dei* [likeness of God]. The experience of God becomes an inherent possibility and necessity."[46] If the *analogia entis* postulates being as a common term comprising God and all creation, Barth rejects that as "an invention of the Antichrist" (CD I/1, x). Rejection of the *analogia entis* is part of Barth's relentless campaign against natural theology in all its forms.[47] Instead, Barth's analogy of faith begins with God, not with being; indeed, when he wants to stress God's initiative rather than human reception of revelation, Barth often uses the term *analogia gratiae*, analogy of grace, to refer to the analogy. Thus the nature of God as love provides the definition and paradigm of what a truly human love would be in the creaturely world. And the divine community, the Kingdom of God, as *God's* society, provides the model of which policies in human society are to be signs and parables (see "The Christian Community and the Civil Community" below, 280ff.). The analogy of faith, then, rests on God's revelation; faith is tutored by God, as it were, to know what behavior and activities in the world are truly "like," analogous to, God.

> In faith and confession the Word of God becomes human thought and human word, certainly in infinite dissimilarity and inadequacy, yet not in utter alienation from its prototype; but in all its human-sinful perversion of a real copy, [and hence] as the veiling of the divine, its unveiling at the same time (CD I/1, 276).

Human creatureliness and sinfulness thus distort the relation between the divine prototype and the human "copy," rendering the analogy a "veiling"; nevertheless, in spite of this, by the grace of God, there is a real analogy between the divine prototype and the human counterpart.

Now we must focus on the central *content* of God's revelation, beginning with the observation that Barth's mature position is a Christocentric trinitarian theology.[48] A glance at an outline of the *Church Dogmatics* (see below, 168ff.) discloses that volumes III, IV and V on creation, reconciliation and redemption correspond to the three persons of the Trinity: God the Creator, Christ the Reconciler, and the Holy Spirit as Redeemer. Volume I deals with the foundation of the following volumes, namely God's revelation, and is itself trinitarian and Christological in character; Barth argues, incidentally, that the threefold form of the Word of God (see above) is the only proper analogy of the trinitarian life of God. On this foundation, and before dealing with the special subjects of creation, reconciliation and redemption, Barth devotes volume II to the Doctrine of God, the one God, which includes his radical re-interpretation of the doctrine of election (predestination).

Another fundamental characteristic of Barth's theology is the integration of theology and ethics. Each volume of the *Church Dogmatics* concludes with a section on "the command of God." Christian ethics is not rooted in some natural law any more than knowledge of God is rooted in natural theology. Rather, Christian life and action is a showing forth of God's grace in Jesus Christ. As Barth describes the relationship of theology and ethics, the imperative follows the indicative.

To take an example from the Doctrine of Creation, in Paragraph 45 (CD III/2) Barth speaks of human life as being a covenant partner of God, and in the ethics of volume III (Chapter 12, "The Command of God the Creator") he deals in Paragraph 54 with "freedom in community," specifically with the co-humanity of man and woman. Thus in the theological section human life is interpreted as life in co-humanity with God and in the ethical section the specifics of this co-humanity in the sphere of sexuality are explored. The indicative of God says: "This is what it means to be truly human"; and the imperative says: "Live out the human life your Creator has given you to live!" This illustration also exemplifies Barth's analogical method at work.

So ethics is neither a false human autonomy apart from God's grace, nor is it the authoritarian imposition of commands contrary to human nature by an arbitrary God. Nor is God's command divorced from God's grace, nor God's grace lacking in an imperative for human action in the world. Barth made the point in a neat formulation in his 1935 essay, "Gospel and Law": law is the gospel, whose content is grace, in its form of demand and claim.[49]

At the center of Barth's theology is *Christology*. Following the ecumenical councils of the early church, especially Nicaea (A.D. 325) and Chalcedon (A.D. 451), Christology for Barth is the central Christian paradigm. For in Christology the church formulated its understanding of Jesus as this embodies the biblical revelation of the relation of God to humanity and the relation of humanity to God. The Council of Chalcedon confessed "one Lord Jesus Christ" perfect in divinity, perfect in humanity, truly God and truly human, "like us in all things except sin," one Christ "acknowledged in two natures [i.e. divine and human] without confusion, without change, without division, without separation."[50]

We can summarize some of Barth's central themes, and translate the meaning of the classical confession, as follows:

1 God does not choose to be God apart from Jesus of Nazareth. The God of the church, the God of the Christian faith, is the God who is God in Jesus. Do not look outside of Jesus to know who God is. God chooses to be God in Jesus, with Jesus and for Jesus. That means: God chooses to be God by being present in this human being. And being present in, with and for Jesus means precisely this: being present for us and with us − indeed, being present for all humanity, for our history, for the universe. In Jesus we meet the sociable God, the God of pro-humanity. And God's pro-humanity is the basis of our co-humanity.

2 Jesus does not choose to be human in and by himself alone, in isolated autonomy or narcissistic self-preoccupation. Jesus is not a religious Prometheus. Rather, Jesus is fully and truly human in being himself in, with, and for God. In being fully human himself, Jesus is fully for God and for all humanity at the same time.

3 So, in this reality and paradigm, God is present for us, and humanity is engaged by God as our Creator, Reconciler and Redeemer. The central message of this Jesus paradigm is twofold: (i) that God in the fullness of divine love, glory and power is free to be with and for us; and (ii) that humanity, embraced by God's grace, is free to be with and for God. And in this freedom for God we are freed to be most fully human, to be

our true selves with and for God, and with and for each other.

Again, in Jesus, God's being-for-humanity is God's co-humanity, and this is the basis of our humanity which is likewise co-humanity and pro-humanity. So human being is essentially a being-in-community, and a being-for-one-another in community — like the trinitarian life of God. Therefore being-in-Christ is inseparable from being-in-the-community-of-Jesus. And this community is God's promise of community to the broken and suffering world. It is the presence of God's eschatological community in the midst of the history of the old age.

This Christological paradigm governs the whole of Barth's mature theology, and is simultaneously the heart of the content and methodology of the *Church Dogmatics*. So it shapes not only the doctrine of the person of Christ and reconciliation, where we would expect to find it, but also Barth's doctrine of revelation, his understanding of Scripture, his doctrine of God — especially his radical re-interpretation of predestination — his discussions of creation, the church, ethics, and even his treatment of sin.

The Christological paradigm also highlights another distinctive Barthian teaching: God also reveals true humanity in Jesus of Nazareth. It is not as if humanity were self-evident and God problematic, and therefore only God needed to be revealed. It is not as if authentic humanity were already apparent to us through biology, psychology, sociology, economics and philosophy; through Darwin, Freud, Marx, existentialism, liberalism, conservatism or natural law. For what it means to be a creature is only known face to face with the Creator; what it means to be sinner is only known not from natural guilt or anxiety but in encountering God's judgment in the true humanity of Jesus; and what it means to be redeemed is not known from political messiahs or therapeutic saviors but from the resurrection of the crucified Jesus. If the human story of the twentieth century is the story of conflict between human nobility and the "rough beast" (Yeats), Barth presents the story of Jesus, humanity with God, to disclose the depths of evil and the heights of hope that is humanity's peril and promise before God.

From this central point Barth develops his biblical interpretation and his exposition of the classical Christian doctrines. At the heart of his *doctrine of God* is the statement that God's Lordship is defined, not from unreconstructed human ideas of rule and power magnified to the absolute, but in terms of God's actual dealing with humanity in Jesus Christ: God is "the One who loves in freedom." Free love and loving freedom are thus the basic characteristics of God's Lordship; and these derive from the most basic Christian statement: in Jesus Christ we know God as the God of grace. Under these two terms, divine loving and divine freedom, Barth treats the "perfections" of God, what tradition usually called God's attributes (CD II/1, Paragraphs 30-31). Preferring "perfection" as more fitting for the living, acting God of biblical revelation, Barth treats under the perfections of divine loving God's grace, mercy, patience and holiness, righteousness and wisdom; under the perfections of divine freedom are treated God's unity, constancy, eternity and omnipresence, omnipotence and glory. But, as always, the specific Christian meaning of these perfections is not derived from free-floating speculation about what, for example, omnipotence abstractly conceived might entail, or what eternity could — or might, or might not — mean; the test of their meaning is that they help to describe and illuminate the God revealed in Jesus Christ.

A dramatic example of this Christological method is Barth's doctrine of *election*. Traditional doctrines of predestination (e.g., those of Augustine and Calvin) involved an inscrutable if not arbitrary divine will, and gave rise to agonizing questions. Why did God predestine only certain souls to salvation? Why, as in Calvin, did God predestine some to damnation as well as some to salvation? Is grace partial? Is there a conflict between the saving God of grace revealed in Christ and some unrevealed, deep, hidden will of God? Even Calvin himself described his own teaching on predestination as the "horrible decree."

Barth addresses the problem from the conviction that God is *fully* revealed in Jesus Christ; there is no hidden "remainder," as it were, no other will and nature of God which is undisclosed or in conflict with what is revealed in Jesus Christ. "There is no greater depth in God's being and work than that revealed in these happenings and under this name" (CD II/2, 54). Instead, what is disclosed in him is both the *electing God* and the *elect human being*.

Jesus Christ reveals that God is the *electing God*, and God's election is grace. The doctrine of election bears witness to "eternal, free and unchanging grace as the beginning of all the ways and works of God" (CD II/2, 3). In Christ, God chooses humanity in divine loving freedom. Jesus Christ is the *elect human being*, not only as an individual person but above all as the representative, the head, the personification of all humanity. That is to say, *all* humanity — and precisely all *sinful* humanity — is chosen, elect, predestined by God in Jesus Christ. This is Barth's radical reconstruction of the traditional doctrine of predestination! It is so radical a revision that critics began accusing Barth of teaching universalism, that is, the salvation of everybody. To this Barth replied, first, that passages like Colossians 1.19f. do, after all, speak of God reconciling "all things unto himself"; and, second, "there is no theological justification for setting any limits on our side to the friendliness of God towards humanity which appeared in Jesus Christ" (HG; below 63f.).

This does not mean that the note of judgment which was so severe in the traditional doctrine of predestination is ignored by Barth. There is indeed a rejection of sin, there is a No in God's eternal will; it is the power of God by which the power of evil is overthrown and negated, denying it ultimacy and denying it a future. This No is in the service of God's Yes, so that there is no ontological dualism, and God's grace is the beginning and end of all God's ways. While the unbelievers' opposition to God is rejected, even unbelievers are elect no matter if they live as though they were not elect. It is God's election, not human belief or unbelief, which is fundamental and decisive. This teaching had very practical consequences for Barth personally, leading him to deal even with hardened atheists as people who, like himself, were elected by God in Jesus Christ.

God's *creation* is rooted in electing grace, for God's free love and loving freedom establishes the covenant with humanity. This covenant is, as Barth puts it, "the internal basis of creation"; correspondingly, creation is "the external basis of the covenant." What it means to be a creature is not, in the first or last analysis, something that can be learned from the natural or social sciences, or from the humanities. Illuminating though their insights may be, we understand our creaturely existence as we encounter our Creator. Indeed, creaturely existence is precisely a history of encounter, of dialogue, of hearing and response, to God our Creator.

What we learn from Jesus is that the true God is God *with* us human beings, and that true human being is being with God. Jesus does not try to be human apart from and without God in isolated self-sufficiency. Given that, Barth states that "basically and comprehensively, therefore, to be human is *to be with God*." This being with God is the "ontological determination of humanity" (CD III/2, 134f.). Because God becomes human in Jesus, because he is neighbor, companion and brother, to be human means first and foremost to live in this companionship with God.

Creaturely life is thus an intrinsically *sociable* existence, participating in covenant with God, which simultaneously means living in relationship with our human companions, near and far. Since God in Jesus Christ is a God of pro-humanity and co-humanity, so human life is essentially co-humanity and mutuality. Here Barth is revising the traditional doctrine of the *imago Dei* along lines pioneered by Dietrich Bonhoeffer.[51] The image of God is not some individually possessed quality, such as reason, which likens a human being to God; rather, our likeness to God is our co-humanity. The analogy is this: as God is the God who is not solitary but is God in covenant and community, so "humanity in its basic form is co-humanity" (CD III/2, 285). Since human life "is modelled on the human being Jesus, on his being for human companions [*Mitmenschen*]" (CD III/2, 324), so the life of women and men is life with and for others; it is not isolated, self-sufficient and self-serving, but life with and for others, co-humanity in community. In the ethics of his Doctrine of Creation, Barth tries to work out concretely the life of "freedom in community" (the title of Par. 54) in the relations of men and women, parents and children, and near and distant neighbors (CD III/4, 116ff.).

Barth's concern in his doctrine of creation, then, is not to give a theological explanation of the origins of the world and human life, not to develop a would-be "biblical" theory as an alternative or in opposition to the theories of natural scientists. Rather, moving out from the Christological center of his thinking he focuses on the relation of Creator and creature. To be God's creature is not to want to be more than a creature (the sin of pride), nor to be content with being less than a creature (the sin of sloth), but to affirm creaturely life in its limits and its freedom. Barth himself lived and enjoyed life robustly, as John Updike rightly noted, and in his theology he took pains to affirm bodily life against all false dualism and asceticism. Echoing the liturgical refrain of Genesis 1, "and God saw that it was good," Barth describes creation as *benefit*. Creation comes from God's affirmation, God's Yes, not from any negation; nor is God ambivalent about creation, saying both Yes and No. "Creation is a blessing because it has unchangeably the character of an action in which the divine joy, honour and affirmation are turned toward another" (CD III/1, 331). It is no accident that Barth wrote yet another mini-essay on Mozart in his Doctrine of Creation (see below, 322ff.). With Calvin he could gladly proclaim that the chief end of God's creatures is to glorify and enjoy their Creator for ever — and, more than Calvin, he really meant enjoy!

We have already met the central Christological paradigm of Barth's theology (above, 29f.) and see how, following the Council of

Chalcedon, Christ means both God who comes to humanity and the true human being Jesus in union with God. Barth summarizes this Christology and gives a brief introduction to his doctrine of *reconciliation* in the first reading on "The Humanity of God":

> In his one person Jesus Christ is at once as true God humanity's faithful partner, and as true human being God's faithful partner, both the Lord abased to community with humanity and the servant exalted to community with God. . . . Thus in this *unity* Jesus Christ is the Mediator, the Reconciler between God and humanity. Thus, demanding and awakening faith, love and hope, he acts for God before humanity — and, representing, atoning and interceding, for *humanity* before God (below, 53).[52]

With the ancient church Barth teaches that Jesus is truly and fully human. Christ was not a demi-god, a mixture of divine and human; nor was he only seemingly human, a god in disguise as it were. Jesus was truly and fully human. He was born, lived, was tempted, suffered and died like all of us. As truly human, Jesus was like us in all things, sin only excepted. For sin does not belong to our created human nature, but to its corruption and alienation from God.

And yet Jesus identified totally with the human condition, taking our sin upon himself.

> He was not a sinful human being. But inwardly and outwardly his situation was that of a sinful person. He did nothing that Adam did. But he lived life in the form it must take on the basis and assumption of Adam's act. He bore innocently what Adam and all of us in Adam have been guilty of. Freely he entered into solidarity and necessary association with our lost existence (CD I/2, 152).

Knowing who Jesus is, what Barth means is this: *God* entered into solidarity with our lost existence.

We cannot pierce the mystery of how God encounters us in the person of the human Jesus of Nazareth.[53] But Barth's affirmation is clear and unequivocal that

> we have to do with *God himself* when we have to do with this person. *God himself* speaks when this person speaks in human speech. *God himself* acts and suffers when this person acts and suffers as a human being. *God himself* triumphs when this One triumphs as a human being (CD IV/2, 51; below, 201).

There is no law which requires God to be God in isolation from humanity, there is no alien limit to God's love or foreign constraint upon God's freedom. God can be, and graciously is, "God in his unity with this creature, this human being, in his human and creaturely nature — and this without ceasing to be God, without any alteration and diminution of his divine nature" (CD IV/1, 183; below, 202).

Barth's doctrine of reconciliation is the story of the great reversal. The sin of humanity is taken by God, and humanity is freed to share in God's glory. In the seventy-eight Paragraphs of the *Church Dogmatics* only three headings expressly speak of sin, under the themes of pride, sloth and falsehood.[54] The pattern of Barth's doctrine of reconciliation shows that even his understanding of sin is Christologically structured. For God's self-abasement exposes overweening human pride, the servant's exaltation exposes human sloth, and the unity of humanity with God in Jesus Christ exposes the falsehood of isolation from God in sinful self-sufficiency. Barth's focus on God rather than human sin does not mean that he minimizes the power or evil of sin, as will become apparent in his treatment of the Cross and reconciliation. It means, consistent with his whole theology, that sin is not truly known as *sin* until it is exposed in the light of God's judgment. So great is human "perversion and corruption, . . . *offence* and *plight*" (CD IV/1, 13; below, 214), that only God's personal bearing away of sin can bring salvation.

Already in his striking re-working of the doctrine of election Barth had in mind his doctrine of reconciliation. The thesis for Paragraph 33 on "The Election of Jesus Christ" reads as follows:

> The election of grace is the eternal beginning of all the ways and works of God in Jesus Christ. In Jesus Christ, God in his free grace determines himself for sinful humanity and sinful humanity for himself. He therefore takes upon himself the rejection of humanity with all its consequences and elects humanity to participation in his own glory (CD II/1, 94).

Like the prodigal in the parable, God comes into the far country. In Jesus Christ, God the Creator and Lord of all becomes servant. In the Incarnation God enters not just the world of creation and finitude, but above all the world of sin. The rejection of sinful humanity is borne by Christ. The judgment upon sin is taken by God. When Jesus dies, he dies in the place of humanity. The meaning of this passion depends entirely on

> the person and mission of the One who suffered there and was crucified and died. *His person*: it is the eternal God himself who has given himself in his Son to be human, and as human being to take upon himself this human passion. *His mission*: it is the Judge who in this passion takes the place of those who ought to be judged and allows

himself to be judged in their place (CD IV/1, 246; below, 225). This is the beginning of the story of the great reversal.

Following the story line of Philippians 2, the second volume of the Doctrine of Reconciliation treats "Jesus Christ, the Servant as Lord." The emphasis is now on the the resurrection and "The Exaltation of the Son of Man," the title of Paragraph 64. From the parable of the prodigal now comes another theme: "The Homecoming of the Son of Man." The story of the great reversal continues with the vindication of Jesus and, in him, of God's cause. But God's cause is precisely the cause of humanity, so that the "homecoming" of the Son also means the reconciliation of humanity to God, for Jesus is the representative of all humanity. God's reconciliation means for humanity justification, sanctification and vocation, and the Christian life these create is a life of faith, love and hope — the typical order Barth always uses. This is the life in the community of the people of Jesus created by the Holy Spirit.

Barth's discussions of the *church* characteristically prefer to speak of "the Christian community" (see, for example, CD Paragraphs 62, 67 and 72). Part of the meaning of the doctrine of the Trinity is that community belongs to the very essence of God. Again, creation is rooted in the *covenanting* nature of God whose love wills to create community with the creatures. Consequently, human life is life in co-humanity. Finally, Jesus and the kingdom, God's eschatological community, belong together. So, community is the appropriate word for the Christian people. There is no solitary Christianity or individualistic faith — personal, yes; isolated and self-sufficient, no.

The community is created by the Holy Spirit, the Spirit of the resurrected Jesus. It is not an organization Jesus set up, and it is not a society people join. It is not created by human religious striving; on the contrary, religion in the first instance is unbelief — idolatry and self-justification (CD I/2, 280ff.). Nor is the Christian community created by the faith of believers; rather, faith is the response to the activity of the Spirit. Here, once again and as always, Barth's critique of natural theology shapes his exposition. Positively stated, once again and as always, Barth points to God's gracious initiative.

From this perspective we can see why the German Christians of the Hitler period were anathema to Barth, since attempting to weld together Christ and National Socialism finally meant enslaving the church to the ideology of blood, soil and the thousand year Reich. If that was a temptation in a demonic yet very seductive form, it also appears in more and less subtle guises, as when churches by doctrine or habit become vehicles of race, class or nationalist interests, or when they are uncritically domesticated to a particular economic system, or become partisans in a power struggle like the Cold War. The Christian community is the free community of the Spirit; it is not a creature of these "principalities and powers."

So the church does not possess and control its being in and of itself. It cannot guarantee its true being as church, for example, by its ministry and order, or its claim to possess the Word of God in the Bible. Scripture and ministries, like the index finger of John the Baptist, point to Christ and the Spirit as the only source of the community's life.

Another way to say this is that for Barth the church is an *event* and a movement, rather than an institution. Not everything that calls itself church *is* church, any more than all talk about "God" is really talk about God. Through sin, the witness of the church is always equivocal, and in the worst cases the witness can be "either omitted or obscured and falsified" so that we have but "the semblance of a church" (below, 244). (The critical function of theology is to guard against just this danger.)

To say that the church is event, ever dependent on the Holy Spirit awakening faith and obedience, is not to reject organization, order, form, rite, tradition, teaching and leadership. Barth does not evaporate the church into some imaginary "spiritual" existence; he has no time for "ecclesiastical Docetism" (below, 237). Rather he stresses that it is the Spirit of the living Christ who gives the community its life in and through all these forms.

Since, in Jesus, all humanity is elected by God to be reconciled and restored to community with its Creator, the Christian community bears a promise and a calling for all people: in Barth's language, the Christian community is "a provisional representation of the whole world of humanity" (CD IV/1, 643; IV/2, 614; CD IV/3 ii, 681). What the church "represents," what it embodies and portrays to all humanity, is the universality and inclusiveness of God's grace. It is a promise of justification and forgiveness to all people, of the sanctification of all human life; and so it is also a calling for all to enter into the covenant of God with all human beings. The Christian community is a "provisional" representation, it is not the fullness of God's eschatological community. But it bears witness that God's covenant and community is the ground and goal of human life, the meaning of human history. In so far as the Christian community in history represents God's promising future here and now, in spite of everything in the world which appears to deny God's purpose and reign, it is a beacon of hope to the world, a "great, effective and living hope" (CD IV/3 ii, 681).

Helmut Gollwitzer, Barth's Berlin student, friend and interpreter, commented on this point nicely:

> the community is not an end in itself, not a little flock of the saved in Noah's ark while all those around her drown.... She is totally directed toward her co-existence with the rest of humanity ... [to] "perform the service which the world most needs" (RP, 88f.).

Gollwitzer continued by pointing out that when Barth spoke of the Christian community called to be a "living hope" for the world, he was not talking piously, but politically. If the church is to be a "provisional representation" of humanity reconciled to God, then concretely this means, *inter alia*, that

> true church law is exemplary law. For all its particularity, it is a pattern for the formation and administration of human law generally, and therefore of the law of other political, economic, cultural and other human societies (CD IV/2, 719).... In the form in which she exists among them she can and must be to the human world around her a reminder of the justice of the kingdom of God already established on earth in Jesus Christ, and a *promise* of its future manifestation. *De facto*, whether they realize it or not, she can and should show them that there already exists on earth an order based on that great transformation of the human situation, and directed towards its manifestation. To those outside she can and should not only say, but also demonstrate by deed, ... that *things can be different*, not merely in heaven but on earth, not just some day but even now....[55]

From here it is a short step to the topic of the next group of readings. "Don't forget to say that I have always been interested in politics, and consider that it belongs to the life of a theologian," Barth told an interviewer near the end of his life.[56] In discussing Barth's ethics we focus on *politics*, and once again the theme of Christian freedom is central. I have already noted the public orientation of Barth's theology, and pointed out that ethics is an intrinsic part of dogmatics for Barth. Next the basis of Christian ethics must be considered.

In the *Church Dogmatics* the order is always dogmatics — ethics; that is, first comes discussion of God's nature and activity and then of the human activity which corresponds to God's being and initiative. The same point was made by Barth in 1935 when he reversed Luther's famous formula "law and gospel" and published his essay on "Gospel and Law."[57] Another way to make the point is to say: the imperative follows the indicative. This means that for Barth Christian ethics no more rests on natural law than its theology rests on natural theology. Nor does Christian ethics rest on an innate "conscience" which is then construed to be the internal voice of God.

Yet another way to state Barth's approach is to say that for him the Christian ethic is an ethic of gratitude. One does not obey the command of God to earn God's grace, or to prepare for it. Grace is God's love freely given, and gratitude is the response which leads the Christian to free and willing obedience to God's command. At the same time, since God is the Creator and Reconciler of humanity, what God commands is that creatures affirm and live out that humanity which is most truly their own. Christian ethics has nothing to do with the imposition on men and women of an alien law; rather, it concerns God's "gift of freedom."[58]

There is a clear methodological implication of this approach to Christian ethics: what *analogy* is to dogmatics, *parable* is to ethics. The function of Christian ethical behavior is to tell a story, as it were, which witnesses to God's being and action in Jesus Christ, and its great promise for human life and community. The essay on "The Christian Community and the Civil Community" (below, 265ff.) is an excellent example of this "parabolic ethics." After describing the relationship between church and state, Barth devotes eleven sections to showing the way God's revelation in Christ shapes Christian behavior in the political order. These sections develop the following explicit theological themes: incarnation; justification[59]; Jesus' coming to the lost; Christian freedom; commitment to Christ; Christian unity; the gifts of the Spirit; God's revelation; the freedom of the Word of God; service as the model for power and rule; and the judgment of God. The political action which corresponds to these themes is the ethical parable.

The fundamental purpose of such parabolic behavior — fragmentary, provisional and even sinful though it may be — is to point indirectly but truly to Christ and the kingdom of God as they give specific form to human life. The state is God's ordinance for an unredeemed world; indeed, both church and state will be superseded by the kingdom of God, so neither in its own life nor in the state can the church expect to find the perfection of the eschatological community. Therefore the parables will be indirect, partial and imperfect. Here are some examples. The political parable which corresponds to God's revelation and self-disclosure is accountable public disclosure and debate by government, not secret policies. That Christ came not to be served but to serve, and warned his disciples against seeking power like "the Gentiles,"[60] requires that power be an instrument of just law, rather than law being an instrument of naked power. Again, the violent overthrow of a tyrannical regime or a defensive war against an unjust aggressor "must be approved, supported and if necessary even suggested by the Christian community" (below, 288) in exceptional circumstances; however, God's wrath is momentary but mercy eternal, and therefore such actions must be exceptions to the church's overriding, imaginative and energetic commitment to peace.[61]

Another characteristic of Barth's ethics and politics, namely its historical-social concreteness, is illustrated in his response to Emil Brunner on the subject of communism (below, 296ff.). In an open letter Brunner had demanded that Barth explain why he was not combatting "totalitarian Communism" in the same way he fought against Nazi totalitarianism. Brunner presumed that "opposing totalitarianism" was a timeless ethical principle which had informed Barth's resistance to Nazism in the 1930's and which should be consistently followed by Christians with regard to communism also. Barth's reply presupposes that there are no such timeless ethical principles which embody the will of God regardless of historical and social circumstances, and which are controlled and wielded by those who always have them ready to hand. As he points out in a careful historical comparison, Nazism had a mesmerizing, seductive effect, not least on the churches and Christian people, which communist governments have never had. If he, or the church, were to witness against "the evils of totalitarianism," it would only be echoing what everybody knew, rather than bringing some new insight from the gospel to the political situation. Worse, it would be giving Christian legitimation to the Cold War and its hypocrisies. Christian speech and action which is truly a parable of God's rule and blessed community will be historically pertinent, not abstract and timeless, because it listens for the Word of the living God which is new every morning.

In "The Church Between East and West" (below, 301ff.) Barth gave his constructive approach to the East-West conflict. The United States and the Soviet Union are engaged in a global power struggle. Each is engaged in a polemic against the other, with critiques sometimes penetrating, often self-serving, and with several points of striking resemblance. It is a service for Christians to be able to see and say this, standing freely in an independent position and not being co-opted as uncritical partisans. Barth's recommendation of "No partisanship!" for the church (which deeply antagonized Americans like Reinhold Niebuhr) was not advocating that Christians neutrally ignore international politics. In calling the church to be *free from* captivity to a power bloc and its ideology, he was calling the Christian community to be *free for* its own, independent, third way which he called "reconstruction." Conceptually Barth understood that peace, justice and freedom were inseparably joined together, that Western talk about freedom degenerated into individualism while Eastern talk about justice degenerated into collectivism, and that so-called peace was a precarious balance of terror. The task of reconstruction requires the church to pursue in practical ways both human justice and human freedom, free from hypocrisy as well as godlessness. In this way the church can be an advocate for humanity, and in this direction, Barth believed, lay the path to peace.

Barth was active in the peace movement after the war, and this is reflected in the final reading of this section. Recently, a number of church leaders have issued statements declaring an unequivocal No! to the use of nuclear weapons. Barth and his colleagues from the Confessing Church had reached that position thirty years ago. "The church and the individual Christian can say nothing but an *a priori No* to a war with atomic weapons. Even preparation for such a war is under all circumstances *sin against God and the neighbor*, for which no church and no Christian can accept responsibility" (below, 320f.).

In the light of his early socialist addresses and activities, we cannot leave the discussion of political ethics without giving special attention to the recent debate about Barth's *socialism*. It was launched in 1972 by the German theologian Friedrich-Wilhelm Marquardt with his book *Theologie und Sozialismus: das Beispiel Karl Barths* (Theology and Socialism: The Example of Karl Barth).[62] The essence of his position is that Barth was a socialist, that the life-context of his theology was socialist activity, and that Barth's theology was seeking the organic connection between God's biblical kingdom and a new world to follow the collapse of the bourgeois capitalist order — in short, that theology and socialist politics were two sides, the theory and praxis, of the one life project for Barth. This thesis set off a storm of controversy, with able Barth scholars and friends backing the main thrust of Marquardt's thesis and others severely criticizing it.[63] How should we assess the early socialist activities and writings, like the essay printed below? What was Barth's mature position? Is Marquardt correct in maintaining that socialism was the formative influence for Barth's theology?

First, a quick review of some of Barth's activities and statements. To begin with, his socialist activities and beliefs did not stop after he left Safenwil. When he was teaching in Germany he joined the German

Social Democratic Party on May Day, 1931, in protest against the increasing influence of the National Socialists. This was not an abstract ideological commitment, for Barth's theology would not permit him to adopt any system of ideas, philosophical or political, that would constrict the freedom of the gospel; rather it was a practical decision to support the party with the most healthy political position.

Given this caveat, we continue to find regular references to socialism and the church in his mature work; here is a sampling. To his son Christoph he wrote in 1950: "Anyone who does not want communism — and none of us do — should take socialism seriously" (KB, 382).[64] In a 1956 interview he said: "I decided for theology because I felt a need to find a better basis for my social action."[65] In 1961 he wrote that God's command is "a call for counter-movements on behalf of humanity, . . . a call for the championing of the weak against every kind of encroachment on the part of the strong." The church has been too tardy to do so in the face of capitalist injustices towards workers, and too quick to criticize state socialism, in spite of its obvious faults. The church in the West should "keep to the 'left'" in opposing the defenders of capitalist injustices, without dogmatically and uncritically espousing all socialist solutions, such as public ownership of the means of production. Barth goes further:

> The Christian community both can and should espouse the cause of this or that branch of social progress or even socialism in the form most helpful at a specific time and place and in a specific situation. But its decisive word cannot consist in the proclamation of social progress or socialism. It can consist only in the proclamation of the revolution of God "against all ungodliness and unrighteousness of man" (Rom. 1.18), i.e., in the proclamation of his kingdom as it has already come and comes (CD III/4, 544f.).[66]

Yet it is obvious that Barth's socialism was not as evident in the teaching of the university professor as it had been in the Safenwil pastor. As noted by Helmut Gollwitzer: "he, without changing his political views, pursued his theological work without making visible the previous connection to his political position. . . ." (RP, 114). Gollwitzer interpreted this largely, and ironically, in terms of Barth's changed social location in the university world and his separation from day-to-day socialist praxis.

The anti-bourgeois elan of the Safenwil pastor lost its force when, upon his entering the academic milieu, the previous praxis could no longer be continued. Our classes hold us tenaciously fast. The counterweight of our ideas cannot offset the influence of our social existence on our consciousness, the bourgeois slant even to a theology anti-bourgeois in tendency (RP, 106).

To this we must add Barth's need to do fundamental theological work, for which he was not yet prepared, when he first became a professor. Further, Barth's expectations of socialist politics had been sobered by the role of socialist parties in World War I and the aftermath of the Russian revolution.

Barth himself tended to confirm Gollwitzer's view, as well as his own continuing socialist commitment, when he wrote to Eberhard Bethge (Bonhoeffer's biographer) somewhat wistfully near the end of his life. Reflecting on the time of *Romans* and his move to Germany, he said that the political theme slipped into the background while reinterpreting the Reformation preoccupied him. Nevertheless, he continued, Lutheran Germany really needed "the direction which I now silently presupposed or only incidentally stressed: ethics — co-humanity — servant church — discipleship — socialism — peace movement — and, hand in hand with all that, politics."[67] So he clearly still intended socialism, though it was a presupposition he did not consistently argue but only stressed "incidentally."

To summarize: Marquardt is right in drawing attention to Barth's socialism, and in reinforcing the point that his critique of liberalism was a move in a radical, not conservative, direction; but he is wrong in arguing that socialism is the ground of Barth's theology. Rather, the reverse is true: theology is the ground of Barth's socialism — and the basis of his critique of practical socialist (and capitalist!) politics. The Kingdom of God is true socialism, not the reverse.[68] Another way to make the point is to say that socialism is one of the parables of the Kingdom of God, as are other social forms such as the relation of man and woman, and the church. In other words, *community* comes first, then socialist politics; socialism is a *consequence* of community which is theologically grounded, rather than *the* hermeneutical key to the theology; socialism is in the service of, and measured by, the Kingdom of God, not vice versa.

The last brief selections come from the writings on Mozart who, though Catholic and even Freemason, was the consummate composer who early made his way into the inner sanctum of Barth's study to a place of honor beside John Calvin, and who accompanied the theologian day by day throughout his life. Barth felt that whereas Bach's music was a message and Beethoven's a personal confession, Mozart "just sings and sounds" (M, 37).[69] But precisely his freedom from the need to preach or to express himself allowed Mozart to sing and sound the grace of God. Poor Schleiermacher once more gets his ears boxed, this time by Mozart! For Barth holds that the center for Schleiermacher was "a matter of balance, neutrality, and, finally, indifference," while for Mozart it was always God's Yes — not a Yes which ignored the sorrow, evil and death in the world, but the Yes of God's free love which overcomes the No.

Mozart once said of Protestants — and Barth quotes him approvingly — that they had their religion too much in their heads. Those who are a little intimidated by the mass of Barth's texts might explore a non-literary approach to his theology via music. I recommend substituting another mass, namely the Missa Longa in C (K.262), after reading Barth's essays on Mozart. The attentive listener, who has learned the words of the mass, cannot fail to understand Mozart's singing and sounding and why Barth found his music a parable of the kingdom of heaven.

The subtitle of this book describes Barth as a "theologian of freedom," and that theme recurs in numerous forms, as in a musical composition, again and again throughout the texts and this introduction. It has long commended itself to me as a useful summary of Barth's theology, certainly more than outmoded or ponderous names such as "theology of crisis," dialectical theology" and "neo-orthodoxy." Eberhard Jüngel also chose this theme to conclude his tribute to Barth at the time of his death, and his words are a fine conclusion for this essay.

Barth's life work is a free theology worthy of a free man. This is ultimately due to the fact that his work was nothing less than an essay in the theology of freedom, speaking of the sovereign freedom of a gracious God and of the justified freedom of the human being who receives that grace. Barth consciously responded with a Yes to both this freedom of God and this freedom of the human being. And it was on their behalf that he said No. He was an enemy of the enemies of freedom. He was never shy about recruiting friends of freedom. Even in the last year of his life he sought and found the friendship of an author who had impressed him with his free candor. And the express purpose of his teaching was to cultivate students who would be friends of freedom.

The success of this undertaking is attested by the fact that Barth found friends of freedom, not only in Protestant Christianity, nor even simply in all Christian confessions, but even beyond the pale of the church. They by no means had to become Barthians.

The freedom of God: for Barth, that was God himself. The unmistakable greatness of his theology arises from his unwavering intention to think of God himself. The polemical aspect of his theology is directed against all surrogates. No idea, no ideology, no pious postulate, and especially no theological concept may take the place of God. God confides in no one. He speaks for himself. He reveals himself. Barth uncompromisingly demanded that we think of God himself!

It is only when our attention is directed to God himself that we can correspondingly think of the human being as a self. Here, too, "the human being" is no general conception of humanity, no ideal humanity, no theoretical or practical substitute, no liturgical or sacramental surrogate, but the free person himself or herself, a living, irreplaceable, responding being.

Karl Barth lived a life of response. He was himself. His entire life and thought as a whole announced that "God" is a cheerful word.

With nothing more than this announcement, Karl Barth edified the community of Jesus Christ and helped to shape a century. At the very least, Barth's life work was to provoke us — and not just theologians — to continue to build in the same way.[70]

SELECTED TEXTS

1

BARTH INTRODUCES HIS THEOLOGY

THE HUMANITY OF GOD

This 1956 lecture gives Barth's own interpretation of his theological development. He first looks back to his Romans *with its emphasis on the deity of God over against humanity. He continues to affirm the "180 degrees" change of course that his commentary represented against the direction of 19th century protestant theology in Europe. But he is also quite self-critical of his early work: he has been required to make a major revision and new start, a "retraction".[1]* This means a greater Christological concentration because, in Jesus Christ, God cannot be understood apart from humanity, nor humanity apart from God.[2] Hence Barth's title, for the deity of God in light of Jesus Christ includes the humanity of God: the divine God is the God of pro-humanity.*

Parts II and III of the lecture sketch out the implications of this revision for Barth's mature theology. In fact Barth himself had been engaged in this revision for many years before this lecture, perhaps beginning as early as his Anselm *book in 1931 (see below) and certainly by his doctrine of election in* Church Dogmatics *II/2, published in 1942.[3] Accordingly this first selection introduces all Barth's work, from the early fiery polemics to the constructive work of the mature* Dogmatics.

The translation used here is by James Strathearn McNab in God, Grace and Gospel *(Edinburgh: Oliver and Boyd, 1959). Another, by John Newton Thomas, is found in* The Humanity of God *(London: Collins; Richmond: John Knox, 1961).*

The humanity of God — that, rightly understood, must mean: God's relationship and approach to humanity; God, who speaks to human beings in promise and commandment; God's existence, intervention and action for them; the community which God has with them; God's free grace, in which he desires to be and is God not otherwise than as the God of humanity.

I do not think that I am mistaken in assuming that the theme set us

* Footnotes indicated by figures are on pp. 334ff.

today is partly meant to point to a *change of direction* — in which we are today involved or should be — in the thinking of evangelical theology, not in opposition to a former critical turn but in *distinction* from it. What began to force itself stormily upon us, some forty years ago now, was less the humanity than the *divinity* of God. By this I mean that property of God which in his relation to humanity and to the world is absolutely his own. It is the overwhelmingly high and distant, the strange, the totally other, with which people find themselves dealing when they take the name of God upon their lips, when God confronts them, when they have to do with God. It is that mystery, comparable only with the impenetrable darkness of death, in which God veils himself at the very moment when he unveils himself to humanity, makes himself known, reveals himself. It is the judgment which human beings must encounter because God is gracious and desires to be and is the God of humanity. What we discovered in the revolution in those days was the majesty — so illuminating in all its horror — of the Crucified, as Grünewald had seen and represented him, and the same artist's finger of John the Baptist mightily pointing into this sanctuary: *Illum oportet crescere, me autem minui* ["He must increase, but I must decrease"]. There is no mistaking the fact that the *humanity* of God then moved from the center to the margin, from the emphatic principal clause to the less emphatic subordinate clause. It would, I fancy, have embarrassed me somewhat if I had been asked, say in the year 1920 — the year in which I confronted in this very hall my great teacher, Adolf von Harnack — to speak about the humanity of God. We should have sensed evil behind this theme. In any case we were not engaged with it. The fact that it has been given us today and that I could not today refuse to say something on it is a symptom, showing that the earlier critical turn was not a final word. It could not be. Even the change of direction in which we are now involved cannot be a final word. That may, however, become the concern of a future generation. Our task is this: the knowledge of God's *humanity* on the basis of, starting out from, the knowledge of the *divinity* of God.

I

Permit me in my exposition to give this theme first of all the form of a report. We shall look back to the critical turn of those days. And then our looking back will of itself change into a looking forward upon the new task that has been pressing upon us from that day to this.

The critical turn of those days had avowedly a *critical-polemical* character. Looked at from the temporal point of view it certainly developed gradually, but in terms of its content, it was a sudden conversion. It took the shape of an impetuous movement to dethrone the then dominant, more or less liberal, or even positive theology, which indeed only represented the mature stage of a development that had been going on apparently irresistibly for the past two or three centuries.

Today it is necessary — and also easier — to do a greater historical justice to that earlier theology and to the whole development culminating in it than, in the vehemence of the first onset and conflict of that time, appeared to us possible or advisable. But there is one thing which, in any unprejudiced estimate of its legitimate aim and undoubted services, cannot be concealed even in the most friendly retrospect. It is, that things could not go on as they were doing. It was inevitable that bounds should be set to the then prevailing theological conception by new and at the same time older and original Christian knowledge and language. Along almost the whole front, at any rate in all its representative figures and groups, evangelical theology had become religionistic and so anthropocentric and so, in this sense, humanistic. I mean, the phenomenon and theme about which everything circled was an outer and inner disposition and emotion in human piety — which could well be Christian piety. That is what it circled around in the principles it formulated, in its representation of the Christian past and in its practical understanding of the Christian present, in its ethics and in what it was pleased to call its dogmatics, in the church proclamation and instruction which it shaped, but, first and foremost, in its exposition of the Bible. And apparently it had so to circle without having any exit into the open air. What did it know and what had it still to say about God's divinity? To think of God meant for them, with scarcely any attempt to hide the fact, to think of human experience, particularly of the Christian religious experience. To speak about God meant to speak about humanity, no doubt in elevated tone, but once more and now more than ever about human revelations and miracles, about human faith and human works. Without doubt *human beings* were here magnified at the expense of *God* — the God as One who is sovereign Other standing over against humanity, as the immovable and immutable Lord confronting humanity, Creator and Redeemer. This God who is the free partner of humanity in a history which he himself inaugurated and in a dialogue ruled by him — this divine God was in danger of being reduced to a pious notion: the mythical expression and symbol of human excitation oscillating between its own psychic heights or depths, whose truth could only be that of a monologue and its own graspable content.

Here some of us took fright — after having, with all the rest, drunk the various cups of this theology to the last dregs. Here (somewhere about the middle of the second decade of our century) we felt we had reached the parting of the ways. Had the pious human being, had religion of whose history and present state we had at the university heard so much that was glorious and afterwards tried to say it ourselves, become, in our own person, problematical? Was it the encounter with socialism as interpreted by Kutter and Ragaz that opened our eyes to the fact that God might want to be God and to speak quite otherwise than in the fusty shrine of the Christian self-consciousness? Was it the aspect of the world, so suddenly darkened just then, compared with the preceding long peace period of our youth, which made us note that human distress might be too great to find in the advice to turn to one's religious possibilities a word that brought comfort and direction? Was it — and for me personally this played a decisive role — the failure of the ethics of modern theology at the outbreak of the First World War which led to our discontent with its exegesis, its conception of history and its dogmatics? Or, positively, was it the Blumhardt message of the Kingdom of God, which was only then, strange to relate, becoming actual? Was it Kierkegaard, Dostoyevsky, Overbeck, read as commentaries to that message, through whom we found ourselves summoned to search out and to make for new shores? Or more fundamental than all that, was it the discovery that the theme of the Bible — contrary to the critical and the orthodox exegesis, in which we had been brought up — definitely could not possibly be human religion and religious ethics — could not possibly be humanity's own secret divinity, but — this was the rock on which we first foundered — the divinity of *God*, precisely God's *divinity*, God's own peculiar nature over against not only the natural, but also the spiritual cosmos, God's absolutely unique existence, power and initiative above all in his relationship to humanity? We felt that it was in this way, and only in this way, that we could understand the voice of the Old and New Testaments, that it was from here, and only from here, that we could from now on be theologians and particularly preachers, *ministri Verbi Divini*.

Were we right or wrong? Undoubtedly we were right. Just read the *Glaubenslehren* of Troeltsch and Stephan! Read even a Dogmatics so fine in its way as that of Lüdemann or even that of Seeberg! Blind alleys! What was needed then was without doubt not any further rearrangement within the traditional discipline, such as was finally attempted by Wobbermin, Schaeder, Otto, but nothing less than this radical turning.

49

The ship threatened to run on to the sands. The moment had come to turn the helm through this angle of 180 degrees. And in view of what is to be said later, let it be at once premised: "What is past is past." So there can be no question later, there can be no question now, of denying that critical turn or cancelling it out. No doubt there was later and there is today a "retraction." A genuine retraction, however, does not by any means consist in a retrospective withdrawal, but in a new start and attack in which what was said before has now to be said properly — in a better way. If what we then thought we had discovered and what we brought forward was no final word, but one that needed retraction, it was nonetheless a true word, which as such must keep its ground, which still today cannot be passed by, which rather forms the basis of what we have today to reflect further upon. Assuredly whoever did not share in that earlier critical turn, or who still does not find it impressive that God is God, would not get a sight of what has now to be said further as true word about his humanity.

But just in view of that critical turn which then took place, there might well have been sung: "You see the moon aloft the sky? It's only half that meets the eye." It must now be asserted equally openly that we were then — even *vis-à-vis* the theology from which we derived and from which we had to detach ourselves — only to a limited extent in the right. Limited in the sense in which all movements, attitudes and positions that are predominantly critical and polemical, however significant they may be, are accustomed to be right only to a limited extent. What mighty formulations were there partly taken over, partly newly fabricated! In the forefront of all — "and as they warbled, a thousand voices struck up and echoed them in the field" — the famous *totaliter aliter* breaking in "vertically from above" and the no less famous "infinite qualitative difference" between God and humanity; the vacuum; the mathematical point and the tangent, in which alone they were supposed to touch each other; the bold assertion that there is generally only one theological interest in the Bible, namely God, that there is visible in it only one way, namely, that from above downwards, and there is audible only one message, namely that of forgiveness of sins — immediate, without before or after — while the problem of ethics as such is identical with human sickness unto death; the view of redemption which consists in the cancellation of the creatureliness of the creature, in the swallowing up of this world by the world beyond; correspondingly the summons to faith as to a leap into the abyss, and the like. All, no matter how well meant it was, and how much was to be said for it, yet somewhat cruelly inhuman, and itself also — only on the other side — running to some extent in a heretical direction. What a clearance was made — and almost nothing else! Everything that even from afar smelt of mysticism and morals, of pietism and romanticism or even of idealism, how suspect it was and how strictly prohibited or confined in the strait-jacket of restrictions that sounded prohibitive! What derisive laughter there was where there need only have been a sad and friendly smile! Might the whole not often appear more like the news of an enormous execution than the message of the Resurrection which was indeed its aim? Was there no foundation for the impression of many contemporaries that it all might amount to making Schleiermacher, for a change, stand on his head, that is, making God, for a change, great at the expense of human beings: so here not so very much fundamentally would be gained, perhaps in the last resort only a new titanism be at work? Was it only obduracy when alongside the many who listened and took part with a sense of emancipation, so many others preferred to shake their heads, dumbfounded or even — as Harnack then — angry at such innovation? Did that attitude not proclaim the dim suspicion that something indispensable might be at stake in the religionism, the anthropocentrism, the doubtful humanism of that theology of the preceding period — namely , the humanity of God which in all the unmistakable weakness, indeed, perversity of its conception did not get justice when we — immersed in the spectacle of the mighty deployment of Leviathan and Behemoth in the book of Job — focused all attention on his divinity.

Looking at things from our side, where was our position false? Where had, and therefore where has, the new change of direction to begin? The acute friend[4] from the other side of the stream has, as is well known, laid his finger on the fact that then almost the only concept employed was that of diastasis, only seldom and on occasion the complementary concept of analogy. That is no doubt correct. But was this formal failing not really only a symptom of a deeper seated material trouble afflicting our thought and language? What I mean is: it consisted in our being wrong at the very point where we were right, namely, in our not knowing how to carry into effect carefully enough and completely enough the new recognition of the *divinity* of God which so deeply stirred us and then also others. It was no doubt good and timely to return to it and to assert it with great force. But in this matter, Master Calvin especially gave us not only good instruction. The allegation that we had taught that God was all, and humanity nothing, was, of course, a pure invention of those who were then dumbfounded or angry. It was not as bad as that. Even then on

occasion certain hymns of praise to humanism had been struck up —
Platonic humanism especially, from which even Calvin derived. But it
is true, we were fascinated then above all by the image and the conception of a "totally other" which we had no right without more consideration to identify with the divinity of him who is called Yahweh-Kyrios in
the Bible. In the isolation, abstraction and absolutism in which we
viewed it and opposed it to humanity, poor wretches — not to say boxed
their ears with it — it still had or required greater similarity to the
divinity of the God of the philosophers than to that of the God of
Abraham, Isaac and Jacob. Was there not again a threat of a molten
image appearing? What if — this was the concern and objection of
Leonhard Ragaz — the end of the hymn to the Majesty of God was to be
a new confirmation of the hopelessness of all human action, and with
that a new justification of human autonomy and therefore of secularism
in the sense of the Lutheran doctrine of the two kingdoms? God forbid!
That is not what we aimed at or desired. But did we not largely fail to
perceive that the *divinity* of the *living* God — and it was with him that we
wanted to deal — has its meaning and power only in the context of his
history and of his dialogue with *humanity*, and therefore in his *togetherness* with humanity? Yes, indeed — and that is the point from which
there must be no going back. I refer to *God's* sovereign togetherness with
humanity, based on himself, and determined, delimited, arranged only
by himself. It is something that happens and is knowable in that context
thus and not otherwise. But it is God's *togetherness* with humanity. God
shows and reveals who he is and what he is in his divinity, not in the
vacuum of a divine self-sufficiency, but genuinely just in this fact that he
exists, speaks and acts as partner (without doubt the absolutely superior
partner) of humanity. He who does that is the living God. And the freedom in which he does *that* is his divinity. It is the divinity which as such
has also the character of humanity. It is in this form and only in this form
that the statement of the divinity of God was and is to be opposed to that
theology of the preceding period — in positive acceptance, not in
thoughtless rejection of the elements of truth which cannot be denied it,
even when its weakness stands revealed right down to the foundation.
God's *divinity* rightly understood includes his *humanity*.

II

Where do we learn this? How is this statement justified and what indeed
demands it? It is a *Christological* statement, or rather, a statement based
on and to be developed out of Christology. After that first critical turn

there would have been no need of a second if we had, then at the very beginning, possessed the presence of mind to risk making the whole counter-movement that had become inevitable start from that point, so that it would have been based, better and more accurately, on the central and total witness of Holy Scripture. One thing is certain, that in *Jesus Christ*, as we know him from the witness of Holy Scripture, we have not to do with *humanity* in the abstract — people who, in their little bit of religion and religious morality, could satisfy themselves without God and therefore be God to themselves. Nor, on the other hand, with *God* in the abstract — a God who in his divinity is nothing else than separated from human beings, nothing else than far from them and strange to them and therefore non-human, if not quite inhuman. In Jesus Christ there is no barrier on the human side upwards nor one on God's side downwards. Rather, what we have in him is the history, the dialogue, in which God and humanity meet and are together, the reality of the *covenant* concluded, kept and completed by them *mutually*. In his one person Jesus Christ is at once as true God humanity's faithful partner, and as true human being God's faithful partner, both the Lord abased to community with humanity, and the servant exalted to community with God, both as the Word spoken from out of the highest, most glorious Beyond, and the Word heard in the deepest, darkest Here and Now: both unconfused, but also undivided, wholly the One and wholly the Other. Thus, in this *unity* Jesus Christ is the Mediator, the Reconciler between God and humanity. Thus, demanding and awakening faith, love and hope, he acts for *God* before *humanity* — and, representing, atoning, interceding, for *humanity* before *God.* Thus he attests and guarantees to humanity God's free *grace*, but he also attests and guarantees to God free human gratitude. Thus he establishes in his person God's right *vis-à-vis* humanity, but also humanity's right before God. Thus he is in his person the covenant in its fulness, the close at hand Kingdom of Heaven, in which God speaks and humanity hears, God gives and humanity receives, God commands and humanity obeys. God's glory shines in the highest — but also from the highest into the depths — and peace on earth eventuates among the people of his good pleasure. And just in this way, as this mediator and reconciler between God and humanity, Jesus Christ is for both *revealer.* Who and what God is in truth, and who and what humanity, we have not to explore and construct by roving freely far and near, but to read it where the truth about both dwells, in the fulness of their union, their covenant, that fulness which manifests itself in Jesus Christ.

Who and what *God* is — it is just that in particular which, in the new change of direction of evangelical light and language which has become necessary, we have to understand more accurately and better in view of that earlier critical turn. But who and what is God in *Jesus Christ*? — this is how the question must be framed if we are going to push forward to a better answer.

And no doubt it is God's *divinity* which is the first and the fundamental thing that meets the eye as we view the existence of Jesus Christ attested in Holy Scripture. And God's divinity in Jesus Christ consists in God's being in him sovereign *subject*, who speaks and acts: *he* is the One who is free, in whom all freedom has its ground, its meaning, its prototype. *He* is the initiator, founder, maintainer and fulfiller of the covenant, he the sovereign Lord of the amazing situation in which he is not only different from humanity, but becomes and is one with us: *he*, who is also the Creator of this partner of his, he, through whose faithfulness the corresponding faithfulness of this partner of his is awakened and brought into action. This was especially clearly worked out by the early Reformed Christology in its doctrine of the "hypostatic union": God sits in power. His speaking, giving, commanding, comes absolutely *first* in the existence of Jesus Christ; human hearing, receiving, obeying, can and must only *follow* this. Human freedom is in Jesus Christ completely included in the freedom of God. Without God's condescension no exaltation of humanity could be achieved. As the Son of God, and not otherwise, Jesus Christ is also the Son of Man. This sequence is irreversible. God's independence, omnipotence and eternity, his holiness and righteousness and therefore his divinity are in their original and peculiar form the power of this sequence, "superordination" and "subordination,"[5] which are effective and visible in the existence of Jesus Christ. It is therefore no general divinity, to be conceptually reached; it is this concrete God — actual and recognizable in the condescension — that is peculiar to the existence of Jesus Christ and that comes from that sequence. But here something still more concrete is to be seen. God's deep freedom is in Jesus Christ his freedom for *love*. That divine ability, which works out and is represented in his existence in that "superordination" and "subordination" is manifestly also God's ability to humble himself, to adjust himself to something else and to adjust this something else to himself — no doubt in that irreversible sequence, but in it in perfect reality. It is just in that sequence that there arises and exists in Jesus Christ the fullest *community* of God with humanity. God's divinity therefore is no prison in which he could exist only in himself and for himself. It is rather his freedom to be in himself and for himself, but also to be with us and for us, to assert himself, but also to surrender himself, to be both completely august and also completely insignificant, not only omnipotent but also omnipotent compassion, not only Lord but also servant, not only Judge but also himself the condemned, humanity's eternal King, but also our brother within time. All that, without losing his divinity in the smallest degree! Rather, all that just in the highest proof and manifestation of his divinity! He who does all that and therefore clearly can do it, he and no other is the living God. That is the nature of his divinity — the divinity of the God of Abraham, Isaac and Jacob. It is thus that it is effective and recognizable in Jesus Christ. If he is the Lord of truth, then the very truth of God is this and no other.

But it is just in view of Jesus Christ that the judgment is made that God's divinity does not exclude, but includes his humanity. If only Calvin had continued thinking more energetically at this point in his Christology, in his doctrine of God, in his doctrine of predestination and then logically in his ethics! Then his Geneva would not have become such a dismal affair. Then his letters would not have contained so much bitterness. Then it would not be so obvious to play off a Henri Pestalozzi and, among his contemporaries, a Sebastian Castellio against him. How should God's divinity *exclude* his humanity? For it is God's freedom for love, and therefore his ability to be not only in the heights but also in the depths, not only great but also small, not only in and for himself but also to be with another who is different from himself, to give himself for this other, since there is room enough in it for community with humanity. And precisely, in his relationship to this other — it is indeed his work! — God has and holds the absolute priority. The first and decisive Word is and remains *his* — *his* the initiative, *his* the direction. How else could we see or say it in view of Jesus Christ, in whom we find humanity accepted into community with God? No, God needs no exclusion of humanity, no non-humanity or inhumanity, in order to be truly God. But we may and must go on to see and affirm that rather his divinity *includes* in itself his humanity. Not the fatal Lutheran doctrine of the two natures and their *idiomata*,[6] though its essential aim here is not to be turned down but accepted. It would be a false God's false divinity, in which and with which we did not at once encounter his humanity also. Such false divinities are once and for all turned to derision in Jesus Christ. In him the judgment is once and for all given that God is not without humanity. Not as if God needed something else, and

55

particularly human beings, in order as partners to him to be truly God. "What is man that thou art mindful of him? And the son of man, that thou visitest him?"[7] How should God as the eternal love not be able to be sufficient to himself? Even without humanity, even without the whole created cosmos, he would truly in his life as Father, Son and Holy Spirit, be no solitary or egoistic God. And there is no necessity for his being *for* humanity; he could — one even thinks, he would rather have to be against us. But that is the mystery in which we actually meet him in the existence of Jesus Christ; in his freedom he actually does not desire to be without humanity, but *with* us, and in the same freedom to be not against us but, regardless of and contrary to our desert, to be *for* us — he desires in fact to be humanity's partner and our omnipotent pitying Savior. He chooses to make his power, comprehending as it does, the heights and the far off, the depths and the near, to be to our advantage, to keep community with us in the area secured through his divinity. He decides to love precisely us, to be precisely God, *our* Lord, *our* Pitier, *our* Upholder and Saviour unto eternal life, to desire precisely *our* praise and service. In this divinely free willing and choosing, in this sovereign decision (in this decree, as they used to put it), God is *human*. His free affirmation of humanity, his free sympathy with us, his free intervention for us — that is God's humanity. We recognize it precisely where we also, and first of all, recognize his divinity. Is it not the case that in Jesus Christ, as we see him in the witness of Holy Scripture, genuine divinity includes also genuine humanity? There we see the Father who has compassion on his lost son, the King who pities his insolvent debtor, the Samaritan who has compassion on the man who fell among thieves and espouses his cause in an act of compassion which is as noble and effective as it is unexpected. And the act of compassion to which all these parables as parables of the Kingdom of Heaven point is this: there stands One — the very One who speaks in these parables — whose heart is moved by the weakness and perversity, the perplexity and misery of the human folk around him, who does not despise this human folk as it is, but incomprehensibly honors it, who takes it to his heart, puts himself in its place, who perceives it to be the will of God — that commanding will to which he gives complete submission — that he has to sacrifice himself for this human folk, and seeks his glory in the doing of this very thing. In the mirror of this humanity of *Jesus Christ* is revealed the humanity of *God* which is included in his divinity. As he is, so is God. It is thus that he affirms humanity, that he sympathizes with us, that he interests himself in us. The God of Schleiermacher cannot

56

have compassion. The God of Abraham, Isaac and Jacob can and does. If Jesus Christ is the Word of Truth, the "mirror of the fatherly heart of God" [Luther], then Nietzsche's saying, that man is something that has to be overcome, is an impudent lie, and the *truth* of *God* is just this and nothing else — his *friendliness to humanity* (as Titus 3.4 puts it).

III

But we should not yet have carried what we learned to a proper conclusion, at any rate we should be short of a full grasp of it, if its content were not made clear for us along the lines which all Christian thought and language, starting from there, must follow. What has been stated about God's humanity, the Immanuel to which we have advanced from the Christological center, cannot but involve the widest-ranging *consequences*. These come to light when we are questioned about the *correspondence* — here the concept of analogy could come into its own — of our thought and discourse with the humanity of God. These consequences — not all of them, but the most fundamental and important — must now be set forth in a sketchy way.

From God's being human, in the sense described, there follows a quite definite *distinction of humanity* — of all that bear the human countenance, of the sum of those capabilities and possibilities which human beings have partly in common with other creatures partly in contrast to them, and finally, of human work and its products. The recognition of this distinction has nothing to do with any optimistic estimate of human beings. They get it as the beings whom God was pleased to make his covenant-partners, and for no other reason. But they actually get it and cannot be deprived of it by any pessimistic judgment, however well founded, for the simple reason that God is in this sense human.

We have to regard all *human beings*, even the oddest, most infamous or wretched, from the point of view that, on the basis of the eternal decision of God, Jesus Christ is also their brother, God himself is also their Father. On that assumption we have to associate with them. If that is already known to them, we have to strengthen them in it. If they do not yet know it or know it no longer, it is our job to impart this knowledge to them: When the humanity of God is perceived, no other attitude is possible to any human companion. It is identical with the practical recognition of their human rights and their human dignity. If we refused it to them, we should, on our side, be renouncing Jesus Christ as our brother and God as our Father.

The distinction which accrues to human beings from the humanity of God extends also to all that with which they as humans are endowed and equipped by God their Creator. This gift, their humanness, is not extinguished by the Fall of humanity, nor suffers any diminution even of its goodness. It is not because human beings deserved such a privilege in virtue of their humanity that they are elected for intercourse with God. They are so only by God's grace. But they are elect as those who have been so endowed by God — in their special corporality in which they certainly have a great deal in common with plant and animal, and as rationally thinking, willing, speaking beings who have to act on their own responsibility and reach spontaneous decisions and who above all are from the start socially constituted, bound by obligation to their human companions. It is as such beings in their special totality, that God means, loves and calls them. It is as such beings, realizing their special nature, that they may and must praise him and put themselves thankfully at the service of his grace. It would not do to blacken, to esteem lightly or run down even partly, this humanity — this gift of God, which marks them as such beings. We can meet God only within the bounds of the human which he has determined. But just within these bounds we may meet him. He does not spurn what is human. Quite the contrary. This is what we have to hold on to.

But human distinction goes still further. It extends to the special human activity which comes from that endowment, to what is usually called human *culture* in its higher as well as its lower branches. We all participate in it, whether as producers or as consumers, in any case as having responsibility for it. In regard to it we could not exercise any abstinence, even if we would. But we must not even want that. Each of us has a place and a function in its history. Certainly it has to be borne in mind here that the use of the good gift of God and therefore human work and its great and small results have been most grievously compromised by humanity's perverted attitude to God, to neighbor and to self. Civilization both in the past and at present clearly and truly shows that human beings, far from being good, are nothing short of monstrous. But even the sceptic who was in this respect most extreme in view of the humanity of God directed towards human beings who are not good, who are indeed monstrous, would not dare to say that civilization shows only that. What else is civilization than the endeavor of human beings to be human, and therefore to bring to honor and to set to work the good gift of their humanity? That in this endeavor we again and again go to pieces, and indeed achieve the opposite, is another matter by itself. But this does not alter the fact that the endeavor is unavoidable; above all, the fact that people who take part in this endeavor in one way or another, as producers or as consumers, are the beings in whom God is interested; or finally the fact that God as *humanity's* Creator and Lord is still at liberty on occasion to make of human activity and its results, in spite of their problematic character, *parables* of his own eternally good willing and doing, in face of which there could be no place for any arrogant abstinence, but for reverence, joy and gratitude.

As a second consequence we have to assert that, through the humanity of God, a quite definite *theme* is presented especially to *theological* culture — for that also exists alongside of pyramid building, pre-Kantian and post-Kantian philosophy, classical poetry, socialism and theoretical and practical atomic physics. Since God in his divinity is human, it has to do neither with God in himself nor with humanity itself, but with the God who encounters human beings and with the human beings who encounter God; with their dialogue and history, in which their community eventuates and reaches its objective. Just for that reason theology can think and speak only in view of Jesus Christ, and by starting out from him. It cannot bring him into the field. Nor can it carry that dialogue, history and community to completion. These are not at its disposal. It is thrown back on the Holy Scriptures, according to which the covenant has been completely ratified, and in which he — in which Jesus Christ — bears witness to himself. It listens to this witness. It trusts it and is satisfied with it. It was in this way that it received through the centuries, and also receives today, its object, its theme and along with it the introduction to that theoretical and practical realism which is suited to it. In what does this "*objectivity*" [*Sachlichkeit*] consist, which theology has to establish in its exegesis, in its investigation, representation and interpretation of Christian past and present, in its dogmatics and ethics, in its preaching? It consists in its attempt, without allowing itself to be enticed into error to the right or to the left, to see, to understand and to express that *intercourse* — the intercourse of God with humanity which involves the intercourse of humanity with God — namely, the Word and act of the grace of God and the word and deed of human gratitude, evoked, awakened and nourished by it, the first not without the second and the second not without the first, both of them in the order, difference and unity given in the divinity and thus in the humanity of God. When it keeps to this theme, it is even in its most modest form good — let us say for once, cultivated theology.

Whether the theological existentialism of Bultmann and his followers, in proximity to which we here find ourselves, advances us in this "objectivity" which is indispensable to a good theology has still to be demonstrated. It is not yet clear whether, and in what sense, a genuine concrete dialogue, history and fellowship between God and humanity, come there into the field of vision, or whether we have only a repristination of the theology of the devout individual, engaged in self-reflection (this time about one's authenticity or inauthenticity), self-expression and self-explanation. Misgivings are aroused by the fact that neither the people of Israel nor the Christian Church seem to have had up to now any constitutive importance. And what is the value of the "overcoming of the subject-object scheme" which has lately been proclaimed with particular zeal, so long as it is not settled and assured that this undertaking will not in the long run issue again in the anthropocentric myth and will not anew make just that *intercourse* between God and humanity and so the object of theology problematical ? Certainly existentialism may have reminded us yet again of the elements of truth of the older school in impressing on us again and yet again that one cannot speak of God without speaking of humanity. It is to be hoped that it will not lead us back into the old error that one could speak of humanity without having first, and that very concretely, spoken of the living God.

There is a third consequence: that God's humanity and the recognition of it demand that the thought and discourse of Christian theology take up a definite *attitude* and be carried out in a particular way. Theology can never deal with its objective in a vacuum, in mere theory. It cannot affirm, consider and express truths that rest or are moved within themselves — not an abstract truth about God, or about humanity, or even about the intercourse between God and humanity. It can never substantiate, reflect, report in a monologue. There is no such thing as a theological pictorial art. The humanity of God, just because it is an event, is not to be fixed in a picture. In correspondence with its object, the basic form of theology is prayer and sermon. It can itself only take the form of a dialogue. Its outer presupposition and motive consist in the fact that this intercourse between God and human beings concerns all people. What is dealt with in him, in Jesus Christ, is the most intimate matter for all of them; what is decided is everybody's life or death. It is necessary that all should know him, in order to have a right relation to him, to share in him. But many, far too many, do not yet know, or no longer know, or do not rightly know of him. In one way or another that holds of everybody. Therefore it is necessary and it is commanded that there should be proclaimed, shouted out, imparted: *tua res agitur!* [This concerns you!]. Christian thought circles around both God's Word of the covenant of peace, and about human beings who have in this way or in that not heard, or not rightly heard, this Word, to whom therefore it must be spoken. And Christian discourse is at once prayer to God and address to these people. As the exegesis of Form-history [*Form-geschichte*[8]] has shown, it is *kerygma*, herald's call, message. That is what it is in the New Testament — and there by way of example for the whole time, following the resurrection of Jesus Christ, and preceding his direct, universal, concluding revelation. This *kerygma* does not invite or summon to any sort of freely roving speculation but to the special reflection of faith and obedience, in which one passes over from the mere "interest" of the spectator to the genuine *inter-esse*; then we know our own God in the divinity of Jesus Christ and ourselves in his humanity — ourselves under God's judgment and grace, ourselves as recipients of his promise and his commandment; in which therefore we ourselves enter into the event of that intercourse with our own understanding, will and feeling. Theological thought and discourse can never bring it about that this happens to us; just on that account, it can have not only the character of address, but must also have the character of prayer. For this it can be of service to us, and it must therefore be directed to this service-ableness, corresponding to the humanity of God himself. If this practical performance is lacking, it would mean that it was not only acting out of character, but that it was betraying its true nature, prostituting itself, and that, however "Christian" its content might be, it would be becoming a profane thought and discourse.

The question of *language*, which has to be discussed with a special view to the so-called "outsiders," is not so burningly serious as is maintained these days from various sides. For one thing, starting out again from the humanity of God, there can be no counting seriously on real "outsiders," on a "world that has come of age,"[9] but only with one that thinks itself of age (and daily proves that that is just what it is not). Further, if we start from here, there can only be those who have not yet conceived and apprehended themselves as "insiders." And again in the latter sense even the most convinced Christians must and will recognize themselves anew as "outsiders." So then there is no need of any special language for insiders and for outsiders. Both are — we all are — people of the world of our time. A little bit of "non-religious" language of the streets, of the newspaper, or literature or — at the dizziest heights — of philosophy may therefore, when the address is in question, no doubt on occasion be quite in place. But that must not be in any case a matter of special concern. A little bit of the language of Canaan, a little bit of "revelation positivism" can also be a good thing in the address to us all, and from my experience — and in this I do not stand alone — this is, not always, but often, better understood by the most alien strangers than if one had the idea of encountering them — as "Jesuit in Gütterli," certainly no sympathetic figure! — with any jargon that at the moment sounded "modern." What we have to say to them — and first to ourselves — is in any case a surprising novelty. If we see to it that it is the great novelty — the message of the eternal love of God, directed to us human beings, as we were, are and shall be at all times — then we shall decidedly be very well understood by them, whatever they may or may not do with it. Those whose hearts are really with God and so really with men and women, can be confident that the Word of God which they are attempting to declare, will not return void.

A fourth consequence: the sense and tone of what we say must be fundamentally *positive*. Proclamation of the covenant of God with humanity, declaration of the place which has been opened up and assigned to human beings once and for all in this covenant, message of Immanuel, message of Christ — that is the task. That dialogue and encounter which is our theological theme, are concerned with God's grace and human gratitude. It is no task of ours to tear open again the abyss which Jesus Christ closed. Once again and no doubt truly, human beings are not good. God does not turn towards them without saying No to their transgression with inexorable sharpness. Thus it cannot but be that theology also must introduce this No within the framework of its theme. But it must not do so otherwise than as the No which Jesus Christ has taken on himself for us human beings, so that it may no longer fall upon us and so that we might no longer place ourselves under it. What takes place in God's humanity is, in including that No in itself, the *affirmation* of humanity. That gives the direction our word should have. While people with whom we have to do in ourselves and in others are the rebels, the rotters, the hypocrites that they are, at the same time they are the creatures to whom their Creator is faithful and not unfaithful — still more, the beings. whom God has loved and will love, for whom he has pledged himself and made himself surety. "Jesus is victor" and "you people belong to God" — these two watchwords of Blumhardt hold. And in this exposition, there may also hold, as a proposition of defiant, happy proclamation: *Anima humana naturaliter christiana*! [Tertullian] That is the testimony we must make to people in view of the humanity of God, without regard to the more or less gross godlessness of their humanity — all else only within the framework of this statement and promise. Just as the bitterest accusations and the darkest threats of judgment of the Old Testament prophets are uttered only in the context of the history of the covenant founded by Jahweh and faithfully maintained in spite of all the unfaithfulness of Israel — and as the Baptist's preaching of repentance had its basis and significance only in the Kingdom of Heaven that was near at hand; as also certain dreadful passages at the end of the Apocalypse of John have their place and so their limit in the book's very last words: "Amen. Even so, come, Lord Jesus. The grace of our Lord Jesus Christ be with you all." It is good tidings which the Word of God preaches to the poor, freedom to the captives, eyesight to the blind, justification and sanctification and even a call to service to sinners, whether gross or refined. What follows from this is to be borne in mind. It is one thing to unveil and expose misunderstandings as such; it is another to understand and to guide towards understanding; and in this way moral seriousness is a praiseworthy thing, in this way the gift of penetrating and perhaps brilliant analysis of the times, of the situation, and of the psyche is certainly a fine gift. But the task of making the Gospel shine forth is more urgent than that of making that seriousness visible or putting this gift into action. Anyone to whom this positive task is not absolutely the chief task, who might be inclined to shout at, disconcert or laugh at people above all for their foolishness and wickedness, had better be silent. In this respect there is only one analogy to the humanity of God — the message — at once establishing and judging — of the great joy which is prepared for humanity by God and which we on our part may have in God: "All my springs are in thee" (Ps. 87.7).

Therefore "*universalism*" (*apokatastasis*)? I should like here to make just three brief observations that present a point of view which cannot be interpreted as for or against what goes under that name amongst us.

1. It would be well not to yield to that panic fright which this word seems to have a way of spreading around it, at least before one has come to an understanding with regard to its possible sense or nonsense.

2. It would be well to let oneself be spurred on by the passage, Col. 1.19, where it is stated that God resolved, through his Son, as his image and as the first born of the whole creation, "to reconcile all things ($\tau\grave{\alpha}$ $\pi\acute{\alpha}\nu\tau\alpha$) unto himself" and by the parallel passages, to consider whether the conception is not susceptible of a good interpretation.

3. It would be well, in view of the "danger" with which the expression

is ever and again seen to be encompassed, to ask for a moment, whether on the whole the "danger" from those theologians who are forever sceptically critical, who are again and again suspiciously questioning, because they are always fundamentally legalistic, and who are therefore in essentials sullen and dismal, is not in the meantime always more threatening amongst us than that of an unsuitably cheerful indifferentism or even antinomianism, to which one could in fact yield oneself on one definite understanding of that conception. One thing is sure, that there is no theological justification for setting any limits on our side to the friendliness of God towards humanity which appeared in Jesus Christ — it is our theological duty to see and to understand that as even greater than we had done before.

And now in conclusion, still a fifth consequence: When the humanity of God is perceived, Christendom, the *church*, is to be taken seriously and affirmed, and one must thankfully profess oneself a member of it. We have, each in his place, to participate in its life, fit into its service. One of the exaggerations of which we made ourselves guilty around 1920 was that we were able to see the theological relevance of the church properly only in its character as negative counterpart to the Kingdom of God, then so fortunately rediscovered by us. We were inclined then to regard as "not so very important," because "human all too human," the form of its teaching, of its public worship, of its legal arrangements. We declared all earnestness or zeal directed to them as superfluous or even pernicious. In all this we, at least, came near to the theory and practice of a spiritual insurgency and of an esoteric *gnosis*. At the present moment, in view of the unceasingly actual Roman temptation, as well as the ecclesiastical, clericalistic and liturgistic restoration and reaction going around in the Germany of today and perhaps one day encroaching on our own territory, it would certainly not be fitting to silence or even to subdue today the note sounding ultimately through the whole Bible of the judgment beginning at the house of God. And it was and is definitely no good undertaking to reverse the order, *event*, then *institution*, which is likewise secured in the Bible. But we had and have to see and understand that, in maintaining this order and remembering that judgment, there can be no neglect or renunciation of our solidarity with the church. Criticism of the church can be significant and fruitful only when it comes from insight into — I am not exaggerating — the necessity for salvation of the existence and function of the church, and when it is uttered to further its ministry in its gathering, upbuilding and mission. The humanity of God has to do with the old and the new Israel, with the individual existing within it and not in any empty space. Jesus Christ is the Head of his Body and only so the Head of his members. Our confession of faith in God's work accomplished in him states that it was done *pro nobis*, and only so also *pro me*. The Lord's Prayer is a we-prayer, and only so also an I-prayer. "We" are the church. The church is the special human community, the congregation, or to use Calvin's expression, the *compagnie*, which has been constituted, appointed and called to be his witness in the world by a knowledge of the gracious God manifest in Jesus Christ, a knowledge which is rather miserable, but which is invincible because the Holy Spirit has the making of it. And what else is the existence of this special human community than the mirroring — certainly everywhere obliterated and obscured and all too often with the continuity broken — of the humanity of God, whose kindness to humanity goes so far as to call and waken some, many of these, as provisionally representing the rest and as his messengers to them for his worship, for his praise and service? We should be inhuman where God is human, we should be ashamed of Jesus Christ, if we felt like being ashamed of the church. For what Jesus Christ is for God and for us on earth and in time, that he is as Lord of this congregation, as King of this people, as Head of this Body and of all its members. This he is, within this poor-looking, painfully torn and generally so questionable Christendom; this he is with, under and in Christians, admiration and even love for whom is beset with such serious difficulties. This he is as Reconciler and Redeemer of the whole world, but he is it within the strange community of these strange saints. For him it is not so mean, but rather it is in all its good and evil so dear and precious that he entrusts to it the bearing of witness to himself and so his cause in the world, indeed, his very self. So great is God's friendliness to humanity! For this reason there is no private Christianity. For this reason the position is that we take this community in its strangeness seriously, affirm it, love it, and critically but seriously regard as *important* in all details its human, all too human concern about better knowledge and better confession of faith, about its assemblies, about its internal organization and about its mission to the outside. For this reason, also, theology cannot be pursued in the private lighthouses of any kind of merely personal discoveries or views. It can only be church theology, which means that in all its elements it can only be set to work within the context of the questions and the answers which that community raises and in the hard service of its commission to all people. It may possibly be that one must oneself have taken part in difficult times in the church in order to know that in its work, its struggle and sufferings there are hours when not less than all depends on some human, very human iota or little item in its decisions and so also in its thinking and speaking. That makes one more circumspect where there is a disposition to see all around only adiaphora. In a really live church there are perhaps no adiaphora at all. But, however that may be, our *credo in Spiritum sanctum* would be empty, if it did not include concretely, practically and bindingly the *credo unam, sanctam, catholicam et apostolicam ecclesiam.* We believe the church as the place where in Christocratic brotherhood the crown of humanity, namely the co-humanity of human beings, can become visible — and more than that, as the place where God's glory will dwell on earth, where, namely, the humanity of God will assume palpable form already in time and here on earth. Here the humanity of God is recognized. Here joy is felt over it. Here it is celebrated and attested. Here Immanuel is gloried in as One, who, just in view of the world, is not willing to repudiate the burden of the church, but to take it on himself and carry it, has done it in the name of all its members — Rom. 8.31: "If God be for us, who can be against us?"

(H: 31-52)

*

CONCLUDING UNSCIENTIFIC POSTSCRIPT ON SCHLEIERMACHER

Schleiermacher was Barth's first theological love, and even this late critical essay contains paragraphs of warm appreciation. But he came to symbolize for Barth the fundamental problem of modern neo-protestant theology, namely its theological "turn to the subject," its "anthropologizing of theology." "Schleiermacher," Barth writes, "made the christianly pious person into the criterion and content of his theology." Schleiermacher defined theology as "the Christian religious affections set forth in speech." For Barth the church's language about God is address, proclamation of the Word of God, and the task of theology is to test the responsibility of such language by measuring it against Scripture.[10] In contrast to Schleiermacher's focus on the believing subject, Barth's focus is on God as speaking and acting Subject.

This essay also serves to review in more historical detail Barth's theological development, and shows how his critique of Schleiermacher determined his negative evaluation of the Bultmann school, "a new and vigorous Schleiermacher renaissance."[11]

Several other writings of Barth on Schleiermacher are available in English. Theology and Church[12] *contains two Schleiermacher essays from 1924 and 1926. Barth wrote a long chapter on Schleiermacher in his 1952 book on 18th and 19th century protestant theology, eleven chapters of which were translated into English in 1959 as* From Rousseau to Ritschl; *the complete work was published in 1972 as* Protestant Theology in the Nineteenth Century.[13] *Barth's lectures on Schleiermacher from 1923-24 were edited by Dietrich Ritschl and translated into English by Geoffrey Bromiley as* The Theology of Schleiermacher[14], *which also contains the selection below. The German original of our text was first published in 1968 as an "Afterword" to a reader of Schleiermacher texts; this translation by George Hunsinger originally appeared in* Sciences Religieuses/Studies in Religion, *Spring, 1978, and was reprinted in Barth,* The Theology of Schleiermacher *(Grand Rapids, Michigan: Eerdmans, 1982).*

Having been invited to write an "Introduction" to this selection from Schleiermacher's writings, I have decided (after initial hesitations) that I could most conscientiously contribute, in the form of an "Afterword," a brief overview of the history of my own relationship to this "church father of the nineteenth (and also the twentieth?!) century" — or, if you will, an "unscientific postscript." What follows thus somewhat presumptuously describes a not unimportant segment in the course of my own life.

The temptation for some thus might not be slight to begin reading this book here, whereas it would be more meaningful for them to take in and digest the selection from Schleiermacher's expressions of his own life which has been so capably and creatively compiled by H. Bolli (without any involvement on my part). So, the curious are warned! Whoever takes a different view from the one here solemnly advised does so with my express disapproval. *Dixi et salvavi animam meam* [I speak and save my soul].

There was once a time, so I must begin, in my youthful occupation with theology when — after first having worked through Immanuel Kant's *Critique of Practical Reason* several times and (only then, but equally intensively) his *Critique of Pure Reason* — I knew how to swear no higher than by the man, Daniel Ernst Friedrich Schleiermacher.

I had highly respected my father, Professor Fritz Barth in Bern — his picture still hangs directly before me today — as a sound scholar, quite apart from all personal and spiritual ties. But I myself could not adopt, as one said at that time, his (moderately) "positive" theological attitude and direction, determined in his youth through J. T. Beck. Neither my first New Testament teacher, Rudolf Steck, with his amiable but rather tediously exact analyses (he considered even Galatians to be "inauthentic") nor my first dogmatics teacher, Hermann Lüdemann, with his ever ill-tempered systematic acuity (he was, like Steck, a direct pupil of F. C. Baur), was able to make a deeper and enduring impression on me. The same was true of the Old Testament scholar, Karl Marti, who was also a greatly learned man: what he (a pupil of Wellhausen) had to say about Israel's history and religion was a hopelessly dry kind of wisdom. That the Old Testament was concerned with something exciting I did not begin to discover until Berlin under Gunkel. What I owe despite everything to those Bern masters is that I learned to forget any fears I might have had. They gave me such a thorough grounding in the earlier form of the "historical-critical" school that the remarks of their later and contemporary successors could no longer get under my skin or even touch my heart — they could only get on my nerves, as is only too well known.

In Berlin, where by the way I learned to esteem Harnack even higher than Gunkel, I then bought myself, along with Wilhelm Herrmann's *Ethics*, a copy of Schleiermacher's *Speeches on Religion to its Cultured Despisers*, in the edition by R. Otto, which I still use. Eureka! Having apparently sought for "The Immediate," I had now found it, not through Hermann Kutter, who wrote his first book under that title, but through Schleiermacher. That those *Speeches* were the most important and correct writings to appear since the closing of the New Testament canon was a fact from which I did not allow my great Marburg teacher [Herrmann] to detract — just as little as I did his denigration of Schleiermacher's later and late writings. I did not see, yet I sensed, the line of continuity which runs through Schleiermacher's life's work from the *Speeches* to the so-called *Glaubenslehre* (a rather un-Schleiermacherian designation), and was implicitly inclined to give him credit all down the line. Anyway, as was certainly quite in order, I also loved Eichendorff and was especially fond of Novalis. Was I (am I!) a bit of a romantic myself? (By the way, what I wrote in the first edition of my *Romans* on pp. 195-204 about the evils of romanticism with explicit reference to the young Schleiermacher is something of which I "repent and suffer in my heart," just as in my holy zeal at that time I did not really do justice to pietism.) One thing, however, is certain, that even before 1910 I was a stranger in my innermost being to the bourgeois world of Ritschl and his pupils. In the year when the first edition of *Romans* appeared (1919),

I could still produce the provocative sentence: "We can afford to be more romantic than the romantics." But even the "historicism" by which Ernst Troeltsch and the historians of religion of that time thought they could outbid the Ritschlians (and thus also the teacher whom I still regard so highly, Wilhelm Herrmann) struck me as being too sterile, and at any rate was not what I was looking for. I had just now (not without direct and indirect instruction from Schleiermacher) tasted something of what "religion" itself was supposed to be. And the pallid "Schleiermacher renaissance" which began to emerge around 1910 was also a more literary affair which did not take me any further, nor could it take me any further. The only one of its representatives who made any impression on me as an interpreter of Schleiermacher, and who gave me something lasting to think about, was Heinrich Scholz, who then later became my close friend. At any rate, that Schleiermacher renaissance was superseded a few years later by a Luther renaissance, which, at least in its beginnings (around the anniversary celebrations of 1917), despite and because of Karl Holl, struck me as rather unfortunate.

Now, as to what concerned me, in 1909 I moved from Marburg to Geneva, and in 1911 to Safenwil. At both places the relatively few writings of Schleiermacher's which I owned received a special place of honor on my still rather modest bookshelves. But then came certain turning points which also touched my relationship to him.

Although in Geneva I had still lived completely and utterly in the religious atmosphere which I brought with me from Marburg, and especially from the circle of the *Christliche Welt* and its friends, when I moved to the industrial village of Safenwil, my interest in theology as such had to step back noticeably into second place (even though it continued to be nourished by my eager reading in the *Christliche Welt*, the *Zeitschrift für Theologie und Kirche*, and even in the works of Troeltsch, etc.). Because of the situation I found in my community, I became passionately involved with socialism and especially with the trade union movement. At that time I did not yet know that, in his later years, Schleiermacher also had become involved in the beginnings of these things, at least on the periphery — even though here and there I might have gathered that from his sermons! Those now came into my possession, along with his letters, his *Christian Morals*, and other of his writings — after a foray I conducted into my maternal grandfather's estate in Basel. This grandfather had studied in Berlin during the forties of the nineteenth century under, among others, the later Schelling, and afterwards in Heidelberg under R. Rothe; thus, he had still been able to take in something of

Schleiermacher's atmosphere, but then in the following period had gone over, like so many of his contemporaries, to a rather primitive theological conservatism, which was softened only by the mild pietism of my good grandmother. He had indeed purchased Schleiermacher (good for me that he did!), but had hardly read him seriously, and, judging from a few biting notes in the margins, had not loved him. So now those books had landed in my lap. But then, I had to read Sombart and Herkner. I had to read the Swiss trade union newspaper and the *Textilarbeiter*. Indeed, I also had to prepare my weekly sermon and my confirmation classes. Although in these pastoral activities I was decisively stimulated by Schleiermacher, it goes without saying that, like Schleiermacher himself as he proceeded, I did not exactly express myself in the language, or even exclusively in the original sense, of the *Speeches*. Even so, I really had neither the time nor the desire to pursue further research into his work.

Then came the beginning of my friendship with Eduard Thurneysen. He was committed to what was then the "modern" theology of his Basel teachers, P. Wernle and B. Duhm; beyond that, however, he was connected with Hermann Kutter and, further back, with Christoph Blumhardt. He made them both better known to me; before that my knowledge of them had only been cursory. From Kutter I simply learned to speak the great word "God" once again seriously, responsibly, and forcibly. From Blumhardt I learned just as simply (at least at the beginning) what it meant to speak of Christian hope. Ragaz and his "religious socialists" interested Thurneysen, and they interested me too, but only from a certain distance. The concept of "God's kingdom" was portrayed in various ways (sometimes more transcendently, sometimes more immanently) — but certainly no longer in the form familiar to us from Ritschl and his followers. The question lay in wait for me at the door: Had not even "my" Schleiermacher perhaps used that concept in a way which to me was now becoming increasingly strange?

And then the First World War broke out and brought something which for me was almost even worse than the violation of Belgian neutrality — the horrible manifesto of the ninety-three German intellectuals who identified themselves before all the world with the war policy of Kaiser Wilhelm II and Chancellor Bethmann-Hollweg. And to my dismay, among the signatories I discovered the names of almost all my German teachers (with the honourable exception of Martin Rade). An entire world of theological exegesis, ethics, dogmatics, and preaching, which up to that point I had accepted as basically credible, was thereby shaken to the foundations, and with it everything which flowed at that time from the pens of the German theologians. And Schleiermacher? Had not even he in the first of his *Speeches* from 1799 written impossible things about the British and the French? Had he not also been a leading Prussian patriot from 1806 to 1814? Would he also perhaps have signed that manifesto? Fichte certainly, perhaps Hegel too, but Schleiermacher? According to what I know of his letters from the period after 1815, I remain convinced that, no, he would not have done that. Nevertheless, it was still the case that the entire theology which had unmasked itself in that manifesto, and everything which followed after it (even in the *Christliche Welt*), was grounded, determined, and influenced decisively by him.

"My child, what are we now to speak?" These well-known words from *The Magic Flute* continue: "The truth, the truth, lest she also be complicit." But that was easier said than done. It was Thurneysen who once whispered the key phrase to me, half aloud, when we were alone together: what we needed for preaching, instruction, and pastoral care was a "wholly other" theological foundation. It seemed impossible to proceed any further on the basis of Schleiermacher. I can still see Thurneysen's contemptuous gesture to my Schleiermacher books in Safenwil. But where else could we turn? Kutter was also impossible, because he, like Ragaz later on, would have nothing to do with theology, but wanted only to know and to preach the "living God." He was also impossible for me, because, with all due respect for him and his starting point, his "living God" had become extremely suspicious to me after his wartime book *Reden an die deutsche Nation* [Speeches to the German Nation]. During that period Thurneysen once even broached the strange question of whether we shouldn't study Hegel. But nothing came of that then. We did not even reach for the Reformers at first, although in Geneva I had worked through Calvin's *Institutes* closely and from an earlier period had come to know (or thought I had come to know) the chief writings of Luther. The "old orthodoxy" was present to us only in the caricatures in which it had been taught to us at the university. In fact and in practice, as is well known, something much closer at hand forced itself upon us. We made a fresh attempt to learn our theological ABCs all over again. More reflectively than ever before, we began reading and expounding the writings of the Old and New Testaments. And behold, they began to speak to us — very differently than we had supposed we were obliged to hear them speak in the school of what was then called "modern" theology. The morning after Thurneysen had whispered to me our commonly held conviction, I sat down under an apple tree and began, with all the tools at my disposal, to apply myself to the Epistle to the Romans. That was the text which as early as my own confirmation classes (1901-02) I had heard was supposed to be concerned with something central. I began to read it as if I had never read it before — and not without deliberately writing out the things which I was discovering. Only now did I begin to regard my father, who had died in 1912, with, as I put in the preface to the first edition of *Romans*, "respect and gratitude" theologically as well. He belonged to those who were disregarded and slightly disdained in the theological lecture halls and seminar rooms of his time. And regardless of the warning at the end of Mozart's *Seraglio* that "Nothing is so hateful as revenge," I will not conceal the fact that for a moment the thought raced through my head that I could and would now exact a kind of reprisal from those who had placed my father in the shadows, even though he had been just as learned as they (only from a different point of view). Be that as it may, I read and read and wrote and wrote. Meanwhile, we published a bundle of sermons. True, among the books I had inherited from my father, I found many by J. T. Beck which were fruitful to use. True, at that time we also read huge amounts of Dostoyevsky (here again at Thurneysen's prompting) as well as Spittler, Kierkegaard, and even Overbeck — who had not been "disposed of" and whom one merely needed to mention in Basel at that time to make everyone's hair bristle. My philosopher brother, Heinrich, took care that I should once again seriously confront the wisdom of Plato as well. And Father Kant, who had provided the initial spark for me once before, also spoke in a remarkably new and direct way to me in those years. Even Kutter, despite everything, doubtless continued to speak to me. So at that time (and indeed later), I read the biblical text with many different kinds of spectacles, as I unhesitatingly made known. But by using all those different kinds of spectacles, what I honestly wanted to express (and was convinced I was expressing) was the word of the Apostle Paul. That is how *The Epistle to the Romans* originated and appeared, in a first, and then immediately in a second edition, in which, at the beginning of a long and pugnacious preface, I at once confessed that "no stone" of the first edition was left "standing upon the other." During the time when I was at work on the second edition, our eldest daughter, today an energetic grandmother, but then a little girl of six years, explained to anyone who was willing to listen that Daddy was now working on "a much better Epistle to the Romans"! What the angels might have been saying to themselves on this occasion is another matter. At any rate, the second edition, the one which became "famous," thus came into being. Whoever might want to pursue further the beginnings and progress of the so-called dialectical theology may turn to the volumes prepared by J. Moltmann and W. Fürst.[15]

However, in this whole story what about my relationship to — Schleiermacher? It is certain, for one thing, that neither in his youth nor in his maturity could he have preached a sermon like the one I preached and then published in 1916 under the title, "The Pastor Who Does Right by the People." It is also certain that what I thought, said, and wrote from that year on, I simply did without him, and that his spectacles were not sitting on my nose as I was expounding the Epistle to the Romans. He was no longer a "church father" for me. It is further certain, however, that this "without him" implied a rather sharp "against him." On occasion, I intentionally made that explicit. Yet I really did not do it — since "old love never fades" — without a deep inner regret that it could not be otherwise.

But then it came about in the course of this change, which my friend Emil Brunner also made, that in his book *Die Mystik und das Wort* (1924) he gave very drastic expression to our departure (which was unavoidable) from Schleiermacher. I had to review the book in *Zwischen den Zeiten*, and found myself in something of a quandary over it. Although it contained a great deal which I also held in my heart against Schleiermacher, I was not very happy with the way in which Brunner presented his case. I did not regard the term "mysticism" as an adequate designation of Schleiermacher's intentions. Moreover, in his fight against Schleiermacher and his victory over him (and here there were already some first indications of my later conflict with Brunner), I saw him relying just as forcefully on F. Ebner's anti-idealistic logology (a forerunner of contemporary linguistic philosophy) as on the validity of the "Word" (of God). (It is not without reason that J. Moltmann has so happily stressed this in his edition of the writings of "dialectical theology.") Above all, although certainly "against" Schleiermacher in my own way, I for my part was neither so certain nor so completely finished with him as Brunner undoubtedly was after he had completed that book.

I owe to his book, nonetheless, that it had an extraordinarily stimulating effect on me in the new and comprehensive study of Schleiermacher which I had meanwhile undertaken. For almost overnight in 1921 I found myself transposed into a newly founded chair for Reformed theology at Göttingen. I had now cheerfully decided — Ragaz and Kutter gave me no applause for this decision — in my own way and style to pursue theological research and teaching with grim seriousness. To carry out this task I was of course only very partially equipped. And so, before venturing on dogmatics, I announced some purely historical lectures — essentially for my own instruction, but not without a considerable influx of students. First I offered a two-hour course on the Heidelberg Catechism, then some four-hour courses on Calvin, on the Reformed confessions, on Zwingli, and finally on Schleiermacher! As far as I know, no one either before or since has attempted to interpret Schleiermacher in the light of his sermons. That was precisely what I first tried to do in my lectures, moving on from there to his *Speeches*, to the *Soliloquies*, to the *Dialogue on Christmas*, to the *Brief Outline on the Study of Theology*, to his *Hermeneutics* and finally, as far as time allowed, to *The Christian Faith*. Certainly it did not remain hidden that I was not exactly satisfied with the things which were appearing before our wondering eyes. But I attained the main purpose toward which I strove: I now understood Schleiermacher a little better than before (as I hope my students did as well). So without presupposing that I could pronounce an anathema over him, I was then in a position during my last three semesters at Göttingen to begin working out, and lecturing on, my own dogmatics. However, the posture of the Göttingen theological faculty was so Lutheran at that time that I was only allowed to teach that topic under the completely different heading of "Instruction in the Christian Religion." Laughing up my sleeve, I carried out this charade for three semesters. In the period which followed I then wrote various essays on Schleiermacher — for example, on "Schleiermacher's *Celebration of Christmas*" (1924) — in part with a certain irony, but on the whole with a straightforward respect for his achievement, for his humanity and spirituality, and for the greatness of his historical impact. Indeed, with all the distance I had gained from him, I was not without a certain love for this person who had evidently perceived "human nature" in its totality. Through my probings into Schleiermacher, I also learned to appreciate from afar certain matters where I stood (or again came?) much closer to him theologically than I had ever supposed could be the case after 1916. Has not Paul Seifert even gone so far as to assert that my growing, and increasingly noticeable, interest in Schleiermacher's theology was "certainly indicated by the surprisingly positive evaluation" of him in my *Protestant Theology in the Nineteenth Century*?"[16] "Positive" is no doubt somewhat too strong a term for what I really said there. Nevertheless, when faced with such a slight exaggeration, I do not want to deny that for all my opposition to Schleiermacher, I could never think of him without feeling what Doctor Bartolo so well articulated in *The Marriage of Figaro*: "An inner voice always spoke to his advantage"; or at least, never without confirming the rather coarse popular expression, "A criminal always returns to the scene of the crime." And did I not even openly boast in 1947 that on the basis of my presuppositions I was actually in a much better position to illuminate Schleiermacher than, say, Horst Stephan (who, by the way, was among my teachers at Marburg)? However, it must not be overlooked that after praising everything worthy of praise in my writings on Schleiermacher, I still had ringing in my ears the venerable "Apostles" and Nicene Creeds. Theologically speaking, I could not revert to Schleiermacher.

This phase in my relationship to him is noteworthy for the following reason: it was determined not only by a much better knowledge of his work, but also by a conscious distancing of myself from him which could no longer be reversed.

Then a further and presumably final phase unexpectedly developed. That is, it came to pass that we "old fighters" from the second and third decades of our rather eventful century suddenly saw ourselves overtaken and overwhelmed by a new theological movement. "Demythologization" and "existentialization" of theological language were its catchwords. And the one who had inaugurated it was none other than our erstwhile companion of old, Rudolf Bultmann.

As far as *demythologizing* was concerned, the enterprise left me cold. For one thing, it was only too well known to me — not the term but the matter itself — from my theological beginnings. Furthermore, I found it much too humorless. Finally, after my experiences with "modern man," who was after all the object of the exercise, I could not regard it as a fruitful instrument for conversation with this creature. Apologetics is something of which I am deeply suspicious, something alien to me in all its forms, and therefore also in this reductionist approach.

However, I certainly listened to the other news, so vigorously presented, that theological language was supposed to need *existentializing*. For I had indeed known for a long time, and had even said myself in the first and then especially in the second edition of *Romans* (occasionally even with the use of the term), that genuinely theological language could not talk about its object in merely intellectual terms, but could only express what it had to say *existentially*, that is, in terms which directly and unavoidably confronted persons in their human existence. Even before I read Kierkegaard, that had been thoroughly pounded into me by Wilhelm Herrmann, and in fact had not been entirely unknown to me before that. For me that belonged to the obvious formal conditions, to the moral presuppositions of my "theological existence," to which in one way or another I tried to do justice and to which I tried to adhere. But now I was receiving what at first (but only at first) glance seemed to be fabulously new tidings, that theology had to be *existential* theology in a material, technical, and fundamental sense as well. Apart from his knowledge and confession as a baptized member of the Christian community, thus apart from the way he was engaged in his own human existence, the theologian was first supposed to orient himself toward and clarify that which was supposed to be at stake for human existence and human engagement in general and as such. Only then, in that context, and according to the standards of such "existential" instruction, might he consider and articulate the Christian engagement of his existence, and thus his Christian faith. His task as a theologian was supposed to be to understand and proclaim precisely the faith which had become credible in this way. Tertullian's dictum that *Deus non est in genere*[17] was in error: *Deus est in genere.* That was what struck me as something really novel in my first encounter with this most recent theology. One of the most unforgettable experiences of my life was the time when Bultmann (it may have been around 1922 — he was still amiably disposed toward me in a view of the second edition of *Romans*) once visited me in Göttingen in order to read to me for more than an hour over coffee and almond-cake from the lectures of Martin Heidegger which he had attended and transcribed. The purpose of this exercise: just as we had to apply ourselves to any great spiritual achievement in precisely this ("existential") direction, so we also had to apply ourselves to the gospel documented in the New Testament. Delighted by this basic systematic teaching of his, as well as by the "historical-critical" method which he himself so masterfully represented (in this respect a true pupil of his Marburg predecessor, Jülicher), many older and younger students gathered themselves around him. Instead of orienting oneself to Heidegger, or Jaspers, or M. Buber, or finally even to fifty pages of D. Bonhoeffer,[18] one could most recently even as a Roman Catholic theologian become a Bultmannian. And, as many from the younger generation in particular experienced (in connection with the general spiritual exhaustion after the Second World War), to a certain extent one could even concur with him (the master) instinctively or intuitively. Among themselves Bultmann's pupils then became a rather various and even splintered group. But on the basis of Bultmann's systematic starting point, they remained a group and a school. On the basis of that starting point, they can no doubt be brought together under a common denominator.

What is that common denominator? Now I must speak of the impression which the whole phenomenon made on me from the beginning and which has only increased with time: the common denominator was and is indeed Schleiermacher — not the very image of him, but certainly in a new form which accommodated itself to the "contemporary spiritual situation" or "linguistic situation" and to the contemporary (or rather one contemporary) vocabulary. Unmistakably, my old friend and enemy, Schleiermacher! Once again, the Christian exhortation relegated to that cozy nook where the contemporary society and world pretend to their authoritative claim! Once again, the symbiosis of theology and philosophy so characteristic of Schleiermacher! Once again, an anthropologizing of theology, just as obviously as in Schleiermacher, who had thereby simultaneously brought the theological learning of the eighteenth century to completion while establishing that of the nineteenth century! Once again, the tension-in-unity between subject and object which he had so masterfully described in the second of his *Speeches*! And once again, the original and ultimate unity of both which he there so triumphantly proclaimed, the glorious elimination of the "subject-object schema." Once again, the move found in *The Christian Faith* of granting supremacy to "feeling," in whose place of course one could then set "faith" in order to move somewhat closer to the Bible or the Reformation: "faith" on which was conferred sovereignty over everything which might be its ground, object, and content. So that is more or less (the list could easily be extended) how, in attentively considering its rise and development, I supposed and suppose that this most recent "modern" theology ought to be understood — as a new and vigorous Schleiermacher renaissance!

Now, allow me one more citation from *The Marriage of Figaro*: "What I said about the noble youth was only a suspicion, it was only a matter of distrust." Was it in this case only a matter of suspicion and distrust? Yet I found it remarkably confirmed by the fact that I occasionally ran across utterances from the representatives of this (for the present) new direction in which they openly enough acknowledge precisely the same kinds of parallels. Consider what Martin Redeker writes in the introduction to his excellent reissue of *Der christliche Glaube* [Schleiermacher, *The Christian Faith*]:

The feeling of absolute dependence thus means being engaged by the transcendent as something infinite and unconditioned. If one wanted

77

to interpret the concept of feeling and of immediate self-consciousness in contemporary terms so as to rule out psychologistic misunderstandings, then perhaps this primal act of human existence could be characterized through modern existentialist philosophy in terms of care for being, for the foundation and meaningfulness of existence, as Tillich has already suggested in his dogmatics. The theology of the experience of faith thus means connecting all theological utterances to these basic questions of human existence.

Or consider carefully what Friedrich Hertel writes in the preface to his recent book on Schleiermacher's theology (dedicated to G. Ebeling): "If theology and proclamation are to be guided today by the task of a 'non-religious' interpretation, and thus if nothing else is to be considered as speaking humanly, then one may not forget that it was Schleiermacher — despite his employment of the concept of religion — who paved the way for this striving!" Or consider just as carefully the disposition and conceptuality with which Hertel analyzes Schleiermacher's first two and decisive *Speeches*. And what had I already run across in 1922, the time of the "beginnings of dialectical theology," from the pen of Bultmann himself in the very year he had discovered Heidegger, at the outset of his long review of the second edition of *Romans*?

Karl Barth's *Epistle to the Romans* may be characterized by one sentence, the phraseology of which he would disagree with, but which would still be valid in terms of the usage that has been prevalent in the present time: the book attempts to prove the autonomy and absoluteness of religion. It thus takes its place . . . in the same line with such works as Schleiermacher's *Speeches on Religion* and Otto's *Idea of the Holy*, with modern attempts to demonstrate a religious a priori, and finally with the Epistle to the Romans itself, which . . . basically has no other intention than this. However different all these attempts may be in detail, they seek to give verbal expression to the consciousness of the uniqueness and absoluteness of religion.[19]

The disposition and conceptuality in this review were also noteworthy. It was "faith," again and again it was "faith," which was at the center of those things which Bultmann found interesting and now praiseworthy in my book (whose first edition two years before he had rejected rather contemptuously). What (according to him) I had expressed about faith, he supposed he could effortlessly place in a series with what Schleiermacher, R. Otto, and E. Troeltsch had treated under the heading of "religion." Then in this very same series he even dared to place Paul's

Epistle to the Romans itself! At that time he had not yet learned to use the language of Heidegger. But what does it matter? In that book review the outlines of the whole Bultmann, even the later and latest Bultmann, can clearly be recognized. No wonder that the closeness, and even the alliance, which once supposedly existed between us, could only be something apparent and transitory, as later became painfully evident: Bultmann was and is a continuator of the great tradition of the nineteenth century, and thus in new guise, a genuine pupil of Schleiermacher.

And this is precisely the common denominator under which I see him as well as his followers, who are otherwise so diverse among themselves: what connects them with him, and with each other, is the consciously and consistently executed anthropological starting point which is evident as the focus of their thought and utterances. And that was and is precisely a clear recurrence of Schleiermacher. Was it not Schleiermacher who had already made the distinction, so remarkable in the second "speech" even though it was capable of supersession [*aufhebbar*], between "intuition" and "feeling" — a distinction which later disappeared in favor of the "feeling" which incorporated "intuition" within itself (absolute dependence!)? Had he not already described the Christian faith as a particular form of this "feeling," in which all objectivity, and all contents characteristic of it, were supposed to be sublated [*aufgehoben*] and supplied? Hadn't he already known nothing of the Old Testament as an indispensable positive presupposition of the New? Hadn't he already reduced the function and meaning of Jesus to that of a great prototype of faith, and thus of that feeling? Hadn't he already reduced the proper relationship postulated between Christians and Jesus to that which today is proclaimed as the "discipleship" owed him? Wasn't his eschatology as devoid of all concrete content as that which today is known as the "theology of hope"?

Certainly many existentialist theologians (as Wilhelm Herrmann had already done) ardently appealed to Luther, to whom Schleiermacher appealed only seldom or not at all (having found him too rough-hewn and contradictory). Still others reverted more to Kierkegaard, to whom of course Schleiermacher could not yet have appealed. As to Luther, no doubt out of the Weimar Edition of his works, that great Pandora's box, one can extract a theologically existentialist, and thus indirectly Schleiermacherian, thread! But how many other threads one must then leave unconsidered or must even decisively cut off! And as to Kierkegaard, I must confess that the appeal of the existentialist theologians to him as their great and direct forerunner has made me a little reserved toward him. Why did he actually delimit himself — in his original manner, but yet also in conformity to the spirit of the middle of the nineteenth century — so sharply against Hegel, but hardly at all, to my knowledge, against Schleiermacher? In short, despite the fact that the vocabulary of this recent theology included concepts which Schleiermacher certainly would not have cherished — such as Word, encounter, occurrence, cross, decision, limit, judgment, etc. — I could not allow myself to be deceived that within their own context they did not break with the narrowness of Schleiermacher's anthropological horizon, that there under the pretext of being so correctly "human," in that certainly unromantic sobriety, his path was once again traversed. That Schleiermacher made the christianly pious person into the criterion and content of his theology, while, after the "death of God" and the state-funeral dedicated to him, one now jubilantly wants to make the christianly impious person into its object and theme, these certainly are two different things. In the end and in principle, however, they probably amount to the same thing. And because, despite all remaining admiration, I for my part had decisively departed from Schleiermacher's path, it was not possible to join with those multitudes who, openly or secretly, consciously or unconsciously, were following in his train. Rather, as it says in the song, I had to "make my wayward path through the woods, a mangy little sheep" — I, the poor neo-orthodox theologian, the supernaturalist, the revelational positivist, as I had to hear from so many quarters on both sides of the Atlantic. Until better instructed, I can see no way from Schleiermacher, or from his contemporary epigones, to the chroniclers, prophets, and wise ones of Israel, to those who narrate the story of the life, death, and resurrection of Jesus Christ, to the word of the apostles — no way to the God of Abraham, Isaac, and Jacob and the Father of Jesus Christ, no way to the great tradition of the Christian church. For the present I can see nothing here but a choice. And for me there can be no question as to how that choice is to be made.

So, just as I finally could not hold fast to the old Marburg, so could I catch hold of the new Marburg even less. Even less? Yes, for at the risk of seeming malicious, I must here add something else — a "merely" humanistic, or if you will, a "merely" aesthetic question, which irresistibly pressed itself upon me in the course of comparing Schleiermacher with his contemporary followers. Given the fact that I might be able to attach myself to Schleiermacher theologically (something I cannot now do) on some kind of grounds (which are not now visible to me) and then of course to join forces with those who follow him in our own day, nonetheless I would still remain deeply alarmed at the simple contrast between the stature, the weight, and the quality of Schleiermacher's personality and achievements — human, Christian, and academic — and those corresponding qualities which have so far appeared in the framework of the new Schleiermacher renaissance. To cite a tolerably similar example at least for the sake of clarity: what a shockingly different niveau between Schleiermacher's definition of God, still impressive in its own way, as the "source of the feeling of absolute dependence," and the definition from one of his contemporary epigones, at first glance so similar and apparently dependent on Schleiermacher's, but then so terribly wretched and banal by comparison: God as the supposed "source of my involvement with my fellow humans"! To this example could easily be added a multitude which are similar and even worse. But no, I will resist the malicious desire to characterize Schleiermacher by comparing him in any further detail with his contemporary pupils. Rather, setting aside everything which I have *in petto* [in private] against the being, acting, and stirring in the sphere of today's swaggering theologians, I want to turn now to something positive, in the form of a little song of praise for the human greatness of Schleiermacher and his work, and thus without in any way referring too closely to the greatness or smallness of our own day.

"Small of stature" like Zaccheus, and beyond that, after his sister Charlotte (who later became so close to him) had once dropped him as a small child, somewhat misshapen, Schleiermacher was an open, expansive, and truly comprehensive spirit. Pressing beyond all mere "diagnosis" and analysis, he aimed toward synthesis. He had the freedom to take part with hearty affirmation in the style, the language, and the ideals of his contemporaries, or just as freely to step back from them, or even decisively to oppose his special knowledge to them as something novel. He was inclined toward peace, even when he became very cutting. Many things troubled and angered him which he saw and heard and read, but I can recall no passage in his letters or even in his books where he expressed himself peevishly, acidly or poisonously with regard to them. That was certainly related to the fact that at every stage of his life, and in all the branches of his life's work, he had something positive to say. His youthful writings (the *Speeches* and the *Soliloquies*) served, of course, as a prelude, but one which established the melody. When he spoke and wrote he was thus not experimenting, but was proceeding on the basis of well-considered tenets and themes, which he never styled or formulated stiffly, but in which he displayed, rather, an astonishing suppleness of thought. If his style often approached the limits of the tolerable, especially in his earlier years, yet he never became tasteless. He discovered and represented in personal union a consistent philosophy and just as consistent a theology. And in both fields he worked out a remarkable coherence between the whole and the parts, as well as between his earlier and later writings. Beyond that, he was also in a position to produce, with his left hand as it were, a complete translation of Plato with introductions to all of the dialogues. And, after listening to a flute concert, he was able to depict the most difficult point in his dogmatics in the form of a short novel.

There was, in addition, his humanity in the stricter sense: he knew the meaning of friendship and love. And although he was not spared disappointments here (Friedrich Schlegel!) and there (Eleonore Grunow and the rather immature, dependent, and opaque young widow who then became his spouse), he endured them with manly forbearance and dignity — refined and gallant, a gentleman to the end. In those two fields he was acquainted with more than mere play. He displayed a similar humanity toward the two colleagues in Berlin who so spitefully fought him: Hegel the philospher, and Marheineke the Lutheran dogmatician. Furthermore, in the *Sendschreiben an Lücke* [Open Letter to Lücke] and in the notes and supplements to the later editions of the *Speeches*, it may be observed how capable he was of self-criticism and of unfolding new and corrective aspects of his previous work (even if one must admit that, had he really put that into practice, then — such was indeed precisely his strength! — he would have remained terribly true to himself). At any rate, according to K. A. Varnhagen von Ense's *Denkwürdigkeiten* (1848), which are generally so illuminating for that period, Schleiermacher also possessed the wonderful ability to laugh, above all at himself. He was an ethicist on the basis of a profound ethos which did not restrict him either to the philosophical or (even less) to the theological sphere in formal and methodological questions (which he wonderfully mastered!), but rather which permitted and demanded (happily or unhappily) that he dare to take up the most difficult particular problems of human and Christian, individual and social existence.

And now we come to the center of his humanity, which must be kept firmly in mind in any consideration of the range of issues which he represented, when we go on to say that Schleiermacher was outspokenly a man of the church. Throughout the course of his life, he thought, spoke, and acted in the consciousness of his concrete responsibility precisely on that front. It drove him, from his youth to the days of his old age, irresistibly to the pulpit. And whatever one may think of it theologically, he not only talked about the "feeling of absolute dependence," but had that feeling himself — rather, it had him. He himself was one of those who were moved by what he said about it in the pulpit (as well as in the podium and in the salon!), carried away at times to the point of tears. And that no doubt hangs together with the fact that while he certainly conceded to the "worthy men called rationalists" those things which at that time were to be conceded, he himself — no pietist, but certainly a "Moravian of a higher order" — had a personal relationship to Jesus which might well be characterized as love. Although constantly engaged with the question of John the Baptist, "Are you he who is to come, or shall we look for another?", he never broke free from Jesus, but had to return to him again and again. I suspect that on that basis (and contrary to the malign appearance in particular of his Christology), and only on that basis, was it given to him to depict the "Christian faith" not only in aphoristic excurses, but also "in its context."

As this particular man — thinker, preacher, teacher, and writer — Schleiermacher determined the nineteenth century. Not in the field of philosophy! In those textbooks, as is well known, he figures only as an "also ran." Certainly, however — and precisely this will be drawn in as a positive point in any evaluation of his scholarly intention — in the field of theology. Here his influence has survived. It has survived not only his being badly compromised by Feuerbach, and then his being compromised even worse by Ritschl and his followers, but also that catastrophe which broke out in 1914 for the whole theology which followed him, and even the onslaught of "our" so-called dialectical theology. Here, even in the middle of our century, he was able to produce, as shown, those "existentialist" epigones. Truly a great man and a great achievement!

That, then, is the song of praise from one who is able to concur with Schleiermacher *rebus sic stantibus* in *no* fundamental sense whatsoever. Nor, therefore, with the liberal, mediating, and conservative theology of the nineteenth century. And thus especially not, and even less, with the Schleiermacher-epigones of the present. At this point, on the same purely humanistic level, let me pose a brief question to them: Where and when among you, in your school and in what you have produced, has a personality and a life's work emerged whose calibre and stature would be worthy of mention in the same breath with those of Schleiermacher, even if only from afar? In this respect I place myself among you, but the question pertains to you especially who are in a particular way to be measured against him. Perhaps I have overlooked someone or something up to now. Perhaps those who and that which are here missed are still to come. If it can be shown to me in good time, then I would also want to praise you, if not your theology, on a similarly humanistic plane. Until then, I will think of you in terms of what is written in Psalm 2.4, whereas despite everything I could not think of Schleiermacher in such terms. Schleiermacher impresses me (I notice that here I am involuntarily lapsing into the style of the ironic-polemical passages of the *Speeches*), whereas you — although and because I am sincerely striving to love even you as myself — impress me not at all.

It may be surprising that I have declared myself to be at odds with Schleiermacher only with reservations: *rebus sic stantibus,* "for the present," "until better instructed." Something like a reservation, a genuine uncertainty, may rightly be detected here. The door is in fact not latched. I am actually to the present day not finished with him. Not even with regard to his point of view. As I have understood him up to now, I have supposed and continued to suppose that I must take a completely different tack from those who follow him. I am certain of my course and of my point of view. I am, however, not so certain of them that I can confidently say that my "Yes" necessarily implies a "No" to Schleiermacher's point of view. For have I indeed understood him correctly? Could he not perhaps be understood differently so that I would not have to reject his theology, but might rather be joyfully conscious of proceeding in fundamental agreement with him?

In what follows I will attempt to formulate and ventilate two questions four times in order to make my perplexity known. By answering them dialectically, perhaps my history with Schleiermacher can now go further.

1. Is Schleiermacher's enterprise concerned (a) necessarily, intrinsically, and authentically with a Christian *theology* oriented toward worship, preaching, instruction, and pastoral care? Does it only accidentally, extrinsically, and inauthentically wear the dress of a philosophy accommodated to the person of his time? It is clear that in that case — regardless of details — I would at least have to entertain the possiblity of affirming the enterprise. But would I then have understood it correctly? Up to now I have supposed that Schleiermacher cannot be understood in this way, thus finding myself materially at odds with him.

Or is his enterprise concerned (b) primarily, intrinsically, and authentically with a *philosophy* which turns away from Aristotle, Kant, and

Fichte in order to locate itself in the vicinity of Plato, Spinoza, and Schelling, mediating between logos and eros while aesthetically surmounting both, a philosophy indifferent as to Christianity and which would have wrapped itself only accidentally, extrinsically, and inauthentically in the garments of a particular theology, which here happens to be Christian? It is clear that in that case I could only take and maintain my distance from Schleiermacher. But in this way have I understood him correctly? And if in this way I have not understood him correctly, then am I acting properly by distancing myself from him and his enterprise?

2. In Schleiermacher's theology or philosophy, do persons feel, think, and speak (a) in relationship to an indispensable [*unaufhebbar*] Other, in accordance with an *object* which is superior to their own being, feeling, perceiving, willing, and acting, an object toward which adoration, gratitude, repentance, and supplication are concretely possible and even imperative? Were that the case, then I would prick up my ears and be joyfully prepared to hear further things about this Other, in the hopes of finding myself fundamentally at one with Schleiermacher. But then, if I supposed I could find such things in him — perhaps in the dark passages of the *Speeches* where he expresses an "intimation of something apart from and beyond humanity" or in that later, famous definition of God as "the source of the feeling of absolute dependence" — would I have understood him correctly? Up to now I have supposed I had to understand him differently, thus not being able to attach myself to him. Was and is that supposition foolish or indeed quite wise?

Or, for Schleiermacher, do persons feel, think, and speak (b) in and from a sovereign consciousness that their own beings are conjoined, and are indeed essentially *united*, with everything which might possibly come into question as something or even someone distinct from them? If that were the case, then the door between him and me would indeed be latched, and substantial communication would then be impossible. But have I understood him correctly if up to now I have supposed that I ought to understand him in this way? Would I need to understand him in a completely different way in order to regard substantial communication between him and me as something which is not impossible?

3. According to Schleiermacher, do persons feel, think, and speak (a) primarily in relationship to a reality which is *particular* and concrete, and thus determinate and determinable, and about which, in view of its nature and meaning, they can abstract and generalize only secondarily? In that case Schleiermacher and I would be in profound agreement. But

have I understood him correctly here when I interpret him in this way? How wonderful and hopeful that would be! However, if I would then have attributed something to him which does not at all accord with his own outlook and intention, then how could my outlook and intention, which would not at all be in concordance, to say nothing of coincidence, possibly be reconciled with his?

Or, according to Schleiermacher, do human feeling, thinking, and acting occur (b) primarily in relationship to a *general* reality whose nature and meaning have already been derived and established in advance, so that on that basis only secondary attention is paid to its particular, concrete, determinable, and determinate form? In that case, of course, I would immediately have to issue a protest. In that case Schleiermacher and my humble self would be completely separated from the outset. But in that case — having so understood him up to now — would I have understood him correctly? If he could be understood in some other way, then my protest would be left hanging in the air. I would then have to meet him with a *Pater, peccavi!* and to accept modestly the instruction he would have to impart to me. Oh, if only I were in such a position!

4. Is the spirit which moves feeling, speaking, and thinking persons, when things come about properly, (b) an absolutely *particular* and specific Spirit, which not only distinguishes itself again and again from all other spirits, but which is seriously to be called "holy"? If this is the correct way to understand Schleiermacher, that is, if it accords with his own standpoint, then — instead of disputing with him — what is to prevent me from joining him and deliberating further with him about its basic content and consequences? But then, in this way have I understood him correctly? Could I, as a conscientious interpreter, be responsible for this understanding of Schleiermacher's position?

Or, according to Schleiermacher, is the spirit which moves feeling, thinking, and speaking persons rather (b) a *universally effective* spiritual power, one which, while individually differentiated, basically remains diffuse? In that case we would be and remain — he, the great, and I, the little, man — separated from each other. But in this way have I understood him correctly, i.e., congenially? Or have I burdened him with an alien point of view? If I could dispense with this viewpoint, would I not have to recognize and confess that he and I are not quite so far apart?

Whoever has followed carefully this fourfold explanation of my two questions will not fail to recognize that in each case I would greatly prefer to have understood Schleiermacher in terms of the first question, and just as greatly to have misunderstood him in terms of the second. When my life is over I would certainly like to live at peace with Schleiermacher with regard to these issues. Yet in all four cases I had to end each question with a question! And that means that all along the line I am not finished with Schleiermacher, that I have not made up my mind, whether on the positive or even on the negative side! Even though and because I find myself embarked upon a course, clear as day to myself and others, which certainly is not his. With regard to this man's basic standpoint, I find myself in a great, and for me very painful, perplexity. And to illuminate it even more sharply, I will not fail to pose a final pair of questions:

5. Are the two questions which I have posed four times (a) *correctly* formulated as such, i.e., so as to correspond to Schleiermacher's intentions? Would the possible answers to these questions be sufficient for a substantive judgment (positive, negative or critical) about the standpoint he represented? Do these questions provide a basis for a meaningful and relevant discussion about the way he worked out the details of his position?

Or are all the questions I have posed (b) *incorrectly* formulated, i.e., so as not to correspond to Schleiermacher's intentions? Thus, would their possible answers be insufficient for a substantive judgment about his point of view? Do they fail to provide a basis for a substantial and relevant discussion of the particular tenets and themes by which Schleiermacher worked out his position?

The only certain consolation which remains for me is to rejoice that in the kingdom of heaven I will be able to discuss all these questions with Schleiermacher extensively — above all, of course, the fifth — for, let us say, a couple of centuries. "Then I will see clearly *that* — along with so many other things, also that — which on earth I saw through a glass darkly." I can imagine that that will be a very serious matter for both sides, but also that we will both laugh very heartily at ourselves.

Incidentally — moving away from the earlier humanistic plane — that which can be viewed as waiting in the eschatological distance with the "old sorcerer" also pertains, of course (including the fifth and final set of questions), *mutatis mutandis*, to those lesser sorcerer's apprentices of his who are today making villages and cities insecure. I know what I have intended, and continue to intend, in distinction from them as well, but I confess that even concerning them do I find myself in a certain perplexity. In their own way, without possessing Schleiermacher's significance, they certainly mean well, too. If those who follow in his footsteps (at a great human distance from him) are to fall with him, then they might also be able to stand with him. And I certainly would not want to exclude them from my eschatological peace with Schleiermacher, to which I previously alluded. The only thing is that I cannot take my "reunion" with them quite so seriously, nor can I imagine it quite so joyfully, as I can my "reunion" with their ancestor, Schleiermacher. When contemplating the great then-and-there of the coming revelation, it is probably not only permitted, but also imperative to think in terms of a certain gradation.

As to a clarification of my relationship to Schleiermacher, what I have occasionally contemplated for here and now — and thus not only with respect to a theological event in the kingdom of glory (which will then form the triumphal ending to my history with Schleiermacher), but, so to speak, with respect also to a millennium preceding that kingdom — and what I have already intimated here and there to good friends, would be the possibility of a theology of the third article, in other words, a theology predominantly and decisively of the Holy Spirit. Everything which needs to be said, considered, and believed about God the Father and God the Son in an understanding of the first and second articles might be shown and illuminated in its foundations through God the Holy Spirit, the *vinculum pacis inter Patrem et Filium* [bond of peace between the Father and the Son]. The entire work of God for his creatures, for, in, and with human beings, might be made visible in terms of its one teleology in which all contingency is excluded. In *Church Dogmatics* IV/1-3, I at least had the good instinct to place the church, and then faith, love, and hope, under the sign of the Holy Spirit. But might it not even be possible and necessary to place justification, sanctification, and calling under this sign — to say nothing of creation as the *opus proprium* of God the Father? Might not even the Christology which dominates everything be illuminated on this basis (*conceptus de Spiritu Sancto!*)? Isn't God — the God confessed by his people through the revelation of his covenant and who is to be proclaimed as such in the world — essentially Spirit (John 4.24, 1 Cor. 3.17), i.e., isn't he the God who in his own freedom, power, wisdom and love makes himself present and applies himself? Was it perhaps something of that sort which, without having gotten beyond obscure intimations, was so passionately driving my old friend Fritz Lieb in the last decades of his life, a life which was moved and moving on that basis all along? And is that perhaps also what in our day the promising young Catholic dogmatician Heribert Mühlen in Paderborn is getting at? Be that as it may, interpreting everything and everyone *in optimam partem,* I would like to reckon with the possibility of a theology of the Holy Spirit, a theology of which Schleiermacher was scarcely conscious, but which might actually have been the legitimate concern dominating even his theological activity. And not his alone! I would also like to apply this supposition in favor of the pietists and (!) rationalists who preceded him, and, of course, in favor of the "Moravians of a lower order" of the eighteenth century, and beyond that, in favor of the "Enthusiasts" who were so one-sidedly and badly treated by the Reformers, and still further back, in favor of all those agitated and contemplative souls, the spiritualists and mystics of the Middle Ages. Could it not be that so many things which for us were said in an unacceptable way about the church and about Mary in Eastern and Western Catholicism might be vindicated to the extent that they actually intended the reality, the coming, and the work of the Holy Spirit, and that on that basis they might emerge in a positive-critical light? And then even (*in etwa* ["more or less"] — as one is wont to say today in bad German) Schleiermacher's miserable successors in the nineteenth century and the existentialist theologians in our twentieth century as well? The whole "history of sects and heretics" could then be discovered, understood, and written not "impartially" but quite critically as a "history" in which everything is thoroughly tested and the best retained, a history of the *ecclesia una, sancta, catholica et apostolica* gathered by the Holy Spirit.

This is merely a suggestion, as is only proper, of what I dream of from time to time concerning the future of theology in general, and in particular concerning the perplexity in which I find myself as I attempt to evaluate Schleiermacher as well as also those who preceded and succeeded him. I will no longer experience this future, to say nothing of leading the way into it or taking its work in hand.

Not, however, that some gifted young person — in the supposition that he or she is called to it — should now immediately run down the path and into the marketplace for me with a buoyantly written brochure entitled "Toward a Theology of the Holy Spirit" or something of that sort! And how misunderstood my beautiful dream would be if anyone supposed that what is at stake is now to say "the same thing from an anthropological standpoint" once again! As if that were not precisely what is so deeply problematic about Schleiermacher, that he — brilliantly, like no one before or after him — thought and spoke "from an anthropological standpoint"! As if it were precisely the Holy Spirit which encouraged him to do so, or would encourage anyone to do so! As if pneumatology were anthropology! As if I, instead of dreaming of a possibility of better understanding Schleiermacher's concern, had dreamed quite crudely of continuing in his path! I warn! If I am not to have dreamed sheer nonsense, then only persons who are very grounded, spiritually and intellectually, really "well-informed Thebans," will be capable of conceiving and developing a theology of the third article. Those who are not or not yet to that point, instead of boldly wanting to actualize a possibility of the millennium, should prefer to persevere for a little while with me in conscious "perplexity."

*

FEUERBACH

Theology, declared Feuerbach, is anthropology. All talk about God is really indirect, projected talk about human beings. Exactly right, said Barth: Feuerbach is the true doctor of modern neo-Protestant theology, and he diagnosed its fatal illness. In his "anti-theology" he simply said candidly and clearly what others, Barth believed, were implying obliquely. In an earlier lecture than the present selection, Barth asked if Feuerbach were not "really a very sharp-sighted but not too intelligent spy" who had revealed the secret of the modern theological priesthood.[20]

But Barth does not regard Feuerbach only as a symptom of theological ills. In this brief essay he finds that Feuerbach's thesis provokes real questions about the theological tradition, especially Luther, and about the resurrection of Jesus and the theological affirmation of human bodiliness over against a false spiritualism. Barth, who opposed spirit-body dualism and its political implications, praised Feuerbach on his affirmation of the whole person because it had an "unconscious but evident affinity to the ideology of the socialist workers' movement."[21]

Feuerbach was the catalyst who led Marx to turn Hegel on his head, to turn dialectical idealism into dialectical materialism. Feuerbach the anti-theologian provoked Barth not so much to turn anthropology on its head — as if theology and anthropology were opposites — as to seek in Christology a better theology and anthropology.

Another essay on Feuerbach by Barth in English may be found in Barth's Theology and Church, translated by Louise Pettibone Smith; a translation by James Luther Adams appears as an Introduction to Feuerbach's The Essence of Christianity.[22] *The following text is from Barth, Protestant Theology in the Nineteenth Century (London: SCM, 1972), 534-40.*

Feuerbach was an outsider; not a theologian, but a philosopher engaging in theology. There are few philosophers who have not at some time and in some way engaged in theology. But Feuerbach, the philosopher, engaged in nothing but theology. "Strictly speaking, all my writings have only one aim, one sole motivation, and one sole theme. This theme is religion and theology and everything connected with it," he once said. His love seems to have been an unhappy one, for in effect what he practised was anti-theology. But he practised it so knowledgeably, and with such relevance to the theological situation of his age, throwing such clear light upon it, and, moreover, in a way so interesting in itself, that we must allow him to speak together with the theologians.

Ludwig Feuerbach was born in Landshut in 1804, studied under Daub and Hegel, became a *Privatdozent* (unsalaried lecturer) at the University of Erlangen in 1828, and died near Nuremberg in 1872 as a private scholar. Of his numerous writings the most important are: *Das Wesen des Christentums* (The Essence of Christianity, 1841) and *Das Wesen der Religion* (The Essence of Religion, 1851). His aim was a simple, but big one: he sought to take Schleiermacher and Hegel seriously, completely seriously, at the point where they concurred in asserting the non-objective quality of God. He wanted, that is, to turn theology, which itself seemed half-inclined towards the same goal, completely and finally into anthropology; to turn the lovers of God into lovers of humanity, the worshippers into workers, the candidates for the life to come into students of the present life, the Christians into complete people; he wanted to turn away from heaven towards the earth, from faith towards love, from Christ towards ourselves, from all, but really all, supernaturalism towards real life.

In his eyes even Kant, Fichte and Hegel are still supernaturalists, to the extent that they are seeking the divine Being in reason, separate from humanity. True humanity is not sundered from nature, abstracted from the world of the senses; true human being is identical with the totality of bodily life. Feuerbach wants to assert the right of such a human being. Feuerbach does not want to think as a thinker, but to think, as he expressly says, in "existence," i.e. as the living, actual being which he finds present, as himself, in the world, and co-existing with it. Only the distinction of I and Thou is real. And it is precisely in the experienced unity of this distinction that the essence of human being is to be found. The concept of the object is nothing else but the concept of an objective I, and thus of a Thou. By the consciousness of the Thou I become conscious of the world, and with the world, of myself. And this consciousness is imparted by means of the senses; truth, reality, the world of senses, and humanity are identical concepts. The secret of being is the secret of love in the most comprehensive meaning of the word; which means that ultimately head, heart and stomach jointly seek and find one object. With this premise as his starting-point Feuerbach sets out to transform the theologians into anthropologists — but this time in earnest.

Feuerbach does not deny either God or theology. In denying the existence of an abstract divine Being, divorced from nature and human being, he is merely affirming God's nature as humanity's true nature. And in denying a false theology distinguishing theological and anthropological tenets, he is merely affirming anthropology as the true theology. The weight of Feuerbach's feeling is positive. He, too, is singing his *Magnificat*. He affirms, loves and praises the human will for life, the will revealed in the needs, desires and ideals which prompt human beings to rise above their dependence, their limited and threatened state, to distinguish between the valuable and the worthless, to struggle for what is valuable, and against what is worthless. And he affirms, loves and praises the human tendency to make absolute the reason, necessity and right of this will for life, and thus to become religious in the most diverse ways. Feuerbach would wish us only to perceive and acknowledge that the name of "God," in which all the highest, worthiest and most beloved human names are concentrated, actually first sprang from the human heart, and that religion is thus in the deepest sense concerned with humanity itself; he would have us perceive and acknowledge that with God it is a question of the human will for life, and not of a second, different thing in opposition to it. "God, as the quintessence of all realities or perfections, is nothing else but the quintessence, comprehensively summarized for the assistance of the limited individual, of the qualities of the human species, scattered among human beings, and manifesting themselves in the course of world history." The interest I feel in God's existence is one with the interest I feel in my own existence, and indeed in my own everlasting existence, and this latter interest is fulfilled in the consciousness of the species, the consciousness to which I exalt myself in positing God as existing. God is my hidden, assured existence as a member of the human species. There is no quality or capacity attributed by theological dogmatics to God, which would not be better, or more simply conceived of as a quality and capacity of the human species, of humanity as such, which I have occasion in varying degrees to affirm, to aim at, and to believe in my concrete existence as a human being. Theology itself in fact admits in Christology that God is entirely human. He is human — and that is the true Christ — in the consciousness of the species, in which we actually partake together of redemption, peace and fellowship. The Word of God should be understood as the divinity of the human word, in so far as it is a true word, a self-imparting of the I to the Thou, and thus essential human nature, and hence the essence of God. Baptism and Holy Communion, in which Feuerbach took a special interest, are manifestly a ceremonial recognition of the divinity and healing power of nature, the divinity of the objects of the pleasure of the senses. And thus the Holy Spirit is the personification of religion itself, the groaning of the creature, the religious feeling's mirrored self. In short: Why search afar? Behold, the good things lie at hand! What people, through a thousand contradictions and self-violations, seek in and from a divine object — these things are their own predicates, or alternatively those of the species.

That is the liberating truth Feuerbach seeks to express, at a time when, as he never tires of stressing, this truth has long since shown itself to be self-evident, through the actual historical course which religion, the church, and theology have taken. "Theology has long since become anthropology" — from the moment when Protestantism itself, and Luther in particular, ceased to be interested in what God is in himself and became emphatically interested in what God is for humanity. Theology's course of development has irresistibly proceeded in such a way that human beings have come more and more to renounce God, in proportion as they have come to proclaim themselves. And it is an open secret that Christianity in its theological form has long since disappeared, not only from the sphere of reason, but also from the actual life of human beings; and that humanity's awakened self-consciousness has meant that Christianity in this form is no longer taken seriously. Religion exists. Religion is possible and necessary. But it is humanity which is the beginning, middle and the end of religion — humanity and only humanity.

Whatever else it may imply, this anti-theology of Feuerbach represents a question; a question put by him to the theology of his time, and perhaps not only in his time. In our previous discussions we have seen how theology was influenced by the belief in humanity which was developing in opposition to it and suffered itself to be driven into the corner of apologetics. We saw that its whole problem had become how to make religion, revelation and the relationship with God something which could also be understood as a necessary human predicate, or at any rate how to demonstrate that humanity had a potentiality, a capacity, for these things. To Feuerbach at all events the meaning of the question is whether the theologian, when he thus formulates the problem, is not after all affirming the thing in which the ascent of humanity seems to culminate in any case, namely the apotheosis of humanity. It was in this sense that, making up his mind quickly and fully approving of it, he wanted to understand and adopt the true aim of that theology. If theology was to be understood in that sense, he wanted to be a theologian himself.

Was he in fact completely in the wrong? Had not the theologians themselves tended to work in this same direction before him? We are reminded of Schleiermacher's doctrine of the relationship between God and pious excitement, which, as he expresses it, is manifestly not one which has lost all the characteristics of an encounter. We are reminded further of Schleiermacher's doctrine of the three dogmatic forms, of which the second and third, the utterances concerning God and the world, might just as well have been left out; and we are reminded of the same author's Christology and doctrine of atonement, seemingly projected back from the personal experience of the human subject. We think too of de Wette, who had already caused the word "anthropology" to be pronounced and adopted as a slogan within theological circles themselves. We think of Hegel and his disciples, and of the might they bestow upon the human mind in its dialectic self-movement; a might which eventually and finally prevails over God too, and his revelation. We think of Tholuck, with his proclamation that it was the "heart" which was the seat of divine wisdom in human beings. The question arises whether Feuerbach does not represent the point of intersection where all these lines converge, little as this may have been the intention of their originators; the question whether, taking into account the premises established at that time, the drawing of this unwelcome conclusion could effectively be avoided; the question whether the theologians themselves could at least protest to this anti-theologian that he had mistaken their intentions, and that they were seeking something else.

But it is not only in the relevance of what he said for his own time that Feuerbach is interesting. The question he represents becomes acute whenever incautious use is made in theology of mystical ideas, of the union of God and humanity; in fact, whenever these ideas are used other than in an eschatologically ensured connection. And there is something here which should give us Protestant theologians special food for thought. Feuerbach preferred to call to witness for his interpretation of Christianity, not his theological contemporaries but Luther of all people. First he called to witness Luther's concept of faith, in which faith had acquired the nature of a divine hypothesis, and might upon occasion be called the "creator of the Godhead" in us. Secondly, and chiefly, he called upon Luther's Christology and doctrine of the Lord's Supper. Luther taught, with the over-emphasis of genius, that the Godhead should not be sought in heaven but on earth, in the man Jesus, and then again that Christ's nature as the God-Man should substantially be sought in the sacred elements of Holy Communion. And Lutheran orthodoxy has cast this inspired doctrine into the dogma of the *communicatio idiomatum in genere majestatico*, according to which the predicates of the divine glory, omnipotence, omnipresence, eternity, etc., are to be attributed to the humanity, as such and *in abstracto*, of Jesus; and this it has expressly called the "apotheosis" of Christ's humanity. In principle this clearly meant that the higher and lower positions, those of God and humanity, could be reversed. And what the theologians of old had seen as being right for the person of Christ was now, to more modern and even less restrained speculating minds, capable of seeming proper for human beings in general. German theology had for centuries guarded itself perhaps all too rigidly against the Calvinist corrective, so that it was bound to become uncertain now whether the relationship with God had really in principle to be thought of as irreversible. Hegel, as we saw, emphatically declared that he was a good Lutheran, and so did Feuerbach, in his own way and upon his own level. In the light of Feuerbach's interpretation of Luther, we must ask whether it may not be advisable for us to reflect, as regards the non-reversibility of the relationship with God, upon some things which Luther, in establishing his doctrine, seems to have neglected to ponder. And today especially it should certainly be useful for us at least to be aware that the doctrine of I and Thou was put forward as early as 1840 in the strongest possible form, with Luther as its authority, as the true *via regia* of faith and revelation. But it was put forward, be it noted, with this particular interpretation.

The question raised by Feuerbach further becomes acute at the point where it is opposed to all spiritualist understanding of Christianity. The very thing which might at first sight seem to be the weakness of Feuerbach's position, namely its sensualism and naturalism, might at any rate be also its particular strength. In speaking of human reality as consisting in the unity of head, heart and stomach, Feuerbach is obviously concerned with the same ideas as Menken. It was human existence, and indeed, as he stressed with passionate exaggeration, human sensory existence, which interested him. He sought to have God's Beyond transposed into this human life. This might have been a denial of God's Beyond and thus a denial of God himself. But a denial or neglect of the relationship of God's Beyond with human life might also signify a denial of God; it is precisely a one-sided idealism and spiritualism which might cause us in a particularly dangerous way to suspect that the teaching of God is a human illusion. The question arises whether it might not in fact be this whole human being, soul and body, of whom Feuerbach clearly sought to speak, who really corresponds to God. The question arises whether Feuerbach, with his protest, might not after all have upon his side the radical Easter belief, the belief in the resurrection of the flesh, which prevailed in early Christendom and still exists today in the Eastern Churches. One thing is certain here: the fact that a common concern unites him with J. T. Beck and the two Blumhardts, and with the theology typical of Würtemberg as a whole. It is doubtful whether we can answer Feuerbach, who might upon this point also be in the stronger Christian position, if we fail to take this concern fully into account. Perhaps, to serve as a basis whereby a standpoint inwardly superior to Feuerbach's illusionism might be gained, a very real faith in resurrection corresponding to a real faith in God is necessary.

Feuerbach's doctrine was possible because there were several things which he failed to see, just like his contemporaries and opponents in theology. It was impossible for his contemporaries at any rate to point out his mistakes to him. It would have been possible to object, in terms just as basic and sweeping as those Feuerbach himself used in speaking of human existence, that "essential human being," the "consciousness of the species" which he made the measure of all things and in which he thought he saw humanity's true divinity, might be a supernatural fiction in exactly the same way as Hegel's concept of reason, or any other abstraction. This objection was in fact raised by Max Stirner, an Hegelian living at the same time as Feuerbach, and tending even further to the left than Feuerbach himself. The true human being, if thought of in completely existentialist terms, should surely be individual person. Like the theology of his time, Feuerbach discussed humanity in general, to which he attributed divinity, but in fact he said nothing about real human beings. And Feuerbach's tendency to make the two largely interchangeable, so that he speaks of the individual person as humanity in general, and thus dares to attribute divinity to the individual, is evidently connected with the fact that he does not seem sincerely and earnestly to have taken cognizance either of the wickedness of the individual, or of the fact that this individual must surely die. If he had been truly aware of this, then he might perhaps have seen the fictitious nature of this concept of humanity in general. He would then perhaps have refrained from identifying God with human beings, real people that is, who remain when the abstraction has been skimmed off. But the theology of the time was not so fully aware of the individual, or of wickedness or death, that it could instruct Feuerbach upon these points. Its own hypotheses about the relationship with God were themselves too little affected by them. In this way they were similar to Feuerbach's, and upon this common ground his rivals could not defeat him. That was why the theology of his time found it ultimately possible to preserve itself in face of him, as it had preserved itself in face of D. F. Strauss, without summoning an energetic cry of "*God* preserve us!"

2

ON THE WAY TO
THE *CHURCH DOGMATICS*

JESUS CHRIST AND THE
MOVEMENT FOR SOCIAL JUSTICE

Three months after he arrived in his parish Barth began giving lectures at the Workers Association. This lecture, the earliest piece of Barth by a decade in this book, is an excellent example of his early socialism. To be sure, we can still hear tones from liberal theology ("the spiritual power which . . . entered into history and life with Jesus"), and the relation of Jesus and socialism is portrayed fairly comfortably without the strong note of judgment we will hear in Romans. Nevertheless, Barth does not simply identify socialism with Jesus, but rather claims socialist intent as embodying much of the teaching of Jesus in the Gospels. His critique here of individualism, idealism and subjectivism will be prominent in his developed critique of liberal theology. Further, his critique of capitalism, and of a "spiritualized" Christianity, his call for the church to be a champion of the weak and exploited, and his communal understanding of Jesus and the Kingdom of God are consistent themes through all his writings.

Barth's lecture was published in December, 1911 in the socialist daily of his canton, Der Freie Aargauer, and has not yet been republished in German. Its first republication was in the English translation of 1976 by George Hunsinger in his Karl Barth and Radical Politics, 19-37; that volume, currently out of print, also contains an attack on Barth by a local factory owner, Walter Hüssy, and Barth's rebuttal.

I am happy to be able to speak to you about *Jesus*, especially because the initiative for it has come from your side. The best and greatest thing I can bring to you as a pastor will always be Jesus Christ and a portion of the powers which have gone out from his person into history and life. I take it as a sign of the mutual understanding between us that you for your part have come to me with a request for this best and greatest thing. I can say to you, however, that the other half of our theme lies just as much on my heart: *the movement for social justice*. A well-known theologian and author has recently argued that these two ought not to be joined together as they are in our topic: "Jesus Christ *and* the movement for social justice," for that makes it sound as if they are really two different realities which must first be connected more or less artificially. Both are seen as *one and the same*: Jesus *is* the movement for social justice, and the movement for social justice *is* Jesus in the present. I can adopt this view in good conscience if I reserve the right to show more precisely in what sense I do so. The real contents of the person of Jesus can in fact be summed up by the words: *movement for social justice*. Moreover, I really believe that the social justice movement of the nineteenth and twentieth centuries is not only the greatest and most urgent word of God to the present, but also in particular a quite direct continuation of the spiritual power which, as I said, entered into history and life with Jesus.

But against these ideas, there are objections from two sides, and I would guess that both are represented among us gathered here. The one side is formed by so-called *Christian* circles in the narrower sense of the term, with which the majority of bourgeois churchgoers are affiliated. If they read or hear that "Jesus Christ and the movement for social justice" have been linked together, they will protest more or less energetically that Christ is being made into a Social Democrat. "But please don't paint the Savior too 'red,' will you?" a worthy colleague said to me when I told him of my present theme. Then the assertion customarily follows, almost with a certain enthusiasm, that it is completely impossible to associate Jesus with a political party. His person remains nonpartisan, *above* social conflicts, indeed, indifferent to them. His significance is eternal and not historically limited like that of the Social Democratic Party. And so it becomes an untruth and a profanation to draw him into the conflicts of the day, as supposedly occurs in our theme. From the "Christian" side matters can be made still *easier*, however, and that is what usually happens — unfortunately even among many of my colleagues. One points with outstretched finger at this or that gross error or mistake committed by the Social Democratic side. Here the workers beat up a strikebreaker; there someone perpetrated a poisonous newspaper article, abounding in hatred; elsewhere assembly representative Naine made a fool of himself through anti-militaristic tirades; and so on. What does all that — along with all the other irritating things socialists do — what does all that have to do with Jesus Christ? All that obviously has nothing at all to do with Jesus Christ. It has just as little to do with him as those problems found on the free-thinking or conservative side, such as philistine narrow-mindedness, brutal self-seeking, and the self-glorifying exercise of violence. The errors and mistakes of individual persons are found on all sides, and I would not like to point the finger at others.

What concerns us here, however, is not individual persons, but rather the subject matter itself. It is just as cheap as it is unjust to pound away again and again, saying: "Look what the socialists are doing!" It is precisely Christians who ought to know that *we all* fall short when we look at what we're *doing*. When I talk about the movement for social justice, I am not talking about what some or all Social Democrats are *doing*; I am talking about what they *want*. As Christians we should like to be judged by God and by people according to what we *want*, not just according to what we *do*. What concerns us, therefore, are not the words and deeds of Bebel or Jaures, of Greulich or Pflüger or Naine, nor even the words and deeds of socialists in Aargau and Safenwil. Rather, what concerns us is what all these persons have in *common*, what is left over after everything personal and accidental, good or evil, is taken into account, what they all with their words and deeds *want*. What they want comes to a few very simple thoughts and motifs, which together amount to a historical phenomenon which is self-contained and independent of the behavior of socialists and the tactics of the socialist parties, and which stands completely *beyond* the controversy of the day: namely, the movement for social justice. I find it difficult to see how it becomes a profanation of the eternal to associate this movement with Jesus Christ. Indeed, we just said that we did not want to talk about what is temporal and accidental in this movement. In the same sense that we are accustomed to linking "Jesus and the Reformation" or "Jesus and Missions," in the same sense we now say: "Jesus and the Movement for Social Justice." We don't want to make Jesus into a German, French, or Aargau Social Democrat — that would be absurd — but rather we want to demonstrate the inner connection that exists between what is eternal, permanent, and general in modern social democracy [socialism] and the eternal Word of God, which in Jesus became flesh.

However, I still need to point out the objection that comes from the *other* side. Among you yourselves, dear friends of the labor union, or perhaps among your comrades in the canton outside, at least one or two persons thought quietly at the announcement of this topic: "Oh, no! Jesus Christ and the movement for social justice! They are still trying to capture us socialists for an antediluvian world view or even for the church." A social-democratic author, Joseph Dietzgen, has warned against connecting Christianity and socialism, for he sees it as a conservative maneuver. And in fact many a "Christian" approach to socialism does seem like a maneuver designed to "bring the people around" and make them once again into "pious little sheep." While socialism was the means, the Christian church and world view were the actual purpose for which one worked. I would not be surprised if you quietly held a little suspicion toward me as well in this regard. And at this point it would be insufficient to assure you that I really don't want to "bring anyone around." Rather, I must also give you the reason why it isn't so: I must explain why I would like to talk about the inherent connection between Jesus and socialism, and why the purpose of my lecture — that this connection may become clear to you — has nothing to do with your attitude toward the church. Perhaps you will have understood the connection between Jesus and socialism about which I want to speak. Perhaps — and this much I would wish for you — you will enter into a personal, inner relation with this man. Yet, afterward as before, it is still possible to make a wide arc around the church, even around the Safenwil church. The church can help you in your relationship to Jesus, but that is all. At all times there have been people who have managed without this help. Perhaps you are among those people. The church has often performed her service badly. That is quite certainly true of our church and of myself. Of the church, therefore, I can only say to you: "She is there in order to serve you. Do what you think is right." The church is not Jesus, and Jesus is not the church.

The same holds true of the so-called Christian world view. If you understand the connection between the person of Jesus and your social-ist convictions, and if you now want to arrange your life so that it corre-sponds to this connection, then that does not at all mean you have to "believe" or accept this, that, and the other thing. What Jesus has to bring to us are not ideas, but a way of life. One can have Christian ideas about God and the world and about human redemption, and still with all that be a complete heathen. And as an atheist, a materialist, and a Darwinist, one can be a genuine follower and disciple of Jesus. Jesus is not the Christian world view and the Christian world view is not Jesus. If I would like to interest you in Jesus today, then I can say to you gladly that I am not thinking of capturing you in order to "bring you around" to Christian ideas. I invite you to put them aside, and to concentrate your attention with me upon the one point we want to talk about: the bridge between Jesus and socialism. I would like nothing more from my lecture than that you all, my dear listeners, would *see* this bridge and attempt to *go* across it, some from this side to that, others from that side to this.

Now let us get into the subject matter. Socialism is a movement from below to above. In the discussion after my last lecture, someone put forth the claim that "we are the party of the poor devil!" As I look at you sitting before me, it seems to me that this indeed says a little too much; even you yourselves will not take it all too literally — but we both understand what was meant. Socialism is the movement of the economically dependent, of those who earn wages working for someone else, for a stranger; the movement of the *proletariat*, as the literature calls it. The proletarian is not always poor, but is always dependent in his existence upon the means and the goodwill of his brother, the factory owner. Here socialism sets in: It is and wants to be a proletarian movement. It wants to make independent those who are dependent, with all the consequences for their external, moral and cultural life which that would bring with it. Now one cannot say that Jesus also began precisely at this point. The reason is quite simply that two thousand years ago a proletariat in the contemporary sense of the term did not exist: There were still no factories. And yet it must strike everyone who reads his New Testament without prejudice that that which Jesus Christ was and wanted and attained, as seen from the human side, was entirely a *movement from below*. He himself came from the lowest social class of the Jewish people at that time. You all recall the Christmas story of the crib in Bethlehem. His father was a carpenter in an obscure town in Galilee, as he himself was during his entire life with the exception of his last years. Jesus was a worker, not a pastor. In his thirtieth year he laid down his tools and began to move from place to place, because he had something to say to the people. Once again, however, his position was fundamentally different from that of us pastors today. We have to be there for everyone, for high and low, for rich and poor; our character frequently suffers from this two-sided aspect of our calling. Jesus felt himself sent to the poor and the lowly; that is one of the most certain facts we encounter in the gospel story. Above his work stands that word in which we can still discern today the fire of a genuinely social spirit: He grieved when he saw the people, "because they were like sheep without a shepherd" (Mark 6.34). Occasionally, we also hear of rich people who became his followers. If they did not turn back again after brief enthusiasm, like the rich young ruler (Matt. 19.16-22) — he knew why! — then in Jesus' presence they felt more like guests than like those who actually belonged to him. Nicodemus (John 3.1-2), "a ruler of the Jews," who came to him by night, is a typical example of this. Indeed, in the last weeks of his life Jesus even turned to the rich and the educated with that which moved him — he went from Galilee to Jerusalem — but as you know, that attempt ended with the cross at Golgotha. What he brought was good news to the poor, to those who were dependent and uneducated: "Blessed are you poor, for yours is the kingdom of God" (Luke 6.20). "Whoever is least among you all is the one who is great" (Luke 9.48). "See that you do not despise one of these little ones; for I tell you that in heaven their angels always behold the face of my Father who is in heaven" (Matt. 18.10). Such sayings may not be interpreted as words of consolation from a philanthropic man who spoke thus from on high. "Yours is the kingdom of God!" said Jesus, and what he meant was this: You should rejoice that you belong to those who are least; you are nearer to salvation than those who are high and rich. "I thank thee, Father, Lord of heaven and earth, that thou hast hidden these things from the wise and understanding and revealed them to babes" (Matt. 11.25). That clearly was Jesus' own attitude: He found his friends among the fishermen of the Sea of Galilee, among the despised tax collectors who worked for the Romans, indeed among the prostitutes of the sea cities. One cannot reach lower down the social scale in the choice of one's associates than Jesus did. To him there was no one underneath who was too low or too bad. And I repeat: That was not a cheap pity from above to below, but the eruption of a volcano from below to above. It is not the poor who need pity, but the rich; not the so-called godless, but the pious. It was at those *above* that Jesus directed his scandalous saying: "The tax collectors and the harlots go into the kingdom of God before you" (Matt. 21.31). And again: "Woe to you that are rich, for you have received your consolation" (Luke 6.24). To those *below*, however, he says: "Come to me, all who labor and are heavy laden, and I will give you rest" (Matt. 11.28).

The kingdom of God has come to the poor. But what is "the kingdom of God"? I hear the objection: Social democracy wants only the external, *material* betterment of persons; by contrast, the kingdom of God that Jesus preached is *spirit* and inwardness. Social democracy preaches *revolution*; the gospel preaches *conversion*. The kingdom of God for social democracy is *earthly* and *immanent*; the kingdom of God for Jesus is *transcendent*; it is not called the *kingdom of heaven* without reason. Jesus and socialism are thus as different as night and day. At first glance there seems to be something to this objection. An outstanding and non-partisan student of socialism, Werner Sombart, has said that the "quintessence of all socialist doctrines of salvation" is contained in the lighthearted poem by Heinrich Heine:

A new song, a better song,
I want, O friends, to compose for you:
We want even here upon the earth
To build the kingdom of heaven.

We want to be happy upon the earth
And want to starve no more;
No more shall idle bellies squander
What industrious hands have earned.

Enough bread grows here below
For all the children of men;
And roses and myrtles, beauty and air,
And, not least, sweet peas.

Yes, sweet peas for everyone,
Plant the pods right away;
Heaven we will leave
To the angels and the sparrows.

And then one places next to this poem such words of Jesus as these: "Man shall not live by bread alone, but by every word that proceeds from the mouth of God" (Matt. 4.4); or "Therefore, do not be anxious, saying, 'What shall we eat?' or 'What shall we drink?' or 'What shall we wear?' for the Gentiles seek all these things; and your heavenly Father knows that you need them all. But seek first his kingdom and his righteousness, and all these things shall be yours as well" (Matt. 6.31-33); or "What will it profit a man, if he gains the whole world and forfeits his life?" (Matt. 16.26). And then one juxtaposes social democracy's endless agitation for economic justice with that scornful reply of Jesus: "Man, who made me a judge or divider over you?" (Luke 12.14). One then goes on to remark: "'Jesus and socialism' — as if the one were not diametrically opposed to the other!"

Everything now seems to be crystal clear, yet perhaps nowhere else has Christianity fallen farther away from the spirit of her Lord and Master than precisely in this estimation of the relation between spirit and matter, inner and outer, heaven and earth. One might well say that for eighteen hundred years the Christian church, when confronted by social misery, has always referred to the spirit, to the inner life, to heaven. The church has preached, instructed, and consoled, but she has *not helped.* Indeed, in the face of social misery she has always commended help as a good work of Christian love, but she has not dared to say that help is *the* good work. She has not said that social misery *ought not to be* in order then to summon all her power for the sake of this conviction that *it ought not to be*. She has entrenched herself behind a falsely understood saying of Jesus, taken out of context, which says that "the poor you always have with you" (John 12.8). She has accepted social misery as an accomplished fact in order to talk about spirit, to cultivate the inner life, and to prepare candidates for the kingdom of heaven. That is the great, momentous apostasy of the Christian church, her apostasy from Christ. When social democracy then appeared with its gospel of heaven on earth, this very church dared to stand in judgment over it, because it had denied spirit. She referred with smug horror to the little verse about angels and sparrows, and to similar expressions. She accused social democracy of vulgar materialism, and beat upon her breast: "Lord, we thank you that we are not as they are, that we are still idealists who regard spirit as the highest value and believe in heaven." Thus spoke and wrote the pastors — who would then sit down and eat a hearty midday meal!

The whole picture of the relationship between Spirit and matter, between heaven and earth, becomes completely different when we come to Jesus. For him there are not those two worlds, but the one reality of the kingdom of God. The opposite to God is not the earth, not matter, not the external, but evil, or as he put it in the forceful manner of his day: the demons, the devils who live in human beings. And that is why redemption is not the separation of spirit from matter; it is not that humanity "goes to heaven", but rather that God's kingdom *comes to us* in matter and on earth. "The World became flesh" (John 1.14), and not the other way around! The heavenly Father's love and justice come to rule over all things external and earthly. His will is to be done "*on earth* as it is in heaven" (Matt. 6.10). All those sayings which are often employed against socialism about the unsurpassed significance of spirit, of the interior are completely right: Jesus knows and recognizes only the kingdom of heaven that is *within* us. But the kingdom must obtain dominion over the external — over actual life — otherwise it does not deserve the name. The kingdom is not *of* this world, but of God. It is *in* this world, however, for *in* this world God's will is to be done. Humanly considered, the gospel is a movement from below to above, as I said. Seen from the divine side, however, it is wholly and completely a movement from above to below. It is not that we go to heaven, but that heaven comes to us.

This kingdom of heaven that comes to earth is by no means "purely spiritual," as is sometimes said. Rather, it is said very simply that we will "sit at table in the kingdom of God" (Luke 13.29). "Blessed are you that hunger now, for you shall *be satisfied*" (Luke 6.21). "Blessed are the meek, for they shall *inherit the earth*" (Matt. 5.5). To all those who have left everything for the sake of the gospel, it is promised that in time they will receive houses and fields a hundredfold once again (Matt. 19.29). The way to the kingdom of God is, however, by no means a merely spiritual and inward imploring of "Lord, Lord!"; rather, "you will know them by their fruits" (Matt. 7.21, 16). Again and again, however, the fruit is nothing but social help in material terms. This supposition of Jesus becomes clear from the great parable of the world's judgment: It is not according to the quality of their "spirit" that people are separated out to the right or the left. Rather, "I was hungry and you gave me food, I was thirsty and you gave me drink, I was a stranger and you welcomed me, I was naked and you clothed me, I was sick and you visited me, I was in prison and you came to me." For "as you did it to one of the least of these my brethren, you did it to me"; and "as you did it not to one of the least of these, you did it not to me" (Matt. 25.32-46). The spirit that has value before God is the *social* spirit. And social help is *the* way to eternal life. That is not only how Jesus spoke but also how he acted. If one reads the gospels attentively, one can only be amazed at the way it has become possible to make Jesus into a pastor or a teacher whose goal was supposedly to instruct persons about right belief or right conduct. Power came forth from him which healed them all (Luke 6.19). That was his essential effectiveness. Whether his healings of the sick are explained in a more supernatural or a more natural way, it is in any case a fact that he healed people and that this ability stood far more in the *center* of his life than is usually realized. He was an itinerant preacher who went about doing good and making people well (Acts 10.38). Many people came to him bringing with them the blind, the dumb, the crippled, and many others, and they put them at his feet, and he healed them (Matt. 15.30). We hear things like this again and again.

I ponder these facts known to every Bible reader and fail to see how one has a right to call social democracy unchristian and materialist because its goal is to introduce an order of society that would better serve the material interests of the proletariat. Jesus by word and deed opposed that material misery which *ought not to be*. Indeed, he did so by instilling people with the Spirit which transforms matter. To the paralytic in Capernaum, he said first: "Your sins are forgiven!" And then: "Stand up, take up your bed, and walk!" He worked from the internal to the external. He created new people in order to create a new world. In this direction the present-day social democracy still has infinitely much to learn from Jesus. It must come to the insight that we first need people of the future to create the state of the future, not the reverse. But regarding the goal, social democracy is one with Jesus: It has taken up the conviction that social misery *ought not to be* with a vigor which has not been seen since the time of Jesus. It calls us back from the hypocritical and slothful veneration of spirit and from that useless Christianity which intends to come only "in heaven." It tells us that we should really believe what we pray every day: "Thy Kingdom come!" With its "materialism" it preaches to us a word which stems not from Jesus himself, yet certainly from his Spirit. The word goes like this: "*The end of the way of God is the affirmation of the body (ist die Leiblichkeit)*" [Oetinger].

Something stands in the way of the coming of God's kingdom to earth, says Jesus. Indeed, answers social democracy, what stands in the way is capitalism. Capitalism is the system of production which makes the proletariat into the proletariat, i.e., into a dependent wage earner whose existence is constantly insecure. The materials necessary for production (investment capital, factories, machines, raw materials) are the *private property* of one of the co-workers, namely, the boss, the factory owner. The other co-worker (the "worker") possesses nothing but the power of his work, which he furnishes to the factory owner, while the net profits of the common work are accounted as capital — as the factory owner's *private property*. Socialism declares that it is unjust to pay the one co-worker for his production so disadvantageously, while the other pockets the full actual gain of the common production. It is unjust that the one becomes a distinguished person, amasses capital upon capital, lives in a beautiful house, and is granted all the pleasures of life, while the other must live from hand to mouth, at best manages to save a little, and, if for one reason or another this is impossible for him, remains a "poor devil," who is consigned finally to charity. This class contradiction, says socialism, is the daily crime of capitalism. This system of production must therefore *fall*, especially its underlying principle: *private property* — not private property in general, but private ownership of the means of production. Just as the work is collective or common, so must its net profits be shared in common. For that, however, the boundless *competition* between individual producers must fall; and the state, the whole, must itself become the producer and therefore the owner of the means of production. This in the briefest of words is the anticapitalist theory of social democracy. We could certainly search for a long time until we found a similar theory, or anticipations of one, in the Gospels. We do not want to search for that at all. The capitalist economic system is a modern phenomenon, as is the socialist counter-theory. But in these modern phenomena we have to do with a problem that is as old as humanity, namely, the question of *private property*. What was Jesus' attitude toward that? Here is a question we may pose quite legitimately and from that basis infer his attitude toward capitalism and socialism in the present. Let us first take a look around. What does the Christian church say about that? And what about the state, which, through the support of a state church, to a certain extent passes itself off as a Christian state? Here we notice that both church and state shroud the concept of private property with an amazing aura of sanctity and unassailability. It has been impressed upon all of us down to the marrow of our bones that what's mine must remain mine. In our penal code, property enjoys far greater protection than, for example, a good reputation or morality. What's mine is mine, and no one can change that! Not ony have Christians become used to this notion, because temporarily perhaps it could not be otherwise, but they even act as if it were a divine law and have fallen into the deepest dismay regarding the intention of social democracy largely to eliminate private property and to transform private capitalism into social capitalism.

The dismay could well be on the other side. If one lets the words of Jesus say what they really say without watering them down or weakening them, then one finds that precisely the notion that "what's mine is mine" is condemned with a greater force than perhaps found anywhere in all of socialist literature. Jesus is more socialist than the socialists. You know the saying: "It is easier for a camel to go through the eye of a needle than for a rich man to enter the kingdom of God" (Matt. 19.24). Here clever theologians have made the discovery that the eye of a needle is not really the eye of a needle, but a Palestinian name for a narrow gate through the city wall. A camel could pass through such a narrow gate only with great difficulty; thus a rich man, if otherwise virtuous, could supposedly enter the kingdom of God, albeit with great difficulty. Thus is the Bible watered down! No, no, the eye of the needle is and remains the eye of the needle, and Jesus really wanted to say that a rich person, a possessor of worldly goods, does *not* enter into the kingdom of God. You know the story of the rich man and poor Lazarus. It nowhere says that the rich man committed some sort of particularly evil deed and for that reason ended up in hell and torment. No. Rather, his fate was the consequence of the contrast — of the class contradiction — in his life, which consisted in the fact that he was rich and had it good, while Lazarus was poor. "Now he is comforted here, and you are in anguish" (Luke 16.19-31). And it is not accidental that we are reminded of modern capitalism when we hear of the rich man (Luke 12.16-21) whose land brought forth so plentifully that he no longer had room to store his crops and who decided to tear down his barns to build larger ones. Why shouldn't he? His profits were certainly his property! And we hear nothing more evil about him than that he was so satisfied in his possessions. Yet the parable continues: "Fool! This night your soul is required of you; and the things you have prepared, whose will they be?" (v. 20). Then there is the rich young ruler (Matt. 19.16-22) who had kept all the commandments from his youth. Jesus said to him: "One thing you still lack. Sell all that you have and distribute to the poor." But when he heard this he went away sorrowful, for he was very rich. Moreover, there is the entire section from the Sermon on the Mount, which begins with the words. "Do not lay up for yourselves treasures on earth" (Matt. 6.19), where we hear that such gathering of treasure turns the human inner light into darkness; where we are placed before the great Either/Or: "No one can serve two masters; for either he will hate the one and love the other, or he will be devoted to the one and despise the other. You cannot serve God and mammon" (Matt. 6.24). One can only be continually amazed if one realizes how easily Christendom of all confessions and types has glossed over these words, while it has often been so zealously strict and precise in dogmatic questions which had no meaning at all in the life of Jesus. Jesus rejected the concept of private property; of that, it seems to me, there can be no doubt. He rejected precisely the principle that what's mine is mine. Our attitude toward material goods should be that of the famous steward in the parable (Luke 16.1-12): "Make friends for yourselves by means of the mammon of unrighteousness." We should not possess it, but we should be "faithful" with it. And "being faithful" in this context means quite clearly: We should make others into its common owners. As private property it is and remains precisely the mammon of unrighteousness. The fact that this was Jesus' belief is finally most clearly illuminated by the position which he himself adopted in practice, and which he also enjoined upon his disciples. There was a man who declared that he was ready to follow Jesus wherever he went. Jesus answered him: "Foxes have holes, and birds of the air have nests; but the Son of Man has nowhere to lay his head" (Luke 9.57-58). Indeed, the abolition of private property goes farther: His mother and his brothers called to him as a crowd was sitting around him. But he no longer knew of any familial bonds that had some personal, private value in themselves: "'Who are my mother and my brothers?' And looking around on those who sat about him, he said, 'Here are my mother and my brothers!'" (Mark 3.31-35). The same held for his disciples: "Take no gold, nor silver, nor copper in your belts, no bag for your journey, nor two tunics, nor sandals, nor a staff" (Matt. 10.9-10). Do we want once again to wriggle off the hook by saying that these words apply only to those who were missionaries in the earliest era of the gospel, or do we detect in them the heartbeat of the gospel itself? It says to us: Thou shalt become free from everything that begins with "I" and "mine," absolutely free, in order to be free for social help. Do the two go together, Jesus and capitalism, the system of boundlessly increasing private property? Joseph Dietzgen, mentioned earlier — by his own words a despiser of Jesus and Christianity — says at one point: "The real original sin, from which the human race has suffered up to now, is self-seeking. Moses and the prophets, all the law givers and preachers of morality together, have not been able to liberate us from it. . . . No fine phraseology, no theory and rule, has been able to abolish it, because the constitution of the whole society hangs on this nail. Bourgeois society depends upon the self-seeking distinction between 'mine' and 'yours,' on the social war, on competition, on the defraudation and exploitation of the one by the other." This despiser of Jesus has understood Jesus *correctly*. Jesus' view of property is this: Property is sin, because property is self-seeking. What's mine is absolutely not mine!

However, social democracy does not only say that the material situation of the proletariat must become a different and better one. It does not only say that for this purpose human work must cease being a way merely to increase private capital. Rather, it seizes and employs a means to lead this goal to realization. The means is called *organization*. The historic programmatic text of socialism, the Communist Manifesto of 1848, concludes with the famous words: "Workers of the world unite!" Socialism proceeds from the *solidarity* that is actually already imposed by the capitalist system. In distinction to the crafts of the old guild type, modern factory work is collective work under conditions of solidarity. Twenty pairs of hands and more take part in producing a single shoe! Now socialism wants to bring to the worker's consciousness this (in itself necessary) solidarity as the source of his power and progress. He should learn to think collectively, solidarily, commonly, socially, just as he has actually been long since working socially. He should become a class-conscious worker. It is customary in this context to speak of the "battalion of workers." The individual worker can achieve nothing, but the battalion of workers will in an unremitting assault bring down the fortress of capitalism. To be a socialist means to be a "comrade" in consumers unions, in labor unions, and in political parties. He ceases to be an individualist, to be something for himself. He takes seriously that fine Swiss saying: "One for all, and all for one." As a socialist, he no longer thinks and feels and acts as a private person, but rather as a member of the forward-striding, fighting totality. Solidarity is the law and the gospel of socialism. Or to speak once again with Joseph Dietzgen: "Conscious and planned organization of social work is what the longed-for savior of the modern period is called."

As Christians we will at first be inclined to say that the gospel and the Savior of the New Testament are something quite different. There what is concerned is not a matter of the masses, but of the individual soul. Do we not hear from Jesus' lips of the shepherd who leaves ninety-nine sheep in the wilderness to go after the one which is lost, until he finds it (Luke 15.3-7)? The socialist call to solidarity and Jesus' call to repent and believe the gospel stand in rather strange contrast to each other. Unfortunately, in fact they really do — not for Christ, however, but for those who call themselves by his name. It is thus also one of the current misunderstandings that religion is a means of making the individual quiet, cheerful, and where possible blessed in the midst of the anxieties of life. Because Jesus said, "When you pray, go into your closet" (Matt. 6.6), we act as if Christianity as a whole were a matter of the closet, and indeed of *our* private closet. One finds oneself together with other persons in the church in order to secure the consolation and joy of the gospel, but the community extends no farther: Religion beforehand and afterward remains a matter between God and the soul, the soul and God, and only that. This attitude is found today especially among the Christians of Germany, above all to the extent that they stand under the influence of Luther. They then distinguish themselves without exception by a complete failure to understand social democracy. In that regard we Swiss, even if we don't realize it, are brought up differently through our Reformers, Zwingli and Calvin. To these men, religion was from the outset something cooperative, something social, not only externally, but also internally. It is therefore no accident that among us, Christianity and socialism have never come to the kind of rift that exists between them in Germany. Rather, with ever-increasing clarity one begins from both sides to become aware of the correlation, indeed of the *unity* between them.

111

This unity is found already in Jesus. We believe, without wanting to derogate others, that we understand Jesus better than our fellow Christians in Germany. Certainly, Jesus wanted to bring the heavenly Father to the soul *and* the soul to the heavenly Father. But what do we pray: "my Father" or "our Father"? Isn't that the whole point? For Jesus there was only a social God, a God of solidarity; therefore there was also only a social religion, a religion of solidarity. In Jesus' view, do we have eternal life in a secluded retreat or in the *kingdom of God*? Does the *gospel* really say that *I* attain life, eternal life, blessedness? What does Christ say? "Whoever would save his life will *lose* it; and whoever loses his life for my sake and the Gospel's will *save* it" (Mark 8.35). It is not for our own sake that we are called; it is not for the sake of the soul's self-seeking that we are to repent, be converted, and believe in God. Rather: "Follow me and I will make you become fishers of men" (Mark 1.17). "You are the light of the *world*." "You are the salt of the earth" (Matt. 5.13-16). Against the Pharisees, who took piety with the utmost seriousness, Jesus directed the saying of the prophets: "I desire mercy, and not sacrifice" (Matt. 9.13). God's law is blotted out when we want to be pious instead of practicing *love* (Matt. 15.3-6). "Woe to you scribes and Pharisees, hypocrites! for you tithe mint and dill and cummin, and have neglected the weightier matters of the law, justice and mercy and faith" (Matt. 23.23). There is no other greatness before God than the greatness of helping others: "Whoever would be great among you must be your servant" (Matt. 20.26). All this does not stand *beside* faith in God the Father in heaven as something added onto it afterward; rather, it is inextricably bound to it. In answer to the question, "Which commandment is the first of all?" Jesus named two: "You shall love the Lord your God with all your heart," and "you shall love your neighbor as yourself" (Mark 12.28-31). From this awareness of the collective, solidary, communal, social God, the rule of corresponding action follows of itself: "Whatever you wish that men would do to you, do so to them" (Matt. 7.12). And Jesus added: "This is the law and the prophets," God's love should flow into us in order to transform us in love into human beings again. And now we look once again from Jesus' words to his life. We step here into the most sacred areas of our faith. Above our religion stands the sign of the *cross*. This sign stands first over the life of Jesus: "The Son of Man . . . came not to be served but to serve, and to give his life as a ransom for many" (Mark 10.45). He gives up life unto death, not for his own sake, or for the sake of his own eternal happiness, but rather in order to help many. You know the story of how Jesus washed his disciples' feet:

"I have given you an example, that you also should do as I have done to you" (John 13.4-19). You know the words of institution at the Last Supper: "Take, this is my body"; and "This is my blood of the covenant, which is poured out for many" (Mark 14.22-24). This was the climax and end of his life, an act of *faithfulness* to his disciples. Have we understood the word of the cross when we so conduct ourselves as if there were something in life even higher than the *giving* of one's life for others, than this consciousness of solidarity which makes the neighbor equal to oneself? Indeed, this word of the cross is a scandal and folly, just as it was at the time of Paul (I Cor. 1.18). Let him take it in who can, that one must lose one's life in order to find it, that one must cease being something for oneself, that one must become a communal person, a comrade, in order to be a person at all. "But to those who are being saved the word of the cross is the power of God." I find something of this power of God in social democracy's idea of organization. I also find it elsewhere, but here I find it more clearly and purely, and here I find it in the way in which it must be worked out in *our* time.

And now, in conclusion, allow me a few personal words which I would like to say to you as a pastor of this community.

First, to those friends present who up to now have related themselves to socialism in an indifferent, reserved, or *hostile* way: At this moment you are perhaps feeling somewhat disappointed and upset, so that it would not be inconceivable that one or another might go out from here and report: "He said that the socialists are right." I would be sorry if anyone said that. I repeat once again: I have spoken about what socialists *want*, not about the manner in which they *act* to attain it. *About what they want, I say: That is what Jesus wanted, too.* About the manner in which they *act* to attain it, I could not say the same thing. It would be easy for me to come up with a broad critique about the manner in which the socialists act to attain it. But I fail to see what good such an easy exercise would accomplish. Therefore, I have not said that the socialists are right! Nonetheless, I do not want to say that you nonsocialists should now go home comforted and reassured. If you feel upset, then that is good. If you have the feeling that "Oh, no, Christianity is a hard and dangerous matter if one gets to the roots of it," then you have rightly understood me — or, rather, not me, but *Jesus.* For I did not want to tell you my view, but the view of Jesus as I have found it in the Gospels. Consider, then, whether as followers of Jesus you ought not to bring more understanding, more goodwill, more *participation* in the movement for social justice in our time than you have up to now.

And now to my *socialist* friends who are present: I have said that Jesus wanted what you want, that he wanted to help those who are least, that he wanted to establish the kingdom of God upon this earth, that he wanted to abolish self-seeking property, that he wanted to make persons into comrades. Your concerns are in line with the concerns of Jesus. *Real* socialism is real Christianity in our time. That may fill you with pride and satisfaction about your concerns. But I hope you have also heard the rebuke implied in the distinction I have made between Jesus and yourselves! He wanted what you want — as you *act* to attain it. There you have the difference between Jesus and yourselves. He wanted what you want, but he *acted* in the way you have heard. That is generally the difference between Jesus and the rest of us, that among us the greatest part is program, whereas for Jesus program and performance were one. Therefore, Jesus says to you quite simply that you should carry out your program, that you should *enact* what you *want.* Then you will be Christians and true human beings. Leave the superficiality and the hatred, the spirit of mammon and the self-seeking, which also exists among your ranks, behind: They do *not* belong to your concerns. Let the faithfulness and energy, the sense of community and the courage for sacrifice found in Jesus be effective among you, in your whole life; then you will be true socialists.

However, the unrest and the sharpening of conscience which Jesus in this hour has hopefully brought to us all should not be the last word in this beautiful Christmas season. I think we all have the impression that Jesus was someone quite different than we are. His image stands strangely great and high above us all, socialists and nonsocialists. Precisely for that reason he has something to say to us. Precisely for that reason he can be something for us. Precisely for that reason we touch the living God himself when we touch the hem of his garment. And if we now let our gaze rest upon him, as he goes from century to century in ever-new revelations of his glory, then something is fulfilled in us of the ancient word of promise which could also be written of the movement for social justice in our day: "*The people who walked in darkness have seen a great light.*"[23]

*

THE EPISTLE TO THE ROMANS

Disillusioned during his Safenwil pastorate with the liberal theology in which he had been trained, Barth was impressed with his friend Thur-

neysen's remark that their preaching, teaching and pastoral care needed "a 'wholly other' theological foundation." Surely not thinking of any parallel with Newton, "the morning after Thurneysen had whispered to me our commonly held conviction, I sat down under an apple tree and began, with all the tools at my disposal, to apply myself to the Epistle to the Romans."[24]

Theology for Barth was always biblical interpretation. The Church Dogmatics contains hundreds of pages of "excurses" with studies of biblical texts. This was a theological method Barth adopted with Der Römerbrief. (Barth's biblical text is his own German translation from the Greek, while the translator uses a lightly altered text of the English Revised Version.) The first edition of the commentary was dated 1919, though it actually appeared in December, 1918. It was never translated into English since Barth completely re-wrote the book in 1920-21, and it was this second edition of 1922 that brought him notoriety. Subsequent editions were virtually unchanged, and the sixth edition was translated into English in 1933. There is a deep irony here for, while it was this translation that gave rise to impressions — and stereotypes — of Barth that prevailed for decades,[25] Barth in 1933 had already moved far beyond his Romans, had published the first volume of his Church Dogmatics, and was already engaged in the "revision" described in the essay on "The Humanity of God."

The two selections exemplify the negations which led to the label "dialectical theology"; they also show Barth's thesis that the Word of God creates a permanent crisis in human affairs, and this gave rise to the label "theology of crisis"; the Greek κρισις which Barth transliterates Krisis is printed KRISIS in Edwyn Hoskyns' translation. Yet its author, who was so busy with this "enormous execution" as he later put it (see above, 51), was not without a healthy dose of humor and self-criticism. He wrote as an inscription in his own copy a quotation from Luther: "If you feel or imagine that you are right and suppose that your book, teaching or writing is a great achievement . . .then, my dear man, feel your ears. If you are doing so properly, you will find that you have a splendid pair of big, long, shaggy asses' ears. . . ."[26]

THE NIGHT

Its Cause: 1.18-21

v. 18. For the wrath of God is revealed from heaven against all ungodliness and unrighteousness of men, who hold the truth imprisoned in the chains of their unrighteousness.

In the name of God! We know not what we should say to this. The believer knows our ignorance. With Job, the believer loves the God who in his unsearchable eminence is only to be feared: with Luther, he loves the *deus absconditus*.[27] To him is manifested the righteousness of God. He shall be saved, and he alone. "Only the prisoner shall be free, only the poor shall be rich, only the weak strong, only the humble exalted, only the empty filled, only nothing shall be something" (Luther). But against the ungodliness and unrighteousness of humanity there is revealed the wrath of God.

The wrath of God is the judgment under which we stand in so far as we do *not* love the Judge; *it* is the "No" which meets us when we do *not* affirm it; it is the protest pronounced always and everywhere against the course of the world in so far as we do *not* accept the protest as our own; it is the questionableness of life in so far as we do *not* apprehend it; it is our boundedness and corruptibility in so far as we do *not* acknowledge their necessity. The judgment under which we stand is a fact, quite apart from our attitude to it. Indeed, it is the fact most characteristic of our life. Whether it enters within the light of salvation and of the coming world depends upon the answer we give to the problem of faith. But it is a fact, even should we choose the scandal rather than faith (1.16). That time is nothing when measured by the standard of eternity, that all things are semblance when measured by their origin and by their end, that we are sinners, and that we must die — all these things *are*, even though the barrier be not for us the place of exit. Life moves on its course in its vast uncertainty and we move with it, even though we do not see the great question-mark that is set against us. Human beings are lost, even though they know nothing of salvation. Then the barrier remains a barrier and does not become a place of exit. The prisoner remains a prisoner and does not become the watchman. Then is waiting not joyful but a bitter-sweet surrender to what is inevitable. Then is the contradiction not hope, but a sorrowful opposition. The fruitful paradox of our existence is then that which consumes it like a worm. And negation is then — what is normally meant by the word. In the place of the Holy God there then appear fate, matter, the universe, chance, ἀνάγκη [necessity]. Indeed, a certain perception is betrayed when we begin to avoid giving the name "God" to the "No-God" of unbelief (1.17). That which we, apart from faith in the resurrection, *name* "God," is also a final consequence of the divine wrath. But the God who, contradicting his own name, affirms the course of this world, is God — God in his wrath, God who sorrows on our behalf, God who can only turn himself from us and say only "No." And yet, for this very reason, no upright person can unreservedly name him "God." For the wrath of God cannot be his last word, the true revelation of him! "Not-God" cannot seriously be named "God." Nevertheless, it is, in fact, always God against whom we are thrust. Even the unbeliever encounters God, but he does not penetrate through to the truth of God that is hidden from him, and so he is broken to pieces on God, as Pharaoh was (9.15-18). "Everything that thwarts and damages the life that has been made by God, all the frailty and bondage of the creaturely life, including the sentence of death under which it lies, is a reaction of the power of God" (Zündel). Yes, but we must add that, if we do not make the apprehension of this divine reaction our own, we must perish at its hands. The whole world is the footprint of God; yes, but, in so far as we choose scandal rather than faith, the footprint in the vast riddle of the world is the footprint of his wrath. The wrath of God is to unbelief the discovery of his righteousness, for God is not mocked. The wrath of God is the righteousness of God — apart from and without Christ.

But what does "apart from and without Christ" mean? **The wrath of God is revealed against all ungodliness and unrighteousness of men.** These are the characteristic features of our relation to God, as it takes shape on this side of the resurrection. Our relation to God is *ungodly*. We suppose that we know what we are saying when we say "God." We assign to him the highest place in our world: and in so doing we place him fundamentally on one line with ourselves and with things. We assume that he *needs something*: and so we assume that we are able to arrange our relation to him as we arrange our other relationships. We press ourselves into proximity with him: and so, all unthinking, we make him nigh unto ourselves. We allow ourselves an ordinary communication with him, we permit ourselves to reckon with him as though this were not extraordinary behavior on our part. We dare to deck ourselves out as his companions, patrons, advisers, and commissioners. We confound time with eternity. This is the ungodliness of our relation to God. And our relation to God is *unrighteous*. Secretly we are ourselves the masters in this relationship. We are not concerned with God, but with our own requirements, to which God must adjust himself. Our arrogance demands that, in addition to everything else, some super-world should also be known and accessible to us. Our conduct calls for some deeper sanction, some approbation and remuneration from another world. Our well-regulated, pleasurable life longs for some hours of devotion, some prolongation into infinity. And so, when we set God upon the throne of the world, we mean by God ourselves. In "be-

117

lieving" in him, we justify, enjoy, and adore ourselves. Our devotion consists in a solemn affirmation of ourselves and of the world and in a pious setting aside of the contradiction. Under the banners of humility and emotion we rise in rebellion against God. We confound time with eternity. That is our unrighteousness. Such is our relation to God apart from and without Christ, on this side of the resurrection, and *before* we are called to order. *God* himself is not acknowledged as God and what is called "God" is in fact *humanity* itself. By living to ourselves, we serve the "No-God."

Who hold the truth imprisoned in unrighteousness. This second characteristic is in point of time the first. One falls a prey first to oneself and then to the "No-God." First one hears the promise — *ye shall be as God!*[28] — and then loses the sense for eternity. First one exalts humanity, and then obscures the distance between God and ourselves. The nodal point in the relation between God and ourselves apart from and without Christ is the unrighteousness of slaves. Thinking of ourselves what can be thought only of God, we are unable to think of him more highly than we think of ourselves. Being to ourselves what God ought to be to us, he is no more to us than we are to ourselves. This secret identification of ourselves with God carries with it our isolation from him. The little god must, quite appropriately, dispossess the great God. Men have imprisoned and encased the truth — the righteousness of God; they have trimmed it to their own measure, and thereby robbed it both of its earnestness and of its significance. They have made it ordinary, harmless, and useless; and thereby transformed it into untruth. This has all been brought to light by their ungodliness, and this ungodliness will not fail to thrust them into ever new forms of unrighteousness. If humanity be itself God, the appearance of the idol is then *inevitable*. And whenever the idol is honored, it is *inevitable* that human beings, feeling themselves to be the true God, should also feel that they have themselves fashioned the idol. This is the rebellion which makes it impossible for us to see the new dimensional plane which is the boundary of our world and the meaning of our salvation. Against such rebellion there can be revealed only the wrath of God.

vv. 19-21. **Because that which may be known of God is manifest to them; for God manifested it unto them. For the invisible things of him since the creation of the world are clearly seen, being perceived through the things that are made, even his** everlasting power and divinity; so that they are without excuse: because that, in spite of knowing God, they glorified him not as God, neither gave thanks; but became vain in their reasonings, and their senseless heart was darkened.

That which may be known of God is manifest unto them. The truth concerning the limiting and dissolving of humanity by the unknown God, which breaks forth in the resurrection, is a *known* truth: this is the tragic factor in the story of the passion of the truth. When our limitation is apprehended, and when he is perceived who, in bounding us, is also the dissolution of our limitation, the most primitive as well as the most highly developed forms of human self-consciousness become repeatedly involved in a "despairing humiliation," in the "irony of intelligence" (H. Cohen). We know that God is he whom *we do not* know, and that our ignorance is precisely the problem and the source of our knowledge. We know that God is the personality which *we are not*, and that this lack of personality is precisely what dissolves and establishes our personality. The recognition of the absolute heteronomy under which we stand is itself an *autonomous* recognition; and this is precisely that which may be known of God. When we rebel, we are in rebellion not against what is foreign to us but against that which is most intimately ours, not against what is removed from us but against that which lies at our hands. Our memory of God accompanies us always as problem and as warning. He is the hidden abyss; but he is also the hidden home at the beginning and end of all our journeyings. Disloyalty to him is disloyalty to ourselves.

For the invisible things of God are clearly seen. This we have forgotten, and we must allow it to be brought once more to our minds. Our lack of humility, our lack of recollection, our lack of fear in the presence of God, are not in our present condition inevitable, however natural they may seem to us. Plato in his wisdom recognized long ago that behind the visible there lies the invisible universe which is the Origin of all concrete things. And moreover, the solid good sense of people of the world had long ago perceived that the fear of the Lord is the beginning of wisdom.[29] The clear, honest eyes of the poet in the book of Job and of the Preacher Solomon had long ago rediscovered, mirrored in the world of appearance, the archetypal, unobservable, undiscoverable majesty of God. The speech of God can always be heard out of the whirlwind.[30] Always it requires of us that we should perceive how unwisely we speak of that which is too high for us, too far beyond our

119

understanding, when, in praising God or in complaining of him, we plead with him as with One who is like unto us. The insecurity of our whole existence, the vanity and utter questionableness of all that is and of what we are, lie as in a text-book open before us. What are all those enigmatic creatures of God — a zoological garden, for example — but so many problems to which we have no answer? But God only, God himself, he is the answer. And so the boundary which bars us in and which, nevertheless, points beyond itself, can since the creation of the world be clearly seen through the things that are made by God. By calm, veritable, unprejudiced religious contemplation the divine "No" can be established and apprehended. If we do not ourselves hinder it, nothing can prevent our being translated into a most wholesome crisis by that which *may be known of God.* And indeed, we stand already in this crisis if we would but *see clearly.* And what is clearly seen to be indisputable reality is the invisibility of God, which is precisely and in strict agreement with the gospel of the resurrection — his everlasting power and divinity. And what does this mean but that we can know nothing of God, that we are not God, that the Lord is to be feared? Herein lies his preeminence over all gods; and here is that which marks him out as God, as Creator, and as Redeemer (1.16). And so through all history there runs the line of intersection between time and eternity, between the present and the future world (1.4). Long ago it was proclaimed (1.2); always it was visible. The wrath of God needed not to be revealed to those who stood already under his judgment, for they could have known and loved the Judge. *So that,* when they fail to see and fail to hear, they are without excuse. Having eyes to see and ears to hear they are doing what they are doing. Inexcusable is their godlessness, for the *clearly seen* works of God speak of his *everlasting power* and they have already risen up in protest against the service of the known "No-God," by which God is ranged in the midst of the natural and religious and other forces of this world. Inexcusable also is their unrighteousness, for the *clearly seen* facts bear witness to the *everlasting divinity* of God, and have already risen up in protest against the arrogance of religion, by which human beings, speaking of God from the welter of their experiences, mean in fact themselves. We have, therefore, encased the truth of God and evoked his wrath. But this was not because no alternative was open to us. *God is not far from each one of us:* "*for in him we live, and move, and have our being*" (Acts 17.27, 28). The situation might, therefore, have been very different.

But — in spite of knowing God. The knowledge of God attainable through a simple observation of the incomprehensibility, the imperfection, the triviality of human life, was not taken advantage of. The invisibility of God seems to us less tolerable than the questionable visibility of what we like to call "God." We make of the eternal and ultimate presupposition of the Creator a "thing in itself" above and in the midst of other things, of that which is living and abstracted from all concreteness a concrete thing — no doubt the highest — in the midst of other concrete things, of the Spirit *a* spirit, of what is inaccessible and therefore so nigh at hand an endlessly uncertain object of our experiences. Rather than see in his light — eternal and which no man can approach unto[31] — the Light, we allow him to become *a* light — no doubt the most brilliant and, indeed, immaterial and supernatural — at which we kindle our *own* lights and then, quite consistently, seek to find in concrete things their *own* light. If, then, God is to us no longer the Unknown, what has become of the **glory** we owe him? If God is to us no longer what we are not, what has become of the **thanks** which are due to him? The revolt of Prometheus is wholly justified when once Zeus — the "No-God" — has been exalted to the throne of God.

And so the light has become in us darkness, and the wrath of God is inevitable — **They became vain in their reasonings, and their senseless heart was darkened.** The barrier is now indeed a barrier, and the "No" of God is now indeed negation. Bereft of understanding and left to themselves, people are at the mercy of the dominion of the meaningless powers of the world; for our life in this world has meaning only in its relation to the true God. But this relation can be re-established only through the — *clearly seen* — memory of eternity breaking in upon our minds and hearts. There is no other relation to God save that which appears upon the road along which Job traveled. If this "breaking in" does not occur, our thought remains empty, formal, merely critical and unproductive, incapable of mastering the rich world of appearance and of apprehending each particular thing in the context of the whole. Unbroken thought thereby divests itself of any true relation to the concrete world, and, contrariwise, the unbroken heart, that is to say, that sensitiveness to things which is guarded by no final insight, divests itself of the control of thought. Dark, blind, uncritical, capricious, humanity becomes a thing unto itself. Heartless, perceiving without observing and therefore empty, is our thought: thoughtless, observing without perceiving and therefore blind, is our heart. Fugitive is the soul in this world and soulless is the world, when people do not find themselves within the sphere of the knowledge of the unknown God, when they avoid the true God in whom they and the world must lose themselves in order that both may find themselves again.

This is the cause of the night in which we are wandering: this also is the cause of the wrath of God which has been manifested over our heads.

Its Operation: 1.22-32

v. 22. **Professing themselves to be wise, they became fools.**

The picture of a world *without* paradox and *without* eternity, of knowing *without* the background of not-knowing, of a religion *without* the unknown God, of a view of life *without* the memory of the "No" by which we are encountered, has much to be said in its favor. It evokes confidence, for it is simple and straightforward and uncramped; it provides considerable security and has few ragged edges; it corresponds, generally speaking, with what is required by the practical experiences of life; its standards and general principles are conveniently vague and flexible; and it possesses, moreover, a liberal prospect of vast future possibilities. Once the possibility that things can be *clearly seen* (1.20) is abandoned, people are able against this background to profess that they are wise. The night, too, has its wisdom. But, nevertheless, the vanity of the mind and the darkness of the heart still remain facts to be reckoned with. The brilliance of this unbroken wisdom cannot be maintained in the actual course of events, for they have passed inevitably under the wrath of God. That God is not known as God is due, not merely to some error of thought or to some gap in experience, but to a fundamentally wrong attitude to life. Vanity of mind and blindness of heart inevitably bring into being corrupt conduct. The more unbroken people march along their road secure of themselves, the more surely do they make fools of themselves, the more certainly do that morality and that manner of life which are built up upon a forgetting of the abyss, upon a forgetting of their true home, turn out to be a lie. It is indeed not difficult to show that this is so.

vv. 23, 24. **And changed the glory of the incorruptible God for an image made like to corruptible man, and to birds, and four-footed beasts, and creeping things. Wherefore God gave them up in the lusts of their hearts unto uncleanness, that their bodies should be dishonoured among themselves.**

They changed the glory of the incorruptible — for an image of the corruptible. That is to say, the understanding of what is characteristic of God was lost. They had lost their knowledge of the crevasse, the polar zone, the desert barrier, which must be crossed if they are really to advance from corruption to incorruption. The distance between God and humanity had no longer its essential, sharp, acid, and disintegrating ultimate significance. The difference between the incorruption, the pre-eminence and originality of God, and the corruption, the boundedness and relativity of our being had been confused. Once the eye, which can perceive this distinction, has been blinded, there arises in the mist, between here and there, between us and the "Wholly Other," a mist or concoction of religion in which, by a whole series of skilful assimilations and mixings more or less strongly flavored with sexuality, sometimes human or animal behavior is exalted to be an experience of God, sometimes the being and activity of God is "enjoyed" as a human or animal experience. In all this mist the prime factor is provided by the illusion that it is possible for people to hold communication with God or, at least, to enter into a covenant relationship with him without miracle — vertical from above, without the dissolution of all concrete things, and apart from *the* truth which lies beyond birth and death. But, on whatever level it occurs, if the experience of religion is more than a void, or claims to contain or to possess or to "enjoy" God, it is a shameless and abortive anticipation of that which can proceed from the unknown God alone. In all this busy concern with concrete things there is always a revolt against God. For in it we assist at the birth of the "No-God," at the making of idols. Enveloped in mist, we forget not merely that all that passes to corruption is a parable, but also that it is *only* a parable. The glory of the incorruptible God has been confused with the image (Psalm 106.20) of corruptible things. Some one of the relationships of people to the objects of their fear or of their desire, to some means of their subsistence, to some product of their own thought or action, to some impressive occurrence in nature or in history, is taken to be *in itself significant* and of supreme importance, as though even this selected relationship were not broken by the witness it bears to the unknown Creator whose glory cannot be confused with the known glory of an image, however pure and delicate. From such supposed direct communion with God — genuine only when it is not genuine, when it is not romanticized into an "experience," when it is at once dissolved and claims to be merely an open space, a sign-post, an occasion, and an opportunity — there emerge precisely all those intermediary, collateral, lawless divinities and powers and authorities and principalities (8.38) that obscure and discolour the light of the true God. In the realm of romantic direct communion — in India, for example — these divinities are thrown up in the most extravagant numbers. Wherever the qualitative distinction between humanity and the final Omega is overlooked or misunderstood, that fetishism is bound to appear in which God is experienced in birds and fourfooted things, and finally, or rather primarily, in the likeness of corruptible man — "personality," the "child," the "woman" — and in the half-spiritual, half-material creations, exhibitions, and representations of his creative ability — Family, Nation, State, Church, Fatherland. And so the "No-God" is set up, idols are erected, and God, who dwells beyond all this and that, is "given up."

Wherefore God gave them up. The confusion avenges itself and becomes its own punishment. The forgetting of the true God is already itself the breaking loose of his wrath against those who forget him (1.18). The enterprise of setting up the "No-God" is avenged by its *success.* Deified nature and deified spirits of men are, in truth, very gods; like Jupiter and Mars, Isis and Osiris, Cybele and Attis, they *come to be* the very breath of our life. Our conduct *becomes* governed precisely by what we desire. By a strict inevitability we *reach* the goal we have set before us. The images and likenesses, whose meaning we have failed to perceive, become themselves purpose and content and end. And now people have really become slaves and puppets of things, of "Nature" and of "Civilization," whose dissolution and establishing by God they have overlooked. And now there is no higher power to protect them from what they have set on high. And, moreover, the uncleanness of their relation to God submerges their lives also in uncleanness. When God has been deprived of his glory, human beings are also deprived of theirs. Desecrated within their souls, they are desecrated also without in their bodies, for human beings are one. The concreteness of the creatureliness of their lives becomes now dishonour; and libido — sexuality both in the narrower and in the wider sense of the word becomes, as the primary motive-power of their whole desire and striving, altogether questionable and open to suspicion. The whole ignominy of the course of the world they must now bear and bemoan and curse as ignominy; and further, in their separation from God they must continue to give it ever new birth. They have wished to experience the known god of this world: well! now they have experienced him. *(R:42-51)*

*

Jesus: 3.21-6

vv. 21, 22a. But now apart from the law the righteousness of God hath been manifested, being witnessed by the law and the prophets; even the righteousness of God through his faithfulness in Jesus Christ unto all them that believe.

But now. We stand here before an irresistible and all-embracing dissolution[32] of the world of time and things and people, before a penetrating and ultimate crisis, before the supremacy of a negation by which all existence is rolled up. The world is the world; and we now know what that means (1.18-3.20). But whence comes this crisis? Whence comes our recognition of it and our ability to comprehend it? Whence comes the possibility of our perceiving that the world is the world, and of our thus limiting it as such by contrasting it with another world which is unknown to us? Whence comes the possibility of our describing time *only* as time, and things *only* as things, and human beings *only* as human beings? and whence the possibility of our assigning a value to history and existence by sternly recognizing that they are concrete, limited, and relative? From what lofty eminence do all these critical opinions descend? And out of what abyss arises our knowledge of these last, unknown things, by which everything is measured, this shattering knowledge of the invisible Judge in whose hands lies our condemnation? All these questions revolve round one point, which is our origin, and sound one presupposition, from which our existence has emerged. From this presupposition we have come, and, regarded from this point, the world and we ourselves are seen to be bounded, dissolved, rolled up, and judged. But this one point is not a point among other points, and this one presupposition is not one among many presuppositions. Our origin evokes in us a memory of our habitation with the Lord of heaven and earth; and at this reminiscence the heavens are rent asunder, the graves are opened, the sun stands still upon Gibeon, and the moon stays in the valley of Ajalon.[33] *But now* directs our attention to time which is beyond time, to space which has no locality, to impossible possibility, to the gospel of transformation, to the imminent Coming of the Kingdom of God, to affirmation in negation, to salvation in the world, to acquittal in condemnation, to eternity in time, to life in death — *I saw a new heaven and a new earth: for the first heaven and the first earth are passed away.*[34] This is the Word of God.

Apart from the law. That God speaks, that we, known by him, see

125

ourselves and the world in his light, is something strange, peculiar, new; and this "otherness" runs through all religions, all experience, and every human disposition, when these are directed towards God. This "otherness" cuts sharply through all human sense of possession and semi-possession, even through all sense of not-possessing. It is the meaning of all ecclesiastical and religious history, nay, of all history; meaning which, for this reason, cannot be identified with any period or epoch of history or even with any underlying experience in history — for even such experience itself shares in the general ambiguity of all history. It is the confirmation of all these concrete and spiritual factors in the history of religion which we have named the impress of revelation, of all forms of worship, and, in the broadest sense of the word, of all "beliefs;" confirmation which, for this reason, must not be identified with the things which are confirmed, as though it were a visible thing in the midst of other visible things, and not, on the contrary, visible only in its invisibility. The *voice* of God which is his *power* (1.16) is and remains the voice of *God*; were it not so, and did it not remain beyond all other voices, it would not be the *power* of God. God speaks where there is *law*; but he speaks also where there is no law. He speaks where law is, not because law is there, but because he willeth to speak. God is *free*.

The righteousness of God. The word of God declares that he *is* what he *is*. By committing himself to humanity and to the world which has been created by him, and by his unceasingly accepting them and it, he justifies himself to himself. Even the wrath of God is his righteousness (1.18). To unbelief, his righteousness is necessarily manifested as divine negation. God makes himself known as Creator and Lord of all things through his anger against unbelief, through the compulsion by which he drives people helplessly on to the barrier which hems them in, and hands them over to the god of this world (1.22f.). In this negation God affirms himself and pronounces his claim upon humanity to be decisive, permanent, and final. Beyond the barrier at which we stand is — God. This is the theme of the Word of God. The more we become aware of the piercing irresistibility of this Word, the more powerfully and clearly will God speak to us of *his* justice and of his kingdom; the more everything human — our good and evil, our belief and unbelief — becomes transparent as glass, the more pronouncedly do we — as we are seen and known by God — stand under his sovereignty and under the operation of his power. The righteousness of God is that *nevertheless*! by which he associates us with himself and declares himself to be our God. This "nevertheless" contradicts every human logical "consequently," and is itself incomprehensible and without cause or occasion, because it is the "nevertheless!" of God. The will of God brooks no questioning: because he is God, he wills. The righteousness of God is his *forgiveness*, the radical alteration of the relation between God and humanity which explains why, though human unrighteousness and ungodliness have brought the world to its present condition and are intolerable to him, he nevertheless continues to *name* us his people in order that we may *be* his people. The righteousness of God is righteousness from outside — *justitia forensis, justitia aliena*; for the Judge pronounces his verdict according to the standard of his righteousness only. Unlike any other verdict, his verdict is creative: he pronounces us, his enemies, to be his friends. "Here therefore is the sermon of sermons and the wisdom of heaven; in order that we may believe that our righteousness and salvation and comfort come to us from outside; in order that we may believe that, though in us dwells naught but sin and unrighteousnes and folly, we are, nevertheless, acceptable before God, righteous and holy and wise" (Luther). The righteousness of God is the action which *sets free the truth* that we have imprisoned (1.18), and which is wholly independent of every attempt, or imaginable attempt, that we could make to achieve liberty. The righteousness of God is therefore the sovereign and regal display of the power of God: it is the miracle of resurrection. The righteousness of God is our *standing-place in the air* — that is to say, where there is no human possibility of standing — whose foundations are laid by God himself and supported always by him only; the place where we are wholly in his hands for favor or disfavor. This is the righteousness of God; and it is a *positive* relation between God and humanity. "We can neither doubt nor surrender this article of faith — though heaven and earth and every corruptible thing fall in ruins about us" (Luther). In the light of some 150,000 years of human insecurity, can we even consider any other positive relation? Can we even for one moment conceive of the emergence of some concrete or direct, historical or spiritual, relation? European history apart, can Asiatic or African or American history provide any other answer than God alone, God himself, and the mercy of God?

That God is righteous — **hath been manifested**. This is the answer to our question "whence?," the meaning of our "thence," our *But now*. The mercy of God triumphs! It has been *given* to us. The positive relation between God and humanity, which is the absolute paradox, veritably *exists*. This is the theme of the Gospel (1.1, 16), proclaimed in fear and trembling, but under pressure of a necessity from which there is no escape. It proclaims eternity as an event. We declare the knowledge of the Unknown God, the Lord of heaven and earth, who dwelleth not in temples made with hands, who needeth not anything, seeing that he himself giveth to all life and breath and all things. We set forth everything given by God to human beings, as given in order that they may seek *him* who is not far from each one of us, in whom we live and move and have our being, who is beyond all our life and movement and existence, and whose nature is to remain faithful, in spite of human depravity. We proclaim that, because it is his nature to remain faithful, the Godhead cannot be graven into any likeness by the skill and device of men; that God has overlooked the times of ignorance, *but* that *now* he commandeth everybody everywhere to repent. We announce the dawning of the day in which he will judge the world of men in righteousness — in *his* righteousness! (Acts 17.23-31). The righteousness of God *hath been manifested.* We can no longer omit to reckon with it; we can no longer see what has been given otherwise than in the light of this previous giving. We can come from nowhere except from this presupposition. Henceforward the negation in which we stand can be understood only in the light of the divine affirmation from which it proceeds. This means that the marks of human unrighteousness and ungodliness are crossed by the deeper marks of the divine forgiveness; that the discord of human defiance is penetrated by the undertones of the divine melody "Nevertheless." Once the revelation is given, our situation can never be otherwise; if, that is to say, we believe what has been revealed, and if we perceive that humanity has been dissolved *by* God, and therefore exalted to be *with* him. By faith in the revelation of God we see humanity bounded, confined, and barred in, but even this is the operation of God. We see humanity under judgment, yet nevertheless thereby set aright. We see sense in the non-sense of history. We see that truth has burst its bonds. We see in humanity more than "flesh." We see salvation breaking through. We see the faithfulness of God remaining firm, even though the noblest human hopes and expectations are dashed to the ground. And so, now that we have beheld what has appeared, been manifested, and displayed, we advance to meet the world, our conversation is of this revelation, and we are occupied in bringing the revelation of God to the notice of those who have eyes to see and ears to hear.

The revelation of the righteousness of God is — **witnessed by the law and the prophets**: it has been *proclaimed long ago* (1.2). Abraham saw the day when God would judge the world in righteousness; Moses saw it also; the Prophets saw it; Job and the Psalmists saw it. We are encompassed by a cloud of witnesses who stood, all of them, in the light of this day; for the meaning of every epoch in history is directly related to God.[35] In his righteousness every promise is fulfilled. The righteousness of God is the meaning of *all* religion, the answer to *every* human hope and desire and striving and waiting, and it is especially the answer to *all* that human activity which is concentrated upon hope. The righteousness of God is that upon which the whole existence and inevitability of the world is founded, and it is peculiarly visible when the world stands under the negation of judgment. It is the meaning of *all* history, and especially of the complaint of history against its own inadequacy. It is the redemption of *all* creation, and most particularly when the creature knows itself to be more than a creature, and so points beyond itself. Wherever there is an impress of revelation — and does anything whatsoever lack this mark? — there is a witness to the Unknown God, even if it be no more than an ignorant and superstitious worship of the most terrible kind (Acts 17.22, 23). Where have there not been *certain of your own poets who also* have said it (Acts 17.28)? Where there is experience, there is also the possibility of understanding. We proclaim no new thing; we proclaim the essential truth in everything that is old; we proclaim the incorruptible of which all corruptible is a parable. Our theme, therefore, is the theme concerning which the parables speak and to which they bear witness; the theme which eyes have seen and ears heard, and in which people have veritably believed; we proclaim the theme of the church of God which has been believed by everyone, everywhere, and at all times.

The righteousness of God is manifested — **through his faithfulness in Jesus Christ**. The faithfulness of God is the divine patience according to which he provides, at sundry times and at many divers points in human history, occasions and possibilities and witnesses of the knowledge of his righteousness. Jesus of Nazareth is the point at which it can be seen that all the other points form one line of supreme significance. He is the point at which is perceived the crimson thread which runs through all history. Christ — the righteousness of God himself — is the theme of this perception. The faithfulness of God and Jesus the Christ confirm one another. The *faithfulness of God* is established when we meet the Christ in Jesus. Consequently, in spite of all our inadequacy, we are able to recognize the veritable possibility of the action of God in all his divers witnesses in history; consequently also, we are able to discover in the traces of the righteousness of God in the world more than mere chance occurrences, and are in a position to see that our own position in time is pregnant with eternal promise, if — nay, because! — we meet truth of another order at *one* point in time, at one place in that time which is illuminated throughout by reality and by the answer of God. The day of Jesus Christ is the day of *all* days; the brilliant and visible light of this one point is the hidden invisible light of all points; to perceive the righteousness of God once and for all *here* is the "hope of righteousness" (Gal. 5.5) everywhere and at *all* times. By the knowledge of Jesus Christ all human waiting is guaranteed, authorized, and established; for he makes it known that it is not human beings who wait, but God — in his faithfulness. Our discovery of the Christ in *Jesus of Nazareth* is authorized by the fact that every manifestation of the faithfulness of God points and bears witness to what we have actually encountered in Jesus. The hidden authority of the Law and the Prophets is the Christ who meets us in *Jesus*. Redemption and resurrection, the invisibility of God and a new order, constitute the meaning of every religion; and it is precisely this that compels us to stand still in the presence of *Jesus*. All human activity is a cry for forgiveness; and it is precisely this that is proclaimed by *Jesus* and that appears concretely in him. The objection that this hidden power of forgiveness and, in fact, the whole subject-matter of religion, is found elsewhere, is wholly wide of the mark, since it is precisely we who have been enabled to make this claim. In Jesus we have discovered and recognized the truth *that* God is found everywhere and *that*, both before and after Jesus, humanity had been discovered by him. In him we have found the standard by which all discovery of God and all being discovered by him is made known as such; in him we recognize that this finding and being found is the truth of the order of eternity. *Many* live their lives in the light of redemption and forgiveness and resurrection; but that we have eyes to *see* their manner of life we owe to the *One*. In *his* light we see light. That it is *the Christ* whom we have encountered in Jesus is guaranteed by our finding in him the sharply defined, final interpretation of the Word of the faithfulness of God to which the Law and the Prophets bore witness. His entering within the deepest darkness of human ambiguity and abiding within it is the faithfulness. The life of Jesus is perfected obedience to the will of the faithful God. Jesus stands among sinners as a sinner; he sets himself wholly under the judgment under which the world is set; he takes his place where God can be present only in questioning about him; he takes the form of a slave; he moves to the cross and to death; his greatest achievement is a negative achievement. He is not a genius, endowed with manifest or even with occult powers; he is not a hero or leader of men; he is neither poet nor thinker: — *My God, my God, why hast thou forsaken me?*[36] Nevertheless, precisely in this negation, he is the fulfilment of every possibility of human progress, as the Prophets and the Law conceive of progress and evolution, because he sacrifices to the incomparably Greater and to the invisibly Other every claim to genius and every human heroic or aesthetic or psychic possibility, because there is no conceivable human possibility of which he did not rid himself. Herein he is recognized as the Christ; for this reason God hath exalted him; and consequently he is the light of the Last Things by which everybody and all things are illuminated. In him we behold the faithfulness of God in the depths of hell. The Messiah is the end of humanity, and here also God is found faithful. On the day when humanity is dissolved the new era of the righteousness of God will be inaugurated.

Unto all them that believe. Here is the necessary qualification. The vision of the New Day remains an indirect vision; in Jesus revelation is a paradox, however objective and universal it may be. That the promises of the faithfulness of God have been fulfilled in Jesus the Christ is not, and never will be, a self-evident truth, since in him it appears in its final hiddenness and its most profound secrecy. The truth, in fact, can never be self-evident, because it is a matter neither of historical nor of psychological experience, and because it is neither a cosmic happening within the natural order, nor even the most supreme event of our imaginings. Therefore it is not accessible to our perception: it can neither be dug out of what is unconsciously within us, nor apprehended by devout contemplation, nor made known by the manipulation of occult psychic powers. These exercises, indeed, render it the more inaccessible. It can neither be taught nor handed down by tradition, nor is it a subject of research. Were it capable of such treatment, it would not be universally significant, it would not be the righteousness of God for the whole world, salvation for all. Faith is conversion: it is the radically new disposition of the person who stands naked before God and has been wholly impoverished in order to procure the one pearl of great price; it is the attitude of the person who for the sake of Jesus has lost his own soul. Faith is the faithfulness of God, ever secreted in and beyond all human ideas and affirmations about him, and beyond every positive religious achievement. There is no such thing as mature and assured possession of faith: regarded psychologically, it is always a leap into the darkness of the unknown, a flight into empty air. Faith is not revealed to us by *flesh and blood* (Matt. 16.17): no one can communicate it to himself or to any one else. What I heard yesterday I must hear again today; and if I am to hear it afresh tomorrow, it must be revealed by the Father of Jesus, who is in heaven, and by him only. The revelation which is in Jesus, because it is the revelation of the righteousness of God, must be the most complete veiling of his incomprehensibility. In Jesus, God becomes veritably a secret: he is made known as the Unknown, speaking in eternal silence; he protects himself from every intimate companionship and from all the impertinence of religion. He becomes a scandal to the Jews and to the Greeks foolishness. In Jesus the communication of God begins with a rebuff, with the exposure of a vast chasm, with the clear revelation of a great stumbling block. "Remove from the Christian religion, as Christendom has done, its ability to shock, and Christianity, by becoming a direct communication, is altogether destroyed. It then becomes a tiny superficial thing, capable neither of inflicting deep wounds nor of healing them; by discovering an unreal and merely human compassion, it forgets the infinite[37] qualitative distinction between humanity and God" (Kierkegaard). Faith in Jesus, like its theme, the righteousness of God, is the radical "Nevertheless." Faith in Jesus is to feel and comprehend the unheard of "love-less" love of God, to do the ever scandalous and outrageous will of God, to call upon God in his incomprehensibility and hiddenness. To believe in Jesus is the most hazardous of all hazards. This "Nevertheless," this unheard of action, this hazard, is the road which we show. We demand faith, no more and no less; and we make this demand, not in our own name, but in the name of Jesus, in whom we have encountered it irresistibly. We do not demand belief in our faith; for we are aware that, in so far as faith originates in us, it is unbelievable. We do not demand from others our faith; if others are to believe, they must do so, as we do, entirely at their own risk and because of the promise. We demand faith in Jesus; and we make this demand here and now upon all, whatever may be the condition of life in which they find themselves. There are, however, no preliminaries necessary to faith, no required standard of education or intelligence, no peculiar temper of mind or heart, no special economic status. There are no human avenues of approach, no "way of salvation"; to faith there is no ladder which must be first scaled. Faith is its own initiation, its own presupposition. Upon whatever rung of the ladder of human life people may happen to be standing — whether they be Jews or Greeks, old or young, educated or uneducated, complex or simple — in tribulation or in repose they can believe. The demand of faith passes diagonally across every type of religious or moral temperament, across every experience of life, through every department of intellectual activity, and through every social class. For all faith is both simple and difficult; for all alike it is a scandal, a hazard, a "Nevertheless"; to all it presents the same embarrassment and the same promise; for all it is a leap into the void. And it is possible for all, only because for all it is equally impossible.

vv. 22b-24. For there is no distinction: for all have sinned, and fall short of the glory of God; being justified freely by his grace through the redemption that is in Christ Jesus.

"Note: here is the very center and kernel of the Epistle and of all Scripture" (Luther).

There is no distinction. The reality of the righteousness of God is attested by its universality. It is not irrelevant that it is precisely Paul, who, daring, in Jesus, to put his trust boldly in grace alone, is able, in Jesus, also to perceive the divine breaking down of all human distinctions. Indeed, Paul's courage proceeds from his insight. Because he is the Apostle of the Gentiles, he is the Prophet of the Kingdom of God. Once this interdependence was obscured, there came into being what was afterwards known as "missionary work." But this is something quite different from the mission of Paul. His mission did not erect barriers; it tore them down. God can be known only when people of all ranks are grouped together upon one single step; when those of the highest rank regard "suffering with the whole social order of their age and bearing its heavy burden" (S. Preiswerk) as the noblest achievement of which they are capable; when the rich in spirit think nothing of their wealth — not even in order to share it — but themselves become poor and the brothers of the poor. The Pharisee who prays can indeed become a missionary, but not a missionary of the Kingdom of God. The strange *union* — of people one with another — must assert and expose the strange, and yet saving, *separation* — between God and humanity. In this separation is displayed the righteousness of God. The paradox must be maintained absolutely, in order that the scandal may not be obscured, and in order that Christianity may be disclosed in its true nature as "a problem which is itself essentially a riddle, and which sets a question-mark against every human achievement in history" (Overbeck). Nothing must be allowed to disturb this paradox; nothing must be retained of that illusion which permits a supposed religious or moral or intellectual experience to remove the only sure ground of salvation, which is the mercy of God. The illusion that some people have an advantage over others must be completely discarded. The words *there is no distinction* need to be repeated and listened to again and again. Faith, faith *alone* is the demand that is laid upon *all. All* must proceed along the road of faith, and must proceed only along that road; yet it is a road along which nobody can go. *All* flesh must be silent before the inconspicuousness of God, in order that all flesh may see his salvation.

All have sinned, and fall short of the glory of God. Here is exposed the cause of the dissolution of every distinction. The remarkable union is attested by a remarkable separation. There is no positive human possession which is sufficient to provide a foundation for human solidarity; for every positive possession — religious temperament, moral consciousness, humanitarianism — already contains within itself the seed of the disruption of society. These positive factors are productive of difference, since they distinguish people from one another. Genuine human community is grounded upon a negative: it is grounded upon what people lack. Precisely when we recognize that we are sinners do we perceive that we are brothers. Our solidarity with others is alone adequately grounded, when with others — or apart from them, since we may not wait for them! — we stretch out beyond everything that we are and have, and behold the wholly problematical character of our present condition. All *fall short of the glory of God.* The glory of God is his conspicuousness (Gloria divinitas conspicua — Bengel). For us this conspicuousness is lacking; and herein we are united. Consequently, all that is exalted must become abased; and blessed are they who already stand far below. The problem of faith appears where the conspicuousness of God is lacking — *they that have not seen, and yet have believed;*[38] and forgiveness of sins, which is the only relevant salvation, then emerges as a highly significant possibility. The recognition of the need of the forgiveness of sin has nothing in common with pessimism, with contrition and the sense of sin, or with the "heavy depression" of the "preachers of death" (Nietzsche); it has no relation to eastern asceticism contrasted with the merriment of the Greeks. The need of the forgiveness of sin might in fact be regarded as a Dionysiac enthusiasm, were it not that it can be placed in no such human category. True negation is directed as much against the denial of this life as it is against the acceptance of it. Both Jew and Greek are set under one condemnation. Our deepest and final deprivation — a deprivation just as real whether we accept or deny the world as it is! — is recognized when we perceive the true and original humanity which lies beyond this world. In this *pure* humanity human beings are in the hand of divine mercy.

Being justified (declared righteous) **freely by his grace.** When we are enabled to hear nothing except the word of the Judge, by which he asserts himself and by which he upholds all things (Heb. 1.3), we know that we stand assuredly and genuinely before God. Our hearing can then be nothing more than faith in God, faith *that* he is *because* he is. So long as we are swayed by any other motive except faith, we do not stand before God. Thus all distinctions between us human beings are seen to be trivial. *God declares*: He declares *his* righteousness to be the truth behind and beyond all human righteousness and unrighteousness. He declares that he has espoused our cause, and that we belong to him. He declares that we, his enemies, are his beloved children. He declares his decision to erect his justice by the complete renewal of heaven and of earth. This declaration is *creatio ex nihilo*, creation out of nothing. Uttered by God from his tribunal, it is grounded in him alone, and is without occasion or condition. Such creation is assuredly genuine creation, the creation of the divine righteousness in us and in the world. When God speaks, it is done. But the creation is a *new* creation; it is not a mere eruption, or extension, or unfolding, of that old "creative evolution" of which we form a part, and shall remain a part, till our lives' end. Between the old and the new creation is set always the end of this person and of this world. The "Something" which the Word of God creates is of an eternal order, wholly distinct from every "something" which we know otherwise. It neither emerges from what we know, nor is it a development of it. Compared with our "something" it is and remains always — nothing. However true it is that — *this* mortal must put on immortality, and *this* corruptible must put on incorruption; nevertheless — *Flesh and blood cannot inherit the Kingdom of God* — inasmuch as the *putting on* is an act of God, and not a human action, this mortal remains mortal and subject to corruption: he *awaits* a radical and qualitative change, a transformation; he awaits, in fact, the resurrection of the dead (1 Cor. 15.50-7). *We await a new heaven and a new earth.* The righteousness of God in us and in the world is not a particular form of human righteousness competing with other forms; rather, *your life is hid with Christ in God* (Col. 3.3). If it be not hidden, it is not Life! The Kingdom of God has not "broken forth" upon the earth, not even the tiniest fragment of it; and yet, it has been *proclaimed*: it has not come, not even in its most sublime form; and yet, it is *nigh at hand.* The Kingdom of God remains a matter of faith, and most of all is the revelation of it in Christ Jesus a matter of faith. It is heralded and it is nigh at hand as a new world, not as the continuation of the old. "Our" righteousness can be genuine and permanent only as the righteousness of *God.* By *new* must always be understood the *eternal* world in the reflection of which we stand here and now. The mercy of God which is directed towards us can be true, and can remain true, only as a *miracle* — "vertical from above." When the mercy of God is thought of as an element in history or as a factor in human spiritual experience, its untruth is emphasized. We stand really before God, inasmuch as we *await* in faith the realization of his Word, and inasmuch as we perpetually recognize that the declaration that we are justified by God in his presence takes place *freely by his grace,* and *only* by his grace. Grace is the generous and free will of God, his will to accept us; its necessity proceeds from him and from him only. The necessity of the promise of God that those who in a pure heart lack his glory shall see him face to face; the necessity that the imprisoned truth of God shall break its chains; the necessity that God shall maintain and show forth his faithfulness, without any provision by us of an occasion for its display — but simply because he is God; all this necessity is the majestic pre-eminence of grace. Grace is, then, no psychic power residing in the people of this world; no physical energy residing in nature; no cosmic power in this earth. Grace is and remains always the power of God (1.16), the promise of a new person, of a *new* nature, of a *new* world: it is the promise of the Kingdom of *God.* Grace is and remains always in this world negative, invisible, and hidden; the mark of its operation is the declaration of the passing of this world and of the end of all things. Restless, and terribly shattering, grace completely overthrows the foundations of this world; and yet, on the day of days, the creative Word of God veritably declares the operation of grace to be no mere negation. Grace is altogether "Yes"; it is salvation, comfort, and edification. Through the dissolution of the outer self the inner self is renewed day by day. But all this is true on the day of all days through the creating Word; and it must be believed on, because the creative Word of God has promised it; and we can believe in it, if our eyes be fixed upon the day of fulfilment which has been announced in Jesus.

This creative word is spoken — **through the redemption that is in Christ Jesus.**

What is there, then, in Christ Jesus? There is that which horrifies: the dissolution of history in history, the destruction of the structure of events within their known structure, the end of time in the order of time. *Hallowed be Thy name! Thy kingdom come! Thy will be done in earth as it is in heaven!* The Son of Man proclaims the death of the human being, he proclaims God as First and Last; and the echo answers: *He taught them as one that had authority — He is beside himself — He deceiveth the people — A friend of publicans and sinners.*[39] The answer bears unmistakable witness to the truth of what has been proclaimed. Jesus of Nazareth, *Christ after the flesh,* is one amongst other possibilities of history; but he is *the* possibility which possesses all the marks of impossibility. His life is a history within the framework of history, a concrete event in the midst of other concrete events, an occasion in time and limited by the boundaries of time; it belongs to the texture of human life. But it is history pregnant with meaning; it is concreteness which displays the beginning and the ending; it is time awakened to the memory of eternity; it is humanity filled with the voice of God. In this fragment of the world there is detached from this world — before the very eyes of people and in their actual hearing! — something which gleams in the darkness and gives to the world a new brilliance; and this "something" is — Glory to God in the highest, and on earth peace among people in whom he is well pleased![40] — God himself, who willeth to draw the whole world unto himself, and to fashion a new heaven and a new earth. As yet we see but the image of this world and of its dominion. Mighty it is, and lifted up, and very magnificent, terrible to behold, an image of gold and silver, of iron and clay and brass. But in the hidden life of Jesus we see also the stone fashioned and detached, which smites the image upon its feet and, without any aid from human hands, breaks it in pieces. The whole image is crushed, and the wind carries it away like the chaff of the summer threshing-floors. *But the stone that smote the image became a great mountain, and filled the whole earth* (Dan. 2.24-35). Satan as lightning is fallen from heaven,[41] his dominion is ended; the Kingdom of God is at hand, and the heralds of his Kingdom are assuredly present: *The blind receive their sight, and the lame walk, the lepers are cleansed, and the deaf hear, the dead are raised up, and the poor have the gospel preached to them; and — blessed is he, whosoever shall not be offended in me.*[42] Whoever gazes upon this earthly fragment of the world, and *perceives* in the "life of Jesus," and beyond it, the redemption which shall come; they are those that hear the creative voice of God, and look henceforward for no other, but await *all* from this redemption and from this voice of God (Matt. 11.1-4). Blessed are those who believe what can only be *believed,* and what *can* only be believed because of that which is — in Christ Jesus.

vv. 25, 26. Whom God set forth to be a covering of propitiation, through his faithfulness, by his blood, to shew his righteousness, because of the remission of sins done aforetime, in the forbearance of God; for the shewing, I say, of his righteousness at this present time: that he might be just, and the justifier of him that is grounded upon the faithfulness which abides in Jesus.

Whom God set forth to be a covering of propitiation, through his faithfulness, by his blood. In the Old Testament cultus the *covering of propitiation* (EV. *mercy seat*; Hebr. *Kapporeth*; LXX *Hilasterion*) was the sheet of gold, overshadowed by the wings of the two angel-figures (cherubim), which covered and marked the place where the contents of the ark, the oracles of God, were deposited (Exod. 25.17-21). In 1 Sam. 4.4, 2 Sam. 6.2, Ps. 80.1, it is the *place* above which God himself dwells; in Exod. 25.22, Num. 7.89, it is the *place* from which God speaks to Moses; it is pre-eminently, however, the *place* where, on the great Day of Atonement, the people were reconciled to God by the sprinkling of blood (Lev. 16.14, 15). The analogy with Jesus is especially appropriate, because the mercy seat is no more than a particular, though very significant, *place*. By the express counsel of God, Jesus has been appointed from eternity as the *place* of reconciliation above which God dwells and from which he speaks; now, however, he occupies a position in time, in history, and in the presence of humanity. The life of Jesus is the place in history fitted by God for reconciliation and fraught with eternity — *God was in Christ reconciling the world unto himself* (2 Cor. 5.19). At this place the Kingdom of God is come nigh: so near is it, that here his coming and his redeeming power are recognized; so near, that here God dwells with humanity and his communing is unmistakable; so near, that here the pressure of faith is a commanding necessity. But, just as in the Old Testament the *Kapporeth* covered the testimonies of God as well as marked their presence, so here the Kingdom of God, his reconciling activity, and the dawning of the day of redemption (3.24), are in Jesus covered as well as displayed. Jesus is presented to us unmistakably as the Christ, but his Messiahship is also presented to us as a sharply defined paradox. It is a matter for *faith* only. The reconciliation occurs at the *place* of reconciliation — only by *blood*, whereby we are solemnly reminded that God gives life only through death. Consequently, in Jesus also atonement occurs only through the faithfulness of God, *by his blood*: only, that is to say, in the inferno of his complete solidarity with all the sin and weakness and misery of the flesh; in the secret of an occurrence which seems to us wholly negative; in the extinguishing of all the lights — hero, prophet, wonderworker — which mark the brilliance of human life, a brilliance which shone also in his life, whilst he lived a human being among other human beings; and finally, in the absolute scandal of his death upon the Cross. By his blood, then, Jesus is proved to be the Christ, the first and last word to the human race of the faithfulness of God. By his death he declares the impossible possibility of our redemption, and shows himself as the light from light uncreated, as the herald of the Kingdom of God. "In the picture of the Redeemer the dominant color is blood" (Ph. Fr. Hiller), because, in the way of the Cross, in the offering of his life, and in his death, the radical nature of the reconciliation which he brings and the utter novelty of the world which he proclaims are first brought to light. Brought to light — nay, rather, put in the shade, when once we recognize that to comprehend either this radicalism or this novelty of God's world or the necessary transformation of human hearts, lies beyond our competence — *Behold, this child is set for the fall and rising up of many in Israel; and for a sign which shall be spoken against — yea and a sword shall pierce through thine own soul — that the thoughts of many hearts may be revealed* (Luke 2.34, 35). The secret of reconciliation by the blood of Jesus is, and remains, the secret of *God.* Its manifestation also, which is the invisibility of God becoming visible, is always the action of God, an act of his faithfulness, or, what is the same thing, an act of faith. In so far as this occurs and his faithfulness persists, in so far as the hazard of faith is ventured, the dawn of the new world, the reality of the mercy of God and of our salvation, of our future being-clothed-upon with our habitation not made with hands, eternal, in the heavens (2 Cor. 5.1ff.), is displayed and announced, secured and guaranteed to us, in the blood of Jesus. We stand already, here and now, in the reflection of the things which are to come; we are perplexed, but not hopeless; smitten by God, but nevertheless, in this crisis, under his healing power. "Therefore we must nestle under the wings of this mother-hen and not rashly fly away trusting in the powers of *our own* faith, lest the hawk speedily tear us in pieces and devour us" (Luther).

For the showing of his righteousness. Everywhere there *has been* forgiveness of sins, the miraculous outpouring upon people of the wealth of the divine mercy, signs of the forbearance and longsuffering of God (2.4). Everywhere people *are* being healed of the divine wounds. But it is through Jesus that we have been enabled to see that this is so; through him the righteousness of God has been exposed and presented to us; through him we have been placed so that we can apprehend history — sins done aforetime — as God sees it, that is to say, in the light of his dissolving mercy; through him we know the mercy of God to be the end of all things and the new beginning, and we know what this means for us — it means that we must be led unto repentance (2.4, 6.2-3). Only through him is the righteousness of God clearly seen to be the unmistakable governance of humanity and the real power in history. By the presupposition which has been given us in Jesus we now see always and everywhere not only the flesh and the sin, as the law sees (3.20), but the Judge who, in his condemnation, speaks the word of forgiveness wherever he finds in the *human secrets* (2.16) faithful recognition of his faithfulness. God is just; and he is the justifier of those who dare to leap into the void. Believing in Jesus, we believe in the universal reality of the faithfulness of God. Believing in Jesus, to us the righteousness and justification of God are manifested and displayed. This is the presupposition by which we can see ourselves as we are and advance to meet people as they are. In the light of this presupposition we can dare to do what otherwise we could never do — to believe in ourselves and in all people. For this reason and with this presupposition we demand courageously of all people (3.22) faith — faith in the presupposition. We have peace with God (5.1), because he is just, and because he justifies.

(R: 91-107)

*

ANSELM: FIDES QUAERENS INTELLECTUM

Most commentators on his work, Barth wrote, "have completely failed to see that in this book on Anselm I am working with a vital key, if not the key, to an understanding of that whole process of thought that has impressed me more and more in my Church Dogmatics *as the only one proper to theology."* [43] *The book is a farewell to*

the last remnants of a philosophical, i.e., anthropological (in America one says "humanistic" or "naturalistic") foundation and exposition of Christian doctrine. The real document of this farewell is, in truth, not the much read brochure Nein!, directed against Emil Brunner in 1934, but rather the book about the evidence for God of Anselm of Canterbury. Among all my books I regard this as the one written with the greatest satisfaction. And yet in America it is doubtless not read at all and in Europe it certainly is the least read of any of my works. [44]

The method Barth describes, in the words that Anselm modified from Augustine, is "faith seeking understanding," that is, human thought seeking to understand the intelligibility of what God reveals and which is believed in faith. Human knowledge of God is analogical. But this is not an *"analogy of being"* (analogia entis) *as if "being" were a general category, accessible to human reason generally, and comprising not only all creatures but God as well. Rather, the analogical thinking and language of theology is a response to what God reveals; it is the methodological procedure of a theology of grace. Barth understands Anselm's argument in his famous* Proslogion *as a truly theological presentation. As for the common view that it is an "ontological" proof of the existence of God, followed by some philosophers (Descartes, Leibniz) and rejected by others (Kant), "all that," said Barth, "is so much nonsense on which no more words ought to be wasted"!*

PREFACE TO THE FIRST EDITION

. . . About this Proof much has already been written. Its interpretation, traditional since Gaunilo and all but canonized through Thomas Aquinas and still influential even in our day, always struck me as being a kind of intellectual insolence concealing or distorting everything vital. On the other hand, neither was I convinced of the value of the other interpretations that have been expounded to us in the last few decades from the widest variety of sources, more subtle and more accurate as they undoubtedly are. When I looked around for the causes of my dissatisfaction the following two formal questions more or less forced themselves upon me concerning the literature to date. Is it possible to assess Anselm's *Proof of the Existence of God* unless it is read, understood and explained within the series of the other Anselmic proofs, that is within the general context of his "proving," the context of his own particular theological scheme? And is it possible to assess it without an exact exegesis of the whole passage (*Proslogion 2-4*) which is to be regarded as the main text — an exegesis that investigates every word and that also gives as full consideration as possible to Anselm's discussion with Gaunilo? I have tried to give effect to both these presuppositions, which up until now seem to have been left out of account as much by Anselm's critics as by his friends. Whatever position one may wish to take up with regard to the interpretation to which this path has led me, I hope that at least it will be granted that this path is in fact the right one and that even the champions of other interpretations have to start out along this same road.

From all this I cannot deny that I deem Anselm's Proof of the Existence of God in the context of his theological scheme a model piece of good, penetrating and neat theology, which at every step I have found instructive and edifying, though I would not and could not identify myself completely with the views of its author. Moreover, I believe that it is a piece of theology that has quite a lot to say to present-day theology, both Protestant and Roman Catholic, which, quite apart from its attitude to its particular form, present-day theology ought to heed. In saying that, I may be suspected of reading this or that idea into the eleventh-century thinker, so that under the protection of his century I might advance it in the twentieth. But I have no qualms. Who can read with eyes other than his own? With that one reservation I think I am able to say that I have advanced nothing here but what I have actually read in Anselm.

(A: 8-9)

*

INTRODUCTION

The Proof of the Existence of God comprises the first and disproportionately shorter of the two parts (*cap. 2-4* and *5-26*) of Anselm's *Proslogion*. The second and longer part goes on to deal with the Nature of God. The purpose behind this arrangement of the book is quite obvious: *Da mihi ut, quantum scis expedire, intelligam quia es sicut credimus, et hoc es quod credimus* [Grant me to understand — as much as Thou seeest fit — that Thou dost exist as we believe Thee to exist, and that Thou art what we believe Thee to be] — thus begins the exposition proper after the great introductory invocation of *Prosl. 1*. Before this the Prologue of the book had described how the author had long sought and, after many a digression, eventually found *unum argumentum . . . ad astruendum, quia Deus vere est et quia est summum bonum* [one argument . . . to prove that God truly exists and that he is the supreme good]. Now this *argumentum* must not be identified with the proof which is worked out in *Prosl. 2-4* but rather it is one technical element which Anselm has made use of in both parts of the book. Therefore, all that he can have meant by it is the formula for describing God, by means of which he has in fact proved the existence of God in the first part and the nature of God in the second part: *Id quo maius cogitari non potest* [that than which greater cannot be conceived]. The sub-title *De Existentia Dei* which appears in some manuscripts, is due to a mistaken identity, caused, as Gaunilo's reply shows, by the tremendous impression that the short first part made on the very earliest readers. Anselm never meant that the part should thus be taken for the whole. The joy he speaks of in the Prologue sprang from the discovery of the formula by which he considered himself to be in a position to prove, on the one hand: *quia es, sicut credimus* (with the result: *vere es*); and on the other hand: *quia hoc es, quod credimus* (with the result: *summum bonum es*). So far as he is concerned *Prosl. 5-26* is in actual fact no less important than *Prosl. 2-4*. However, the aim of our inquiry should be confined to these three first chapters — the celebrated Proof of the Existence of God.

What has to be said in explanation of the Proof will only make sense if we may assume a firm grasp of what "to prove" means in Anselm generally. Too much has been said about this proof, for it and against it, without there being any real appreciation of what Anselm was trying to do, and in fact doing, when he explained "was proving" and when he justified this particular proof. What is set out in *Prosl. 2-4* is first described as a "proof" (*probare, probatio*) by Anselm's opponent Gaunilo, but this designation is adopted by Anselm himself. This concept can be found elsewhere in Anselm but always in passages where he is speaking of a definite result that his work has actually produced or is expected to produce. Anselm is bent on this result and strives to achieve it. But in point of fact his own particular description of what he is doing is not *probare* at all but *intelligere* [understand]. As *intelligere* is achieved it issues in *probare*. Here we can give a general definition: what to prove means is that the validity of certain propositions advocated by Anselm is established over against those who doubt or deny them; that is to say, it means the polemical-apologetic result of *intelligere*. How exactly he conceived this result and what he did and did not anticipate from it, can be ascertained only after detailed analysis of his thoughts on *intelligere*, that is to say, of his theological scheme. Therefore it is to these that we must first of all turn. *(A: 13-14)*

*

THE NAME OF GOD

In *Prosl. 2-4* Anselm wants to prove the existence of God. He proves it by assuming a name of God the meaning of which implies that the statement "God exists" is necessary (that means, that the statement "God does not exist" is impossible). In *Prosl. 5-26* Anselm wants to prove the nature of God (that means his perfection and unique originality). He proves it on the presupposition of a name of God, the meaning of which implies that the statements, "God is perfect and originally wise, mighty, righteous, etc.", are necessary (that is, all statements to the opposite effect are impossible). The lever in both cases, the *argumentum* in his analysis of both parts of the *Proslogion* is therefore the name of God that is presupposed concerning which the author tells us in the Prologue how he sought it and how, after he had abandoned the search, he suddenly found it.

At the beginning of *Prosl. 2*, where it appears for the first time, this name is rendered by the words: *aliquid quo nihil maius cogitari possit.* The actual formulation is not fixed either in the *Proslogion* itself or in the essay against Gaunilo: instead of *aliquid* Anselm can also say *id.* It can even be further abbreviated by omitting the pronoun. *Possit* can be replaced by *potest* and occasionally by *valet*; *nihil* also by *non*; *nihil* (or *non*) . . . *possit* (or *potest*) also by *nequit* and also, quite frequently, *melius* instead of *maius.* Only this last variant is important for an understanding of the formula. In the first place the literal meaning of the formula is clear. It can be quite easily translated into French: "*Un être tel qu'on n'en peut concevoir de plus grand*" or even better, "*Quelque chose dont on ne peut rien concevoir de plus grand.*" In German it can be paraphrased: "*Etwas über dem ein Grösseres nicht gedacht werden kann.*" (Something beyond which nothing greater can be conceived.) Here "great" suggests, as is shown by the variant *melius* and by the whole application of the formula, quite generally the large mass of all the qualities of the object described and therefore as much its "greatness" in relation to time and space as the "greatness" of its mental attributes or of its power, or of its inner and outward value or ultimately the type of its particular existence. The "greater" which cannot be conceived beyond the thing described is therefore quite generally: anything superior to it. And from the application which the conception is given, particularly in *Prosl. 2-4*, the definitive sense can be taken to be: the being that stands over against it as a fundamentally higher mode of being. For a fuller understanding of the literal meaning of this name the first thing that has to be noticed is what it does not say: it does not say — God is the highest that man has in fact conceived, beyond which he can conceive nothing higher. Nor does it say — God is the highest that man could conceive. Thus it denies neither the former reality nor the latter possibility, but leaves open the question of the givenness of them both. Clearly it is deliberately chosen in such a way that the object which it describes emerges as something completely independent of whether men in actual fact conceive it or can conceive it. It is so chosen that its actual conception, as well as the possibility of its conception, emerges as being dependent upon an essentially un-expressed condition. All that the formula says about this object is, as far as I can see, this one thing, this one negative: nothing greater than it can be imagined; nothing can be imagined that in any respect whatsoever could or would outdo it; as soon as anyone conceives anything which in any respect whatsoever is greater than it, in so far as it can be conceived at all — then he has not yet begun to conceive it or has already ceased. It remains to be said: we are dealing with a concept of strict noetic content which Anselm describes here as a concept of God. It does not say that God is, nor what he is, but rather, in the form of a prohibition that man can understand, who he is. It is *"une définition purement conceptuelle."* It contains nothing in the way of statements about the existence or about the nature of the object described. Thus nothing of that sort is to be derived from it on subsequent analysis. If it is to be of any use in proving the existence and nature of God then a second assumption, to be clearly distinguished from this first one, is necessary — the prior "givenness" (credible on other grounds) of the thought of the existence and of the nature of God which with his help is to be raised to knowledge and proof. *Aliquid quo nihil maius cogitari possit* is therefore on no account the condensed formula of a doctrine of God that is capable of later expansion but it is a genuine description (*significatio*), one name of God, selected from among the various revealed names of God for this occasion and for this particular purpose, in such a way that to reach a knowledge of God the revelation of this same God from some other source is clearly assumed. All that can possibly be expected from this name is that, in conformity with the program of Anselm's theology, it should demonstrate that between the name of God and the revelation of his existence and nature from the other source there exists a strong and discernible connection. Only in that way and to that extent will statements about the existence and nature of God inevitably follow from an understanding of this name.

From what has been said we have first of all to establish that the presupposition of this name has without any doubt a strictly theological character. Notice how the formula is introduced — *et quidem credimus te esse aliquid quo [nihil] maius. . . .* [Now we believe that Thou art something than which nothing greater. . . .]. What is said here is confirmed by the conclusive statement in which Anselm later guarded against the possible rejection of this name for God, that is against the fact that it is unknown to the Christian: *quod quam falsum sit, fide et conscientia tua pro firmissimo utor argumento* [Now my strongest argument that this is false is to appeal to your *faith* and *conscience*[45]]. In this statement the *fides* of Gaunilo, who is being addressed, is itself to confirm his acquaintance with this name of God and his *conscientia* is to confirm his acquaintance with the person whose name this is: as a believing Christian Gaunilo knows very well who the *quo maius cogitari nequit* is. With this we ought also to compare the remarkable accounts given by Anselm in the Prologue to the *Proslogion* of the discovery of this concept. He sought it *saepe studioseque*, sometimes thinking he was to find it the next moment; somethings thinking he would never find it. Eventually he gave up the attempt as being an impossible undertaking and decided so as not to waste further time on it, not to think about it any more. As soon as he did that, however, the idea began to force itself upon him for the first time in the right way. *Cum igitur quadam die vehementer eius importunitati resistendo fatigarer, in ipso cogitationum conflictu sic se obtulit quod desperaveram, ut studiose cogitationem amplecterer, quam sollicitus repellebam* [So it was one day, when I was quite worn out with resisting its importunity, there came to me, in the very conflict of my thoughts, what I despaired of finding, so that I eagerly grasped the notion which in my distraction I had been rejecting[46]]. Is this a scientific report on an investigation or is it not rather a — perhaps quite typical — account of an experience of prophetic insight? However that may be: Anselm did not regard this designation for God as a non-essential theologoumenon and certainly not as a constituent part of a universal human awareness of God, but as an article of faith. If we assume for a moment that there were for Anselm, alongside the explicit statements of the text of the revelation, consequences arising directly from these to which he attached equal weight, then we will have no difficulty over the fact that naturally the *quo maius cogitari nequit* does not admit of proof by appeal to any text that was authoritative for him. Thus in no sense is he of the opinion that he produced this formula out of his own head but he declares quite explicitly the source from which he considers it to have come to him: when he gives God a name, it is not like one person forming a concept of another person; rather it is a creature standing before his Creator. In this relationship which is actualized by virtue of God's revelation, as he thinks of God he knows that he is under this prohibition; he can conceive of nothing greater, to be precise, "better," beyond God without lapsing into the absurdity, excluded for faith, of placing himself above God in attempting to conceive of this greater. *Quo maius cogitari nequit* only appears to be a concept that he formed for himself; it is in fact as far as he is concerned a revealed name of God. Thus we see at once (how could it be otherwise after the immediately preceding closing words of *Prosl. 1?*) that at the very outset of his proof of the existence of God and indeed precisely there, Anselm is fully and legitimately engaged in the exposition of his theological program. It goes without saying that for him the existence of God is given as an article of faith. This existence of God which is accepted in faith is now to be recognized and proved on the presupposition of the name of God likewise accepted in faith and is to be understood as necessary for thought. Thus here the name of God is the "*a*" taken from the *Credo* by means of which the existence of God now represented as *X* is to be transformed into a known quantity from one that is unknown (not disbelieved but as yet not realized): *Nullus intelligens id quod Deus est, potest cogitare quia Deus non est* [Nobody who understands what God is can think that God does not exist]. Starting from this point of the *Credo*, the other thing, the existence of God, must make itself — not credible (it is that already) — but intelligible. The choice of this particular point, the discovery of this particular name of God, was the first step along the path that was to commit him to the development of the proof. That it had a vital significance for him follows just as much from the manner in which he reports his discovery in the Prologue as from the manner in which he defended it later against Gaunilo. We can be certain: at all events this first step does not lead away from the constraint of specifically theological thinking but rather leads right into it; it concerns the choice of the concrete limit which so far as this question is concerned appears to make knowledge possible. *(A: 73-78)*

3

THEOLOGY FOR THE CHRISTIAN COMMUNITY

THE BARMEN DECLARATION

Adolf Hitler's seizure of power on January 30, 1933 plunged the German Evangelical Church into crisis. The church, like all other institutions, was to be "co-ordinated" and domesticated to the doctrines of National Socialism with its trinity of nationalism, racism and militarism. The swastika and the cross were to be welded together,[47] Mein Kampf and the Bible placed on the same altar — and in that order. This was the program of the "German Christians," those protestant synthesizers who, by adding a fatal adjective to the name of their Lord, were to prove once again the saying of Jesus about serving two masters. In the church elections of July, 1933 the German Christians won three-quarters of the vote and Ludwig Müller soon proclaimed himself "Reichsbischof," in effect a religious "Führer." The "Aryan paragraph" prohibited people of Jewish ancestry, or those married to "non-Aryans," from serving as ministers.

Barth regarded the German Christians as "the last, fullest and worst monstrosity of neo-Protestantism" (KB, 230). In May, 1934 a group of pastors and theologians met in Barmen to affirm solus Christus, sola Scriptura against the synthesizers. The "official church" was declared heretical and a betrayer of the Reformation. The Barmen Declaration was drafted by Barth "fortified by strong coffee and one or two Brasil cigars" (KB, 245) while his Lutheran co-workers had their afternoon siesta. It was the statement of faith on which the Confessing Church stood in continuity with the Reformation. (The selection below on Barth's doctrine of revelation includes a commentary on the Barmen Declaration.)

For many years the most familiar translation was that of Arthur Cochrane in his The Church's Confession under Hitler,[48] *this was adopted in the* Book of Confessions *of the Presbyterian Church (USA). The present translation was made by Douglas S. Bax in connection with the 50th anniversary celebrations of Barmen, and first published in the* Journal of Theology for Southern Africa, *vol. 47, June, 1984.*

In view of the errors of the "German Christians" and of the present Reich Church Administration, which are ravaging the church and at the same time also shattering the unity of the German Evangelical Church, we confess the following evangelical truths:

1. "I am the Way and the Truth and the Life; no one comes to the Father except through me" (John 14.6).

   "Truly, truly, I say to you, whoever does not enter the sheepfold through the door, but climbs in somewhere else, that one is a thief and a robber. I am the Door; anyone who enters through me will be saved" (John 10.1, 9).

   Jesus Christ, as he is attested to us in Holy Scripture, is the one Word of God whom we have to hear, and whom we have to trust and obey in life and in death.

   We reject the false doctrine that the church could and should recognize as a source of its proclamation, beyond and besides this one Word of God, yet other events, powers, historic figures, and truths[49] as God's revelation.

2. "Jesus Christ has been made wisdom and righteousness and sanctification and redemption for us by God" (1 Cor. 1.30).

   As Jesus Christ is God's comforting pronouncement of the forgiveness of all our sins, so, and with equal seriousness, he is also God's vigorous announcement of his claim upon our whole life. Through him there comes to us joyful liberation from the godless ties of this world for free, grateful service to his creatures.

   We reject the false doctrine that there could be areas of our life in which we would belong not to Jesus Christ but to other lords, areas in which we would not need justification and sanctification through him.

3. "Let us, however, speak the truth in love, and in every respect grow into him who is the head, into Christ, from whom the whole body is joined together" (Eph. 4.15-16).

   The Christian church is the community of brethren in which, in Word and sacrament, through the Holy Spirit, Jesus Christ acts in the present as Lord. With both its faith and its obedience, with both its message and its order, it has to testify in the midst of the sinful world, as the church of pardoned sinners, that it belongs to him alone and lives and may live by his comfort and under his direction alone, in expectation of his appearing.

   We reject the false doctrine that the church could have permission to hand over the form of its message and of its order to whatever it itself might wish or to the vicissitudes of the prevailing ideological and political convictions of the day.

4. "You know that the rulers of the Gentiles exercise authority over them and those in high position lord it over them. It shall not be so among you; but whoever would be great among you must be your servant" (Matt. 20.25-26).

The various offices in the church do not provide a basis for some to exercise authority over others but for the ministry with which the whole community has been entrusted and charged to be carried out.

We reject the false doctrine that, apart from this ministry, the church could, and could have permission to, give itself or allow itself to be given special leaders (*Führer*) vested with ruling authority.

5. "Fear God, honor the King!" (1 Pet. 2.17).

Scripture tells us that by divine appointment[50] the state, in this still unredeemed world in which also the church is situated, has the task of maintaining justice and peace, so far as human discernment and human ability make this possible, by means of the threat and use of force. The church acknowledges with gratitude and reverence toward God the benefit of this, his appointment. It draws attention to God's Kingdom (*Reich*), God's commandment and justice, and with these the responsibility of those who rule and those who are ruled. It trusts and obeys the power of the Word, by which God upholds all things.

We reject the false doctrine that beyond its special commission the state should and could become the sole and total order of human life and so fulfil the vocation of the church as well.

We reject the false doctrine that beyond its special commission the church should and could take on the nature, tasks and dignity which belong to the state and thus become itself an organ of the state.

6. "See, I am with you always, to the end of the age" (Matt. 28.20). "God's Word is not fettered" (2 Tim. 2.9).

The church's commission, which is the foundation of its freedom, consists in this: in Christ's stead, and so in the service of his own Word and work, to deliver to all people, through preaching and sacrament, the message of the free grace of God.

We reject the false doctrine that with human vainglory the church could place the Word and work of the Lord in the service of self-chosen desires, purposes and plans.

The Confessional Synod of the German Evangelical Church

declares that it sees in the acknowledgement of these truths and in the rejection of these errors the indispensable theological basis of the German Evangelical Church as a confederation of Confessional Churches. It calls upon all who can stand in solidarity with its Declaration to be mindful of these theological findings in all their decisions concerning church and state. It appeals to all concerned to return to unity in faith, hope and love.

Verbum Dei manet in aeternum.

*

NO! ANSWER TO EMIL BRUNNER

About the same time as Barmen, Emil Brunner challenged Barth with an open letter which used for its title the famous Thomistic catchword, "Nature and Grace." Brunner argued for a legitimate natural theology. Barth regarded this not only as regression behind the new theological direction he had begun with Romans *(with Brunner and others as allies) and which had been consolidated in the Anselm book in 1931; even worse, natural theology gave aid and comfort to the enemy in the form of the German Christians and those prone to compromise. Barth responded in October, 1934 with his sharp and categorical "Nein!" to all natural theology. He defined it as "every (positive or negative) formulation of a system which claims to be theological, i.e. to interpret divine revelation, whose subject, however, differs fundamentally from the revelation in Jesus Christ and whose method therefore differs equally from the exposition of Holy Scripture." A shorter form is this: "Natural theology is the doctrine of a union of humanity with God existing outside God's revelation in Jesus Christ" (CD II/1, 168).*

In an important section we cannot include here, Barth rejects Brunner's appeal to Calvin in support of natural theology. "The practical nonexistence of St. Thomas in the sixteenth century has had even graver consequences, in that the Reformers could not clearly perceive the range of the decisive connection between the problem of justification and the problem of knowledge of God, between reconciliation and revelation. They remained essentially untouched by the great syntheses of St. Thomas, which later gained such great influence."[51] Consequently, any theology today which appeals to the Reformers' theology of grace must reject natural theology in theological epistemology as vehemently as Luther and Calvin did in their doctrine of justification by grace alone.

The two essays, Brunner's first version (he published a larger version in

151

1935 including answers to Barth) and Barth's response, were translated into English by Peter Fraenkel in 1946 and published together by The Centenary Press, London, under the title Natural Theology. *A facsimile edition was re-issued by University Microfilms (Ann Arbor, Michigan and London) in 1979. The selection is from the Preface and sections II and III of Barth's six-part essay.*

PREFACE

I am by nature a gentle being and entirely averse to all unnecessary disputes. Whoever, faced with the fact of reading here a controversial treatise, should suggest that it would be so much nicer if theologians dwelt together in unity, may rest assured that I heartily agree. Let me also impress upon the reader that, humanly and personally speaking, I have nothing against Emil Brunner. On the contrary I greatly appreciate him, just as I am prepared to be humanly and personally on the best of terms with many another opponent. Emil Brunner is a man whose extraordinary abilities and whose determined will-power I have always sincerely respected. I should like nothing better than to walk together with him in concord, but in the church we are concerned with truth, and today with an urgency such as probably has not been the case for centuries. And truth is not to be trifled with. If it divides the spirits, then they *are* divided. To oppose this commandment for the sake of a general idea of "peace" and "unity" would be a greater disaster for all concerned than such division. Nor must it be a matter for wonder that when this division comes about it appears irrespectively of our formations and groups and appears exceptionally acutely and painfully where before there seemed to be unity, perhaps even far-reaching unity, where perhaps unity really *did* exist or really *can* exist. I can hardly say a clear "No" to Hirsch[52] and his associates, but close my eyes in the case of Brunner, the Calvinist, the Swiss "dialectical theologian." For it seems clear to me that at the decisive point he takes part in the false movement of thought by which the church today is threatened. Is it not true that the danger is greatest where it appears to be least, where error combines with the presentation — a very thorough and skilful presentation — of so many "truths" that at the first, and even at the second and third, glance it looks like the truth itself? My polemic against Brunner is more acute than that against Hirsch because his position is more akin to mine, because I believe him to be in possession of more truth, *i.e.* to be closer to the Scriptures, because I take him more seriously — because for that very reason he seems to me just now to be much more dangerous than a man like Hirsch. The heresies of our time which can be recognized as such at the first glance are, if I am not mistaken, about to go as they have come. Sometimes I am myself amazed that one ever had to defend oneself so explicitly and so decidedly as has been the case in these years. Throughout the struggle which we carried on in these years I have again and again pointed out that the real danger was not to be found in the adversary against whom our struggle was primarily directed. This did not always please the strategists and technicians of the Confessing Church front. The real danger seems to me to lie in a future attitude of the church and of theology which is informed by the spirit of many on both sides today who are undecided and ready for compromise and which might stand at the end of all that we are now going through. Such an end would mean that we would continue comfortably or even busily along the very road which has led us to the present catastrophe and upon which we might meet even greater catastrophes in future. The structure of the church's proclamation must not remain the sort of thing that it became through the developments of the eighteenth and nineteenth centuries. Especially as regards the problem "Nature and Grace," a breath of fresh air must make an end to the compromises by which we have now lived for so long and from which we had almost died. The Evangelical Church and her theology must emerge from the present suffering and strife purer, more united and more determined than when she entered it. Otherwise she has lost the battle in the midst of which we are standing today. Even the blatant abuses which are current today will not trouble her any more. The reason why I must resist Brunner so decidedly is that I am thinking of the future theology of compromise, that I regard him as its classical precursor, and that I have heard the applause with which all who are of a like mind have greeted his essay, *Nature and Grace*. His essay is an alarm signal. I wish it had not been written. I wish that this new and greater danger were not approaching or that it had not been Emil Brunner who had crossed my path as an exponent of that danger, in a way which made me feel that for better or for worse I had been challenged. But all this has now happened, and seen in some greater context it probably has its sense. But I hope that since it has happened I shall not be misunderstood if I act according to the use of our times and treat his doctrine of "Nature and Grace" without much ceremony as something which endangers the ultimate truth that must be guarded and defended in the Evangelical Church.

(N: 67-69)

*

WHERE DO WE REALLY STAND?

Brunner's "counter-theses," in which he develops his view of a "true" natural theology positively, refer to a series of "theses" in which he attempted with great succinctness and lucidity to explain to himself and to his readers my view of the matter as he understands it and as he wishes to correct it: the image of God in humanity is totally destroyed by sin. Every attempt to assert a general revelation has to be rejected. There is no grace of creation and preservation. There are no recognizable ordinances of preservation. There is no point of contact for the redeeming action of God. The new creation is in no sense the perfection of the old but rather the replacement of the old humanity by the new.

That is where I am supposed to stand and to receive Brunner's exhortation and instruction. If I attempt to do this I come immediately upon a fundamental difficulty (quite apart from all the details in which I fail to recognize myself). Not only have I, as Brunner says, never "expounded and defended these theses . . . systematically," but I have never put them forward and do not propose to do so in the future.

By ascribing these theses to me, Brunner imputes to me, apart from all discussion of the pros and cons, a fundamental attitude and position with regard to the whole problem which may be his but is not mine. For I can see no sense in giving to the denial of "natural theology" such systematic attention as appears in these theses. By "natural theology" I mean every (positive *or* negative) *formulation of a system* which claims to be theological, *i.e.* to interpret divine revelation, whose *subject*, however, differs fundamentally from the revelation in Jesus Christ and whose *method* therefore differs equally from the exposition of Holy Scripture. Such a system is contained not only in Brunner's counter-theses but also in the theses ascribed by him to me. Their wording may here and there recall my thoughts and my writings. But this does not mean that I am prepared to accept paternity and responsibility. For they represent — even though negatively — an abstract speculation concerning a something that is not identical with the revelation of God in Jesus Christ. Brunner failed to see that he made a fatal mistake in his initial definitions of my position by treating me as one of his kind. This has made debate difficult, for my first step has to consist in emphasizing the distance between us. Or did he want to set me a trap by inviting me to expose myself that way to his counter-theses and thus to make my position as fundamentally questionable as his? However that may be, I do not think of exposing myself like that. For "natural theology" does not exist as an entity capable of becoming a separate subject within what I consider to be real theology — not even for the sake of being rejected. If one occupies oneself with real theology one can pass by so-called natural theology only as one would pass by an abyss into which it is inadvisable to step if one does not want to fall. All one can do is to turn one's back upon it as upon the great temptation and source of error, by having nothing to do with it and by making it clear to oneself and to others from time to time why one acts that way. A real rejection of natural theology does not differ from its acceptance merely in the way in which No differs from Yes. Rather are Yes and No said, as it were, on different levels. Really to reject natural theology means to refuse to admit it as a separate problem. Hence the rejection of natural theology can only be a side issue, arising when serious questions of real theology are being discussed. Real rejection of natural theology does not form part of the creed. Nor does it wish to be an exposition of the creed and of revelation. It is merely an hermeneutical rule, forced upon the exegete by the creed (*e.g.* by the clause *natus ex virgine*) and by revelation. It is not possible to expand and compound it into a system of special tenets explicating and defending it. Rather does it appear necessarily, but with the same dependence as that of shade upon light, at the edge of theology as its necessary limit. If you really reject natural theology you do not stare at the serpent, with the result that it stares back at you, hypnotises you, and is ultimately certain to bite you, but you hit it and kill it as soon as you see it! In all these matters rejection of natural theology differs from its acceptance even before the rejection takes place. Real rejection of natural theology can come about only in the fear of God and hence only be a complete *lack* of interest in this matter. If *this* matter is allowed to become of interest, though but in order to be rejected, then interest is no longer centred upon *theology.* For this rejection cannot within theology be made for its own sake. For it is not by this rejection that truth is known, the Gospel is expounded, God is praised and the church is built.

(N: 74-76)

*

BRUNNER'S NATURAL THEOLOGY

In order to form a judgment concerning the positive exposition which Brunner gives to his essay of what he means by natural theology, it is indispensable to consider that under the title of "The issue between Karl Barth and myself" he wrote the following:

"We are concerned with the message of the sovereign, freely electing grace of God. Of his free mercy God gives to human beings, who of themselves can do nothing towards their own salvation, to human beings, whose will is not free but in bondage, his salvation in the Cross of Christ and by the Holy Spirit who enables them to assimilate this word of the Cross. We are therefore also concerned with the freedom of the church, which has its basis and its justification, its law and its possibility purely and solely in this divine revelation. Therefore it is not tied at all to nations and states. It is above all nations and states without any possibility of accepting from them any law or commission. We are concerned with the fact that the proclamation of the church has not two sources and norms, such as, *e.g.*, revelation *and* reason or the Word of God *and* history. . . ."

Well, let us proceed. The issue now is this: can the natural theology put forward in Brunner's counter-theses be maintained if measured by the yardstick of his own words? Can these words be taken seriously if viewed against the background of that natural theology?

In order to orient ourselves provisionally we set over against these words the quintessence of what Brunner wants to teach as "natural theology": there is such a thing as a "capacity for revelation" or "capacity for words" or "receptivity for words" or "possibility of being addressed" which people possess even apart from revelation. It would seem that even the first naïve impression would be that either the first or the second pronouncement has to be strangely watered down if they are to be able to stand side by side. What is the meaning of "sovereign, freely electing grace of God" if without it there is a human "capacity for revelation," which is merely supported by grace? What is the meaning of "receptivity for words" if people can do nothing of themselves for their salvation, if it is the Holy Spirit that gives them living knowledge of the word of the Cross? But let us turn to Brunner's own thoughts:

(1) The human capacity for revelation means, according to Brunner, one's "likeness to God." "Humanity's undestroyed formal likeness to God is the objective possibility of the revelation of God." Brunner points out that what matters is the purely formal factor distinctive of human beings within creation, the "*humanum*," the fact that a human person is a subject, one's rationality, one's responsibility, which is the presupposition of one's ability to believe as well as to sin. This presupposition, the "quod of personality," is not abolished by sin. In this formal sense the original image of God in humanity is not destroyed. Indeed not, we may well say. Even as a sinner a human being is human

and not a tortoise. But does this mean that his reason is therefore more "suited" for defining the nature of God than anything else in the world? What is the relevance of the "capacity for revelation" to the fact that a human being is human? The impression given by Brunner's essay has been described roughly like this. If a person had just been saved from drowning by a competent swimmer, would it not be very unsuitable to proclaim the fact of being human and not a lump of lead as his "capacity for being saved"? Unless one could claim to have helped the person who saved him by a few strokes or the like! Can Brunner mean that? Surely not, for we heard "human beings of themselves can do nothing for their own salvation." And according to Brunner, "the possibility of doing . . . that which is good in the sight of God" is also lost. One would have thought that this included the possibility of receiving the revelation of God. "Materially the *imago* is completely lost, human beings are sinners through and through, and there is nothing in them which is not defiled by sin." In face of these strong words it would seem that we have no right to ascribe to Brunner the view that the "capacity for revelation" means that people, as it were, work in concert with the grace which comes to them in revelation. But if he does not mean that, what *does* he mean by "capacity for revelation"? It is obvious that human beings are responsible persons, even as sinners. If it is honestly not proposed to go beyond stating this formal fact, how can the assertion of this fact serve at all to make revelation something more than divine grace? Is Brunner able to say one word beyond what is so obvious, without involving himself in contradiction with his unconditional acceptance of the Reformers' principle of *sola scriptura — sola gratia*?

(2) Brunner next asserts that the world is "somehow recognizable" to humanity as the creation of God, that "human beings somehow know the will of God." "The creation of the world is at the same time revelation, self-communication of God." And the possibility of recognizing it as such is adversely affected but not destroyed by sin. It is not enough to give such knowledge of God as will bring salvation. Moreover, the revelation of God in nature can be known "in all its magnitude" only by those "whose eyes have been opened by Christ." But it is "somehow" recognizable — though but distortedly and dimly — even by those of whom this cannot be said. The idea that revelation is "recognizable" dominates the beginning of that section. But Brunner also says that surprisingly enough "sin makes people *blind* for what is visibly set before our eyes." This makes it not quite clear whether Brunner does not wish to speak of a purely formal possibility of knowing God through his crea-

tion, which is not actualized. But I think that I understand Brunner rightly when I assume that the affliction of the eyes, of which he speaks, is, according to his opinion, very acute, but not to the extent of resulting in total blindness. Hence real knowledge of God through creation does take place without revelation, though only "somehow" and "not in all its magnitude." I think this interpretation is correct. If it is not, I cannot think what Brunner's exposition of the matter intends to convey. Therefore in view of what was said above about the total loss of the "material" *imago*, one is tempted to think that when in this context Brunner speaks of "God" and his "revelation" he means one of those creatures of human philosophical fantasy, one of those principalities and powers of the world of ideas and demons, which most certainly do exist and which reveal themselves and are known to us quite concretely. For if human beings "can do nothing of themselves for their own salvation," only those fantasies can be called the objects of their *de facto* knowledge of God through nature! But what Brunner says and means is different. What would be the significance of the assertion of *such* a knowledge of "God" for his thesis concerning a human capacity for revelation? It would mean that the God revealed in nature is *not* known to, but rather is very much hidden from, humanity. What would then become of the *theologia naturalis*? All that would be left would be a systematic exposition of the history of religion, philosophy and culture, without any theological claims or value. No, when he speaks of the God who can be and is "somehow" known through creation, Brunner does unfortunately mean the one true God, the triune creator of heaven and earth, who justifies us through Christ and sanctifies us through the Holy Spirit. It is he who is *de facto* known by all people without Christ, without the Holy Spirit, though knowledge of him is distorted and dimmed and darkened by sin, though he is "misrepresented" and "turned into idols." There are two kinds of revelation, both revealing the one true God. This is to be affirmed once and for all (on the basis of Scripture!). Only after that may it be asked "how the two revelations, that in creation and that in Jesus Christ, are related." But if that is Brunner's opinion, shall we be able to understand him otherwise than "somehow" distortedly, dimly and darkly? Is it his opinion that idolatry is but a somewhat imperfect preparatory stage of the service of the true God? Is the function of the revelation of God merely that of leading us from one step to the next within the all-embracing reality of divine revelation? Moreover, how can Brunner maintain that a real knowledge of the true God, however imperfect it may be (and what knowledge of God is not imperfect?)

does not bring salvation? And if we really do know the true God from his creation without Christ and without the Holy Spirit — if this is so, how can it be said that the *imago* is materially "entirely lost," that in matters of the proclamation of the church Scripture is the only norm, and that human beings can do nothing towards their salvation? Shall we not have to ascribe to them the ability to prepare themselves for the knowledge of God in Christ at least negatively? Shall we not have to do what Roman Catholic theology has always done and ascribe to them a *potentia oboedientialis* which they possess from creation and retain in spite of sin? Has not Brunner added to a human "capacity for revelation," to what we have been assured is purely "formal," something very material: humanity's practically proved ability to know God, imperfectly it may be, but nevertheless really and therefore surely not without relevance to salvation? Perhaps we can swim a little, after all? If he has really done this, we are happy to know now more clearly what he means by "capacity for revelation." But how can Brunner wish to do this? The echo of his audible confession of the Reformers' doctrines of original sin, justification and the Scriptures is still sounding in our ears! Then he does *not* want to do it? But if not, then what *does* he want to do? No, after all, we still remain rather unhappy.

(3) Next, Brunner asserts a special "preserving grace," *i.e.* the preserving and helping presence which God does not deny even to the fallen and estranged creature. We could easily understand this if Brunner meant to say that it is due to grace that after the fall we and our world exist at all or do not exist in a much worse state of disruption than is actually the case. Creation is the work of the truly free, truly undeserved grace of the one true God, both as an act *and* in its continuance. All very well, we can say. But by what right and in what sense does Brunner speak of another special (or rather "general") grace which as it were precedes the grace of Jesus Christ? If this were not so (but as Brunner wishes to obtain a separate *theologia naturalis* it *has* to be so), one could come to an understanding with Brunner. We could agree that the grace of Jesus Christ includes the patience with which God again and again gives us time for repentance and for the practice of perseverance, the patience by which he upholds and preserves us and our world, not for his own sake but for the sake of Christ, for the sake of the church, for the sake of the elect children of God. We have time, because Christ ever intercedes for us before the judgment-seat of God. How can the preservation of human existence and of the room given us for it be understood

as the work of the one true God unless one means thereby that humanity is preserved through Christ for Christ, for repentance, for faith, for obedience, for the preservation of the church? How can it be understood unless baptism is taken into account? How can one speak of these things unless the one revelation of Christ in the Old and New Testaments is taken into account? And how can one carry the severance of creation and reconciliation into the Bible? Does not the Bible relate all that Brunner calls a special "preserving grace" to prophecy and fulfilment, to law and gospel, to the covenant and the Messiah, to Israel and to the church, to the children of God and their future redemption? Where did Brunner read of another abstract preserving grace? But since he insists on it we must go on to ask how far his "preserving grace" is grace at all. We are ever and again allowed to exist under various conditions which at least moderate the worst abuses. Does that deserve to be called "grace"? Taken by itself it might just as well be our condemnation to a kind of antechamber of hell! If it is anything else — as indeed it is — then not on account of our preservation as such! We must go on to ask: Can we really know that our preservation as such, *e.g.* "what we derive from our people and their history," is a special grace of the one true God? Does this not mean that the principle *sola scriptura* which Brunner accepts, most inopportunely blocks an important source of knowledge? Does it not mean that the church cannot possibly have her basis and her justification, her law and her possibility, purely and solely in divine revelation? Does it not mean — am I dreaming? — that the poor "German Christians" may have been treated most unfairly? We must go on to ask: are not both the preservation of our existence as such and its conditions — Brunner mentions, *e.g.*, the state — so much bound up with our own human possibilities that it cannot be said of this "grace" that we can of ourselves do nothing towards it? Brunner himself declares: "Consequently human activity comes within the purview of divine grace — not of redeeming but of preserving grace. All human activity, which the Creator himself uses to preserve his creation amid the corruption of sin, belongs to this type of activity within preserving grace." Human activity which the Creator uses to carry out the work of his grace? This concept is intelligible on the basis of the Augustinian idea of the indirect identity of human and divine activity or of the Thomist idea of the co-operation of the divine *causa materialis* with a human *causa instrumentalis*. It might be favorably understood if Brunner were speaking of the one justifying and sanctifying grace of Jesus Christ. For in that case also human activity "comes within the purview of divine grace." But that is not what

Brunner wants. He wishes to speak of a special "preserving grace"! Has he not by so doing included in his doctrine an entire sphere (one which is, as it were, preparatory to revelation in the proper sense) in which the Reformers' principle of *sola gratia* cannot possibly be taken seriously? If there really is such a sphere of preparation, will this leave the understanding of revelation proper unaffected? Once Brunner has started to deal in abstractions such as these, will he be able to refrain from joining the Romanists, enthusiasts and pietists of all times in teaching also a special grace of life, a special grace of realization, etc., for the implementation of which God would probably "use" humanity no less than in this area of preparation? And *where* is all this going to lead us?

(4) Brunner's fourth assertion is partly an exposition of the third. It treats separately of the "ordinances," the "constant factors of historical and social life . . . without which no communal life is conceivable, which could in any way be termed human." But among them he wishes to ascribe to matrimony as an "ordinance of creation" a "higher dignity" than to the state which is a mere "ordinance of preservation" relative to sin. Of the "ordinances of creation" it is said that "through the preserving grace of God they are *known* also to natural people as ordinances that are necessary and somehow holy and are by them *respected* as such." Of matrimony in particular it is said that "it is realised to some extent by people who are ignorant of the God revealed in Christ." The believer understands these ordinances of creation "better" than the unbeliever; he even understands them "rightly" and "perfectly." Nevertheless even the believer "cannot but allow his instinct and his reason to function with regard to these ordinances, just as in the arts." What can one say to that? No doubt there are such things as moral and sociological axioms which seem to underlie the various customs, laws and usages of different peoples, and seem to appear in them with some regularity. And there certainly seems to be some connection between these axioms and the instinct and reason which both believers and unbelievers have indeed every reason to allow to function in the life of the community. But what are these axioms? Or who — among us, who are "sinners through and through"! — decides what they are? If we consulted instinct and reason, what might or might not be called matrimony? Do instinct and reason really tell us what is *the* form of matrimony, which would then have to be acknowledged and proclaimed as a divine ordinance of creation? If we were chiefly concerned with the clarity and certainty of knowledge, would not the physical, biological and chemical "laws of nature" or certain axioms of mathematics have a much greater claim

to being called ordinances of creation than those historico-social constants? And who or what raises these constants to the level of commandments, of binding and authoritative demands, which, as divine ordinances, they would obviously have to be? Instinct and reason? And what yardstick have we for measuring these sociological "ordinances of creation," arranging them in a little hierarchy and ascribing to one a greater, to the other a lesser, "dignity"? Do we as "believers" sit in the councils of God? Are we able to decide such a question? On the basis of instinct and reason one person may proclaim one thing to be an "ordinance of creation," another a different thing — according to the liberal, conservative or revolutionary inclinations of each. Can such a claim be anything other than the rebellious establishment of some very private *Weltanschauung* as a kind of papacy? Do theologians do well in taking part in one of these rebellions and in giving their blessing to them by proclaiming them to be divinely necessary? But let us assume for the moment that Brunner is right and that we possess some criterion for establishing here and there divine "ordinances of creation" on the basis of instinct and reason. What are we then to think of Brunner's assertion that these ordinances of creation are not only known but also respected and "to some extent realized" by people who do not know the God revealed in Christ? Of what Christian, however faithful, can it be said that he "to some extent realized" the ordinances of God? Is he not "a sinner through and through" — who would be lost if the law were not realized — but not merely "to some extent" but completely, finally and sufficiently for us all! — in Christ? If people can realize the law "to some extent" without Christ, how much more must "capacity for revelation" mean than merely the formal fact of people being human, *i.e.* responsible and rational subjects! Where, where has the distinction of the formal and the material *imago* got to? It is now purely arbitrary to continue to say that only holy Scripture may be the standard of the church's message, that people can do nothing for their salvation, that it takes place *sola gratia*, that the church must be free from all national and political restrictions! If we are from the start, and without the revelation and grace of Christ even "to some extent" on such good terms with God, if we can swim enough to help our deliverer by making a few good strokes — if all this is so, why are we suddenly so exclusive?

(5) The pot is boiling over. Brunner's aims in the whole matter are beginning to show up: there is a "point of contact" for redeeming grace. What is meant is evidently the "capacity for revelation," which is anterior to, though it only comes alive through, revelation. Brunner pro-

ceeds to discuss this "capacity for revelation" from the point of view that it is the basis on which the Word of God "reaches" humanity. Thus Brunner returns to his original definition: the point of contact is "the formal *imago Dei* which not even the sinner has lost, the fact that a human being is human, the *humanitas*." In order to be responsible and capable of making a decision — as is presupposed by revelation — a person must have "the formal possibility of being addressed." We have already pointed out how unsuitable this definition is for what Brunner wishes to prove. If we are prepared to call the fact that a human being is human and not a cat the "point of contact," "the objective possibility of divine revelation," then all objection to these concepts is nonsensical. For this truth is incontrovertible. Even so, it would be advisable to be careful about statements such as that human beings alone are capable of receiving the Word of God, because this leaves the angels out of account, because there might, after all, exist beings that are unknown to us, and because we have no revelation but only conjectures concerning receptivity or lack of receptivity on the part of such non-human beings as we do know. But be that as it may: what is the relevance of the formal responsibility and ability to make decisions to a "capacity" which human beings possess and which exists in them anterior to divine revelation? Is the revelation of God some kind of "matter" to which people stand in some original relation because as human they *have* or even *are* the "form" which enables them to take responsibility and make decisions in relation to various kinds of "matter"? Surely all their rationality, responsibility and ability to make decisions might yet go hand in hand with complete impotency as regards *this* "matter"! And this impotency might be the tribulation and affliction of those who, as far as human reason can see, possess neither reason, responsibility nor ability to make decisions: new-born children and idiots. Are they not children of Adam? Has Christ not died for them? The fact that God "reaches" people with his Word may well be due to something other than the formal possibility of their being addressed and their *humanitas*. If we are going to stick to the statement that a person is ("materially") "a sinner through and through," then the "formal factor" cannot be anything like a remainder of some original righteousness, an openness and readiness for God. The concept of a "capacity" of humanity for God has therefore to be dropped. If, nevertheless, there is an encounter and community between God and humanity, then God himself must have created for it conditions which are not in the least supplied (not even "somehow," not even "to some extent"!) by the existence of the formal factor. But we have seen that Brunner unfortunately has no intention of stopping at this formal factor. The reason for this is that he departs from the statement that a person is "a sinner through and through," thus contradicting the exposition which precedes it. For he has by now also "materially" enriched and adorned human beings in their relation to God to an amazing extent. "The sphere of this possibility of being addressed" includes not only the *humanum* in the narrower sense, but everything connected with the "natural" knowledge of God. Moreover, "the necessary, indispensable point of contact," which before was defined as the "*formal imago Dei*," has now, as it were, openly become "what the natural people know of God, of the law, and of their own dependence upon God." From afar there sounds across to us like the last echoes of thunder when a storm has passed by without doing harm: "This quid of personality is negated through sin." No doubt the distinction between the "formal" and the "material" *imago Dei*, which at first sight was so impressive, was not meant all that seriously, even in those early passages. The form was probably quite a well-filled form even there. Evidently the "formal *imago Dei*" meant that one can "somehow" and "to some extent" know and do the will of God without revelation. If we had been acute enough to know that right from the start, we should have saved ourselves our amazement at the irrelevance of the statement that a human being is human! How very relevant and full of import it was! But we are not really guilty, since Brunner gave us no indications in this direction and, moreover, had explicitly assured us that he would adhere to the principle *sola scriptura — sola gratia*. That has not happened. If it had happened, it would not have been possible to set humanity over against God, either secretly or openly, as a form that is "somehow" already filled. In that case the purely formal statement that a human being is human would have been seen to be irrelevant and — would not have been made at all or at least not so solemnly! The question of the "point of contact" might then have occurred to Brunner in the context of the doctrine of Christ, of the Spirit, of the church, but not of anthropology. Brunner has been unable to adhere to *sola fide — sola gratia*. He has entered upon the downward path, upon which we find him in *Nature and Grace*, more obviously than in any previous pronouncement. Why then is he angry with me because my objection — which indeed has a wide scope — is that I am no longer able to distinguish him fundamentally from a Thomist or Neo-Protestant? In addition to the applause of the "German Christians" and their ilk he should make a point of reading what my Roman Catholic colleague at Bonn, Gottlieb

Söhngen, wrote concerning his undertaking.[53] This should convince him that I am not wantonly branding him as a heretic, but that this really is how the matter stands.

(6) For a moment Brunner seems to have occupied himself after all with the possibility — upon which we have already touched — that the answer to his question might be found in the doctrine of Christ, of the Holy Spirit, of the church. For he turns to the theme of the death of the old Adam as a condition of the life of the new Adam, to whom the revelation of God is made. Now he remembers Galatians 2.20: "I live; yet not I, but Christ liveth within me," and 1 Corinthians 2.10f.: "But God hath revealed them unto us by his Spirit." But it is now that we meet with the worst surprise. In the counter-theses 2-5 Brunner's view of the human capacity for revelation has become perfectly clear. Moreover, even without revelation a person somehow knows God and, to some extent, fulfils his will. Might we not now expect to be shown how this view is justified and proved when confronted with these two texts? Instead of that, Brunner returns to his original definition of "capacity for revelation" which he had since abandoned. It now signifies the undoubted and indubitable formal definition of the human being as a self-conscious person. And he uses these passages quite superfluously to prove that the death of the old Adam refers always to the material but never to the formal aspect of human nature. The subject as such and the fact of its self-consciousness are not abolished by faith. Faith is not mysticism. The believer does not become Christ. Through the Holy Spirit an act of divine self-consciousness takes place within us, without, however, resulting in an identity between him and us. We receive the Holy Spirit, but our personal identity remains. Who would not agree with that? Though in contrast to an excessively Swiss sobriety some might wish to put in a good word for mysticism and maintain that the act of faith sometimes has taken place and may well take place in mystical forms of consciousness. But apart from that, Brunner would have to be opposed on the following grounds: what he has to prove is that in these passages the life of the person in Christ through the Holy Spirit is said to *presuppose* a knowledge of and respect for the true God and that this presupposition forms its human *point of contact*. Where in Galatians 2 and 1 Corinthians 2 has Brunner found anything of the sort? Which of the sixteen verses of 1 Corinthians 2 could be quoted to show that St. Paul wanted to maintain and proclaim another knowledge of God before and beside "Jesus Christ and him crucified" (v. 2), before and beside the "demonstration of the Spirit and of power" (v. 4), before and beside "the hidden wisdom

in a mystery" (v. 7), before and beside the "revelation by the Spirit" (v. 10) — and not merely as another knowledge beside all these, but as their presupposition and point of contact? In 1 Corinthians 2, St. Paul seems clearly to assume that something of the sort exists. But he does not do so in the way in which Brunner does. Rather does he regard it as "human wisdom" (vv. 5 and 13), as "the spirit of the world" (v. 12), as the ability of "psychical (natural) man" who does not accept "the things of the Spirit of God," who instead regards them as "foolishness" because "he *cannot* know them" (v. 14). Of what help is this person's "formal personality" — which St. Paul does not deny? And — over and above this — of what help is the "wisdom" which intrinsically belongs to this person's nature? What did St. Paul find in this person that might have been of interest to him as a capacity for revelation or a point of contact? In Galatians 2.15-21, St. Paul declares that he is crucified with Christ and dead to the law and that he therefore lives but now only in the faith of the Son of God given for him. He does not deny the continuance of his "formal personality." But is it of any importance to him? Does not the context show clearly that, in spite of this continuance, St. Paul speaks in verse 20 not of continuity but of discontinuity, or rather of the divine miracle of the continuity of his existence without and with Christ, apart from and in Christ? Moreover the text does not go on to say something that it would have to say if Brunner could fittingly quote it in his support. It does not say that though St. Paul is crucified with Christ, but that nevertheless, together with his "formal personality," some general knowledge of God derived from his conscience or from the ordinances of creation, recognizable in the world, accompanied or even led him into that new life which he can but try to explain by the inexplicable expression: "Christ liveth in me". Does he live the life which he lives "in the flesh," the first life, crucified with Christ, in any way but "in the faith of the Son of God, who loved me and gave himself for me"? Is the change in the human situation through the revelation of God, of which 1 Corinthians 2 and Galatians 2 speak, really a *reparatio*, a restoration in the sense in which Brunner employs it: "It is not possible to repair what no longer exists. *But it is possible to repair a thing in such a way that one has to say this has become quite new*"? (Italics mine.) I must confess that I am quite flabbergasted by this sentence. Had one not better at this point break off the discussion as hopeless? Or should one hope for an angel from heaven who would call to Brunner through a silver trumpet of enormous dimensions that 2 Corinthians 5.17, is not a mere phrase, which might just as well be applied to a motor-car that has come to grief and been successfully "repaired"? Or should one implore Brunner to turn his attention again to his rejection of the doctrine of the virgin birth, in order to see from this doctrine — which has been so much misunderstood both by him and by others — what that "hidden wisdom in a mystery" (1 Cor. 2.7) is about, which one has to know if one wants to be able to discuss nature and grace? Or should one ask him to read again quietly the texts which he himself quotes, 1 Corinthians 2 and Galatians 2 (and surely also 2 Cor. 5) in order to convince himself that *that reparatio*, which is mentioned *there*, is one in which there can be no question of a capacity for repair on the part of human beings. This is because the "repair" consists in a *miracle* performed upon us, in a miracle which makes it not a phrase but literal truth to say that we have become new beings, new creatures — because our "formal" aptitude for it is the most *uninteresting* and our "material" aptitude the most *impossible* thing in the world and hence they cannot be problems.

I break off. In Brunner's theology there is as little room for both evangelical and natural theology as anywhere where an attempt has been made to combine those two. And similarly, as always, so in the case of Brunner the conflict ended unequivocally in favour of natural theology. There is no doubt that Brunner could and can go further on the road that he has taken, than he has done so far. I do not know what he proposes to do next. It seems that behind his re-introduction of natural theology a "new" doctrine of the Holy Spirit wants only too logically to break forth. Against this doctrine it will be even more necessary to protest. I do not know whether my words have the power of warning him and making him stop. What is certain is that on *this* road things can only become worse and worse, *i.e.* he cannot but move further and further away from the postulates of evangelical thought which he himself has set down at the beginning of his essay. *(N: 78-88)*

*

AN OUTLINE OF BARTH'S *CHURCH DOGMATICS*

Barth designed the architecture of the Church Dogmatics *to reflect its content. The work was planned to have five volumes, four of which were actually written. Here "volume" does not mean a single book, but rather a series of books devoted to a major doctrine, namely, Word of God, God, Creation, Reconciliation and Redemption. Each of these "volumes" contains several parts which constitute individual books — indeed, IV/3 is itself divided into a first and second half, each requiring a whole book! Hence all references to the* Church Dogmatics *give the volume then the part, e.g., I/2, III/4, IV/3 ii. The chapters within the books are all divided into "Paragraphs," or sections.*

Several aspects of Barth's theology are evident in the following "Outline." First, the trinitarian structure is apparent in volumes III-V, and is also reflected in the first section of Chapter 2 of I/1. Christology is the heart of this theology, and what is expounded at length in volume IV, the Doctrine of Reconciliation, is already anticipated in volume I (especially Paragraphs 8-13 of Chapter 2) and volume II (see especially Chapter 7, Paragraph 33). Volume I on the Word of God, is a methodological introduction (prolegomena) built on the content of what follows; it expressly repudiates the attempt to base theology on an apologetic philosophy of religion or natural theology. Volume II presents the doctrine of the one God, focused on a Christological understanding of God's election of humanity, before the trinitarian teachings of volumes III-V are developed. Typical of Barth's theology is the movement from God to humanity in each volume, in contrast to, for example, Tillich, where the movement goes in the opposite direction. Finally, the Outline reveals the marriage of theology and ethics, indicative and imperative, gospel and law: this is most evident in Chapters 8, 12 and 17 where the command of God is presented on the basis of the previous treatments of God's election, creation and reconciliation.

In the Index Volume to Church Dogmatics[54] *is another thirteen page overview of the whole work, including the summary theses which Barth put at the head of every paragraph.*

This outline was prepared by John D. Godsey and first published in his Karl Barth's Table Talk, 100-101.[55] *It has been supplemented by including paragraph headings under Chapter 17 from the partial* Church Dogmatics *IV/4,[56] and from Barth's other lecture fragments of IV/4 which were published posthumously and translated as* The Christian Life.[57]

AN OUTLINE OF BARTH'S *CHURCH DOGMATICS**

VOL. I: WORD OF GOD

Part 1

Introduction
1. The Task of Dogmatics
2. The Task of Prolegomena to Dogmatics

Ch. 1 *The Word of God as the Criterion of Dogmatics*
3. Church Proclamation as the Material of Dogmatics
4. The Word of God in Its Threefold Form
5. The Nature of the Word of God
6. The Knowability of the Word of God
7. The Word of God, Dogma, and Dogmatics

Ch. 2 *The Revelation of God*
Sect. 1. The Triune God
8. God in His Revelation
9. God's Three-in-Oneness
10. God the Father
11. God the Son
12. God the Holy Spirit

Part 2

Sect. 2. The Incarnation of the Word
13. God's Freedom for Man
14. The Time of Revelation
15. The Secret of Revelation
Sect. 3. The Outpouring of the Holy Spirit
16. The Freedom of Man for God
17. God's Revelation as the Abolition of Religion
18. The Life of the Children of God

Ch. 3 *Holy Scripture*
19. The Word of God for the Church
20. Authority in the Church
21. Freedom in the Church

Ch. 4 *The Proclamation of the Church*
22. The Mission of the Church
23. Dogmatics as a Function of the Hearing Church
24. Dogmatics as a Function of the Teaching Church

VOL. II: GOD

Part 1

Ch. 5 *The Knowledge of God*
25. The Fulfilment of the Knowledge of God
26. The Knowability of God
27. The Limits of the Knowledge of God

Ch. 6 *The Reality of God*
28. The Being of God as the One Who Loves in Freedom
29. The Perfections of God
30. The Perfections of the Divine Loving
31. The Perfections of the Divine Freedom

Part 2

Ch. 7 *The Election of God*
32. The Problem of a Correct Doctrine of the Election of Grace
33. The Election of Jesus Christ
34. The Election of the Community
35. The Election of the Individual

Ch. 8 *The Command of God*
36. Ethics as a Task of the Doctrine of God
37. The Command as the Claim of God
38. The Command as the Decision of God
39. The Command as the Judgment of God

---

* For Editor's introduction see p. 170.

*This was never written.

SELECTIONS FROM THE *CHURCH DOGMATICS*
(1932-1967)

The major themes of the following group of selections have already been discussed in the Introduction. Preliminary comments will therefore be brief.

GOD AS GENUINE COUNTERPART

It is not self-evident that Christian theology should talk about God, probably one of the most abused words in our language. The true start-ing-point of Christian theology is the name of Jesus Christ, as known in the biblical witness.

This brief passage comes from Barth's Doctrine of Creation in a discus-sion of "The Active Life" from Par. 55, "Freedom for Life."

God is indeed the genuine Counterpart which alone can finally and primarily satisfy human beings and all creation as such. Far too often however, this has been said in so general and therefore unconvincing a manner that we cannot be content to make the word "God" our final, or perhaps even our basic, term. Far too often this word is used simply as a pseudonym for the limitation of all human understanding, whether of self or the world. Far too often what is meant by it is some-thing quite different, namely, the unsubstantial, unprofitable and fun-damentally very tedious magnitude known as transcendence, not as a genuine counterpart, nor a true other, nor a real outside and beyond, but as an illusory reflection of human freedom, as its projection into the vacuum of utter abstraction. And it is characteristic of this transcend-ence that, in relation to humanity it neither has a specific will, nor accomplishes a specific act, nor speaks a specific word, nor exercises a specific power and authority. It can neither bind people effectively nor effectively liberate them. It can neither justify them nor satisfy them. It cannot be for their lives either a clear meaning or a distinct purpose.

Its high-priests and prophets usually interrupt those who dare to say such things, telling them that it is only in the form of "mythologization" that we can say anything definite, i.e., that we can ascribe to it a person and form, an ability to act and speak, or even specific words and acts, so that we are better advised not to make any attempts in this direction. Transcendence as they see it cannot mean anything more than that behind and above and before all human action there is this open sphere, this abyss as it were, into which every person is destined to plunge headlong, whether wise or foolish, whether blessed or judged, whether to salvation or perdition. And the only sure and certain result which accrues from contemplating this specter seems to be the rather barren law of toleration, i.e., of refraining from absolutizing, and therefore in fact of avoiding all positive statements concerning its binding content and direction. In the present context we need not join issue with this standpoint and its representatives. We must certainly insist, however, that when we ourselves introduce the term "God" at this point, we necessarily have something totally different in view.

The introduction of the term "God" is not an abuse of this name, but meaningful and helpful, if in respect of it we think of what is attested by Holy Scripture concerning God's speech and action. God is the One whose name and cause are borne by Jesus Christ. Hence there is no question of divinity in the abstract as suprahuman and supracosmic being. Holy Scripture knows nothing of this divinity. To be sure, the God of Holy Scripture is superior to human beings and the world as the Lord. But he has also bound himself to humanity and the world in creating them. God is here introduced to us in the action in which he is engaged, not merely in his superiority over the creature, but also in his relationship to it. What is presented to us is the faithfulness of this God and his living approach to the creature. There is set before us his specific coming, acting and speaking in the creaturely world with the intention of asserting, protecting and restoring his right to the creature, and therefore the creature's own right and honor. In other words, our concern is with what Holy Scripture calls the coming of his kingdom from heaven to earth.

(CD: III/4, 479-480)

*

REVELATION AND KNOWLEDGE OF GOD

Since the heart of Barth's theology is God's gracious action for humanity and self-disclosure in Jesus Christ, we begin with a passage on revelation. "Revelation does not mean that a stone tablet has fallen from heaven with truth written on it. Instead, it is a history between that One [God] and us."[58] This commentary on the Barmen Declaration shows Barth's understanding of the historical, eventful character of God's revelation. The critique of natural theology is found in its full political import as Barth reflects back on the Church Struggle with the German Christians and National Socialism.

The passage also illustrates his doctrine of the "threefold form of the Word of God," and his view that revelation is the giving of "signs" and results in "indirect" knowledge of God.

We will conclude with a short historical commentary on the first article of the *Theological Declaration* of the Synod of Barmen on May 31st, 1934. The text is as follows:

"I am the Way and the Truth and the Life; no one comes to the Father except through me" (John 14.6).

"Truly, truly, I say to you, whoever does not enter the sheepfold through the door, but climbs in somewhere else, that one is a thief and a robber. I am the Door; anyone who enters through me will be saved" (John 10.1, 9).

Jesus Christ, as he is attested to us in Holy Scripture, is the one Word of God, whom we have to hear, and whom we have to trust and obey in life and in death.

We condemn the false doctrine that the Church can and must recognize as God's revelation other events and powers, forms and truths, apart from and alongside this one Word of God.

This text is important and apposite because it represents the first confessional document in which the Evangelical Church has tackled the problem of natural theology. The theology as well as the confessional writings of the age of the Reformation left the question open, and it has actually become acute only in recent centuries because natural theology has threatened to turn from a latent into an increasingly manifest standard and content of church proclamation and theology. The question became a burning one at the moment when the Evangelical Church in Germany was unambiguously and consistently confronted by a definite and new form of natural theology, namely, by the demand to recognize in the political events of the year 1933, and especially in the form of the God-sent Adolf Hitler, a source of specific new revelation of God, which, demanding obedience and trust, took its place beside the revelation attested in Holy Scripture, claiming that it should be acknowledged by Christian proclamation and theology as equally binding and obligatory. When this demand was made, and a certain audience was given to it, there began, as is well known, the so-called German church struggle. It has since become clear that behind this first demand stood quite another. According to the dynamic of the political movement, what was already intended, although only obscurely outlined, in 1933 was the proclamation of this new revelation as the *only* revelation, and therefore the transformation of the Christian church into the temple of the German nature- and history-myth.

The same had already been the case in the developments of the preceding centuries. There can be no doubt that not merely a part but the whole had been intended and claimed when it had been demanded that side by side with its attestation in Jesus Christ and therefore in Holy Scripture the church should also recognize and proclaim God's revelation in reason, in conscience, in the emotions, in history, in nature, and in culture and its achievements and developments. The history of the proclamation and theology of these centuries is simply a history of the wearisome conflict of the church with the fact that the "*also*" demanded and to some extent acknowledged by it really meant an "*only*." The conflict was bound to be wearisome and even hopeless because, on the inclined plane on which this "*also*" gravitated into "*only*," it could not supply any inner check apart from the apprehension, inconsistency and inertia of all interested parties. Actually in these centuries too the church was — as always miraculously — saved because the Bible remained in face of the "also" of invading natural theology and its secret "only." For it threw its own "only" into the scales, and in this way — not without the co-operation of that human apprehension, inconsistency and inertia — did at least maintain the point that for their part God's revelation in Jesus Christ and faith and obedience to him are "also" not actually to be reduced to silence and oblivion. Thus things were not carried as far as the logic of the matter really demands. The logic of the matter demands that, even if we only lend our little finger to natural theology, there necessarily follows the denial of the revelation of God in Jesus Christ. A natural theology which does not strive to be the only master is not a natural theology. And to give it place at all is to put oneself, even if unwittingly, on the way which leads to this sole sovereignty. But during the developments of these centuries this whole state of affairs was almost entirely hidden, particularly from the eyes of those who wanted in good faith to defend the validity and value of the biblical revelation. It is noteworthy that it was conservative movements within the church, like those inspired by Abraham Kuyper and Adolf Stöcker, which acted most naively. But the naiveté reigned at every point. The concept of revelation and that of reason, history or humanity were usually linked by the copulative particle "and," and the most superficial provisos were regarded as sufficient protection against all the possible dangers of such combinations. Happy little hyphens were used between, say, the words "modern" and "positive," or "religious" and "social," or "German" and

"Evangelical," as if the meaning then became self-evident. The fact was overlooked that all this pointed to the presence of a Trojan horse within which the superior enemy was already drawn into the city. For in the long run the fundamentally peaceful acknowledgment of the combination came to be accepted as the true orthodoxy, as the basis of theology (especially of church governments). The resistance occasionally offered to it necessarily came under suspicion as fanatical one-sidedness and exaggeration.

This was how matters stood when the church was confronted with the myth of the new totalitarian state of 1933 — a myth at first lightly masked, but unmasked soon enough. It need not be said that at first the church stood entirely defenceless before this matter and simply had to succumb to it for the time being. Once again, as so often for two hundred years — or so it seemed — the representative of a new trend and movement of the human spirit knocked at the door of the church. Its petition was very understandable in the light of every precedent. It asked simply that its ideas and ideals should be allowed into the church like those of all earlier times and phases. Its argument was that they constituted a more timely form, a new historical hinterland, a point of contact given by God himself, *rebus sic stantibus*, for the proclamation of the Gospel, which in itself, of course, would remain unaltered. Exactly the same thing had happened at the beginning of the 18th century with the reviving humanism of the Stoa; or a century later with Idealism; or, in its train, with Romanticism; and then with the positivism of the bourgeois society and scholarship of the 19th century; and the nationalism of the same period; and a little later socialism: they had all wanted to have their say in the church. And in face of these clear precedents there could be no basic reason for silencing this new nationalism of race. Whether it was as worthy as its predecessors to be heard and to have its say in the church is a matter on which there might be different opinions outside Germany. A negative answer would normally be given where the phenomenon of race nationalism is unknown or known only from a distance, and a different political and philosophical position causes it to be regarded with repugnance. But we must not fail to realize that inside Germany an affirmative answer could be given with what is basically just the same right. If it was admissible and right and perhaps even orthodox to combine the knowability of God in Jesus Christ with his knowability in nature, reason and history, the proclamation of the Gospel with all kinds of other proclamations — and this had been the case, not only in Germany, but in the church in all lands for a long time

— it is hard to see why the German church should not be allowed to make its own particular use of the procedure. And the fact that it did so with customary German thoroughness is not really a ground of reproach. What the "German Christians" wanted and did was obviously along a line which had for long enough been acknowledged and trodden by the church of the whole world: the line of the Enlightenment and Pietism, of Schleiermacher, Richard Rothe and Ritschl. And there were so many parallels to it in England and America, in Holland and Switzerland, in Denmark and the Scandinavian countries, that no one outside really had the right to cast a stone at Germany because the new combination of Christian and natural theology effected there involved the combination with a race nationalism which happened to be rather uncongenial to the rest of the world, and because this combination was now carried through with a thoroughness which was so astonishing to other nations. Now that so many other combinations had been allowed to pass uncontradicted, and had even been affectionately nurtured, it was about two hundred years too late to make any well-founded objection, and in Germany there were at first good reasons to make a particularly forceful stand for this new combination. It had the merit of recommending itself especially to German Lutheranism as, so to say, its distinctive and perhaps definitive solution of the question of the relationship of Christian and natural theology and proclamation. It could seem like the powerful river in which the different separate streams of the older and oldest history of the German Church and religion might possibly unite. It seemed to promise the exponents of culture and fellowship the unexpected fulfilment of their deepest wishes. It seemed to raise like a tidal wave the ship of the church which many people felt had run aground, and at last, at long last to be trying to bear it back again to the high seas of the real life of the nation and therefore into the sphere of reality. Humanly speaking, it was inevitable that in 1933 the German Evangelical Church should accede to the demand made of it, to the new "also," and the "only" which lay behind it, with exactly the same abandon as it had done to so many other demands, and as the church in other lands — wittingly or unwittingly — had continually done to so many other demands. The only question was whether the Bible, which was not at first to be suppressed, and the usual apprehension, inconsistency and inertia of all concerned, would not this time too act as a counter-weight and prevent matters being carried to extremes.

It was, therefore, an astonishing fact — and this is the significance of the first article of the *Barmen Declaration* — that within Germany there arose an opposition to the new combination which was aimed not only at this particular combination, but basically at the long-accustomed process of combination, at the "and" which had become orthodox in Germany and in the whole world, at the little hyphen as such and therefore at no more and no less than the co-dominion of natural theology in the church. For when in Barmen Jesus Christ as attested to us in Holy Scripture was designated as the one Word of God whom we have to trust and to obey in life and in death; when the doctrine of a source of church proclamation different from this one Word of God was repudiated as false doctrine; and when, in the concluding article of the whole *Declaration*, the acknowledgment of this truth and the repudiation of this error were declared to be the indispensable theological foundation of the German Evangelical Church — an assertion was made (far above the heads of the poor "German Christians" and far beyond the whole momentary position of the church in Germany) which, if it was taken seriously, contained in itself a purifying of the church not only from the concretely new point at issue, but from all natural theology. The German Christians were contradicted by the contradiction of the whole development at whose end they stood. The protest — this was expressed with blunt words at Barmen by Hans Asmussen, who had to explain the whole proposal — was "against the same phenomenon which for more than two hundred years had slowly prepared the devastation of the church." The protest was without doubt directed against Schleiermacher and Ritschl. The protest was directed against the basic tendencies of the whole 18th and 19th centuries and therefore against the hallowed traditions of all other churches as well. And it must be noticed that this protest was formulated in a contemporary application of the confession of the Reformation yet without the possibility of appealing to any express formula in that confession. In the unity of faith with the fathers something was expressed which they had not yet expressed in that way. The venture had to be made, even at the risk of the suspicion and later the actual charge of innovation in the church. It was under the sign of this protest that the German Church struggle continued from this point. All its individual and practical problems were and still are directly and indirectly connected with the first article of Barmen. The church was the "confessing" church precisely in the measure that it took this decision seriously in all its aspects. The conclusions of the Synod of Dahlem in November 1934 clarified its position in relation to church law. But this clarification was dependent upon the dogmatic clarification of Barmen and could be carried through only in conjunction with it. The accumulated errors and vacillations in the Confessing Church are connected with the fact that the insight expressed at Barmen — Jesus Christ is the one Word of God whom we have to trust and to obey — did not at first correspond to the flesh and blood reality of the church but contradicted it, and had still to be repeated, attained and practised in a wearisome struggle. Where this did not happen, no other attitude could be reached in practice than that of continual partial retreats and compromises. Where it did happen, it carried with it automatically the will and the power to resist. The German Confessing Church has either the power of the ecumenical gift and task which it received and accepted at Barmen, or it has no power. It either fights for the purification of which the Evangelical Church has long been in need and is everywhere in need, or in reality it does not fight at all. Had it been concerned simply with the German error of 1933, or with certain fatal consequent manifestations of this error, its conflict would have had no less but also no more meaning that the different reactions within the great modern disorder which had never been entirely lacking earlier and are not entirely lacking elsewhere. It would then not have been a real and serious conflict. It is a real and serious conflict so far as it is concerned with the matter as a whole; and not merely because what is at issue is obviously the opponent natural theology in its newest form, but because it is this time a question of the church itself in its repudiation of natural theology as a whole, because it is a question of its own fundamental purification. But the very thing which (in what is best described as a cry of need and of joy) is expressed in the first article of the Barmen *Declaration* is that this is at issue. The fact that in 1934 the basic opposition could be made which is laid down in this article, and that, in spite of all uncertainty and reverses, this opposition could since prove and maintain itself as the nerve of the whole attitude of the Confessing Church in a position of the severest tribulation, is something which, however things may develop, we can already describe as one of the most notable events in modern church history.

It was not the new political totalitarianism, nor was it the methods of beleaguerment which precipitated this event. And it is naive in the extreme to find in "Calvinism" or the activity of this or that professor of theology the effectual power of salvation (or corruption) in this affair. The fact is that, when *nothing else* was left for the church, the one Word of God who is called *Jesus Christ remained.* The fact is that it could not let itself fall into the abyss, as was demanded, but that it could take and had to take a new stand. The fact is that this time the logic of the case worked irresistibly on the other side and therefore this time it was arrested in the church. And all this has to be appraised spiritually or it cannot be appraised at all. What might have been expected was that, having so often blunted the temptation in its earlier, finer forms, the church would now be tired and its eyes blurred and it would be inwardly exhausted, so that it would succumb all the more easily and this time for good to the assault of the blatant temptation. But the fact is that this did not happen. The Word of God still remained, in spite of everything, in the same church in which it had been so often denied and betrayed. People could still be so terrified by the spectre of the terrible form of the new god and his messiah as not to give way to it. They could still come to the position of knowing that there is another possibility than that of crashing into the abyss. In spite of every weakness they could still reach after this other possibility, reading the Bible again, confessing again its clear assertions, and therefore uttering the cry of need and of joy from Barmen. And they could at once stand and hold their position on this ground after all other grounds had crumbled under their feet. That this could be the case certainly has its spiritual-historical, theological and political presuppositions and determinations. But all the same it was impossible, and in the end a miracle, in the eyes of those who saw it at close quarters. And so the first article of Barmen was not merely a pretty little discovery of the theologians. The position in the spring of 1933 was not one in which a fortune could be made in Germany with little theological discoveries. Basically it was quite simply a public statement of the very miracle that, against all expectation, had once again happened to the church. When it had lost all its counsellors and helpers, in the one Word of God, who is called Jesus Christ, it still had God for its comfort. Things being as they were, to whom else could it give its trust and obedience; to what other source of its proclamation could it and should it cling? *Rebus sic stantibus*, any other source could only be myth and therefore the end of all things and certainly the end of the church. But from this very end the church now saw itself pulled back and guarded by the Word of God in contemporaneous self-attestation. What option had it but to confess this Word of God alone? If we want really to understand the genesis of Barmen, we shall be obliged to look finally neither to the Confessing Church as such nor to its opponents. For there is not much to be seen here. The Confessing Church was, so to speak, only the witness of a situation in which simultaneously there took place a remarkable revelation, as there had not been for a long time, of the beast out of the abyss, and a fresh confirmation of the one old revelation of God in Jesus Christ. It was only a witness of this event. Indeed, it was often a most inconspicuous and inconvenient witness. But it was a witness. It was obliged to notice what was going to be seen on this occasion — that Satan had fallen from heaven like lightning and that the Lord is mighty over all gods. What it noticed on this occasion was the fact of the unique validity of Jesus Christ as the Word of God spoken to us for life and death. The repudiation of natural theology was only the self-evident reverse side of this notice. It has no independent significance. It affirms only that there is no other help — that is, in temptation — when it is a question of the being or non-being of the church. What helps, when every other helper fails, is only the miracle, power and comfort of the one Word of God. The Confessing Church began to live at the hand of this notice and at its hand it lives to this day. And it is this notice which it has to exhibit to other churches as the testimony which it has received and which is now laid upon it as a commission. It will be lost if it forgets this testimony, or no longer understands it, or no longer takes it seriously; the power against which it stands is too great for it to meet it otherwise than with the weapon of this testimony. But it will also be lost if it does not understand and keep to the fact that this testimony is not entrusted to it simply for its own use, but at the same time as a message for the world-wide church. And it may well be decisive for other churches in the world, for their existence as the one, ecumenical church of Jesus Christ, whether they on their side are able to hear and willing to accept the message of the Confessing Church in Germany.

For the understanding of what the first article of Barmen has to say in detail, it is perhaps advisable not to pass over the preceding verses from Jn. 14 and Jn. 10, but to understand everything from them as a starting-point. The emphasis of everything said previously lies in the fact that Jesus Christ has said something, and, what is more, has said it about himself: I myself am the way, the truth, and the life. I myself am the door. The church lives by the fact that it hears the voice of this "I" and lays hold of the promise which, according to this voice, is contained in this "I" alone; that therefore it chooses the way, knows the truth, lives the life, goes through the door, which is Jesus Christ himself alone. Moreover, it is not on its own authority, or in the execution of its own security program, but on the basis of the necessity in which Jesus Christ himself has said that no man comes to the father but by him, and that any by-passing of him means theft and robbery, that the church makes its exclusive claim, negating every other way or truth or life or door apart from him. The negation has no independent significance. It depends entirely on the affirmation. It can make itself known only as the affirmation makes itself known. But in and with the affirmation it does and must make itself known. For this reason the positive assertion has precedence even in what follows, and for this reason the resulting critical assertion can be understood only as its converse and unambiguous elucidation. The church lives by the fact that it hears the Word of God to which it can give entire trust and entire obedience, and that in life and in death — that is, in the certainty that it will be sustained in this trust and obedience for time and eternity. Precisely because it is allowed and invited to entire trust and obedience, it knows that the Word said to it is the one Word of God by which it is bound but in which it is also free, alongside whose Gospel there is no alien law and alongside whose Law there is no alien gospel, alongside or behind or above which we do not have to honor and fear any other power as way, truth, life or door. And this one Word is not first to be found, but has already given itself to be found: in him who has the power and the right to call himself the way, the truth, the life and the door because he is these things. This one Word means Jesus Christ from eternity to eternity. In this form it is attested in the Holy Scriptures of the Old and New Testaments. In this form it has founded the church; and upholds and renews and rules, and continually saves the church. In this form it is comfort and direction in life and in death. In this form and not in any other! It is of the "not in any other" that the concluding critical article speaks. We may notice that it does not deny the existence of other events and powers, forms and truths alongside the one Word of God, and that therefore throughout it does not deny the possibility of a natural theology as such. On the contrary, it presupposes that there are such things. But it does deny and designate as false doctrine the assertion that all these things can be the source of church proclamation, a second source alongside and apart from the one Word of God. It excludes natural theology from church proclamation. Its intention is not to destroy it in itself and as such, but to affirm that, when it comes to saying whom we have to trust and obey in life and in death, it can have no sense and existence alongside and apart from the Word of God. Whatever else they may be and mean, the entities to which natural theology is accustomed to relate itself cannot come into consideration as God's revelation, as the norm and content of the message delivered in the name of God. When the church proclaims God's revelation, it does not speak on the basis of a view of the reality of the world and of man, however deep and believing; it does not give an exegesis of these events and powers, forms and truths, but bound to its commission, and made free by the promise received with it, it reads and explains the Word which is called Jesus Christ and therefore the book which bears witness to him. It is, and remains, grateful for the knowledge of God in which he has given himself to us by giving up his Son.

(CD: II/1, 172-1ı δ)

*

GOD'S ELECTION OF HUMANITY

Following his Christological paradigm, Barth says that in the person and event of Jesus Christ we learn both of God in relation to humanity and of humanity in relation to God — and not of one without the other. God's election of humanity is revealed in Jesus Christ; we may not speculate about a doctrine of predestination apart from and behind the God whose grace chooses us in Jesus. In Jesus, God is revealed as the One who chooses human beings to be his covenant partners; in Jesus, true humanity is revealed as affirming that election and living in that covenant of grace.

The selection comes from the opening section of Barth's Doctrine of Election (Par. 32). It concludes by noting the "corrective," and a fundamental one at that, which Barth's Christological doctrine of election makes to the traditional teachings of Calvin and Augustine.

When Holy Scripture speaks of God, it does not permit us to let our attention or thoughts wander at random until at this or that level they set up a being which is furnished with utter sovereignty and all other perfections, and which as such is the Lord, the Law-giver, the Judge and the Savior of the individual person and humanity. When Holy Scripture speaks of God it concentrates our attention and thoughts upon one single point and what is to be known at that point. And what is to be known there is quite simple. It is the God who in the first person singular addressed the patriarchs and Moses, the prophets and later the apostles. It is the God who in this "I" is and has and reveals sovereignty and all other perfections. It is the God who wills to be known and worshipped and reverenced as such. It is the God who created his people Israel by his Word, and separated them from all other peoples, and later separated the church from Israel. It is the God who exercises his rule in what he wills and does with this people, the people first called Israel and later the church. It is he, this God, who as the Lord and Shepherd of that people is also, of course, the World-ruler, the Creator of all things, the Controller of all events, both great and small. But in every way his government of the world is only the extension, the application and the development of his government in this one particular sphere. He does the general for the sake of the particular. Or to put it another way, he does the general through the particular, and in and with it. That is God according to his self-revelation.

We may look closer and ask: Who and what is the God who is to be known at the point upon which Holy Scripture concentrates our attention and thoughts? Who and what is the God who rules and feeds his people, creating and maintaining the whole world for its benefit, and guiding it according to his own good-pleasure — according to the good-pleasure of his will as it is directed towards this people? If in this way we ask further concerning the one point upon which, according to Scripture, our attention and thoughts should and must be concentrated, then from first to last the Bible directs us to the name of Jesus Christ. It is in this name that we discern the divine decision in favor of the movement towards this people, the self-determination of God as Lord and Shepherd of this people, and the determination of this people as "his people, and the sheep of his pasture" (Ps. 100.3). And in this name we may now discern the divine decision as an event in human history and therefore as the substance of all the preceding history of Israel and the hope of all the succeeding history of the church. What happened was this, that under this name God himself became human, that he became this particular human being, and as such the Representative of the whole people that hastens towards this person and derives from him. What happened was this, that under this name God himself realised in time, and therefore as an object of human perception, the self-giving of himself as the covenant-partner of the people determined by him from and to all eternity. What happened was this, that it became a true fact that under this name God himself possesses this people: possesses it no less than he does himself; swears towards it the same fidelity as he exercises with himself; directs upon it a love no less than that with which in the person of the Son he loves himself; fulfilling his will upon earth as in the eternal decree which precedes everything temporal it is already fulfilled in heaven. What happened was this, that under this name God himself established and equipped the people which bears the name to be "a light of the Gentiles," the hope, the promise, the invitation and the summoning of all peoples, and at the same time, of course, the question, the demand and the judgment set over the whole of humanity and every individual person. As all these things happened under this name, the will of God was done. And according to God's self-revelation attested in Scripture, it is wholly and utterly in these happenings that we are to know what really is the good-pleasure of his will, what is, therefore, his being, and the purpose and orientation of his work, as Creator of the world and Controller of history. There is no greater depth in God's being and work than that revealed in these happenings and under this name. For in these happenings and under this name he has revealed himself. According to Scripture the One who bears this name is the One who in his own "I" introduces the concept of sovereignty and every perfection. When the bearer of this name becomes the object of our attention and thoughts, when they are directed to Jesus Christ, then we see God, and our thoughts are fixed on him.

As we have to do with Jesus Christ, we have to do with the *electing* God. For election is obviously the first and basic decisive thing which we have always to say concerning this revelation, this activity, this presence of God in the world, and therefore concerning the eternal decree and the eternal self-determination of God which bursts through and is manifested at this point. Already this self-determination, as a confirmation of the free love of God, is itself the election or choice of God. It is God's choice that he wills to be God in this determination and not otherwise. It is God's choice that he moves towards humanity, that he wills to be and is the covenant-partner of men and women. It is God's choice that under the name of Jesus Christ he wills to give life to the substance of his people's history and to that people itself, constituting himself its Lord and Shepherd. It is God's choice that in this specific form, in one age, in the very midst of that people's history, he acts on behalf of all ages, thus giving to all created time, becoming indeed, its meaning and content. It is God's choice that for the sake of the Head whose name it bears he has created and established this particular body, this people, to be the sign of blessing and judgment, the instrument of his love and the sacrament of his movement towards humanity and each individual person. It is God's choice that at every stage in its history he deals with this people with that purpose in view. It is in the utter particularity of his activity, and therefore of his volition, and to that extent of his self-determined being, that he is the *electing* God. He is so at that one point upon which Scripture concentrates our attention and thoughts. He is so in that he is the Lord and Shepherd of his people. He is so in Jesus Christ, in his only-begotten Son, and therefore from all eternity in himself. To put it the other way round: If we would know who God is, and what is the meaning and purpose of his election, and in what respect he is the electing God, then we must look away from all others, and excluding all side-glances or secondary thoughts, we must look only upon and to the name of Jesus Christ, and the existence and history of the people of God enclosed within him. We must look only upon the divine mystery of this name and this history, of this Head and this body.

It is exactly of a piece with this that when Scripture speaks of *humanity* it does not allow our attention or thoughts to lose themselves in any self-selected generalities. In the Bible we are not concerned with an abstract concept of humanity, or with the human race as a whole, or with the being and destiny of the individual person as such.   *(CD: II/2, 52-55)*

*

If we listen to what Scripture says concerning humanity, then at the point where our attention and thoughts are allowed to rest there is revealed an elect human being, *the* elect human being, and united in him and represented by him an elect people. But just as truly there is revealed at that same point the electing God. The elect One is truly human according to God's self-revelation, and that revelation, being God's, has the decisive word concerning human beings too. And once again we must put it the other way: If we would know what election is, what it is to be elected by God, then we must look away from all others, and excluding all side-glances or secondary thoughts we must look only upon the name of Jesus Christ and upon the actual existence and history of the people whose beginning and end are enclosed in the mystery of his name.

We perceive that the statements of Scripture concerning *God* and those concerning *humanity* converge at this point. And it is as statements concerning what takes place at this point that the statements concerning God's election of humanity must be formulated and understood. For it is at this point that election takes place. If this perception is right, and if we feel bound always to base the doctrine of election upon the self-revelation of God according to the witness of Scripture, then we have answered positively the question of the basis of the doctrine and the standpoint which we ought to take up in relation to it. If our perception has been fundamentally correct in this preparatory survey, then the *necessity* of the doctrine has been decided once and for all. We are not free either to give ourselves to this matter or not to give ourselves to it, either to take seriously the knowledge of divine predestination or not to take it seriously. Election is that which takes place at the very centre of the divine self-revelation. In the light of this fact we can understand the emphasis with which the doctrine of predestination has been presented by all the great teachers of the church. And in particular, we need feel no shame at the witness of the Reformed Church, in which from the outset this doctrine has played so outstanding a role. We must admit rather (not out of mere conservatism or the impulse to imitate, but out of inner necessity) that our forefathers were right. And we shall regard ourselves as bound to follow in their footsteps. But if in this survey our perception has been a right one, then it is also the case that the *form* in which we must take up and present the doctrine has been radically decided. In the face of the whole history, even the Reformed history, of the doctrine, a corrective has been inserted and a standard brought to light. It is the name of Jesus Christ which, according to the divine self-revelation, forms the focus at which the two decisive beams of the truth forced upon us converge and unite: on the one hand the *electing God* and on the other the *elected human being.* It is to this name, then, that all Christian teaching of this truth must look, from this name that it must derive, and to this name that it must strive. Like all Christian teaching, it must always testify to this name.

(CD: II/2, 58-59)

*

GOD THE CREATOR

That God is our Creator is not an inference we make from the world; rather the God who is Creator is revealed in Jesus. This passage comes from the first volume of the Church Dogmatics, *where Barth already introduces the doctrine of the Trinity and develops it Christologically. It is found in the section on "The Eternal Father" in Par. 10.*

Church Dogmatics I/1 was the first volume of the magnum opus *to appear in English, translated by G.T. Thompson in 1936, just four years after the original German text was published. Due to the war it was 1956 before the second half of "The Doctrine of the Word of God" (CD I/2) appeared in English; by then Barth had already reached volume IV/2! After the translation of all the* Church Dogmatics *was completed, volume I/1 was re-translated by G.W. Bromiley. This second edition was published in 1975.*

God is unknown as our Father, as the Creator, to the degree that he is not made known by Jesus.

It is especially the Johannine tradition which expresses this exclusiveness with ever-renewed emphasis: John 1.18; 5.23, 37; 6.46; 8.19; 14.6; 17.25; 1 John 2.23; 2 John [verse] 9; "as the Father knows me and I know the Father" (John 10.15); and therefore "anyone who has seen me has seen the Father" (John 14.9). But in the long run it is to be found with the same unmistakable clarity in the Synoptists too: "Everything is entrusted to me by my Father; and no one knows the Son but the Father, and no one knows the Father but the Son and those to whom the Son may choose to reveal him" (Matthew 11.27).

If this exclusiveness is accepted and taken seriously, if that abstraction between form and content is thus seen to be forbidden, this rules out the possibility of regarding the first article of the Christian faith as an article of natural theology. Jesus' message about God the Father must not be taken to mean that Jesus expressed the well-known truth that the world must have and really has a Creator and was venturing to give this Creator the familiar human name of father. It must not be taken to mean that Jesus had in mind what all serious philosophy has called the first cause or supreme good, the *esse a se* or *ens perfectissimum*, the universum, the ground and abyss of meaning, the unconditioned, the limit, the critical negation or origin, and that he consecrated it and gave it a Christian interpretation and baptized it by means of the name "father," which was not entirely unknown in the vocabulary of religion. In this regard we can only say that this entity, the supposed philosophical equivalent of the Creator God, has *nothing whatever to do* with Jesus' message about God the Father whether or not the term "father" be attached to it. Nor would it have anything to do with it even if the principle: Die and become! were related and perhaps identified with the transcendent origin and goal of the dialectic of losing life and gaining it. An idea projected with the claim that it is an idea of God is from the standpoint of the exclusiveness of the biblical testimonies an idol, not because it is an idea but because of its claim. Even the genuinely pure and for that very reason treacherously pure idea of God in a Plato cannot be excluded. If the exclusiveness is valid, Jesus did not proclaim the familiar Creator God and interpret him by the unfamiliar name of Father. He revealed the unknown Father, his Father, and in so doing, and only in so doing, he told us for the first time that the Creator is, what he is and that he is as such our Father.   *(CD: I/1 (2nd edn., 390-391)*

*

CREATION AND COVENANT

Creation and covenant are mutually related. As Barth puts it, God's covenant of grace with humanity is the "internal basis of creation," its raison d'être. But this covenant is a partnership of God with the creation, "a reality distinct from God." So creation is the "external basis of the covenant." The next two passages from Paragraph 41 treat these two themes.

Creation is the freely willed and executed positing of a reality distinct from God. The question thus arises: What was and is the will of God in doing this? We may reply that he does not will to be alone in his glory; that he desires something else beside him. But this answer cannot mean that God either willed and did it for no purpose, or that he did so to satisfy a need. Nor does it mean that he did not will to be and remain alone because he could not do so. And the idea of something beside him which would be what it is independently of him is quite inconsistent with his freedom. In constituting this reality he cannot have set a limit to his glory, will and power. As the divine Creator he cannot have created a remote and alien sphere abandoned to itself or to its own teleology. If, then, this positing is not an accident, if it corresponds to no divine necessity and does not in any sense signify a limitation of his own glory, there remains only the recollection that God is the One who is free in his love. In this case we can understand the positing of this reality — which otherwise is incomprehensible — only as the work of his love. He wills and posits the creature neither out of caprice nor necessity, but because he has loved it from eternity, because he wills to demonstrate his love for it, and because he wills, not to limit his glory by its existence and being, but to reveal and manifest it in his own co-existence with it. As the Creator he wills really to exist for his creature. That is why he gives it its own existence and being. That is also why there cannot follow from the creature's own existence and being an immanent determination of its goal or purpose, or a claim to any right, meaning or dignity of its existence and nature accruing to it except as a gift. That is why even the very existence and nature of the creature are the work of the grace of God. It would be a strange love that was satisfied with the mere existence and nature of the other, then withdrawing, leaving it to its own devices. Love wills to love. Love wills something with and for that which it loves. Because God loves the creature, its creation and continuance and preservation point beyond themselves to an exercise and fulfilment of his love which do not take place merely with the fact that the creature is posited as such and receives its existence and being alongside and outside the being and existence of God, but to which creation in all its glory looks and moves, and of which creation is the presupposition.

This, then, is a first aspect of creation which Scripture directs us to consider. It is the presupposition of the realization of the divine purpose of love in relation to the creature. Creation is the indispensable presupposition because it is a question of the realization of the *divine* intention of love. . . . God loves the being which could not exist without him, but only does so by him. God loves his own *creature*. This is the absolutely unique feature of the *covenant* in which his love is exercised and fulfilled. Its external basis, i.e., the *existence* and *being* of the creature with which he is covenanted, is the work of his own will and achievement. His *creation* is the external basis of this covenant. So firmly is this covenant established! So trustworthy is its presupposition not only on God's part but also on the part of the creature! So great is the faithfulness and constancy which it can as such expect from God in this covenant! And so transcendent is also the authority of the Founder of this covenant! There is absolutely no external basis that this covenant can have which was not posited by the God who here enters into covenant with humanity. There is no existence of the creature in which it can originally belong elsewhere than to this compact. It has no attributes, no conditions of existence, no substantial or accidental predicates of any kind, in virtue of which it can or may or must be alien to the Founder of this covenant. Nor, of course, are there any claims which it can raise or adduce to a right or dignity which can be asserted in contrast and opposition to the will of the Founder of this covenant. It has no ground on which it can deal with him on an equal footing. In this covenant God gives to it what he undertook to give to it when he first gave it its being and nature. And God wills from it as a partner in this covenant only that for which he prepared and bound and pledged it when he first gave it its being and nature. The creature to whom he has bound himself *belongs* to him. It is only God's free love that makes him bind himself to it. In so doing, he does not in any sense discharge a debt. How can he be impelled by anything but himself, in perfect freedom, really to love the creature which owes its existence and nature to him alone, to enter with it into this relation and therefore to provide this sequel to his creation? But as he does this, as his love is so incomprehensibly high and deep that he is not ashamed to will and do it, his activity has its solid external basis in the fact that what he loves *belongs* to him. In the partner of his covenant he does not have to do with the subject of another nor a lord in his own right, but with his own property, with the work of his will and achievement. The external dynamic of this covenant is that it rests on creation. In virtue of its being and nature, the creature is destined, prepared and equipped to be a partner of this covenant. This covenant cannot be seriously threatened or attacked by the nature of the creature or its surroundings, nor by any attribute of humanity and the world. By its whole *nature* the creature is destined and disposed for this *covenant*. There is no human characteristic or property of the world which does not as such aim at this covenant. As a partner of this covenant, the creature will always have to do exclusively with its Creator on God's side, and exclusively with its own God-given nature on its own. *(CD: III/1, 95-97)*

*

We have already considered the first aspect, to wit, that creation is the formal presupposition of the covenant in which God fulfils the will of his free love. God loves his creature and therefore a being which originally belongs to him as the One who loves, to which nothing that happens from the side of God, the Lord of this covenant, can be foreign, and which in this respect cannot assert or maintain any divergent claims of its own. Creation is one long preparation, and therefore the being and existence of the creature one long readiness, for what God will intend and do with it in the history of the covenant. Its nature is simply its equipment for grace. Its creatureliness is pure promise, expectation and prophecy of that which in his grace, in the execution of the will of his eternal love, and finally and supremely in the consummation of the giving of his Son, God plans for humanity and will not delay to accomplish for our benefit. In this way creation is the road to the covenant, its external power and external basis, because for its fulfilment the latter depends wholly on the fact that the creature is in no position to act alone as the partner of God, that it is thrown back wholly and utterly on the care and intercession of God himself, but that it does actually enjoy this divine care and intercession. What we now see is that *the covenant is the internal basis of creation*. It is certainly not its external basis. Its external basis is the wisdom and omnipotence of God, who is sure of himself as Creator because he is God, who at the creation of the world and humanity, at the laying of the presupposition of the covenant, at the preparation of the creature for his grace, is never at a loss for the right ways and means, but whose Word is sufficient to give being and existence to the creature as the object of his love and as the partner of his covenant. But creation also has — and this is what we have now to consider — its internal basis. This consists in the fact that the wisdom and omnipotence of God the Creator was not just any wisdom and omnipotence but that of his free love. Hence what God has created was not just any reality — however perfect or wonderful — but that which is intrinsically determined as the exponent of his glory and for the corresponding service. What God created when he created the world and humanity was not just any place, but that which was destined for the establishment and the history of the covenant, nor just any subject, but that which was to become God's partner in this history, i.e., the nature which God in his grace willed to address and accept and the people destined for his service. The fact that the covenant is the goal of creation is not something which is added later to the reality of the creature, as though the history of creation might equally have been succeeded by any other history. It already characterizes creation itself and as such, and therefore the being and existence of the creature. The covenant whose history had still to commence was the covenant which, as the goal appointed for creation and the creature, made creation necessary and possible, and determined and limited the creature. If creation was the external basis of the covenant, the latter was the internal basis of the former. If creation was the formal presupposition of the covenant, the latter was the material presupposition of the former. If creation takes precedence historically, the covenant does so in substance. If the proclamation and foundation of the covenant is the beginning of the history which commences after creation, the history of creation already contains, as the history of the being of all creatures, all the elements which will subsequently meet and be unified in this event and the whole series of events which follow; in the history of Israel, and finally and supremely in the history of the incarnation of the Son of God.

(CD: III/1, 230-232)

*

CREATION AS BENEFIT

Rooted in the covenant of grace, God's creation is seen as benefit to all creatures. Under the title "The Yes of God the Creator," Paragraph 42 echoes the refrain in Genesis 1: "And God saw that it was good." The sentence in bold type at the beginning illustrates Barth's practice in the Dogmatics *of starting every section (i.e. "paragraph") with a thesis summarizing its major themes.*

§42 THE YES OF GOD THE CREATOR

The work of God the Creator consists particularly in the benefit that in the limits of its creatureliness what he has created may be as it is actualized by him, and be good as it is justified by him.

Creation as Benefit

We have so far been considering the work of creation in the context in which it is the content of the divine revelation attested to us in Holy Scripture and the object of Christian faith. Its meaning and purpose as the first of all the divine works and the beginning of all things distinct from God, are to be seen in the *covenant* of God with humanity fulfilled in Jesus Christ. From this point we will now return to the question of its distinctive nature in itself and as such. What does creation mean as a divine work undertaken and completed to this end and in this sense? . . . The creation of God carries with it the *Yes* of *God* to that which he creates. Divine creation is divine *benefit*. What takes shape in it is the *goodness* of God. This is the character without which it would not be a work of God. . . .

God the Creator did not say No, nor Yes and No, but Yes to what he created. There is, of course, a divine No as well: the necessary rejection of everything which by his own nature God cannot be; and consequently the necessary rejection of everything which again by his own nature God cannot will and create, and cannot even tolerate as a reality distinct from himself. But the power of this twofold No is only the recoil of his equally twofold Yes: His Yes to himself and to the reality which, although not identical with him, was willed and created by him. The latter is the divine *Yes* to *creation*. Creation is not, then, rejection. It is not the wrathful positing of the non-real by the recoil of the divine No. Creation has to do with this non-real element only in so far as it consists inevitably in its exclusion. Creation as such is not rejection, but election and acceptance. It is God's positing in accordance with his nature of a reality which is distinct from him but willed by him. As a work of God turned outwards it participates in the right, dignity and goodness of the Yes in which he is God by himself. As God in creation manifests his inner being outwardly, as in supreme faithfulness and not unfaithfulness to himself he says Yes not only to himself but also to another, creation is divine *benefit*. For it is the essence of all divine and therefore all true benefit that in supreme faithfulness to himself God rejoices in another which as such has not shared in the divine being; that he honors and approves this other within the limits of its distinct being. Creation is benefit because it takes place according to God's beneficence, and therefore according to the supreme law of all benevolence and *bene esse*. Creation is blessing because it has unchangeably the character of an action in which the divine joy, honor and affirmation are turned towards another. What God has created is as such well done. What he has not created — the whole sphere of the non-real — is clearly to be recognized by the fact that it is not good. And if something is not good, it can be clearly recognized not to have been created by God, but to belong to the kingdom of the non-real. Only the *creation* of God is *really* outside God. And only that which *really* exists outside God is the *creation* of God. But the creation of God and therefore what really exists apart from God is as necessarily and completely the object of the divine good-pleasure, and therefore the divine benefit, as that which has not been created by God and is not therefore real must be the object of divine wrath and judgment.

This affirmation is not an irresponsible venture. It is not only permitted; it is commanded. We cannot understand the divine creation otherwise than as benefit. We are not free to think and speak in this matter otherwise or even uncertainly and equivocally. The Christian apprehension of creation requires and involves the principle that creation is benefit. It shows us God's good-pleasure as the root, the foundation and the end of divine creation. It suggests the peace with which God separated and protected what he truly willed from what he did not will, and therefore from the unreal. It implies that God himself, in and with the beginning of all things, decided for his creation and made himself the responsible Guarantor of it. Creation, as it is known by the Christian, is benefit. To talk otherwise it is necessary to revoke the whole insight afforded by the biblical testimony to creation and to draw upon some other source. We can, of course, arrive at a different view if we try to learn what creation is from human conjectures concerning the beginning of all things. But we are presupposing a willingness to stand by the insights given by the biblical witness to creation. From this standpoint we have no option but to adopt the present line of thought. We may add in explanation that this statement is demanded and supported by Christian knowledge of the Lord who alone can be the *Creator* at the beginning of all things. Who is this Lord? He is the God of Israel who in Jesus Christ has loved humanity, and sought and found us in our lostness and drew us to himself, averting from us the suffering of his righteous judgment, and in grace giving us life with the promise of eternal life. If the God who has expressed and revealed his nature in this way is the Creator, he has already expressed and revealed the same nature as the Creator, not saying No, or Yes and No, but an unqualified Yes to what he has really willed and created. What this God has created is good as such. Only if we lose sight of this God and his nature can we say otherwise. On the other hand we may also add in explanation that the Christian understanding of the *creature* renders this statement unavoidable and unshakeable. Whatever the creature be, it cannot be gainsaid that God has entered into solidarity with the human race in the history of Israel, and that in Jesus Christ he has even become a creature himself, the Son of Man of the seed of Abraham and David. If he did not find this impossible and unworthy of himself, then for all the difference between creaturely being and his own the former was at least an object of his good-pleasure. With a creature negated and rejected by himself, he obviously could not enter into a covenant and even unite himself as he has actually done in the history which finds its consummation in Jesus Christ. The fact that this covenant and union came into being shows the benefit enjoyed by the creature as such because bestowed in the act of creation. *(CD: IV/1, 330-332)*

*

GOD'S PROVIDENCE

Barth's doctrine of providence is expounded through the themes of the creation and creatures being preserved, accompanied and ruled ("conservatio, concursus and gubernatio") by God. God the Creator is not a "first cause," but a covenant partner in a history constituted by spontaneous human activity in relation to the activity of God the Lord. As God says Yes to creation, so the Christian says Yes to being a creature of God; the Christian affirms the goodness of creaturely life. The heading for this selection from Paragraph 49 is "The Christian under the universal Lordship of God the Father."

We have now given an outline of what we are required to believe by the Word of God concerning the great objective reality of the activity and rule of God the Father as Lord of the creature, concerning his divine preserving and accompanying and ruling of the creature, and the basis and meaning of its history. But our sketch would be incomplete if in conclusion we did not expressly consider the *creaturely subject* who participates in the divine lordship, not merely from without, as a creature who is preserved and accompanied and ruled by him like all other creatures, but in some sense from within, as a creature who not only experiences this rule in practice but perceives and acknowledges and affirms and approves it, who is in fact thankful for it and wills to cleave and conform to it. So far we have tacitly presupposed the existence of such a subject, and all our propositions and their elucidation are based upon this presupposition. . . . But who is the subject, and what is this subject's specific *being* and *attitude*, to whom the *conservatio, concursus* and *gubernatio* as we have described them are not empty concepts, but who has actual knowledge of them? We cannot avoid trying to give a right answer to this question, not merely in order to reveal in conclusion what is the basis of our knowledge of this whole matter, but because a right answer to this question is calculated to put the whole matter in a light which is absolutely indispensable if it is to be perceived aright.

The doctrine of providence — at any rate as we have understood and presented it — is with all its elements an integral part of the *Christian confession.* Therefore the subject to whom we are referring is the living member of the Christian community, the Christian. We will not at this point try to explain how this subject is constituted, and how far there can be and is a Christian community, and a Christian as its member. What concerns us now is that Christians are alone the creaturely subjects who can join in a confession of the divine providence because they know this providence, because they participate in the divine world-governance in this special and inward way. What concerns us now is the Christian as the point from which all that we have said in the matter can be understood as actual reality. We are enquiring into the specific being and attitude in which the *conservatio, concursus* and *gubernatio* are just as visible to the Christian in the developed form of the divine operation as are happenings on the street to a person looking out of a window. We are asking how it is that this self-evident manifestness of the divine lordship is both possible and actual in the Christian community.

We can best begin by making the simple assertion that even Christians are only *creaturely subjects,* and that in solidarity with all other people and creatures they stand therefore wholly and utterly *under the universal lordship of God*: with the same disadvantage that this means for every human being or every fly, that they cannot be their own lord; but also with the same advantage, that they do not need to be anxious concerning their own preservation or way or end. Christians, too, are upheld by God without being able to do anything towards it or about it. They, too, have in God an almighty Companion who embraces their whole being, whose activity sovereignly precedes and accompanies and follows their own activity. They, too, can only let themselves be ruled. What, then, distinguishes them from the others? In the first instance, only the fact that with all its consequences they accept and affirm the fact that they are only creaturely subjects like the others, that in this respect there is nothing to distinguish them from others. Of all creatures the Christian is the one who not merely is a creature, but actually says Yes to being a creature. Innumerable creatures do not seem to be even asked to make this affirmation. Human beings are asked. But human beings as such are neither able nor willing to make it. From the very first human beings as such have continual illusions about themselves. They want always to be more than creatures. They do not want merely to be under the universal lordship of God. But Christians make the affirmation that is demanded of human beings. This is their distinction. It is the distinction of renouncing all claim to distinction. They make the common confession of what all creatures really are, sometimes without even being asked, sometimes in defiance of their own wrong answers. The Christian, therefore, is the true creature. All the virtue and activity, all the joy and worth of the Christian must begin with this simple fact, and must finally lead back to it. It is important to assert this at the very outset. The glory of the particular relation and attitude of Christians to the universal lordship of God consists in the fact that it does not give occasion for any glorying in self. It begins and ends with the laying aside of all claim to self-glory. The height of the Christian in this matter is always the depth — and it is no height at all, but a very real depth — of the reality with which they can and may and must and will stand towards the fact that as creatures they are in no sense superior to other people, or to the dust under their feet, but can exist only under the universal lordship of God. Whatever advantage they may have over other people — and they really have a very big advantage — they have it only under the continually present and actual presupposition that as creatures, they have no advantage at all.

How is it that Christians of all people attain to the reality of acknowledging this fact? Our answer can be the very simple one that they see what the others do not see. The world-process in which they participate in solidarity with all other creatures might just as easily be a vain thrusting and tumult without either master or purpose. This is how many see it. But the Christian sees in it a universal lordship. The lordship might just as easily be that of natural law, or fate, or chance, or even the devil. This is how many see it. But Christians see in it the universal lordship of God, of the God who is the Father, who is the Father to them, their Father. They see the constitutive and organizing center of the process. What makes them Christians is that they see Jesus Christ, the Son of God, in the humiliation but also in the exaltation of his humanity, and themselves united with him, belonging to him, their lives delivered by him, but also placed at his disposal. And seeing him, they see the legislative, executive and judicial authority over and in all things. They see it as the authority of God. They see it as the authority of the Father. They see themselves subjected to this authority as those who are united with and belong to the Son. Only the Christian sees this center of the world-process. Only Christians see at this center, as the One who has all power in heaven and on earth, the Son of God, and through him God the Father, and on the circumference themselves as children of the Father for the sake of the Son. The whole Christian community is simply a gathering together by the Word which tells us this and explains and reveals it to us; a gathering together of those whose eyes are opened to the fact of it. Only the Christian is a member of this community, i.e., one who is gathered together with others by this Word, one whose eyes are opened to this fact. There are some creatures which do not need to have eyes for it because even without seeing it they are carried along by the power of this order and are secure in its peace. There are other creatures which have eyes for it but they will not and cannot open them. But Christians have open eyes. That is why they have the reality freely and joyfully to confess their creatureliness and their consequent subjection to the universal rule of God without reserve and without claim. What they see at that center and on that circumference is not something which frightens them, something which they have to reject. God the Father as the ruling Creator is obviously not an oppressor, and Christ as a subject creature is obviously not oppressed. There is nothing here which need frighten them. There is nothing here which need cause them to flee or rebel. To be wholly and unreservedly under the universal lordship of God, to be wholly and unreservedly a creaturely subject, is not in any sense a constraint, a misfortune, an outrage or a humiliation for those who as Christians can see actualized in Jesus Christ both the lordship of God and also the "subordination" [*Unterordnung*] of the creature. For them all attempts to evade this fact are purposeless, and the illusion by which it is obscured or avoided is superfluous. If the relation between the Creator and the creature is the relation which they can see in Jesus Christ, then existence in this relation is the existence which is to be truly desired, an existence in the highest possible freedom and felicity. To have to confess this is not an obscure law, but a friendly permission and invitation. It is not unwillingly but spontaneously, not grudgingly but gladly, that Christians will affirm and lay hold of this relation and their own existence in it. Hence the reality does not cost them anything. They do not have to force it. They do not have to struggle to attain it. It comes to them in the same way as what they see comes to them. And this means that they do not screw themeslves up to a height when they are real creatures. It also means that there does not arise any claim or merit on their part just because they confess so unreservedly what other creatures and other people cannot and will not confess. The fact that they do so is not a kind of triumph for their special honesty. Other people are just as honest, perhaps more so. They are simply made real by what they see. And as such they are simply availing themselves of a permission and invitation. They are going through an open door, but one which they themselves have not opened, into a banqueting hall. And there they willingly take their place at the lower end of the table,[59] in the company of publicans, in the company of beasts and plants and stones, accepting solidarity with them, being present simply as they are, as creatures of God. It is the fact that they see, and that which they are able to see as the center and the circumference, the Creator and the creature, which constitute the permission and invitation and open door to their peculiar reality.

To summarize provisionally, we may say that in virtue of what they (and only they) can see, Christians are those who have a true *knowledge* in this matter of the providence and universal lordship of God. This providence and lordship affect them as they do all other creatures, but they participate in them differently from all other creatures. They participate in them from within. Of all creatures they are those who while they simply experience the providence and lordship of God also consent to it, having a kind of "*understanding*" — if we may put it in this way — with the overruling God and Creator.

In practice, of course, they are faced every day afresh with the riddles of the world-process, with the precipices and plains, the blinding lights and obscurities, of the general creaturely occurrence to which their own life histories also belong. Of course they can only keep on asking: Whence? and Whither? and Why? and Wherefore? Of course they have no master-key to all the mysteries of the great process of existence as they crowd in upon them every moment in a new form, to all the mysteries of their own existences as constituent existences in the historical process of all created reality. On the contrary, they will be the only people who know that there is no value in any of the master-keys which humanity has thought to discover and possess. They are the only people who will always be the most surprised, the most affected, the most apprehensive and the most joyful in the face of events. They will not be like ants which have foreseen everything in advance, but like children in a forest, or on Christmas Eve; those who are always rightly astonished by events, by the encounters and experiences which overtake them, and the cares and duties laid upon them. They are those ones who are constantly forced to begin afresh, wrestling with the possibilities which open out to them and the impossibilities which oppose them. If we may put it in this way, life in the world, with all its joys and sorrows and contemplation and activity, will always be for them a really interesting matter, or, to use a bolder expression, it will be an *adventure*, for the fulfilment of which they for their part have ultimately and basically no qualifications of their own.

And all this is not because they do not know what it is all about, but just because they do know. All this is because they have an "understanding" with the source from which everything derives, from which directly or indirectly everything happens to them; the "understanding" of the creatures with their Creator, which is, for them, that of the children with their father. One thing at least they do not need to puzzle about. About this one thing they have no need to enquire, to be always on the look-out for new answers, new solutions. For they have learned once and for all who is this source, and what basically they can expect from it, and what will always actually come from it. But how the decision is reached, and in what form everything will come as it proceeds from this source, they are as tense and curious as a child, always open and surprized in face of what comes. Yet whatever comes, and in whatever form it comes, they will see that it comes from this one source. However strange it may seem, however irksome is the form in which it comes, they will approve it as coming from this source. They will always be, not perhaps able, but at least willing and ready to perceive the positive — and in the light of its source the most definitely positive — meaning and content of what comes. They will always be willing and ready — again a daring expression — to co-operate with it instead of adopting an attitude of supercilious and dissatisfied criticism and opposition, or, if it were possible, retiring sulkily into a corner as a sceptical spectator. They will always allow everything to concern them directly, and, with all the dialectic of their experiences and attitudes, they will ultimately and basically allow everything to concern them positively. Ultimately and basically they will always be thankful, and in the light of this thankfulness they will look forward to what has still to come. They will always know both what was intended and what is intended. They will always be children having dealings with their father. This is the knowledge of the Christian in matters of the divine lordship. There is nothing arrogant about it. It remains within the bounds of the reality in which Christians can know themselves — know themselves as creatures under the lordship of God like all other creatures. *(CD: III/3, 239-243)*

*

JESUS CHRIST: GOD WITH US

Christology as the center of Barth's theology has determined what he has said about revelation, about election, about creation, and about providence. In Volume IV of the Church Dogmatics *we reach the fullest exposition of Barth's Christology in his Doctrine of Reconciliation.*

The first three excerpts state the theme of the Incarnation. The next selection gives an overview of the Doctrine of Reconciliation. The final passage in this group, from the section on "The Judge Judged in Our Place," is a meditation on the Cross.

We resume the discussion with the second statement in our description of the incarnation: (2) that *the existence of the Son of God became and is the existence of a human being.* There are not two existing side by side or even within one another. There is only the one *God the Son,* and no one and nothing either alongside or even in him. But this One exists, not only in his divine, but also in *human* being and essence, in our nature and kind. He exists, not only like the Father and the Holy Ghost as God, but in fulfilment of that act of humility also as human, as one human being, as this human being. The Son of God becomes and is as humans become and are. He exists, not only inconceivably as God, but also *conceivably* as a human being; not only above the world, but also *in the world,* and of the world; not only in a heavenly and invisible, but in an *earthly* and *visible* form. He becomes and is, he exists — we cannot avoid this statement; to do so would be the worst kind of Docetism — with *objective actuality.* Does this mean, then, that he exists as one thing amongst others, and that as such he can be perceived and may be known like other things? Well, we cannot deny that he is a thing like this, and can be perceived and known as such, if he was and is a human being in the world, with an earthly and visible form. But, of course, a human being is not merely a thing or object. As a human being among human beings he is a human *Thou,* and as such distinct from all mere things. Now as a Thou a human being is not merely an existential determination of the I, but the epitome of all the objective reality of the world. And in Jesus Christ God becomes and is human, the fellow-human being of all people. As God he is not merely one of many such fellow-human beings, nor is he merely the idea of co-humanity. We are speaking of "*the Father's Son, by nature God.*" He became and is human, the fellow-companion of all human beings; and therefore Thou, not merely in a simple, but in a supremely objective reality, *the* human Thou, which as such is also directly the Thou of the one eternal God. It is not that a human being has rightly or wrongly taken it upon himself to be the objective reality of this human Thou, and has been grasped and understood and interpreted by others as the objective reality of this Thou. The fact is rather that God himself, in his deep mercy and its great power, has taken it upon himself to exist also in human being and essence in his Son, and therefore to become and be a human being, and therefore this incomparable human Thou. *God himself* is in the world, earthly, conceivable and visible, as he is this person. We have to do with *God himself* as we have to do with this person. *God himself* speaks when this human being speaks in human speech. *God himself* acts and suffers when this person acts and suffers as a human being. *God himself* triumphs when this One triumphs as a human being. The human speaking and acting and suffering and triumphing of this one person directly concerns us all, and his history is our history of salvation which changes the whole human situation, just because God himself is its human subject in his Son, just because God himself has assumed and made his own our human nature and kind in his Son, just because God himself came into this world in his Son, and as one of us "a guest this world of ours he trod."

(CD: IV/2, 50-51)

*

If God is not truly and altogether in Christ, what sense can there be in talking about the reconciliation of the world with God in him? But it is something very bold and profoundly astonishing to presume to say without reservation or subtraction that *God* was truly and altogether in *Christ*, to speak of his identity with this true human being, which means this person who was born like all of us in time, who lived and thought and spoke, who could be tempted and suffer and die and who was in fact tempted, and suffered and died. The statement of this identity cannot be merely a postulate. If with the witnesses of the New Testament we derive it from what *took place* in this human being, if it only confirms that the reconciliation of the world with God has actually taken place in the existence of this human being, if it can only indicate the mystery and the miracle of this event, we must still know what we are presuming to say in this statement. It aims very high. In calling this human being the Son or the eternal Word of God, in ascribing to this human being in his unity with God a divine being and nature, it is not speaking only or even primarily of him but of *God*. It tells us that God for his part is God in his unity with this creature, this human being, in his human and creaturely nature — and this without ceasing to be God, without any alteration or diminution of his divine nature. But this statement concerning God is so bold that we dare not make it unless we consider seriously in what sense we can do so. It must not contain any blasphemy, however involuntary or well-meant, or however pious. That it does do this is to this very day the complaint of Judaism and Islam against the Christian confession of the deity of Christ. It cannot be taken lightly. It cannot be secured by a mere repetition of this confession. We must be able to answer for this confession and its statement about God with a good conscience and with good reason. We must be able to show that God is honored and not dishonored by this confession. *(CD: IV/1, 183)*

*

We begin with the insight that God is "not a God of confusion, but of peace" (1 Cor. 14.33). In him there is no paradox, no antinomy, no division, no inconsistency, not even the possibility of it. He is the Father of lights with whom there is no variableness nor interplay of light and darkness (Jas. 1.17). What he is and does he is and does in full unity with himself. It is in full unity with himself that he is also — and especially and above all — in *Christ*, that he becomes a creature, human, flesh, that he enters into our being in contradiction, that he takes upon himself its consequences. If we think that this is impossible it is because our concept of God is too narrow, too arbitrary, too human — far too human. Who God is and what it is to be divine is something we have to learn where God has revealed himself and his nature, the essence of the divine. And if he has revealed himself in Jesus Christ as the God who does this, it is not for us to be wiser than he and to say that it is in contradiction with the divine essence. We have to be ready to be taught by him that we have been too small and perverted in our thinking about him within the framework of a false idea of God. It is not for us to speak of a contradiction and rift in the being of God, but to learn to correct our notions of the being of God, to reconstitute them in the light of the fact that he does this. We may believe that God can and must only be absolute in contrast to all that is relative, exalted in contrast to all that is lowly, active in contrast to all suffering, inviolable in contrast to all temptation, transcendent in contrast to all immanence, and therefore divine in contrast to everything human, in short that he can and must be only the "Wholly Other." But such beliefs are shown to be quite untenable, and corrupt and pagan, by the fact that God does in fact be and do this in Jesus Christ. We cannot make them the standard by which to measure what God can or cannot do, or the basis of the judgment that in doing this he brings himself into self-contradiction. By doing this God proves to us that he can do it, that to do it is within his nature. And he shows himself to be more great and rich and sovereign than we had ever imagined. And our ideas of his nature must be guided by this, and not *vice versa*.

We have to think something after the following fashion. As God was in Christ, far from being against himself, or at disunity with himself, he has put into effect the *freedom* of his divine love, the *love* in which he is divinely free. He has therefore done and revealed that which *corresponds* to his divine nature. His immutability does not stand in the way of this. It must not be denied, but this possibility is included in his unalterable being. He is absolute, infinite, exalted, active, impassible, transcendent, but in all this he is the One who *loves* in freedom, the One who is *free* in his love, and therefore not his own prisoner. He is all this as the *Lord*, and in such a way that he embraces the opposites of these concepts even while he is superior to them. He is all this as the Creator, who has created the world as the reality distinct from himself but willed and affirmed by him and therefore as his world, as the world which belongs to him, in relation to which he can be God and act as God in an absolute way and also a relative, in an infinite and also a finite, in an exalted and also a lowly, in an active and also a passive, in a transcendent and also an immanent, and finally, in a divine and also a human — indeed, in relation to which he himself can become worldly, making his own both its form, the *forma servi*, and also its cause; and all without giving up his own form, the *forma Dei*, and his own glory, but adopting the form and cause of the world into the most perfect community with his own, accepting solidarity with the world. God can do this. And no limit is set to his ability to do it by the *contradiction* of the creature against him. It does not escape him by turning to that which is not and losing itself in it, for, although he is not the Creator of that which is not,[60] he is its sovereign Lord. It corresponds to and is grounded in his divine nature that in free grace he should be faithful to the unfaithful creature who has not deserved it and who would inevitably perish without it, that in relation to it he should establish that community between his own form and cause and that of the creature, that he should make his own its being in contradiction and under the consequences of that contradiction, that he should maintain his covenant in relation to sinful humanity (not surrendering his deity, for how could that help? but giving up and sacrificing himself), and in that way supremely asserting himself and his deity. His particular and highly particularized presence in grace, in which the eternal Word descended to the lowest parts of the earth (Eph. 4.9) and tabernacled in the human being Jesus (Jn. 1.14), dwelling in this One human being in the fulness of his Godhead (Col. 2.9), is itself the demonstration and exercise of his *omnipresence*[61], i.e., of the perfection in which he has his own place which is superior to all the places created by him, not excluding but including all other places. His *omnipotence* is that of a divine plenitude of power in the fact that (as opposed to any abstract omnipotence) it can assume the form of weakness and impotence and do so as omnipotence, triumphing in this form. The *eternity* in which he himself is true time and the Creator of all time is revealed in the fact that, although our time is that of sin and death, he can enter it and himself be temporal in it, yet without ceasing to be eternal, able rather to be the Eternal in time. His *wisdom* does not deny itself, but proclaims itself in what necessarily appears folly to the world; his *righteousness* in ranging himself with the unrighteous as One who is accused with them, as the first, and properly the only One to come under accusation; his *holiness* in having mercy on humanity, in taking our misery to heart, in willing to share it with us in order to take it away from us. God does not have to dishonor himself when he goes into the far country, and conceals his glory. For he is truly honored in this concealment. This concealment, and therefore his condescension as such, is the image and reflection in which we see him as he is. His glory is the *freedom* of the *love* which he exercises and reveals in all this. In this respect it differs from the unfree and loveless glory of all the gods imagined by human beings. Everything depends on our seeing it, and in it the true and majestic nature of God: not trying to construct it arbitrarily; but deducing from its revelation in the divine nature of *Jesus Christ*. From this we learn that the *forma Dei* consists in the grace in which God himself assumes and makes his own the *forma servi*. We have to hold fast to this without being disturbed or confused by any pictures of false gods. It is this that we have to see and honor and worship as the mystery of the deity of Christ.

(CD: IV/1, 186-188)

*

THE SUBJECT-MATTER AND PROBLEMS OF
THE DOCTRINE OF RECONCILIATION

§57 The Work of God the Reconciler

The subject-matter, origin and content of the message received and proclaimed by the Christian community is at its heart the free act of the faithfulness of God in which he takes the lost cause of humanity, who have denied him as Creator and in so doing ruined themselves as creatures, and makes it his own in Jesus Christ, carrying it through to its goal and in that way maintaining and manifesting his own glory in the world.

God with Us

We enter that sphere of Christian knowledge in which we have to do with the *heart* of the message received by and laid upon the Christian community and therefore with the heart of the church's dogmatics: that is to say, with the heart of its subject-matter, origin and content. It has a circumference, the doctrine of creation and the doctrine of the last things, the redemption and consummation. But the *covenant* fulfilled in the *reconciliation* is its center. From this point we can and must see a circumference. But we can see it only from this point. A mistaken or deficient perception here would mean error or deficiency everywhere: the weakening or obscuring of the message, the confession and dogmatics as such. From this point either everything is clear and true and helpful, or it is not so anywhere. This involves a high responsibility in the task which now confronts us.

It would be possible and quite correct to describe the covenant fulfilled in the work of reconciliation as the heart of the subject-matter of Christian *faith*, of the origin of Christian *love*, of the content of Christian *hope*. But the faith and love and hope of the Christian community and the Christians assembled in it live by the message received by and laid upon them, not the reverse. And even if we tried to put them in the forefront, we should have to lay the emphasis upon their subject-matter, origin and content, which are not immanent to them, and which do not exhaust themselves in them. For Christian faith is faith *in*, Christian love is love *through*, and Christian hope is hope *in* God the Father, Son and Holy Spirit. There is something prior, outside, different from them which encounters them. It is God whom they encounter, from whom they have their being, whom they can lay hold of but not apprehend or exhaust. Not even the message by which faith and love and hope live, not even the confession with which the community responds to the message, not even the dogmatics in which it gives an account of the message and its own response, and finally of its faith and love and hope as such, can take the place of God. If we tried to start with faith and love and hope, we would still have to go back to that free and higher other in which they have their basis. And in the face of it we should have to say even of them that at their heart they have to do with the covenant fulfilled in the work of reconciliation, and that it is in their relation to this covenant that they are secure or insecure, effective or impotent, genuine or false.

Our first task will be to describe this Christian center in a first and most general approximation. The title "God with Us" is meant as a most general description of the whole complex of Christian understanding and doctrine which here confronts us.

At its heart the Christian message is a common statement on the part of certain people, i.e., those who are assembled in the Christian community. It includes a statement about themselves, about the individual existence of these people in their own time and situation. And it is essential to it that this should be so. But it only includes it. For primarily it is a statement about *God*: that it is he who is with them as God. Only with those who dare to make this statement, who as the recipients and bearers of the Christian message, as members of the Christian community, must dare to make it? With them, to the extent that they know that it is actually the case: God with us. They dare to make this statement because they were able to become and can constantly become again the recipients of this message. God with you, God with thee and thee, was its first form, and they are what they are to the extent that they hear this again and again. But as recipients they are also bearers of the message. And to this extent it is not only to them. They dare to make the statement, that God is the One who is with them as God, amongst people who do not yet know this. And it is to such that they address the statement. They do not specifically include them in that "us." Their aim is to show them what they do not yet know but what they can and should know. What? About themselves, and their individual existence in their own time and situation? That is certainly included. Much depends upon their coming to see that it applies to *them*. But everything depends upon their coming to see that it all has to do with God; that it is God who is with them as God. For it is this that applies to them. "God with us" as the core of the Christian message, the decisive general statement of the Christian community, can indeed be interpreted as "God with us human beings," but with the clear distinction, with us who know it but are always learning it afresh — and as the word of our declaration to all others, and therefore with "us" other human beings who have always to learn it afresh because we do not yet know it, although we can know it. In this movement from a narrower to a wider usage the statement "God with us" is the center of the Christian message — and always in such a way that it is primarily a statement about God and only then and for that reason a statement about ourselves as human beings.

That is the roughest outline of the matter. We must now look at this outline rather more closely in order that we may understand it correctly even in this basic form. . . .

1. Our starting-point is that this "God with us" at the heart of the Christian message is the description of an *act of God*, or better, of God himself in this act of his. It is a report, not therefore a statement of fact on the basis of general observation or consideration. God with us, or what is meant by these three words, is not an object of investigation or speculation. It is not a state, but an *event*. God *is*, of course, and that in the strictest sense originally and properly, so that everything else which is, in a way which cannot be compared at all with his being, can be so only through him, only in relation to him, only from him and to him. Now even when he is "with us," he is what he is, and in the way that he is; and all the power and truth of his being "with us" is the power and truth of his incomparable being which is proper to him and to him alone, his being as God. He is both in his life in eternity in himself, and also in his life as Creator in the time of the world created by him; by and in himself, and also above and in this world, and therefore according to the heart of the Christian message with us men. And he is who he is, and lives as what he is, in that he does what he does. How can we know God if his being is unknown or obscure or indifferent? But how can we know God if we do not find the truth and power of his *being* in his *life*, and of his *life* in his *act*? We know about God only if we are witnesses — however distantly and modestly — of his act. And we speak about God only as we can do so — however deficiently — as those who proclaim his act. "God with us" as it occurs at the heart of the Christian message is the attestation and report of the life and act of God as the One who is.

But if it means that God is with us — and the message of the Christian community certainly implies that it does really apply to us — then that presupposes that we human beings, in our own very different way, which cannot be compared with the being of God, but which on the basis of the divine being and life and act is a very real way, that we also *are*, and that we are in that we live in our time, and that we live in that we ourselves act in our own act. If the fact that God is with us is a report about the being and life and act of God, then from the very outset it stands in a relationship to our own being and life and acts. A report about ourselves is included in that report about God. We cannot therefore take cognisance of it, be more or less impressed by it, and then leave it as the report of something which has taken place in a quite different sphere in which we ourselves have no place. It tells us that we ourselves are in the sphere of God. It applies to us by telling us of a history which God wills to share with us and therefore of an invasion of our history — indeed, of the real truth about our history as a history which is by him and from him and to him. The divine being and life and act takes place with ours, and it is only as the divine takes place that ours takes place. To put it in the simplest way, what unites God and us human beings is that he does not will to be God without us, that he creates us rather to share with us and therefore with our being and life and act his own incomparable being and life and act, that he does not allow his history to be his and ours, but causes them to take place as a common history. That is the special truth which the Christian message has to proclaim at its very heart.

2. We have just said, and this is what is meant in the Christian message, that we have to do with an event, with an act of God. The whole being and life of God is an *activity*, both in eternity and in worldly time, both in himself as Father, Son and Holy Spirit, and in his relation to humanity and all creation. But what God does in himself and as the Creator and Governor of humanity is all aimed at the particular act in which it has its center and meaning. And everything that he wills has its ground and origin in what is revealed as his will in this one act. Thus it is not merely one amongst others of his works as Creator and Governor. Of course, it can and must be understood in this way, in accordance with the general will and work of God. But within this outer circle it forms an inner. The one God wills and works all things, but here he wills and works a *particular* thing: not one with others, but one for the sake of which he wills and works all others. As one with others this act is also the *telos* of all the acts of God; of the eternal ability in which he is both in himself and in the history of his acts in the world created by him. It is of this that the "God with us" speaks.

Therefore even from the standpoint of us human beings the "God with us" does not refer to human existence generally as the creaturely object of the will and work of his Lord. It does refer to it. It includes it. Human being, life and activity is always quite simply our history in relation to the being, life and act of our *Creator*. We can say the same of all creatures. But it is far more than this. For within and beyond this general activity, God himself in his being, life and activity as Creator wills and works a special act. All his activity has its heart and end in a single act. Within and out of the general history, which with all creatures human beings can have in common with God in his being, living and acting, there arises this act of God and that which corresponds to it in human being, life and activity, as qualified history, our true history. And if the "God with us" at the heart of the Christian message speaks of the unifying factor between God and humanity, it speaks of a *specific* conjoining of the two, not always and everywhere but in a single and particular event which has a definite importance for all time and space but which takes place once and for all in a definite *hic et nunc*.

3. From the standpoint of its meaning the particularity of this event consists in the fact that it has to do with the salvation of humanity, that in it the general history which is common to God and humanity, to God and all creation, becomes at its very heart and end a *redemptive history*. Salvation is more than being. Salvation is fulfilment, the supreme, sufficient, definitive and indestructible fulfilment of being. Salvation is the perfect being which is not proper to created being as such but is still future. Created being as such needs salvation, but does not have it: it can only look forward to it. To that extent salvation is its *eschaton*. Salvation, fulfilment, perfect being means — and this is what created being does not have in itself — being which has a part in the being of God, from which and to which it is: not a divinized being but a being which is hidden in God, and in that sense (distinct from God and secondary) *eternal* being. Since salvation is not proper to created being as such, it can only *come* to it, and since it consists in participation in the being of God it can come only from God. The coming of this salvation is the *grace* of God — using the word in its narrower and most proper sense. In the wider sense the creation, preservation and ruling of the world and humanity are already grace. For if this is not proper to created being as such, it can only come to it. Only from God as the One who is originally and properly can it come about that it also has being, that it is, and not that it is not. And by that very fact there is always held out to it the opportunity of salvation: the expectation of being in perfection in participation in the

divine being. But the "God with us" at the heart of the Christian message does not mean this general grace. It means the *redemptive grace* of God. It is this which constitutes, factually, the singularity of the event. It is this which marks out the event within the whole history of the togetherness of God and humanity. Not merely the creating, preserving and ruling of created being, not merely the creating of an opportunity for salvation, but the fact that it actually comes, that God gives it. God gives to created being what can only be given to it and what can be given only by him. And he does really give it: *Take what is mine* — this final, supreme, insurpassable gift; take it, it is meant for you. It is because it has to do with this that the activity of God indicated by the "God with us" is singular and unique. And so, too, is the invasion of the history of our own human being, life and activity described by this "God with us." And so, too, is the whole circle of God in which we find ourselves according to this center of the Christian message. The general grace of God in creation, preservation and ruling still remains. That is already grace. We recognize it distinctly as such only when we see God and ourselves in the inner and special circle of his will and work, in the light of this one, particular, redemptive act of God. It is only from this standpoint that the general grace of being and the opportunity which it offers can and do become a subject for genuine gratitude and a source of serious dedication. For here it is provided that that opportunity is not offered in vain, that it is actually taken, taken by God himself. What concerns us here is the redemptive grace of God, and to that extent something that is more and greater.

4. In the light of this we must now try to outline this particular event with rather greater precision. According to the Christian message "God with us" means God with humanity for whom salvation is intended and *ordained* as such, as those who are created, preserved and ruled by God. It is not as though the expectation belonged to our created being. It is not as though we had any kind of claim to it. God cannot be forced to give us a part in his divine being. The matter might have ended quite well with that general grace of being — which even in itself is great enough. But where God is not bound and humanity has no claim, even more compelling is the will and plan and promise of God. It goes beyond, or rather it precedes his will and work as Creator. Therefore it has to be distinguished from it, as something prior, which precedes it. The ordaining of salvation for humanity and of humanity for salvation is the original and basic will of God, the ground and purpose of his will as Creator. It is not that he first wills and works the being of the world and

humanity, and then ordains it to salvation. But God creates, preserves and rules humanity for this prior end and with this prior purpose, that there may be a being distinct from himself ordained for salvation, for perfect being, for participation in his own being, because as the One who loves in freedom he has determined to exercise redemptive grace — and that there may be an object of this his redemptive grace, a partner to receive it. A further point which we must now make in describing the event indicated by the "God with us" is this. The "God with us" has nothing to do with chance. As a redemptive happening it means the revelation and confirmation of the most original relationship between God and humanity, that which was freely determined in eternity by God himself before there was any created being. In the very fact that humanity exists, and is human, we are as such chosen by God for salvation; that *eschaton* is given us by God. Not because God owes it to us. Not in virtue of any quality or capacity of our own being. Completely without claim. What takes place between God and humanity in that particular redemptive history is fulfilment to this extent too, that in it God — the eternal will of God with humanity — is justified, the eternal righteousness of his grace is active and revealed, in and with the divine right, and so too the right which he has freely given and ascribed to humanity by determining this concerning us. It belongs to the character of this event and its particularity that with the end it reveals the basis and beginning of all things — the glory of God, which is that of his free love, and with it — well below, but eternally grounded upon it — the dignity of humanity, that dignity with which he willed to invest humanity although it is not proper to us.

5. But again we must go further. "God with us" in the sense of the Christian message means God with us human beings who have *forfeited* the predetermined salvation, forfeited it with a supreme and final *jeopardizing* even of our creaturely existence. As the way from that beginning in God to the end of humanity with God is revealed in this particular event, its line is not a straight one, but one which is radically and — if God himself were not there as hope — hopelessly broken. The human situation in this event is this. We occupy a position quite different from that which we ought to occupy according to the divine intention. We do not conduct ourselves as the partners God has given himself to receive his redemptive grace. We have opposed our ordination to salvation. We have turned our backs on the salvation which actually comes to us. We do not find the fulfilment of our being in participation in the being of God by the gift of God. Instead, we aim at another salvation which is to

211

be found in the sphere of our creaturely being and attained by our own effort. Our belief is that we can and should find self-fulfilment. We have ourselves become an *eschaton*. These are the people with whom God is dealing in this particular redemptive history: those who have made themselves quite impossible in relation to the redemptive grace of God; and in so doing, the people who have made themselves quite impossible in their created human being, who have cut the ground from under their feet, who have lost their whole *raison d'être*. What place have we before God when we have shown ourselves to be so utterly unworthy of that for which we were created by God, so utterly inept, so utterly unsuitable? when we have eliminated ourselves? What place is there for our being, our being as humans, when we have denied our goal, and therefore our beginning and meaning, and when we confront God in this negation? Despising the dignity with which God invested us, we have obviously forfeited the right which God gave and ascribed to us as the creatures of God. But it is with this prodigal in a far country, with humanity as fallen and now in this sorry plight, that God has to do in this redeeming event. And this is what reveals the gulf. This is what shows us how it stands between God and humanity. This is where we see the inadequacy of the partner, the point where the relationship breaks down. At a pinch this can be overlooked if we do not think of the redeeming event as the heart and end of their interconnection, if we conceive it abstractly as the interconnection of Creator and creature. We may take this antithesis very seriously, but we shall always have good grounds to think of it as an antithesis which can be bridged. As such it does not contain any breach, any gulf, any enmity, either on the one side or on the other, any judgment and punishment on the part of God or suffering on the part of humanity. But this cannot possibly be overlooked in the redeeming event referred to in the "God with us." On the contrary, what constitutes the particularity of this event is that as a redeeming event, as the fulfilment of the gracious will of God, as the reaffirmation of his right and ours, it can be conceived only in the form of a *Yet*! and a *Nevertheless*! which means that it cannot be conceived at all. If humanity has forfeited salvation, what do we have to grasp in this event but the inconceivable fact that all the same it is given to us? If in so doing we have lost our creaturely being, what do we have to grasp but again the inconceivable fact that all the same we will not be lost? Is it not the case that only here, in the light of the antithesis which is here revealed and overcome, is grace really known as grace, that is, as free grace, as mercy pure and simple, as *factum purum*, having its basis only in itself, in the fact that it is posited by

God? For who really knows what grace is until they have seen it at work here: as the grace which is *for* us when, because we are wholly and utterly sinners before God, it can only be against us, and when in fact, even while it is for us, it is also a plaintiff and judge against us, showing us to be incapable of satisfying either God or ourselves? And looking back once again, it is the grace of God as mercy pure and simple, as a sheer Yet and Nevertheless, which reveals, and by which we have to measure, how it stands with the humanity to whom it is granted. It is not independent human reflection, or an abstract law, but grace which shows incontrovertibly that humanity has forfeited its salvation and in so doing fatally jeopardized its creaturely being — which reveals its sin and the misery which is its consequence. From the *redemption* which takes place here we can gather from what it is that humanity is redeemed; from the *factum purum* of the salvation which comes to humanity without and in spite of our own deserts we may know the *factum brutum* which we for our part dare to set against God. Because the "God with us" at the heart of the Christian message has to do with that *factum purum* of the divine mercy, we must not fail to recognize but acknowledge without reserve that we, and those for whom God is according to this message, are those who have nothing to bring him but a confession of this *factum brutum*: "Father, I have sinned."

6. But if the Christian "God with us" does nevertheless speak, not of a renunciation, but of the *fulfilment* of the redemptive will of God in that event, then no matter how inconceivable may be that which we have to grasp in this connection, it refers to something quite different from the blind paradox of an arbitrary act of the divine omnipotence of grace. We are confronted here by the determination of that event which reveals unequivocally its uniqueness amongst the acts of God, that it declares an absolutely unique being and attitude and activity on the part of God. "God with us" means more than God over or side by side with us, before or behind us. It means more than his divine being in even the most intimate active connection with our human being otherwise peculiar to him. At this point, at the heart of the Christian message and in relation to the event of which it speaks, it means that God has made himself the One who fulfils his redemptive will. It means that he himself in his own person — at his own cost but also on his own initiative — has become the inconceivable Yet! and Nevertheless! of this event, and so its clear and well-founded and legitimate, its true and holy and righteous Therefore! It means that *God* has become *human* in order as such, but in divine sovereignty, to take up our case. What takes place in this work of incon-

ceivable mercy is, therefore, the free over-ruling of God, but it is not an arbitrary overlooking and ignoring, not an artificial bridging, covering-over or hiding, but a real closing of the breach, gulf and abyss between God and us for which we are responsible. God closes it through himself; he becomes and is the human being in whom peace is real. At the very point where we refuse and fail, offending and provoking God, making ourselves impossible before him and in that way missing our destiny, treading under foot our dignity, forfeiting our right, losing our salvation and hopelessly compromising our creaturely being — at that very point God himself intervenes as this human being. Because he is God he is able not only to be God but also to be this *human being*. Because he is God it is necessary that he should be a human being in quite a different way from all the rest of us; that he should do what we do not do and not do what we do. Because he is God he puts forth his omnipotence to be this other, to be human quite differently, *in our place* and for our sake. Because he is God he has and exercises the power as this human being to suffer for us the consequence of our transgression, the wrath and penalty which necessarily falls on us, and in that way satisfy himself in our regard. And again because he is God, he has and exercises the power as this human being to be his own *partner* in our place, the One who in free obedience accepts the ordination of humanity to salvation which we resist, and in that way satisfies us, i.e., achieves that which can positively satisfy us. That is the absolutely unique being, attitude and activity of God to which the "God with us" at the heart of the Christian message refers. It speaks of the peace which God himself in this human being has made between himself and us.

We see the seriousness and force of the divine *redemptive will* in the fact that it is not too little and not too much for him to make peace between himself and us. To that end he gives himself. He, the Creator, does not scorn to become a creature, human like us, in order that as such he may bear and do what must be borne and done for our salvation. On the contrary, he finds and defends and vindicates his glory in doing it. Again, we see our own perversion and corruption, we see what is our *offence* and *plight*, in the fact that God (who never does anything unnecessary) can obviously be satisfied only by this supreme act, that only his own coming as man is sufficient to make good the evil which has been done. So dark is our situation that God himself must enter and occupy it in order that it may be light. We cannot fully understand the Christian "God with us" without the greatest astonishment at the glory of the divine grace and the greatest horror at our own plight.

But even when we understand the entry of God for us in becoming human as the making of peace between himself and us, we have still not said the decisive thing about this action. What he effects and does and reveals by becoming human — for us — is much more than the restoration of the *status quo ante* — the obviating of the loss caused by our own transgression and our restoration to the place of promise and expectation of the salvation ordained for us. God makes himself the means of his own redemptive will, but he is obviously more than this means. And in making peace by himself he obviously gives us more than this peace, i.e., more than a *restitutio ad integrum,* more than the preserving and assuring to us of our creaturely being and this as our opportunity for salvation. For when God makes himself the means of his redemptive will to us, this will and we ourselves attain our goal. What is at first only God's gracious answer to our failure, God's gracious help in our plight, and even as such great and wonderful enough, is — when God himself is the help and answer — his participation in our being, life and activity and therefore obviously our participation in his; and therefore it is nothing more nor less than the coming of salvation itself, the presence of the *eschaton* in all its fulness. The human being in whom God himself intervenes for us, suffers and acts for us, closes the gap between himself and us as our representative, in our name and on our behalf, this One is not merely the confirmation and guarantee of our salvation, but because he is God he is salvation, our salvation. He is not merely the redeemer of our being but as such the giver and himself the gift of its fulfilment and therefore the goal and end of the way of God — and all that as the peacemaker and savior. It is when this great thing takes place that there takes place the even greater. This great thing is included in the "God with us" of the Christian message in so far as this speaks of God's intervening and becoming human, but in this great thing there is also included the even greater, indeed the greatest of all.

7. From all this it is surely obvious that the "God with us" carries with it in all seriousness a "We with God": the fact that we ourselves are there in our being, life and activity.

This does not seem to be apparent at a first glance. For who are we? We have seen already that we are (1) those whose history is absorbed into the history of the acts of God, and (2) made to participate in that event which is the center and end of all the divine acts, and (3) given a share in the grace with which God actually brings salvation to humanity, and (4) that we are such as those whom God has thereto ordained from all eternity, but unfortunately (5) we are those who have refused his salvation and in that way denied their own destiny and perverted and wasted and hopelessly compromised their own being, life and activity, who inevitably therefore find themselves disqualified and set aside as participants in that event, and cannot be considered in relation to it. Yet beyond that and in a sense conclusively (6) we are those whose place has been taken by another, who lives and suffers and acts for them, who for them makes good that which they have spoiled, who — for them, but also without them and even against them — is their salvation. That is what we are. And what is left to us? What place is there for us when we are like that? In what sense is the history of the acts of God at this center and end our history? Are we not without history? Have we not become mere objects? Have we not lost all responsibility? Are we not reduced to mere spectators? Is not our being deprived of all life or activity? Or does it not lack all significance as our life and activity? "God with us" — that is something which we can easily understand even in these circumstances. But how is it to include within it a "We with God"? And if it does not, how can it really be understood as a "God with us"?

The answer is that we ourselves are directly summoned, that we are lifted up, that we are awakened to our own truest being as life and act, that we are set in motion by the fact that in that one human being God has made himself our peacemaker and the giver and gift of our salvation. By it we are made free for him. By it we are put in the place which comes to us where our salvation (really ours!) can come to us from him (really from him!). This actualization of his redemptive will by himself opens up to us the one true possibility of our own being. Indeed, what remains to us of life and activity in the face of this actualization of his redemptive will by himself can only be one thing. This one thing does not mean the extinguishing of our humanity, but its establishment. It is not a small thing, but the greatest of all. It is not for us a passive presence as spectators, but our true and highest activation — the *magnifying of his grace* which has its highest and most profound greatness in the fact that God has made himself human with us, to make our cause his own, and as his own to save it from disaster and to carry it through to success. Human beings as genuine life and activity, the "We with God," are to affirm this, to admit that God is right, to be thankful for it, to accept the promise and the command which it contains, to exist as the community, and responsibly in the community, of those who know that this is all that remains to us, but that it does remain to us and that for all men everything depends upon its coming to pass. And it is this "We with God" that is meant by the Christian message in its central "God with us," when it proclaims that God himself has taken our place, that he himself has made peace between himself and us, that by himself he has accomplished our salvation, i.e., our participation in his being.

This "We with God" enclosed in the "God with us" is Christian *faith*, Christian *love* and Christian *hope*. These are the magnifying of the grace of God which still remain to us — and remain to us as something specifically human, as the greatest thing of all, as action in the truest sense of the word. We do not forget that it is a matter of magnifying God out of the deeps, *e profundis*. Our magnifying of God can only be that of the transgressors and rebels that we are, those who have missed their destiny, and perverted and wasted their being, life and activity. Therefore our magnifying of God cannot seek and find and have its truth and power in itself, but only in God, and therefore in that one human being in whom God is for us, who is our peace and salvation. Our faith, therefore, can only be faith in him, and cannot live except from him as its object. Our love can only be by him, and can only be strong from him as its basis. Our hope can only be hope directed upon him, and can only be certain hope in him as its content. Our faith, love and hope and we ourselves — however strong may be our faith, love and hope — live only by that which we cannot create, posit, awaken or deserve. And although our believing, loving and hoping themselves and as such are in us, they are not of us, but of their object, basis and content, of God, who in that one human being not only answers for us with him but answers for himself with us, who gives it to us in freedom that we may believe, love and hope: open eyes, ears and hearts for himself and his work, knowledge to the foolish, obedience to the wayward, freedom to the bound, life to the victims of death; and all in such a way that the glory of our own being, life and activity is still his, and can be valued, and exalted and respected by us only as his; but all in such a way that in and with his glory we too are really exalted, because in the depths where we can only give him the glory, we find our true and proper place. It is in this way and in this sense that the Christian community proclaims "We with God" when it proclaims "God with us."

In these seven points we have said in rough outline — many things need to be amplified, explained and made more precise — almost everything that has to be said about the "God with us" as the covenant between God and us human beings fulfilled in the work of reconciliation. But we have not yet said it with the concreteness with which it is said at the heart of the Christian message, or at the heart (in the second article) of the creed, and with which it must also be said at the heart of

217

dogmatics, even in the briefest survey, if we are not to speak mistakenly or falsely.

For where does the community which has to deliver the message learn to know and say this "God with us"? And to what does it point those to whom the message is addressed? How far can and must this "God with us," the report of the event which constitutes its meaning and content, be declared and received in truth? How can people come to stand where they obviously have to stand — in that inner circle of the relationship between God and humanity — to dare to make this report as a declaration of *reality*? And how do other men and women come to hear this report in such a way that it is to them a report of reality, and they find themselves challenged and empowered to pass it on to others still? How do they come to stand in the same place as the first men and women, as the Christian community? In other words: How does it come about amongst us human beings that there is a *communication* of this "God with us," of this report, or rather, of that which is reported? That is the question which we can answer only as we say everything once again in the concrete way in which it is said at the heart of the Christian message. Everything depends upon its concrete expression: the whole truth and reality of the report, and the whole secret of the communication of the matter.

We must realize that the Christian message does not at its heart express a concept or an idea, nor does it recount an anonymous history to be taken as truth and reality only in concepts and ideas. Certainly the history is inclusive, i.e., it is one which includes in itself the whole event of the "God with us" and to that extent the history of all those to whom the "God with us" applies. But it recounts this history and speaks of its inclusive power and significance in such a way that it declares a name, binding the history strictly and indissolubly to this name and presenting it as the story of the bearer of this name. This means that all the concepts and ideas used in this report (God, humanity, world, eternity, time, even salvation, grace, transgression, reconciliation and any others) can derive their significance only from the bearer of this name and from his history, and not the reverse. They cannot have any independent importance or role based on a quite different prior interpretation. They cannot say what has to be said with some meaning of their own or in some context of their own abstracted from this name. They can serve only to describe this name — the name of *Jesus Christ*.

This name is the answer to our earlier question. In the Christian "God with us" there is no question of any other source and object than that indicated by this name. Other than in this name — as on the basis of the necessity and power of its conceptual context — it cannot be truth, either on the lips of those who speak it or in the ears and hearts of those who receive it. Without this name it is left insecure and unprotected. It is exposed to the suspicion that it might be only a postulate, a pure speculation, a myth. It is truth as it derives from this name and as it points to it, and only so. Where is it that the people stand who declare this message? The answer is that they stand in the sphere of the lordship of the One who bears this name, in the light and under the impelling power of his Spirit in the community assembled and maintained and ruled by him. They have not placed themselves there but he has placed them there, and it is as they stand there by him that their report is a report of *actuality*. Again, where will those others stand to whom they address their report and witness, who both receive it and then, on their own responsibility, spread it further? The answer is that they too stand in the sphere of the lordship, which has now claimed them, of the One who bears this name, of his Spirit, of the call to his community which has now come to them. They too have not placed themselves there. And those who said to them "God with us" have not brought it about. But, again, it is he himself who bears this name that has called and led and drawn them, and it is as that happens that it is given to them, too, to pass on to others their report of *actuality* as such. Therefore the One who shows and persuades and convinces and reveals and communicates from person to person that it is so, "God with us," is the One who bears this name, *Jesus Christ*, no other, and nothing else. That is what the message of the Christian community intends when at its heart it declares this name. If it were a principle and not a name indicating a person, we should have to describe it as the epistemological principle of the message. Where between person and person there is real communication of the report of what took place in him and through him, he himself is there and at work, he himself makes himself to be recognized and acknowledged. The Christian message about him — and without this it is not the Christian message — is established on the certainty that he is responsible for it, that he as the truth speaks through it and is received in it, that as it serves him he himself is present as actuality, as his own witness. He himself by his Spirit is its guarantor. He himself is the one who establishes and maintains and directs the community which has received it and upon which it is laid. He himself is the strength of its defence and its offensive. He himself is the hope of freedom and enlightenment for the many who have not yet received and accepted it. He himself above all is the comfort, and the restlessness, and yet also the uplifting power in the weakness of its service. In a word, the Christian message lives as such by and to the One who at its heart bears the name of Jesus Christ. It becomes weak and obscure to the extent that it thinks it ought to live on other resources. And it becomes strong and clear when it is established solely in confidence in his controlling work exercised by his Spirit; to the extent that it abandons every other conceivable support or impulse, and is content to rest on his command and commission as its strength and pledge. He, Jesus Christ, is Emmanuel, "God with us." How else can he be proclaimed except as the One who proclaims himself? And how else can human activity and speech and hearing be effective in his service except in the prayer and expectation that he will constantly do it?

The name of Jesus Christ covers the whole power of the Christian *message* because it indicates the whole of its *content*, because at its heart, which is normative for the whole, it is a message about him, and therefore a message about the event of that "God with us."

It means *Jesus Christ* when (1) with this "God with us" it describes an act of God, or rather the being of God in his life and activity. If as a statement about God it is the report of an *event* (not a statement of fact), the report of a *history* in which we have a part with our being, life and activity, which God has in common with us, which inaugurated by him is our own history, then it is so because and in so far as it is a report about *Jesus Christ* as the One who actually unites the divine being, life and activity with ours.

It means *Jesus Christ* again when (2) it describes the "God with us" as an act of God, a particular, once and for all and unique event in the midst of events in general. It is a report of this one event and of this event alone, of its meaning and importance for all of us, for people of all times and places, because and to the extent that it is a report about him as the person who in his existence and work is absolutely unique and therefore universal in effectiveness and significance. It means the event which unites God and humanity and which has been accomplished in him and in him alone, the event of which he alone is the subject and in which we can have a part only by him.

It means *Jesus Christ* again when it describes the event of "God with us" (3) as a redemptive event; as the fulfilment of human being by participation in the divine being which comes to them by the grace of God. It is a message of redemption, and therefore a message of the last and greatest and unsurpassable thing which people can experience from God and have in fact experienced, of the gift of eternal life which has been made to them, because and in so far as it is the message of Jesus Christ — that he is the One who, himself God, is also human, that he therefore was and is and will be the salvation of God for us other human beings, that in one person he is the God who gives salvation and the one to whom it is given and who allows it to be given by him, that as such he is the power and witness of the *eschaton* in the human present — a human present which is itself in the *eschaton*.

But the Christian message again means *Jesus Christ* when (4) it looks through the redemptive event of the "God with us" as through glass to the basis and beginning of all things, of the world and of humanity, in God, to the original ordination of humanity to salvation and of salvation for humanity as the meaning and basis even of the divine creative will. It has the particular emphasis and the specific weight of an original Word which underlies and embraces all other words so that no other word has any independent significance, as one historical report with others, it has none of the contingence of the record of one historical fact with many others, because and in so far as it is a message about Jesus Christ: that he is the One who according to the free and gracious will of God is himself eternal salvation, the last and also the first; our eternal yesterday in God who is the same today and for ever.

But it means Jesus Christ again when (5) it sees and presupposes that we human beings with whom God is are those who have *forfeited* the salvation destined for us from all eternity, letting slip the opportunity for it, and in that way fatally jeopardizing our creaturely being and indeed perishing were it not that God is God and therefore our hope. It is not out of mere pessimism that it sees and understands humanity in this way. As a message about Jesus Christ it cannot do otherwise. This name is the real Emmanuel-sign and therefore — although in the reverse direction from Is. 7.14 — the twofold sign which speaks of both the judgment of God and the grace of God in his dealings with his people. Also and first of all the sign of judgment. The well-deserved and incontestable sentence on humanity, his wrath and punishment, is first introduced and revealed in Jesus Christ. And it is the utterly free and unmerited nature of the grace of God introduced by him as *factum purum* which first reveals the true relationship with God of the people to whom it is granted in him, the *factum brutum* with which we have to do on the part of humanity.

And now it is absolutely clear that the Christian message means *Jesus Christ*, and has to name his name and does not know of any other, when (6) it says that God has made himself the One who fulfils his redemptive will, that he has become *human for us*, that in the power of his Godhead he might take up our cause in our place. Jesus Christ is the man in whom God satisfies himself in face of our transgression and us in face of our plight. It says Jesus Christ when it speaks of this absolutely unique being, attitude and activity of God, of the *peace* which has been made by him between himself and us. And it does so because in speaking of this peace made in this way by God as a human being amongst human beings, in speaking of this great thing, it at once goes on to speak of a greater and of the greatest thing of all, of salvation itself, which has already come to us in and with the opportunity for salvation restored in Jesus Christ, which has already been given to us, which has already become our salvation.

To conclude: How can (7) the reverse side be possible or legitimate, how can a "We with God" be really included and enclosed in the "God with us," how can it be true or actual, if it does not have reference to *Jesus Christ?* It is with reference to him that in spite of all appearances to the contrary the Christian message dares to address *human beings* too as active subjects in the event of redemption, and to its content there belong the praise which we offer to the grace of God *e profundis*, our own faith and love and hope. We have already seen in what sense this by no means self-evident fact is true, to what extent we others who are not that One belong to the redemptive act, that is, to the extent that our human being, life and activity, in the form of the praise of God, of faith and love and hope, live by their object, basis and content, to the extent that it is given to us in that way to be able to praise and believe and love and hope. But in that way means in Jesus Christ, in the community between him and us created by his Spirit, in virtue of our being, life and activity in his, and his in ours. We other men and women are Christians — or prospective Christians — and therefore partakers of his being, life and activity, in so far as Jesus Christ makes us such and wills to maintain and rule us as such. There is a Christian community with its special distinction and service to the extent that Jesus Christ assembles it and is present with it by his Spirit. Therefore this final part of the content of the Christian message stands or falls with him — its characterization and description with the naming of *his* name.   *(CD: IV/1, 3-20)*

*

Jesus Christ was and is for us in that he suffered and was *crucified* and *died*. Along the line that we are following, the witness to Christ in the

New Testament moves towards this statement (in the Gospels) in order
to proceed from it (in the Acts and Epistles). The work of the Lord who
became a servant, the way of the Son of God into the far country, his
appearance in the flesh, his humiliation, all aims at that of which this
statement speaks. The work of his obedience rendered in humility is
when it is completed in this happening. The Judge who judges Israel
and the world by letting himself be judged fulfils this strange judgment
as the man who suffered under Pontius Pilate, was crucified, dead and
buried. It is clear that we must give to this statement our very special
attention.

On the basis of the presuppositions indicated in the two preceding
discussions we now have to do with the true fulfilment of what God had
to do for us in Jesus Christ — the *passion of Jesus Christ*. We must first
emphasize generally that (1) in it as a passion we have to do with an
action. That in it the subject of the Gospel story became an object does
not alter this fact. For this took place in the freedom of this subject.
According to the common consent of the Gospels Jesus Christ not only
knew but willed that this should happen. This distinguishes his passion
from the series of other passions in world history (which we might
describe and understand as one long passion in view of the flood of
blood and tears which it seems always to be). But it also makes it very
puzzling. An offering which offers itself — and that without any obvious
meaning or end! But it is with a free self-offering of this kind and therefore with an act and not a fate that we have to do in this passion. In explanation we must add (2) that we are dealing with an act which took
place on earth, *in time and space*, and which is indissolubly linked with the
name of a certain human being. The history of religious and cultic speculation knows of other suffering and dying gods, and the similarity with
these pictures forces itself upon our attention. But the Gospels do not
speak of a passion which might just as well have been suffered in one
place as another, at one time as another, or in a heavenly or some purely
imaginary space and time. They indicate a very definite point in world
history which cannot be exchanged for any other. They point to its
earthly theater. They do not speak of a passing moment in the occurrence of a myth which is cyclic and timeless and therefore of all times.
They speak of a unique occurrence for which there is no precedent and
which cannot be repeated. They speak of it (3) as an *act of God* which is
coincident with the free action and suffering of a human being, but in
such a way that this human action and suffering has to be represented
and understood as the action and, therefore, the passion of God himself,

which in its historical singularity not only has a general significance for the people of all times and places, but by which their situation has objectively been decisively changed, whether they are aware of it or not. It is, of course, necessarily the case that the knowledge of it as the act of God and the knowledge of the change in the world situation brought about by it can come about for every person only in the decision of faith, in which this act becomes to us a word, the Word of God accepted in obedience, in which the passion of Jesus Christ is attested as having happened for us, and therefore in very truth for the world.

Let us now try to understand it in general terms.

It cannot be ignored that many people have suffered grievously, most grievously, in the course of world history. It might even be suggested that many have perhaps suffered more grievously and longer and more bitterly than did this one in the limited events of a single day. Many who have suffered by human hands have been treated no less and perhaps more unjustly than this man. Many have been willing as he was to suffer in this way. Many in so doing have done something which, according to their intention and it may be in fact, was significant for others, perhaps many others, making a redemptive change in their life. And in face of any human suffering do we not have to think ultimately of the obscure but gracious control of divine providence and therefore of the goodwill of God which becomes act and event in it? Human suffering may be deserved or undeserved, voluntary or involuntary, heroic or not heroic, important for others or not important for others. But even if it is only the whimper of a sick child it has in it as such something which in its own way is infinitely outstanding and moving and in its human form and its more or less recognizable or even its hidden divine basis something which we can even describe as shattering. This is true of the passion of Jesus of Nazareth, but in so far as it is a human passion it is not true in a way which is basically different from that of any other human passion. If this is the scope of the Gospel story and the starting point of Gospel proclamation, it was not the intention of the New Testament, nor was it seriously the intention of the church as it understood itself in the light of the New Testament, that the fundamentally unique occurrence should be found in the human passion as such. If we single out this human passion above others, we may be able to see and to say something which is noteworthy as such, but we shall not be helped forward a single step towards an understanding of what this occurrence is all about. For this reason we have already had to look beyond the human story at every point.

The mystery of this passion, of the torture, crucifixion and death of this one Jew which took place at that place and time at the hands of the Romans, is to be found in the person and mission of the One who suffered there and was crucified and died. *His person*: it is the eternal God himself who has given himself in his Son to be human, and as human being to take upon himself this human passion. *His mission*: it is the Judge who in this passion takes the place of those who ought to be judged, who in this passion allows himself to be judged in their place. It is not, therefore, merely that God rules in and over this human occurrence simply as Creator and Lord. He does this, but he does more. He gives himself to be the humanly acting and suffering person in this occurrence. He himself is the subject who in his own freedom becomes in this event the object acting or acted upon in it. It is not simply the humiliation and dishonoring of a creature, of a noble and relatively innocent man that we find here. The problem posed is not that of a theodicy: How can God will this or permit this in the world which he has created good? It is a matter of the humiliation and dishonoring of God himself, of the question which makes any question of a theodicy a complete anticlimax; the question whether in willing to let this happen to him he has not renounced and lost himself as God, whether in capitulating to the folly and wickedness of his creature he has not abdicated from his deity (as did the Japanese Emperor in 1945), whether he can really die and be dead? And it is a matter of the *answer* to this question: that in this humiliation God is supremely God, that in this death he is supremely alive, that he has maintained and revealed his deity in the passion of this human being as his eternal Son. Moreover, this human passion does not have just a significance and effect in its historical situation within humanity and the world. On the contrary, there is fulfilled in it the mission, the task, and the work of the Son of God: the reconciliation of the world with God. There takes place here the redemptive judgment of God on all people. To fulfil this judgment he took the place of all human beings, he took their place as sinners. In this passion there is legally re-established the covenant between God and humanity, broken by humanity but kept by God. On that one day of suffering of that One there took place the comprehensive turning in the history of all creation — with all that this involves.

Because it is a matter of this person and *his* mission, the suffering, crucifixion and death of this one human being is a unique occurrence. His passion has a real dimension of depth which it alone can have in the whole series of human passions. In it — from God's standpoint as well as ours — we have to do not merely with something but with everything: not merely with one of the many hidden but gracious overrulings of God, but in the fulness of its hiddenness with an action in which it is a matter of his own being or not being, and therefore of his own honor or dishonor in relation to his creation. We are not dealing merely with any suffering, but with the suffering of God and this human being in face of the destruction which threatens all creation and every individual, thus compromising God as the Creator. We are dealing with the painful confrontation of God and this human being not merely with any evil, not merely with death, but with eternal death, with the power of that which is not. Therefore we are not dealing merely with any sin, or with many sins, which might wound God again and again, and only especially perhaps at this point, and the consequences of which this human being had only to suffer in part and freely willed to do so. We are dealing with sin itself and as such: the preoccupation, the orientation, the determination of humanity as it has left its place as a creature and broken its covenant with God; the corruption which God has made his own, for which he willed to take responsibility in this one human being. Here in the passion in which as Judge he lets himself be judged God has fulfilled this responsibility. In the place of all humanity he has himself wrestled with that which separates them from him. He has himself borne the consequence of this separation to bear it away.

The New Testament has this in mind when in the Gospels it looks forward to the passion story of Jesus Christ and in the Epistles it looks forward from it to the future of the community and therefore to the future of the world and of every human being. It is a matter of history. Everything depends upon the fact that this turning as it comes from God for us humans is not simply imagined and presented as a true teaching of pious and thoughtful people, but that it happened in this way, in the space and time which are those of all people. But it is a matter of this history. That it took place once at this time and place as this history is what distinguishes the passion, crucifixion and death of this one Jew from all the other occurrences in time and space with which the passion of Jesus Christ is otherwise similar in every respect. Distinguished in this way, it is the subject of Christian faith and proclamation.   *(CD: IV/I: 244-248)*

*

TRUE HUMANITY

Human reflection has often raised questions about God — while taking humanity for granted. Not so Barth. The question of human existence, what it means to be truly human, is as much a question for him as the question of God. Therefore he looks to the humanity of Jesus Christ in order to develop his theological anthropology. This selection on "The Real Human Being" comes from volume 2 of his Doctrine of Creation.

The ontological determination of humanity is grounded in the fact that one human being among all others is the human Jesus. So long as we select any other starting point for our study, we shall reach only the phenomena of the human. We are condemned to abstractions so long as our attention is riveted as it were on other people, or rather on humanity in general, as if we could learn about real human beings from a study of humanity in general, and in abstraction from the fact that one person among all others is the human Jesus. In this case we miss the one Archimedean point given us beyond humanity, and therefore the one possibility of discovering the ontological determination of humanity. Theological anthropology has no choice in this matter. It is not yet or no longer theological anthropology if it tries to pose and answer the question of true human being from any other angle.

We remember who and what the human Jesus is. As we have seen, he is the creaturely being in whose existence we have to do immediately and directly with the being of God also. Again, he is the creaturely being in whose existence God's act of deliverance has taken place for all other people. He is the creaturely being in whom God as the Savior of all people also reveals and affirms his own glory as the Creator. He is the creaturely being who as such embodies the sovereignty of God, or conversely the sovereignty of God which as such actualizes this creaturely being. He is the creaturely being whose existence consists in his fulfilment of the will of God. And finally he is the creaturely being who as such not only exists from God and in God but absolutely for God instead of for himself.

From this knowledge of the human Jesus we have derived the criteria which indicate the limits within which the attempt to attain knowledge of human existence must always move. We have thus been warned against confusing human reality with mere human phenomena. We have been unable to accept those determinations of humanity in which relationship to God, participation in the history inaugurated between human beings and God, and the glory, lordship, purpose and service of

227

God, are not brought out as the meaning of human life. We have also had to be critical even where the concept of God seemed to play a certainly not unimportant role, but where it remained empty to the extent that there did not emerge anything of his saving action and the related actuality of human being. We have now to show the fact and extent that the ontological determination of humanity results from the fact that one human being among all others is this creaturely being, the human Jesus.

Our first point is that the message of the Bible about this one human being has amongst other things this *ontological* significance. Speaking of this one human being, it says of all other people — those who were before him and those who were after him, those who knew him and those who did not know him or did so only indirectly, those who accepted him and those who rejected him — at least that they were and are creaturely beings whom this human being is like for all his unlikeness, and in whose sphere and community and history this One also existed in likeness with them. This means that a decision has been made concerning the being and nature of every person by the mere fact that among all other people he too has been a human being. No matter who or what or where they may be, they cannot alter the fact that this One is also human. And because this One is also human, all people in their places and times are changed, i.e., they are something other than they would have been if this One had not been human too. It belongs to their human essence that in this One they have their human neighbor, companion and brother. Hence they have no choice in the matter. The question whether and to what extent they know this neighbor, and what attitude they adopt to him, is no doubt important, but it is secondary to that which has already been decided, namely, whether they can be a human being at all without this neighbor. Once for all this question has been decided in the negative for every person. We cannot break free from this neighbor. He is definitively our neighbor. And we as human beings are those in whose midst Jesus is also human, like us for all his unlikeness.

> Theological anthropology must not be so timid that it does not firmly insist on this simplest factor in the situation. Nor must it be so distracted that it suggests every possible and impossible foundation for its thesis except the first and simplest of all, namely, that *every human being as such is the companion of Jesus*. The biblical message to which we must keep is neither timid nor distracted in this respect. It dares to be the message of this one human being, and with all that it tells us concerning him, and obviously in the light of it, it makes the massively self-evident ontological presupposition that *the existence of this*

human being concerns every other human being as such, and that the fact that he too is human is the ground on which every other person is to be addressed and to which every other person is to be kept. It is worth noting that the biblical message never addresses people on any other basis. It does not appeal to their rationality or responsibility or human dignity or intrinsic humanity. No other decisive presupposition is made except that every one who bears the name of human is to be addressed as such in the name of Jesus, and therefore that they stand in an indisputable continuity with him which is quite adequate as a point of contact. The biblical message reckons with a humanity which as such stands in this continuity, and therefore with human persons as beings whom we immediately expect to respond to the call to order, to their own order, addressed in the name of Jesus. It reckons only with a creatureliness constituted by the fact that one human being among all others is this One. This is the ontological undertone which we must not miss if we are to understand why as a message about what this One is and does, and as a message about faith in him, it is so confident and unreserved, and yet not "enthusiastic" but sober. It speaks in fact about the One who not merely *a posteriori* but *a priori*, from the very outset, is the Neighbor, Companion and Brother of every human being.

As an ontological determination of humanity in general, the fact that among many others this One is also human means that we are human as in the person of this One we are confronted by the divine Other. We now adopt this concept. But it is to be noted that we adopt it from the very first as one which has this specific content. Certainly it is a transcendent and divine Other which constitutes humanity, from which we have our being, and in the light of which alone we can be known as real human beings. But this divine Other neither dwells in himself nor is it the transcendence of a deity existing abstractly and to be described in abstract terms. On the contrary, this divine Counterpart of every person, of humanity as such, is concretely this one human being in whose creaturely being we have to do with the existence, the saving act, the glory and lordship and the fulfilment of the will of God — with the creaturely being existing for God. That this being Jesus can be the divine Counterpart of every person is implicit in the fact that he is among all other human beings, that he dwells with them as himself, a human being like others, that he belongs to this community and history. But the same could obviously be said of every other person. Every other human being exists as a person like me, and to that extent in the same community and history as myself. But the co-existence of other people does not mean that I am confronted by a *divine* Other. And this is precisely what the coexistence of this one human being, Jesus, does mean. It is not merely that he can be my divine Counterpart. He *is* this. He is it in all that in which he is unlike other human beings for all his likeness to them. He is it as the one creaturely being in whom God is present as such in his saving action, in the vindication of his glory, in his lordship and in the fulfilment of his will; as the creaturely being who does not exist for himself but for God. In this respect Jesus stands above all other creaturely beings, and especially those which are like him. In this way he confronts them all, and therefore myself. And he does so in a divine manner, in divine existence, action, rule and service. He alone is turned wholly to God. And the ontological determination of all human beings is that Jesus is present among them as their divine Other, their Neighbor, Companion and Brother. In virtue of his unique relation to God, he stands among them in a way which could be predicated of no other. For although all people as individuals and in their particularity are relative others for their fellows, yet all people in their relation to God are always comparable to all others, not standing out in this respect or being among them in such a way as to constitute a true and absolute opposite. But the one human being Jesus does stand in such a relation to all others, confronting them as a true and absolute Counterpart, because he, this individual, is unique in his particularity and his relation to God: as unique as God himself is unique in relation to all creatures. It is in fact the singularity and transcendence of God which finds its creaturely correspondence, reflection and representation in this human being and therefore among all other people. It is in fact the One who in the full majesty of God is *unlike* all other people who is *like* them as this One. In fellowship with Jesus, therefore, to be human is to be with this correspondence, reflection and representation of the uniqueness and transcendence of God, to be with the One who is unlike us. To be human is thus to be in this the true and absolute Counterpart.

Basically and comprehensively, therefore, to be human is *to be with God.* What human beings are in this Counterpart is obviously the basic and comprehensive determination of their true being. Whatever else they are, they are on the basis of the fact that they are with Jesus and therefore with God. We shall have to explain and develop this basic determination — that they are with God. But with it we have already reached the point at which human reality has its origin, in which the whole creaturely being of humanity is summed up, behind which we can never go, and from which we can never abstract in considering any specific determination of this being. If it is not indifferent, incidental or subordinate, but ontologically decisive, that one human being among all others is the human Jesus; if to be human is to dwell with this human being who is our true and absolute Counterpart; if to be human is to be concretely confronted with this human being who is like us for all that he is so unlike in the full majesty of God, then the fact that we are with God is not merely one of many determinations of our being, derivative and mutable, but the *basic determination*, original and immutable.

Godlessness is not, therefore, a possibility, but an ontological impossibility for humanity. Humanity is not without, but with God. This is not to say, of course, that godless people do not exist. Sin is undoubtedly committed and exists. Yet sin itself is not a possibility but an ontological impossibility for humanity. We are actually with Jesus, i.e., with God. This means that our being does not include but excludes sin. To be in sin, in godlessness, is a mode of being contrary to our humanity. For the person who is with Jesus — and this is humanity's ontological determination — is with God. If they deny God, they deny themselves. They are then something which they cannot be in the Counterpart in which they are. They choose their own impossibility. And every offence in which godlessness can express itself, e.g., unbelief and idolatry, doubt and indifference to God, is as such, both in its theoretical and practical forms, an offence with which human beings burden, obscure and corrupt themselves. It is an attack on the continuance of their own creatureliness: not a superficial, temporary or endurable attack, but a radical, central and fatal attack on its very foundation, and therefore its continuance. Their very being as human is endangered by every surrender to sin. And conversely, every vindication and restoration of their relation to God is a vindication and restoration of their being as human. For they themselves as humans are with Jesus and therefore with God. They themselves stand from the very first and inescapably in the order which this fact implies. They themselves are thus upheld if they keep to this order, and they plunge into the void if they fall away from it. . . .

Humanity is with God because we are with Jesus. And everything that is to be said in explanation and expansion of the fact that we are with God will result from the fact that we are with Jesus. But first we must emphasize that the *particularity* of humanity as compared with other creatures is contained in this ontological determination of our being. In a general sense it can and must be said of all other creatures as such that they have their being in the fact that they are with God. God is the Creator of heaven and earth as well as humanity. And whatever is, is at its very roots because God is, and by the fact that he is; that he is the Creator of all creatures, great and small, visible and invisible; that he has willed and posited their being and nature and does not cease but continues to do so. All creatures are as God is with them and they are therefore with God. But not every creature is with God as humanity is with God. This does not mean, of course, that we must rush to the perverse conclusion that the particular thing which is so basically true of humanity is not also true of other creatures in their way, namely, that they are originally and decisively with Jesus, and in this way with God their Creator, and thus participant in being. . . .

We can and must, therefore, say of every creature that it has the same concrete divine Counterpart as humanity; and to that extent the same ontological basis. In respect of all other creatures, we can and must look confidently to the same ontological basis. But in the case of non-human creatures we do not know what it means that they have this basis. We state their (for us) impenetrable secret when, looking in the same direction as we may and must look in regard to ourselves, we say of them too that they are with God. We know only that they are this. We do not know how. For when we say of them, too, that they are with Jesus and therefore with God, the decisive and distinguishing thing is that the God who is also their God did not become like them. He was not made an animal, a plant, a stone, a star or an element of the invisible heavenly world. But he did become human. It was in this way that in his incomparable majesty he was made like the creature. It was in this human being and not in any other creature that he saw the meaning and motive of his whole creative work. It is only in the human and not in any other creaturely sphere that the creaturely correspondence, image and representation of the uniqueness and transcendence of God has been actualized as an event. Of the other created spheres we know only that the God who has created all other people and all other creatures for the sake of this one human being confronts them in majestic dissimilarity. In the other spheres of creation we see no comparable Representative and Revealer of the majestic transcendence of God, no creature to reflect and represent the uniqueness and transcendence of God as distinct from other creatures.

This happens only in the human sphere, and it is only as it happens in this sphere that it is valid and effectual for all other spheres and for the whole of creation. As in the form of a human creature the Creator becomes the true and absolute Counterpart of all other human creatures, he is also the true and absolute Counterpart of all creatures whatsoever. As *humanity* is with Jesus and therefore with God, the same is true of all other creatures. We do not know how, but we know that it is the case. And the very significance for all spheres of what happens in the human sphere forbids us to suppose that there is something similar in others, that there might be a kind of identity between the Creator and the creature. God did not need to become an animal, a plant, or a stone because when he became human everything necessary was done for animals, plants and stones to be with him as their Creator. How and to what extent? We can give no answer by studying animals, plants and stones. And it is the fact that we cannot do so, that this is concealed from us, which from our standpoint distinguishes them from ourselves. No matter how they are with Jesus and therefore with God, the fact remains that they are, quite irrespective of us or anything without. But we for our part are distinguished from them by the fact that the decisive event of the correspondence, repetition and representation of the uniqueness and transcendence of God does not take place among them but in our *human* sphere; that we as human beings have the divine Counterpart before us in that one human being; and that the implied fellowship with God cannot be for us the mystery which it must be when we consider the rest of creation. As human beings, and therefore as direct neighbors, companions and brothers of the human being Jesus, we do not stand indirectly but immediately and directly in the light of this divine Counterpart. *What constitutes the hidden being of all creatures is revealed as human being because Jesus is human.* And it is the fact that human being is revealed as being with God which constitutes its particularity. If we affirm and stress this fact, it is not in arrogance towards other creatures, but as an act of humility in face of the secret of God in other spheres and its revelation in our human sphere. It should not be forgotten that in this way the particularity of other creatures is also emphasized. The glory of other creatures lies in the concealment of their being with God, no less than ours in its disclosure. For all we know, their glory may well be the greater. We do not really know that the outer circle of all other creatures exists for the sake of the inner circle of humanity. The very opposite may well be the case. Or perhaps both circles, the outer and the inner, have their own autonomy and dignity, their distinctive form of being with God. What does this difference amount to as against the fact that the human being Jesus as a creaturely being is the focal point of both circles? But when this is said in rebuttal of human pride we must not fail to recognize as such the special grace conferred upon humanity. Since Jesus as the Bearer of the divine uniqueness and transcendence is like humanity, *God* is revealed to humanity, and in this confrontation with

God humanity is revealed to *us.* Knowing ourselves, and knowing why we can know ourselves, knowing our being as a being with God and knowing why we can know our being as a being with God, we know our singularity among all creatures. For we can know our own being as a being with God because the being of the creature with God is not hidden but revealed in the human sphere. In this sphere the Creator has become a creature, making himself a creature for all his unlikeness to other creatures. On the basis of the election of the human being Jesus, this sphere is singled out from all others. *(CD: III/2, 132-139)*

*

THE CHRISTIAN COMMUNITY

The selections on the church come from Paragraph 62 on "The Holy Spirit and the Gathering of the Christian Community" and Paragraph 67 on "The Holy Spirit and the Upbuilding of the Christian Community." They belong in the Doctrine of Reconciliation because restoring community between God and humanity simultaneously means the re-creating of human community in the world by the Holy Spirit. Indeed, Barth regards the church as a parable and a promise to the whole world: it is a provisional representation of all humanity justified and reconciled to God.

These selections deal, first, with the church as event in its full — and problematic — human visibility, and secondly with the unity of the church. In the third excerpt Barth argues that the church, to be truly the church, is entirely dependent on the activity of the Holy Spirit in its midst; without this it would only be a religious society, a "semblance of a church." The fourth excerpt is on "the growth of the community" which happens not by human techniques, or the following of sociological "laws," but by the presence of Jesus in the Spirit.

The Being of the Community

As the work of the Holy Spirit the Christian community, Christendom, the church is a work which takes place among humanity in the form of a human activity. Therefore it not only has a history, but — like humanity[62] — it exists only as a definite history takes place, that is to say, only as it is gathered and lets itself be gathered and gathers itself by the living Jesus Christ through the Holy Spirit. To describe its being we must abandon the usual distinctions between being and act, static and dynamic, essence and existence. Precisely its act is its genuine being, its dynamic is its stability, its existence is its essence. The church *is* when it takes place that God lets certain people live as his servants, friends and children, the witnesses of the reconciliation of the world with himself as it has taken place in Jesus Christ, the preachers of the victory which has been won in him over sin and suffering and death, the heralds of his future revelation in which the glory of the Creator will be declared to all creation as that of his love and faithfulness and mercy. The church *is* when it happens to these people in common that they may receive the verdict on the whole world of humanity which has been pronounced in the resurrection of Jesus Christ from the dead. By the pronunciation of this verdict, which they can receive and have received by the awakening power of the Holy Spirit, they are gathered and they allow themselves to be gathered, they gather themselves, as they have received it and do receive it. The church *is* when these people subject themselves to the law of the Gospel, "the law of the Spirit of life" (Rom. 8.2), when they become obedient to it, when they keep to the fact, as to an imperative which is true of all of them in common, that God was and is and will be faithful to humanity in his great wrath against human unfaithfulness to him, that he has given himself up for humanity in his Son, that in this One he has re-established his own damaged right and the lost right of humanity, that in him he has maintained and fulfilled his covenant and concluded eternal peace. The church *is* when these people as the first-fruits of all creation can know and have to acknowledge the Lord of the world in his faithfulness as the Lord of the covenant which he has maintained and fulfilled, and therefore as their Lord. The church *is* in the particular relationship of these people, when this is possible and actual under the sovereignty of Jesus Christ in their common hearing and obeying, when they can make a common response with their existence to the work of Jesus Christ received by them as Word. . . .

It is unquestionable that the *communio*, too, is not the being of a state or institution, but the being of an event, in which the assembled and self-assembling community is actively at work: the living community of the living Lord Jesus Christ in the fulfilment of its existence. The church *is* when it *happens*, and it takes place in the form of a sequence and nexus of definite human *activities*. In these human activities as such it can be studied from the very beginning of our era by all those who have the opportunity and give to it the necessary attention. It is a phenomenon of world history which can be grasped in historical and psychological and sociological terms like any other. There is, there takes place, a gathering and separation of certain people to this community. This involves — in varying degrees of strictness or looseness — an ecclesiastical organization and constitution and order. In this gathering and separation there takes place its cultus, teaching, preaching, instruction, theology, confession, and all in definite relationships to the political and economic and social conditions and movements, to the scholarship and art and morality, of the surrounding world. It all develops in and with this world, but according to its own laws, with a tradition which is in many ways related and in many ways differentiated, with its distinctive purpose and stamp, but with obvious connections and similarities and reciprocal actions in relation to other human phenomena and their history. It is a specific and yet also an integrated, a distinctive and yet not a unique element in the whole of human culture, its achievements and its destinies. In all this — to use the term which has become classical — the church is visible, *ecclesia visibilis*. It is one historical factor with others, asserting itself and immediately noticeable as such. Nor is it, as it were, accidental or *per nefas* that it is visible in this way. It is essential to it to be so; just as essential as that in another sense it should be invisible: *ecclesia invisibilis*. The work of the Holy Spirit to which it owes its existence is something which is produced concretely and historically in this world. It is the awakening power of the Word made flesh, of the Son of God, who himself entered the lowliness of an historical existence in this world, who as true God became and is truly human. Like begets like. The Christian faith awakened by him is a definite human activity and therefore a definite human phenomenon. For all the peculiarity of his activity the Christian is an ordinary person among other human companions. Similarly the Christendom in which there are Christians is a human work and as such a human phenomenon which can be generally observed. Where there is this awakening, where the church is born of the Word of God (Zwingli), itself "the mother which conceives and bears every Christian by the Word of God which it reveals and produces, enlightening and kindling the hearts so that they grasp and receive and cling and hold fast to it" (Luther), there there arises in some form a historical quantity which can be observed, which is at work and which can be calculated in historical terms.

According to the Gospels, the church came into being quite visibly with the calling of the twelve apostles who were all named and who correspond in number to the twelve tribes of Israel. It developed visibly with the addition of the thousands on the day of Pentecost, and among the Gentiles in the form of the ἐκκλησίαι of Asia Minor, Greece and Rome, and later the whole Mediterranean littoral, and then the far North and East and South — a very visible counterpart to the visible temporal Empire. In the world of Constantine the

Great and of Charlemagne and later of the Houses of Saxony and Hohen-
stauffen, it assumed visible forms which can only be described as terrifying. It
again took historical form in consequence of the denial of Evangelical renewal in the 16th century, and the necessity to re-establish itself in relation to
this renewal. And the Reformers guarded themselves very carefully against
the idea that by the church they meant only a *civitas platonica*, the pure idea of a
Christian community and therefore only an invisible church. They at once
gave themselves to the task of building on the ruins of the past a new and visible church based on the newly perceived Word of God and in new obedience
to that Word. And they succeeded well enough in a form which is also to some
extent terrifying. And since then, whenever it has been thought that such
reconstruction is necessary and possible, it has always been — and no sect,
however spiritual, can completely escape it — with a certain visibility, with a
separation which every eye can see, with the establishment of certain cultic
and intellectual and legal and social and aesthetic forms which mark it off
more or less distinctively from other temporal or religious societies or from
other forms of the Christian community. The church never has been and
never is absolutely invisible.

There is an *ecclesiastical Docetism*[63] which will not accept this, which
paradoxically tries to overlook the visibility of the church, explaining
away its earthly and historical form as something indifferent, or angrily
negating it, or treating it only as a necessary evil, in order to magnify an
invisible community of the Spirit and of spirits. This view is just as
impossible as Christological Docetism, not only in point of history, but
also in point of substance. For the work of the Holy Spirit as the awakening power of Jesus Christ would not take place at all if the invisible did
not become visible, if the Christian community did not take on and have
an earthly-historical form. The individual Christian can exist only in
time and space as a doer of the Word (Jas. 1.22) and therefore in a concrete human form and basically visible to everyone. Similarly the
Christian community as such cannot exist as an ideal commune or universum, but — also in time and space — only in the relationship of its
individual members as they are fused together by the common action of
the Word which they have heard into a definite human community; in
concrete form, therefore, and visible to everyone. If we say with the
creed *credo ecclesiam*, we do not proudly overlook its concrete form; just
as when we confess *credo resurrectionem carnis* we cannot overlook the real
and whole people who are souls and yet also bodies, we cannot overlook
their hopes as though the resurrection was not also promised them. Nor
do we look penetratingly through this form, as though it was only some-

thing transparent and the real church had to be sought behind it; just as we cannot overlook or look through the pleasing or less pleasing face of the neighbor whom we are commanded to love. We look at the visible aspect of the church — this is the state of it. And as we look at what is seen — not beside it or behind but in it — we see what is not seen. Hence we cannot rid ourselves in this way of the generally visible side of the church. We cannot take refuge from it in a kind of wonderland. The *credo ecclesiam* can and necessarily will involve much distinguishing and questioning, much concern and shame. It can and necessarily will be a very critical *credo.* In relation to the side of the church which is generally visible it can and necessarily will express what does not amount to much more than a hope and a yearning. But it does take the church quite seriously in its common visibility — which is its earthly and historical existence. It confesses faith in the invisible aspect which is the secret of the visible. Believing in the *ecclesia invisibilis* we will enter the sphere of labor and conflict of the *ecclesia visibilis.* Without doing this, without a discriminate but serious participation in the historical life of the community, its activity, its upbuilding, its mission, in a kind of purely theoretical and abstract churchliness, no one has ever seriously repeated the *credo ecclesiam.* Those who try to repeat it in a way which looks above the church, only dreaming of its existence in time and space, must see to it that they are not secretly pandering to a Christological Docetism as well, or, at any rate, that they are really taking seriously the true humanity of Jesus Christ. Faith in his community has this in common with faith in him, that it, too, relates to a reality in time and space, and therefore to something which is at bottom generally visible. If, then, we believe in him, we cannot refuse — however hesitantly or anxiously or contentiously — to believe in his community in its spatio-temporal existence, and therefore to be a member of it and personally a Christian. We will return to the implications of this in the second part of the doctrine of reconciliation under the title of the true humanity of Jesus Christ. For the moment it is enough to point to it by way of demarcation.

When we have done this, the emphasis in the present context must be upon the fact that the community called into being by the Holy Spirit, although it does not exist and must not be sought abstractly in the invisible, also does not exist and must not be sought abstractly in the visible. It does exist openly in a very concrete form, a historical phenomenon like any other. But what it is, the character, the truth of its existence in time and space, is not a matter of a general but a very special visibility. Without this it is invisible. What is visible to all is the event of the *congre-*

gatio and *communio* of certain people, its characteristic activities and achievements, its peculiarities by which it is distinguished from other historical structures, its deficiencies which it has with them in common, its relative advantages. But what actually takes place, what this is in truth, is not visible to all; it is visible to Christians only in this particular way or not at all. Without this special visibility all that can be seen is the people united in it and their common activity, and this will be explained in terms of the categories which are regarded as the most appropriate for the understanding and appraisal of common human activities, with an attempt to subordinate it to some picture of the world and of history. On this view it can be understood as a religious society within human society generally and side by side with other organizations. The attention paid to it will be with reference to its past and present in this connection and on this level. Its structure and message and claims and activity as this particular society within or side by side with others, its greater or lesser, welcome or unwelcome significance and co-operation and power in the spheres of culture and the state, will be registered and either lauded or tolerated, supported or contested, with varying degrees of attention. It will be taken seriously, but within the limits of the two-dimensional view in which it can be generally known, as one earthly-historical factor with others. And when we say that we are already saying too much, because on this view there cannot be any other but earthly-historical factors. . . .

It is plain that fundamentally the church is forced to acknowledge the picture which it offers on this view. Indeed it is essential to it to be external, to exist in the dimensions of this level, and therefore to offer this external picture. It is equally plain that for its own part it cannot agree to be seen and understood for what it is in this external picture as such. It has to know the third dimension of its existence. Yet it also has to know that it is defenceless against the interpretations to which it is subject on this two-dimensional view. For where there is not this special visibility, where there cannot be an insight into its earthly and historical form, even what it can confess and ever so impressively explain concerning its true being as visible in this external picture will, of course, have its greater or lesser interest as its particular ideology and may even be noted with a nod of the head, but it will at once be translated onto the historical and psychological and sociological level and irresistibly absorbed into the external picture as such. No matter what attitude it takes up, what it is will still be invisible, and for the first time genuinely invisible. And then it will always be tempted to give way, to see and understand itself only in this external picture, to acquiesce in it, to be a kind of religious society, to build itself up and to develop as such, to be active, setting itself aims and achieving results as such, to live peaceably with the rest of society on this basis and in this sphere, even to assert itself — perhaps with a certain measure of triumph but certainly with assurance, because, like everything else on this level, religion can always present itself as a necessary human need, and because it is unquestionably in a position to meet that need. But this is a temptation which comes to the church from without, from its own humanity. From within it will never find itself tempted to try to exist only in two dimensions and therefore in an abstract visibility. From within, in the light of its awakening by the Holy Spirit, it will always have to see and understand and confess itself in three dimensions, whether this is understood from without or not.   *(CD: IV/1, 650-656)*

*

Our present question is the gathering of the community by the Holy Spirit, the one single being of the one single community. And we can name only one authority which is fundamentally indispensable, necessary to salvation, infallible and unconditionally effective to guarantee its existence as such in the geographically separate communities: the Lord who attests himself in the prophetic and apostolic word, who is active by his Spirit, who as the Spirit has promised to be in the midst of every community gathered by him and in his name. He rules the church and therefore the churches. He is the basis and guarantee of their unity.

We cannot name any other *legitimate* plurality of churches, one which does not destroy but affirms their unity, other than those which we have mentioned already, the visible and the invisible, the militant and the triumphant church, Israel and the Christian community, and the local congregations. Any other plurality means the co-existence of churches which are genuinely divided. That is, in the event of their gathering, and therefore by their basis and invisible being, in their faith, although they all regard it as the Christian faith, they are so different from one another and confront one another as such strangers that they cannot recognize and acknowledge one another, at any rate seriously, as the community of Jesus Christ. At best they will be able kindly to tolerate one another as believing differently, and at worst they will fight against one another, mutually excluding each other with some definiteness and force. The existence of this kind of plurality of "churches" is in *conflict* with both Eph. 4 and the *credo unam ecclesiam*. Under no head and in no sense can it be regarded as legitimate. Certainly it is possible to understand and explain historically the separation and opposition of such churches. Certainly in the sphere of state and society their co-existence and opposition can be made tolerable for participants and non-participants alike with the assistance or under the supremacy of the doctrine of toleration. Certainly it can be stabilized and canalized in terms of practical law. Certainly among the more enlightened on both sides, or perhaps with some depth even among a majority of those who believe differently, there may arise a tacit or to some extent perhaps even an explicit agreement as to the relative and temporary nature of the opposition, with more or less radical glimpses of a unity which is already present in some point of convergence. It may also be that for good reasons or bad the consciousness of existing differences becomes blunted in whole groups of churches, so that they become an external factor without internal necessity. There is *no* justification — theological, spiritual or biblical — for the existence of a plurality of churches genuinely separated in this way and mutually excluding one another internally and therefore externally. A *plurality* of churches in this sense means a plurality of *lords*, a plurality of *spirits*, a plurality of *gods*. There is no doubt that to the extent that Christendom does consist of actually different and opposing churches, to that extent it denies practically what it confesses theoretically — the unity and the singularity of God, of Jesus Christ, of the Holy Spirit. There may be good grounds for the rise of these divisions. There may be serious obstacles to their removal. There may be many things which can be said by way of interpretation and mitigation. But this does not alter the fact that every division as such is a deep riddle, a scandal. And in face of this scandal the whole of Christendom should be united in being able to think of it only with penitence, not with the penitence which each expects of the other, but with the penitence in which — whatever may be the cost — each is willing to precede the other. Whoever can acquiesce in divisions, whoever can even take pleasure in them, whoever can be complacent in relation to the obvious faults and errors of others and therefore their own responsibility for them, then such people may be good and loyal confessors in the sense of their own particular denominations, they may be good Roman Catholics or Reformèd or Orthodox or Baptists, but they must not imagine that they are good Christians. They have not honestly and seriously believed and known and confessed the *una ecclesia*. For the *una ecclesia* cannot exist if there is a second or third side by side with or opposed to it. It cannot exist in opposition to another church. It cannot be one among many.

241

(CD: IV/1, 674-676)

§67 THE HOLY SPIRIT AND THE UPBUILDING OF THE CHRISTIAN COMMUNITY

The Holy Spirit is the quickening power with which Jesus the Lord builds up Christianity in the world as his body, i.e., as the earthly-historical form of his own existence, causing it to grow, sustaining and ordering it as the community of his saints, and thus fitting it to give a provisional representation of the sanctification of all humanity and human life as it has taken place in him.

The True Church

The upbuilding of the Christian community and then Christian love are the two themes which we have still to discuss at the conclusion of this second part of the doctrine of reconciliation. In these spheres, too, we have to do with the divine work of *sanctification* as a special form of the reconciliation of the world with God which was and is and will be an event in Jesus Christ. The difference in relation to our previous path can consist only in the fact that we are now looking especially at what is effected, and therefore actual, in this divine work. The powerful and living direction of the Resurrected, of the living Lord Jesus, and therefore the Holy Spirit, whom we have had to understand as the principle of sanctification, effects the upbuilding of the Christian community, and in and with it the eventuation of Christian love; the existence of Christendom, and in and with it the existence of individual Christians.

It seems as though we might (and perhaps should) reverse the order and say that the Holy Spirit effects the eventuation of Christian love and therefore the existence of individual Christians, and in and with this the upbuilding of the Christian community and therefore the existence of Christendom. But this is only in appearance. If it is true that Christian love is that which (with Christian faith and Christian hope) makes an individual a Christian, we have to remember that the individual person does not become a Christian, and live as such, in a vacuum, but in a definite historical context, i.e., in and with the upbuilding of the Christian community. One does so on the basis and in the meaning and purpose of the existence of the community, in specific participation in its upbuilding, and in the exercise of its faith and love and hope. Calvin is thus right when he takes up a comparison already used by Cyprian and Augustine and calls the church (*Instit.* IV, 1, 1) the "mother" of all believers. . . .

At the beginning of the previous section we stated that in the work of sanctification God has to do with a community [*Volk*] of humanity (consisting, of course, of individuals); and that this corresponds to the fact that in this work, as in that of reconciliation generally, his purpose is originally and ultimately for the whole world of humanity as such. As Jesus Christ is the Reconciler of all people and in this way (in his community with all) the Reconciler of each individual person, so as the Head of his community he is the Lord of its many members, and in this way (in his special community with these many, with this particular people) the Head of each of its constituents. At a later stage we shall have to raise the question what makes a person a Christian, and speak of Christian love. But we have first to see and understand the context to which this question and the answer to it belong, and thus to consider that what takes place in the work of the Holy Spirit is the upbuilding of the community.

The fact that we are now considering what is *effected* in the work of sanctification cannot mean — either when we speak of the Christian community or of Christian love — that we have to turn our back on the action of God in Jesus Christ by the Holy Spirit and to occupy ourselves *in abstracto* with a human being, doing, and work as its result.

We are, of course, dealing with a work done in common by a group of people within humanity and its history when we speak first of the upbuilding of the community. Sanctification generally is concerned with human being, doing, and work; with the wholly divine stimulation and characterization of the existence of those upon whom it comes as something distinctive. So, too, the form of sanctification which we have now to discuss is concerned with the work of the quickening power of his spirit with which Jesus Christ builds up Christianity within the world; with the divine inauguration, control and support of the human action which takes place among Christians. . . .

It is clear, however, that to see and understand that which is effected by God, the church, in its true reality, we have not to lose sight even momentarily or incidentally of the occurrence of the divine operation, and therefore concretely of the divine work of upbuilding the community of Jesus Christ. The church is, of course, a human, earthly-historical construct, whose history involves from the very first, and always will involve, human action. But it is *this* human construct, the Christian church, because and as God is at work in it by his Holy Spirit. In virtue of this happening, which is of divine origin and takes place for human beings and to them as the determination of their human action, the true church truly is and arises and continues and lives in the twofold sense that God is at work and that there is a human work which he occasions and fashions. Except in this history whose subject is God — but the God who acts for and to and with specific people — it is not the true church. Nor is it visible as such except in relation to this history.

Thus, to see the true church, we cannot look abstractly at what a human work seems to be in itself. This would not be a genuine phenomenon but a false. The real result of the divine operation, the human action which takes place in the true church as occasioned and fashioned by God, will never try to be anything in itself, but only the divine operation, the divine work of sanctification, the upbuilding of Christianity by the Holy Spirit of Jesus the Lord, by which it is inaugurated and controlled and supported. To the extent that it is anything in itself, it is the phenomenon of the mere semblance of a church, and it is only this semblance, and not the true church, that we shall see when we consider this phenomenon. . . .

The Christian community, the true church, arises and is only as the Holy Spirit works — the quickening power of the living Lord Jesus Christ. And it continues and is only as he sanctifies people and their human work, building up them and their work into the true church. He does this, however, in the time between the resurrection and the return of Jesus Christ and therefore in the time of the community[64] in the world, i.e., in this context the human world which participates only in the particular and provisional revelation of Jesus Christ and to that extent is still a prisoner to the flesh and sin and death. Christianity, too, belongs to this world, and works and thinks and speaks and acts in it — even though its action is occasioned and fashioned by that of the Holy Spirit. Even at best, then, its action is an equivocal witness to the fact that it is occasioned and fashioned in this way. And there may be the less good cases, the bad and even the worst, when the witness that it ought to give is either omitted or obscured and falsified; when human pride or sloth, or both together, is what is expressed and revealed as the work of the divine sanctifying and upbuilding. In short, it is to be feared — for this is where its determination by human pride and sloth ultimately leads — that it will express and reveal very little but itself; itself as occasioned and fashioned by God, but with this high consciousness and pretentious claim; itself and not the divine occasioning and fashioning which are its true meaning and power; the semblance of a church, therefore, and not the true church. This is the particular sin which to some extent is always committed where the community arises and continues here and now.

Nor is it something self-evident, but always the omnipotent act of a special divine mercy, if the church is not merely the semblance of a church, but in spite of the sinfulness of the human action of Christians a true church, and expressed and revealed as such. In its own strength this is quite impossible. Its institutions and traditions and even its reformations are no guarantee as such that it is the true church, for in all these things we have to do with human and therefore sinful action, and therefore in some sense with a self-expression in which it can be only the semblance of a church. If the divine occasioning and fashioning of this human action take place in spite of it, i.e., of its sinful tendency, this is not a quality of the church in which it actualizes its reality but the triumph of the power of Jesus Christ upbuilding it; an omnipotent act of the special divine mercy addressed to it, which makes use of the human and sinful action of the community but does not proceed from it and cannot be understood in terms of it. . . .

We have also to consider the relevance of the matter to the question of the *visibility* of the church. Are we not forced to put it as follows, namely, that the true church (its upbuilding by God as the basis and determination of what people want and do and achieve) becomes visible as in the power of the Holy Spirit (the same Holy Spirit by whose victorious operation it is the true church) it emerges and shines out from its concealment both in that which is established and traditional and customary and also in innovation and change? This emergence and shining illustrate the *freedom* of grace; the mighty act of the *particular* divine mercy which takes place when in spite of its sinful tendency the human action of Christians does not attest itself but its basis and meaning, depicting and expressing the divine sanctifying and upbuilding. This takes place only as we can see and read the dark letters of an electric sign when the current is passed through it. We can never see the true church as we can see a state in its citizens and officials and organs and laws and institutions. We can, of course, see the members of the church, and its officials and constitutions and orders, its dogmatics and cultus, its organizations and societies, its leaders with their politics, and its laity, its art and press — and all these in the context of its history. Where else is the church visible if not in these? If it is not visible in these, it is obviously not visible at all. But is it really visible in these? Not immediately and directly. This something which claims to be the church, and is before us all in these manifestations, may well be only the semblance of a church, in which human will and work, although they allege that they are occasioned and fashioned by God, are striving to express only themselves. What is visible in all this may be only a religious society. And if we assume, not only that this is not the case, but that what we have here is really the true church, it is not self-evident that this will be visible as such in all these things; that its actuality will be eloquent truth. As it cannot create or confer its *reality*, the same is true of its *visibility*. It can only be endowed with it. If it is also visible as a true church, this means that the victory of the divine operation, the mighty act of the Holy Spirit in face of the sinfulness of human action, finds further expression in a free emergence and outshining of the true church from the concealment in which it is enveloped by the sinfulness of all human volition (and therefore of ecclesiastical), and in which it must continue to be enveloped apart from this continuation of the operation of the Holy Spirit. It will be always in the *revelation* of God that the true church is visible. And it will be always in *faith* awakened by this revelation that it is actually seen by men and women — at the place where without revelation and faith there is to be seen (perhaps in a very confusing and deceptive way) only this many-sided ecclesiastical entity in all its ambiguity.

It is in this sense that we count on the fact that the church is a true church, and visible as such, and in this confidence thus turn our attention to the history in which its being and visibility as the true church have their living basis. We have called this the divine inauguration and control and support of the human action which takes place in the community and in which Christianity exists in the world. And we will gather up this whole happening under the concept of the upbuilding of the Christian community. In this first sub-section we shall take a comprehensive glance at the whole in explanation of this title.

This history has a *direction* and a *goal*. This is the first point to be noticed if we are to see and understand it. What is at issue has been stated in the concluding part of our introductory thesis. The Holy Spirit is the power by which Jesus Christ fits his community "to give a provisional representation of the sanctification of all humanity and human life as it has taken place in him."

The existence of the true church is not an end in itself. The divine operation by which it is vivified and constituted makes it quite impossible that its existence as the true church should be understood as the goal of God's will for it. The divine operation in virtue of which it becomes and is a true church makes it a movement in the direction of an end which is not reached with the fact that it exists as a true church, but merely indicated and attested by this fact. On the way, moving in the direction of this goal, it can and should serve its Lord. For this reason it will not be the true church at all to the extent that it tries to express itself rather than the divine operation by which it is constituted. As such it will reveal itself, or be revealed, in glory at this goal; yet only as the church which does not try to seek and express and glorify itself, but absolutely to subordinate itself and its witness, placing itself unreservedly in the service and under the control of that which God wills for it and works within it.

The goal in the direction of which the true church proceeds and moves is the revelation of the *sanctification of all humanity and human life* as it has already taken place *de iure* in Jesus Christ. In the exaltation of the one Jesus, who as the Son of God became a servant in order as such to become the Lord of all people, there has been accomplished already in powerful archetype, not only the cancellation of the sins and therefore the justification, but also the elevation and establishment of all humanity and human life and therefore its sanctification. That this is the case is the theme and content of the witness with which his community is charged. It comes from the first revelation (in the resurrection of Jesus Christ) of the reconciliation of the world with God as it has taken place in this sense too. And it moves towards its final manifestation in the coming again of Jesus Christ. Christianity is the holy community of the intervening period; the congregation or people which knows this elevation and establishment, this sanctification, not merely *de iure* but already *de facto*, and which is therefore a witness to all others, representing the sanctification which has already come upon them too in Jesus Christ. This representation is provisional. It is provisional because it has not yet achieved it, nor will it do so. It can only attest it "in the puzzling form of a reflection" (1 Cor. 13.12). And it is provisional because, although it comes from the resurrection of Jesus Christ, it is only on the way with others to his return, and therefore to the direct and universal and definitive revelation of his work as it has been accomplished for them and for all people. The fact that it is provisional means that it is fragmentary and incomplete and insecure and questionable; for even the community still participates in the darkness which cannot apprehend, if it also cannot overcome, the light (Jn. 1.5). But the fact that it is provisional means also — for in this provisional way it represents the sanctification of humanity as it has taken place in Jesus Christ — that divine work is done within it truly and effectively, genuinely and invincibly, and in all its totality, so that even though it is concealed in many different ways it continually emerges and shines out from this concealment in the form of God's people. It is with this provisional representation that we have to do on the way and in the movement of the true church. It is to accomplish it that it is on its way and in this movement. It is in order that it may accomplish it that its time is given; the time between the times, between the first and the final revelation of the work of God accomplished in Jesus Christ. The meaning and content of our time — the last time — is the fulfilment of this provisional representation as the task of the community of Jesus Christ. *(CD: IV/2, 614-621)*

*

As we recognize the life of the community in its growth, and its power of life in its power to grow, we are brought face to face with the question which has not yet been answered in this discussion — that of the nature of this indwelling or immanent (!) power of the community. We may give a preliminary answer in the second and very simple statement that the community lives as the communion of saints because and as Jesus lives. Jesus is the power of life immanent within it; the power by which it grows and therefore lives. This is what we must now explain.

In the thesis at the head of the section we have spoken of the Holy Spirit as the quickening power by which Christianity is built up as the true church in the world. But as we made it clear it is *Jesus the Lord* who is at work in this quickening power of the Holy Spirit. And we must now take up again that which we have already said, and maintain that according to the normative view of the New Testament the Holy Spirit is the authentic and effective self-attestation of the risen and living Lord Jesus; his self-attestation as the Resurrected, the living One, the Lord, the exalted Son of Man, in whom there has already been attained the sanctification of all people, but also the particular, factual sanctification of Christians — their union with him and therefore with one another. In the Holy Spirit as his self-attestation we know him; which means again that we know him as the Resurrected, the living One, the Lord, the exalted Son of Man, in whose exaltation all people are sanctified, and especially, factually and concretely Christians, who are distinguished in the first instance from all other people by his self-attestation and therefore by their knowledge. In the Holy Spirit as the self-attestation of Jesus they thus know themselves in and with him; themselves in their union with him, and also with one another, in the fellowship of faith and love and hope in which they express themselves as his and find self-awareness as this people which has a common descent. It is in this sense that the Holy Spirit as the self-attestation of Jesus is the quickening power by which Christianity is awakened and gathered and built up to a true church in the world. As the self-attestation of Jesus the Holy Spirit achieves the *communio sanctorum* and causes it to grow (intensively and extensively). It lives by his power — from the very first and on all its way and ways in the realization of the relationship of the *sancti* to the *sancta* right up to its goal at the end of all history when it will meet the *eschaton* which will be the *eschaton* of the cosmos. But to understand this in all its fulness of meaning we must be clear that the Holy Spirit by which the community lives and becomes and was and is and will be is the *self-attestation of Jesus.*

The power with which he works is *not*, then, only a remote operation of Jesus. It is indeed this. Risen from the dead, ascended into heaven, seated at the right hand of God the Father, Jesus is remote from earthly history and the community which exists in it. He is unattainably superior to it. He is separated from it by an abyss which cannot be bridged. He is even hidden from it in God (Col. 3.3) — and with him, of course, the true life of the community. He (and its true life) cannot be violated or controlled by it. If in spite of this he is still at work in earthly history, and in the community as it exists in it, by the quickening power of his Holy Spirit, we can certainly call this his operation at a distance. From the point to which there is no way, from heaven, from the throne, from the right hand of God, from his hiddenness in God, he overcomes that abyss in the Holy Spirit, operating here from that exalted status, working in time, in which the *communio sanctorum* is an event and has its history in many events, from the eternity of the life which he has in common with God. The man Jesus has also that form of existence, so that it is quite true that his action towards his community in the quickening power of the Holy Spirit is a remote operation.

But this is only the one aspect of his action, and if we are to understand it as the power of growth and life which does not only reach it from the majesty of God, touching and impelling it from without, but also as that which indwells and is immanent to it, it is the second aspect which we must now consider. It is to be noted that this does not replace the other. The first aspect remains. The human being Jesus is above, superior even to his community and remote from it in absolute transcendence; and with him, so too is its own true life. He has and maintains also that heavenly form of existence characterized by his unique community with God. He exists also at the right hand of God the Father where we human beings, even we Christians are not; where even the *communio sanctorum* is not. Thus the Holy Spirit, too, is the power which quickens from above, from a distance, from God; from the God who dwells in light unapproachable. But the second aspect has also to be considered. For what does it mean to speak of there and here, height and depth, near and far, when we speak of the One who is not only the true Son of Man but also the true Son of God, the human being who, exalted by the self-humiliation of the divine person to human existence, exists in living community with God? It certainly does not mean that these antitheses are .emoved and obliterated and equated in him. But since God is not limited to be there, since he is not the prisoner of his own height and distance, it certainly means that in the human being Jesus who is also the true Son of God, these antitheses, while they remain, are comprehended and controlled; that he has power over them; that he can be here as well as there, in the depth as well as in the height, near as well as remote, and therefore immanent in the *communio sanctorum* on earth as well as transcendent to it. He can have an earthly-historical form of existence as well as a heavenly-historical. He can create and sustain and rule the *communio sanctorum* on earth. He can exist in it in earthly-historical form. We speak of his heavenly form of existence, of the form in which he exists in the height and distance and hiddenness of God, when with the New Testament we speak of him as the Head of his community. But we speak of his earthly-historical form of existence, of the form in which, in the sovereignty of the same God, he also exists here and now with sinners in this history which has not yet concluded, when again with the New Testament we speak of the community as his body.[65] And in both cases, and either way, we speak of the *one* human being Jesus Christ. It is he who is both there and here. It is he who is both the Head and the body. Similarly, the life of Christians as the life of those sanctified in him is one. With him as its Head it is hidden in God, but with him it is also provisionally manifest in the temporal being and activity of the community on earth. Similarly, his Holy Spirit is one. As the quickening power which accomplishes sanctification, he comes down with utter novelty and strangeness from above (as described in the story of Pentecost) and thus constitutes an absolute basis and starting-point. But as the same power he also rules and works in the events, in the sequence and multiplicity, of the temporal history of the *communio sanctorum* which is still the *communio peccatorum*, in all the relativities of that which is called Christian and ecclesiastical and even theological life. All this depends, however, upon the fact that first and supremely the one human being Jesus Christ himself exists both in the first form and also in the second: not in any contradiction of the one to the other and therefore to himself; but because in the one, therefore also in the other, and thus in the whole glory of his being as the true Son of God and Son of Man. Our present concern is with the second form: his earthly-historical form of existence; his body; the community in which, as the One who is with God, he is also with us as the true Son of God and therefore the true Son of Man, in whom we are already united and sanctified.

For a better understanding, let us return to the equation that the Holy Spirit, as the power which quickens the community, is the self-attestation of Jesus. Thus the only content of the Holy Spirit is Jesus; his only work is his provisional revelation; his only effect the human knowledge which has him as its object (and in him the knowing person also). But as the self-attestation of Jesus the Holy Spirit is more than a mere indication of Jesus or record concerning him. Where the human Jesus attests himself in the power of the Spirit of God, he makes himself present; and those whom he approaches in his self-attestation are able also to approach him and to be near him. More than that, where he makes himself present in this power, he imparts himself; and those to whom he wills to belong in virtue of this self-presentation are able also to belong to him. In the Holy Spirit as his self-attestation he reveals and discloses himself to certain people living on earth and in time as the Holy One who represents them before God and therefore in actuality, and also grants them the knowledge that he is theirs; the Holy One in whom they also are holy, and are his — holy in his holy person. He reveals and discloses and grants to them the knowledge of his unity with them and their unity with him. In this knowledge they find that even on earth and in time they are with him, and therefore at unity with one another. It is in this way, by this self-attestation, self-presentation and self-impartation, that he founds and quickens the community, which is the mighty work of the Holy Spirit.

In virtue of and in the occurrence of this mighty work, the community lives and grows within the world — an anticipation, a provisional representation, of the sanctification of all people as it has taken place in him, of the new humanity reconciled with God. Thus it can never be understood as a society which people join of themselves and in which they are active in the pursuit of their own ends, however religious. They are united only by and with Jesus, and only in this way with one another, and only for the fulfilment of his will and purpose. Nor can the community be understood as an organization set up by him, a machine for whose efficient functioning it has to provide, thus having its essential existence in its offices. It exists only as the mighty work of Jesus is done on earth, and as it allows it to take place in itself, and through itself in the world. It can be understood only with reference to him, and only in him can it recognize itself in its true actuality. It *is* only in him. Even in its human being and action and operation it is from him and by him. It cannot recognize and take itself seriously in anything that is not from him. What he is not, it is not, and in what he is not it is not his community, but can only be alien to itself, and withdraw in shame before him and become small and as it were disappear. It does not live apart from the mighty work of his self-attestation. It lives as he himself lives in it in the occurrence of this mighty work; as it is the earthly-historical form of his existence, his body, standing at his disposal, and ruled and impelled by him, in all its members and their various functions.

This brings us back to the statement which was a kind of axiomatic starting-point, anticipating all that was to follow, at the beginning of the prolegomena of our *Church Dogmatics*[66] — that the being of Jesus Christ is the being of the church, and its self-understanding and proclamation and practice and enquiries and conclusions and internal and external politics and theology must all be directed accordingly.

We cannot avoid the statement that Jesus Christ is the community. Nor do we refer only to Jesus Christ in his form as its heavenly Head, in his hiddenness with God. In Jesus Christ as the Head it can only believe. Here and now it can only look up to him from the depths as its Lord. It can only love him as the One whom it has not seen (1 Pet. 1.8). It can only wait for his revelation: "Amen. Even so, come, Lord Jesus" (Rev. 22.20). It can only move towards him. Thus the statement cannot be reversed. It is a Christological statement, and only as such an ecclesiological. The community is not Jesus Christ. It is not the eternal Son of God, the incarnate Word, the Reconciler of the world with God. The justification and sanctification of all people did not and does not take place in it, but only its provisional representation, its attestation by a handful of sinful people amongst others — saints who are holy only in the fact that he is, and has revealed and disclosed himself to them as the Holy One, and that they have been recognized and confess him as such. There does not belong to it the power of the sending and outpouring and operation of the Holy Spirit. It does not "possess" him. It cannot create or control him. He is promised to it. It can only receive him and then be obedient to him. There can be no thought of the being of Jesus Christ enclosed in that of his community, or exhausted by it, as though it were a kind of predicate of this being. The truth is the very opposite. The being of the community is exhausted and enclosed in his. It is a being which is taken up and hidden in his, and absolutely determined and governed by it. The being of the community is a predicate of his being. As it exists on earth and in time in virtue of the mighty work of the Holy Spirit, it is his body; and he, its heavenly Head, the incarnate Word, the incomparable Holy One, has in it his own earthly-historical form of existence; he himself, who is not yet directly and universally and definitively revealed to the world and it, is already present and at work in it. The community is not Jesus Christ. But he — and in reality only he, but he in supreme reality — is the community. He does not live because and as it lives. But it lives, and may and can live, only because and as he lives. "Because I live, ye shall live also" (Jn. 14.19). The sequence and order are all-important. But in this sequence and order it may and must be affirmed that Jesus Christ is the community.

We may say the same with reference to the central New Testament concept of the kingdom of God. The kingdom of God is the lordship of God established in the world in Jesus Christ. It is the rule of God as it takes place in him. He himself is the kingdom of God. Thus we cannot avoid a statement which Protestantism has far too hastily and heedlessly contested — that the kingdom of God is the community. We do not refer to the kingdom or dominion of God in its completed form in which it obtains for the whole world in the person of the one Son of Man, the one Holy Spirit, and in which it will be directly and universally and definitively revealed and known at the end and goal of all history. We refer to it in the guise of the new and obedient humanity, as in the historical time which moves towards this end it is provisionally and very imperfectly but genuinely actualized where in virtue of the mighty work of the Holy Spirit there is an awareness of its incursion and therefore the communion of saints. The community is not the kingdom of God. But — proclaimed and believed in its earthly-historical form of existence by sinners among sinners, as the unholy may become the saints of God in an awareness of its coming — the kingdom of God is the community. It is not for nothing that it comes from the resurrection of Jesus Christ as its first revelation, and goes towards its final revelation in the return of Jesus Christ. As the kingdom of God itself is on the way from the first to the last revelation, it is the community. As the kingdom or rule of God is engaged in this movement, it creates the sphere corresponding to it and is to be found on this way too. And this takes place in the mighty work of the Holy Spirit founding and quickening the community. The community is not the kingdom of God, nor will it ever be before the kingdom encounters it, and is revealed to it, in its glory at the end of all history. It prays for the coming of the kingdom, that encountering it in its true and perfect form it may be directly and universally and definitively revealed. But already on this side of the end, even in the form of the community which prays for its coming, the kingdom is really on earth and in time and history. The community would be nothing if it did not come from the kingdom and go towards it; if the kingdom were not present in this transitional movement. The community can only follow it in this transition; otherwise it surrenders its particularity and betrays its reality as the communion of saints. Its proclamation can only serve the self-proclamation of the kingdom of God which is present here and now because it has come and comes. If it does not stand in this service it is absolutely nothing. If it does, for all its unpretentiousness it is greater than all the greatnesses of world history, for it has to speak the final word among all the words spoken by and to humanity.

In sum, there is a real identity, not present *in abstracto*, but given by God and enacted in the mighty work of the Holy Spirit, between the Holy One, the kingdom of God as perfectly established in him, and the communion of saints on earth, which as such is also a communion of sinners. Thus the power of this Holy One, of Jesus Christ as the heavenly Head, in whom God's rule is perfectly established, is also the indwelling power of life and growth which is immanent in the community on earth. It is in the light of this identity that we have to understand everything that falls to be said concerning its life and growth (both in the extensive and the intensive sense). He, Jesus Christ, must increase (Jn. 3.30), and he does in fact increase. The kingdom of God grows like the seed. It is for this reason that the community also grows — the community of people who with open eyes and ears and hearts come from Jesus Christ, from the kingdom of God, and move towards him. It grows as it gives him room to grow, and to the extent that it "decreases," as the Baptist said of himself. It lives because and as its Lord lives. It lives wholly and utterly as his people.   *(CD: IV/2, 651-657)*

*

FIAT IUSTITIA

Barth's Christocentric theology was always a theology of community — the community of the inner-Trinitarian life of God, expressed in the covenant of God with humanity, and creating the Christian community as a parable of all humanity redeemed in Christ. From his earliest to his latest writings,

Barth always spoke of Jesus and the kingdom of God together. And he always insisted that Christian community was a parable and contained an imperative to act for justice, peace and freedom. This is the overall context for this selection of commentary on the Lord's Prayer under the heading Fiat Iustitia, *"Let there be justice!"*

It comes from the last section (Par. 78) Barth wrote for the Church Dogmatics, *the incomplete Volume IV/4 on the ethics of the Doctrine of Reconciliation. It was published separately by Eerdmans under the title* The Christian Life. Church Dogmatics IV/4. Lecture Fragments;[67] *the selection is from pages 264-271.*

Christians are claimed for action in the effort and struggle for human righteousness. At issue is human, not divine righteousness. That the latter should come, intervene, assert itself, reign, and triumph can never be the affair of any human action. Those who know the reality of the kingdom, Christians, can never have anything to do with the arrogant and foolhardy enterprise of trying to bring in and build up by human hands a religious, cultic, moral, or political kingdom of God on earth. God's righteousness is the affair of God's own act, which has already been accomplished and is still awaited. God's righteousness took place in the history of Jesus Christ, and it will take place again, comprehensively and definitively, in his final manifestation. The time between that beginning and that end, our time as the time of the presence of Jesus Christ in the Holy Spirit, is for Christians the space for gratitude, hope, and prayer, and also the time of responsibility for the occurrence of human righteousness. They have to be concerned about the doing of this righteousness. On no pretext can they escape responsibility for it: not on that of the gratitude and hope with which they look to God and wait for his action; not on that of their prayer for the coming of his kingdom. For if they are really grateful and really hope, if their prayer is a brave prayer, then they are claimed for a corresponding inner and outer action which is also brave. If they draw back here, or even want to, then there is serious reason to ask whether and how far their gratitude, hope, and prayer are to be taken seriously. . . .

Human righteousness! We shall not develop at length here the self-evident point that, measured by God's righteousness and in unconquerable distinction from it, this will always be, even at best, an imperfect, fragile, and highly problematical righteousness. Others may deceive themselves in this regard, but to those who have the prayer for the kingdom in their hearts and on their lips it is indeed self-evident. Nevertheless, it is not so important that they can refrain from doing what they have to do in this relativity. We Protestants have always had a certain inclination to find it too important. We should break free from this. Those who pray that prayer start off with the thesis that the perfect righteousness of God's kingdom is not their own doing, that they can only seek it (Mt. 6.33), as is appropriate, in gratitude for its reality, in hope of its manifestation, in prayer that it may come. This means, however, that any concern for the imperfection of all human action, their own included, is taken from them as idle and pointless. They are also forbidden the lazy excuse of all lazy servants that since all they can do will always be imperfect anyway it is not worth exerting themselves and growing weary in the causes of petty human righteousness. No, precisely because perfect righteousness stands before them as God's work, precisely because they are duly forbidden to attempt the impossible, precisely because all experiments in this direction are prevented and prohibited, they are with great strictness required and with great kindness freed and empowered to do what they can do in the sphere of the relative possibilities assigned to them, to do it very imperfectly yet heartily, quietly, and cheerfully. They are absolved from wasting time and energy sighing over the impassable limits of their sphere of action and thus missing the opportunities that present themselves in this sphere. They may and can and should rise up and accept responsibility to the utmost of their power for the doing of the little righteousness. The only concern should be their awareness of how far they fall short in this sphere of what is not only commanded but also possible for them. But they can quickly rid themselves of this concern by setting to work to snatch the available possibilities of doing what is commanded and thus catching up in God's name where they are in arrears. A little righteousness and holiness of works — there will certainly never be a great deal! — does not have to be an illusion or a danger here. The only danger arising out of the (ill-founded) anxiety that one might become too righteous and too holy, a "works Christian," is the temptation to remain passive where what is required, with a full sense of one's limitations, is to become active.

It is not self-evident, of course, that in the sphere of human activity, alongside and far below divine righteousness, there should be in all seriousness a human righteousness which Christians are freed to do and for whose occurrence they are made responsible. It is not self-evident that the same lofty concept of righteousness, denoting on the one hand perfect divine action and on the other most imperfect human action, should be appropriate or necessary in this context. In relation to human action as such and in general, the analogy is in truth an impossible one. Here, however, we are referring to the obedience of the action of those whom God has freed and summoned to call upon him for the coming of his kingdom and the doing of righteousness. In relation to the action of these people, it cannot be denied that in all its imperfection this action stands related to the kingdom of God, and therefore to the perfect righteousness of God, inasmuch as it derives from the event of the kingdom in Jesus Christ and hastens towards its manifestation in Jesus Christ. Obviously, this whence and whither mean that it cannot be alien to it but is given a determination which it does not have in itself and cannot give itself but which it acquires, which it cannot escape as it takes place in that relation, and which cannot be denied to it. The determination that it acquires and has in that relation is that it can take place only in correspondence with its whence and whither and therefore with God's kingdom and righteousness. If it never can or will be like this, and should not try to aim at equality with it, neither can it be or remain totally unlike it. There is a third possibility. The action of those who pray for the coming of God's kingdom and therefore for the taking place of his righteousness will be *kingdom-like*, and therefore on a lower level and within its impassable limits it will be *righteous* action. Certainly we should not say too much here, yet we should not say too little either. Done in that relation, under that determination, and therefore in that correspondence, the action of Christians may in its own way and within the limits of its own sphere be called and be a righteous action. This is the one talent that is entrusted to Christians, who are neither angels nor archangels but only people, and they must not wrap it in a cloth or bury it anywhere, as did the stupid fellow in Luke 19.20 and Matthew 25.25. Following their prayer, their action can and should be kingdom-like, righteous in its own place and manner. There is not the shadow of a serious reason to contest this.

What do we mean, however, by kingdom-likeness and therefore by the human righteousness of Christian life and thought and speech and action in correspondence with the object of the petition? Anticipating the answer, we may say that according to the measure of what is possible for them, their action must in all circumstances take place with a view to people, in address to people, and with the aim of helping people. The concern of Christians in the coming of the kingdom for which they pray is with doing the perfect righteousness of the God who seeks and magnifies his honor by thinking of human beings, by taking them to himself, by establishing their right as their Creator, Father, Judge, and Deliverer, by creating and giving to them perfect life, freedom, peace, and joy. On the other hand, in the city of the devil, the kingdom of human unrighteousness and disorder which defies God, what is at issue is the work of human hostility in which people fight with one another for their right to live, to live in freedom, peace, and joy, in which they thus deprive themselves of this right, their human right and dignity being constantly overlooked, forgotten, broken, and trampled under the lordship of the released and lordless powers. Praying for the coming of the kingdom of God and his righteousness, and thus empowered, instructed, and summoned to fight against human unrighteousness, Christians can look only where they see God looking and try to live with no other purpose than that with which God acts in Jesus Christ. This means, however, that the true and serious and finally important object of their attention, love, and will, and therefore of their thought, speech, and action, in agreement with their prayer and in correspondence with what they pray for, can only be humanity: humanity as those whose brother God himself willed to become and became; for whom Jesus Christ lived, died, and rose again; to whom he has promised the Holy Spirit; whose cause he will conduct to its goal in his final manifestation. "We are not our own but God's" (Calvin, *Inst.*, III, 7, 1). "We do not belong to ourselves but to the Lord." But because the Lord is the Father, Son, and Holy Spirit who bound and obligated himself to humanity, Christians also belong to humanity and in this concrete sense they belong to themselves. They cannot be for humanity as God was nor do for people what God does; they should not presume to try to be for people or act for them in this way. But they can and should be witnesses of what God is for humanity and does for us. Christians may and can and should reflect and practice God's being and acting for humanity, the distinction with which he treats us, by making humanity the special object of their own interest. What they do therewith — giving and allowing people precedence among all the other things that interest them — is little enough to deprive them of any ground for boasting. As they do it, however, they practice the appropriate human righteousness corresponding to the great divine righteousness. That this should be done and occur (*fiat*) in what they think and speak and do, that it should be the orientation and basis of their lives, is the responsibility they are given.

We do not forget that they are made responsible within the world of unrighteousness and disorder and therefore in the sphere of dominion of these powers and forces. They are made responsible, then, as those who have both a passive and an active share in the evil and corruption of this world, in the unchaining of those demonic factors in world occurrence, in the silent or gloriously tumultuous enterprise of their deification. The only point is that in spite of their situation of shared guilt and oppression they have been required and empowered to pray for the coming of the kingdom. This is what differentiates them from all other people. So too, of course, does their commitment to oppose, resist, and revolt against human corruption in their own sphere, which it is not their affair to transcend. Not led astray by necessity, they have to swim courageously against the stream regardless of the cost or consequences. They do this by looking past and beyond all other things to human beings, whom God loved in spite of all their corruption and misery, by making humanity the proper object of their interest, by making the right and life and freedom and joy of human beings their theme. In this way they fight the fight for human righteousness against human unrighteousness. Since they still move in the sphere of human unrighteousness, and their fight can never be wholly free from it, they are well advised not to make extravagant gestures nor to make too big a song about what they do. But if they look solely at human beings, they are obeying the command that is unquestioningly given them as they may pray for the coming of the kingdom. It is enough if they really do this. In doing it they are in all humility righteous people — sinners, but righteous sinners.

Their concern is with humanity. From the very start they are "humanists." They are not interested in any cause as such. In regard to every cause, they simply look and ask whether and how far it will relatively and provisionally serve or hurt the cause of human beings and their right and worth. No idea, no principle, no traditional or newly established institution or organization, no old or new form of economy, state, or culture, no so-called patrimony, no prevailing habit, custom, or moral system, no ideal of education and upbringing, no form of the church, can be for them the *a priori* of what they think and speak and will, nor can any negation or contesting of certain other ideas and the social constructs corresponding to them. Their *a priori* is not a cause, however great, necessary, or splendid it may appear to be or is. It is the righteousness of God in Jesus Christ and therefore, in correspondence with this, the human persons who are loved by God, their right and worth — solely and simply them.

Certainly in relation to humanity — perhaps temporarily or more permanently, perhaps joyfully or anxiously — they will have to say Yes or No, and say it resolutely, to current ideas and life-forms. Certainly in relation to humanity they will not be afraid of taking sides for and against. But in so doing they will think and speak in terms of theses and not principles. In this field there can be no absolute Yes or No carrying an absolute commitment. One reason for this is that an absolute guarantee of human right and worth cannot be expected from the rule of any idea or the power of any life-form. From one standpoint or another, every idea or life-form will sooner or later prove a threat to humanity. Hence Christians, looking always to the only problem that seriously and finally interests them, must allow themselves the liberty in certain circumstances of saying only a partial Yes or No where a total one is expected, or a total Yes or No where a partial one is expected, or of saying Yes today where they said No yesterday, and vice versa. Their total and definitive decision is for human beings and not for any cause. They will never let themselves be addressed as prisoners of their own decisions or slaves of any sacrosanct consistency. Their Yes and No in this sphere can always be only a relative Yes or No, supremely because if it were more they would be affirming and acknowledging the existence of those absolute or lordless powers, canonizing their deification and instead of resisting the true and most dangerous enemies of human beings and their right, life, and worth, offering them the most hazardous and fateful help. It is another question that they do not topple them, that they do not liberate people from their rule, that they feel their power themselves, and that they can only look on helplessly as countless others fall under their wheels. But how can they confirm them as they would do if they were to indulge in absolute affirmations and negations in this sphere? Christians must resolutely refuse to swallow some of the strengthenings they are offered in order that they may go through world history with a stiffened backbone. In so doing, they will show that they have real backbone. They must not do this because they are themselves possessed by a principial nonconformism, but because they realize that the people about whom they are concerned cannot be helped (even relatively) by such strengthenings, that is, by principles that are enunciated and venerated as divine, that these are rather the works and products of human perversion which can only increase the evil which suppresses and oppresses people. Where do we meet one another more like wolves swallowing one another up than when we come in the name of absolutes and therefore as champions of pseudo-deities, no matter what we call them? Because Christians are dealing with people, they can say to all principles only a relative Yes or No, and they must resist as such all principles that claim to be irrefutable.

As only God himself can be at issue in the prayer of Christians for the coming of the kingdom, so only human beings can be at issue in their other thinking and speech and action. Human beings are those whom God loved, for whom Jesus died and rose again, and for whom he will come again as Judge and Redeemer. To them as such Christians owe righteousness, our whole attention and concern, and mercy. We do not believe at all that "clothes make the man." We cannot be impressed, or deceived, then, by the Sunday clothes or working clothes or fool's clothes in which we will often enough meet them. We will not fear them because of the armor and cut-and-thrust weapons with which they try to impress us and behind which they simply hide their anxiety, and we certainly will not fear them because their coats have too many holes to conceal effectively the emptiness of their vanity and their real needs. We will not see them categorized as political or economic or ecclesiastical beings — the less so the more they claim to be high priests. We will not see people as members of this or that country or sociological stratum, nor as types of this or that psychological category, nor as those who believe in this or that doctrine of salvation or perdition. We will not see a person as a good citizen or a convict, as the representative of a conviction or party that we find agreeable or painful, as a Christian or a non-Christian, as a good or bad, a practicing or non-practicing Christian. Naturally, we will on occasion see people also as the bearers of one or many of these garbs or masks. It will be no accident that they bear them and that they bear this or that particular one of the many that are available. To see them it may be helpful to see them also in these disguises, as worker or at play, or as "business man," or as "organization man," or so-called "modern man." All this is good and right and relevant, but Christians cannot stop here, looking only at people in these disguises. These are not the people themselves. They themselves may act as though they wanted to be addressed in terms of their garbs and masks, but they cannot really be addressed thus. They cannot be nailed to these and judged and treated accordingly. In, with, and under all the apparatus by which they are surrounded and with which they surround themselves and usually hide themselves, they themselves are the beings who, whether they know that God is on their side or not, are to achieve their right, live in dignity, and enjoy freedom, peace, and joy, but who behave with terrible ineptitude and even wickedness in this area, choose crooked and dubious paths — why take the simple course when a complicated one is also available? — act either with total lack of humor or total lack of seriousness, are either as timorous as a gazelle or as relentless as a buffalo, and in any case do not achieve their purpose, being unable to find again what they intend and seek in what they think they sometimes find. People themselves *suffer*, and they fight tooth and nail against admitting this even to themselves, let alone to others. They act — this is the point of their disguises — as if they do not suffer. Those who suffer are real human beings whom God loves. The task of little righteousness which Christians are given praying for the coming of God's kingdom is to see and understand human beings in this plight from which they cannot rescue themselves, but only God can rescue them, to turn to them openly and willingly, to meet them with mercy. What do people need on this side of the deliverance that can be only the work of God? Being hopeless, they need hope. They thus need — this is the mercy that is to be shown to them — the promise that what they intend and seek is really there and is there for them. Christians know and have this promise. We know the God who has already created, and in glory will still create, right, worth, freedom, peace, and joy for humanity. We may hope, and we live by our hope. To bid people hope, and thus to mediate to them the promise that they need, is our task. Concern for this is our conflict. In it we practice the little righteousness which is our affair and portion, in contrast and yet also in correspondence with the great righteousness that God has practiced, practices, and will still practice.

As Christians, obedient to the command that we have been given, busy themselves with this task, whose execution can begin only with the merciful seeing and understanding of real human beings, we confess solidarity at every point with these people, we show ourselves to be their companions and friends without worrying about their garb or mask, and we make their cause our own. Knowing what they for the most part do not know, namely, that those who hunger and thirst after righteousness, that those who, however mistakenly or strangely or impotently, ask after and seek the right and dignity of humanity, have God on their side and will be satisfied (Mt. 5.6), we cannot separate this from them no matter what name they bear or what kind of people they are. It binds us and puts us under obligation to them. We know what we ourselves need. We ourselves, who as humans are also hidden in all kinds of robes and uniforms and rags, go through life wanting our right, though not demanding it by our own efforts. We do not live by the better, which does not wholly evade us and which we may sometimes achieve in favor of others. We live solely by hope and therefore by the promise that human right, worth, freedom, peace, and joy are not a chimera but have already been actualized by God in Jesus Christ and will finally and ultimately be revealed in their actualization. We have to be witnesses, shining lights of hope, to all people. We have to make the promise known to them in its direct wording and sense as a call to faith. There arises here the missionary task of the Christian community in the narrower sense, a task in which each individual Christian will naturally have to have a part. But Christians cannot be content with this. This call needs a practical commentary in the acts of those who issue it to people — just as Jesus Christ himself proclaimed the kingdom of God not only with words but also with significatory acts. People are right in wanting to see the good works of Christians in order to praise our heavenly Father (Mt. 5.16). We also have to be witnesses to them by resolutely being there — and not as the last on the scene — when on this side of the deliverance that God has begun and will complete, in relative antithesis to human disorder and the lordship of demons, there is wrestling and fighting and suffering for a provisional bit of human right. Not with good words alone, not even the best, can we be companions and friends of people who suffer because they seek and cannot find, but who in fact, whether they know it or not, may always and everywhere hope, and therefore cry out for the promise. In order that the promise may not merely be uttered but ring out loudly, Christians must draw alongside people. Nor must we do this as weary sceptics. As we may live by the great hope, we must stand by them even in little things, in hope venturing and taking with them little steps to relative improvements wherever they attempt them, even at the risk of often going astray and being disappointed with them. We should not be afraid, then, to say Yes here and No there in solidarity with them — a relative but still a definite Yes or No. Sometimes in so doing — and there will be plenty of occasion for this — we may really know better and be able to do better, and therefore we can criticize, correct, and instruct. Sometimes we may think or speak or do the same thing but in a slightly or even a very different way. It is more important, however, that in coming to their side we should give them the courage not to be content with the corruption and evil of the world but even within this horizon to look ahead and not back. Shame on us if we let them surpass us in courage for this! The experience, however difficult, of hoping seriously, joyfully, and actively in little things, of doing the relatively better relatively well, will not only be salutary for us but will drive us truly to the great hope, to new prayer that God will take his great step not merely to the better but to the best: "Come, Lord Jesus." But in so praying we may not and cannot abandon people, human beings in spite of all their disguises. We will always see in them companion human beings and not just future brothers, and we must treat them as such. We must assist them in full commitment in this time between the times and thus bring them the promise and be for them credible witnesses that God, like ourselves, has not abandoned them and will not do so, that his kingdom, the kingdom of the Father, Son, and Holy Spirit, has come and will come even for them, that Jesus Christ is their hope too. *(CD: IV/4, 264-271)*

4

PUBLIC THEOLOGY AND POLITICAL ETHICS

THE CHRISTIAN COMMUNITY
AND THE
CIVIL COMMUNITY

1

Barth's is no private theology, confined to the "inner life" or the interpersonal sphere. "This gospel . . . is political from the very outset. . . ." Just as he had argued that the covenant of grace is the internal basis of creation and creation is the external basis of the covenant, so here he argues a similar relation between church and state. Barth's illustration is two concentric circles of which Christ and the Kingdom of God is the center while the church is the inner circle and the state the outer. But he does not advocate a theocratic state: the tasks of the Christian community in the political realm are secular and profane, and there is no such thing as a Christian state. Political systems are human inventions, to be tested experimentally to see if, through law and peaceful order, they provide "an external, relative and provisional humanization" of existence. The positive political task of the church is to witness to the state so that its activities are parables of the Kingdom of God, so that "human politics" and "the politics of God . . . should proceed, however distantly, on parallel lines." So in sections 15-26 Barth gives examples of how specific state policies would reflect, as parables, basic Christian beliefs about the rule of Christ and the Kingdom of God. Theological beliefs can be translated into political terms which serve as analogies, parables of the Kingdom of God. Thus the incarnation implies a state which gives primacy to human beings, not abstract causes; justification finds an analogy in the constitutional state; Christ's seeking the lost finds its parable in the state showing special responsibility for the poor and the socially and economically weak; the community of the church points to a society which is neither individualistic nor collectivist; and one Lord of all translates into a state where all citizens have equal freedom and responsibility, not arbitrarily restricting people because of their religion, class, race or — in particular — their sex.

This essay was first published in Against the Stream (1954), and also reprinted in the volume of three essays on Barth's "social philosophy" edited by Will Herberg in 1960.[68]

By the "Christian community" we mean what is usually called "the church" and by the "civil community" what is usually called "the state."

The use of the concept of the "community" to describe both entities may serve at the very outset to underline the positive relationship and connection between them. It was probably with some such intention in mind that Augustine spoke of the *civitas coelestis* and *terrena* and Zwingli of divine and human justice. In addition, however, the twofold use of the concept "community" is intended to draw attention to the fact that we are concerned in the "church" and the "state" not merely and not primarily with institutions and offices but with human beings gathered together in corporate bodies in the service of common tasks. To interpret the "church" as meaning above all a "community" has rightly become more recognized and normal again in recent decades. The Swiss term "civil community" — in Swiss villages the residential, civil and ecclesiastical communities often confer one after the other in the same inn, and most of the people involved belong to all three groups — the "civil community" as opposed to the "Christian community" may also remind Christians that there are and always have been communities outside their own circle in the form of states, i.e. political communities.

The *"Christian community"* (the church) is the commonality of the people in one place, region or country who are called apart and gathered together as "Christians" by reason of their knowledge of and belief in Jesus Christ. The meaning and purpose of this "assembly" (*ekklesia*) is the common life of these people in one Spirit, the Holy Spirit, that is, in obedience to the Word of God in Jesus Christ, which they have all heard and are all needing and eager to hear again. They have also come together in order to pass on the Word to others. The inward expression of their life as a Christian community in the one faith, love and hope by which they are all moved and sustained; its outward expression is the confession by which they all stand, their jointly acknowledged and exercised responsibility for the preaching of the name of Jesus Christ to all people and the worship and thanksgiving which they offer together. Since this is its concern, every single Christian community is as such an ecumenical (catholic) fellowship, that is, at one with the Christian communities in all other places, regions and lands.

The *"civil community"* (the state) is the commonalty of all the people in one place, region or country in so far as they belong together under a constitutional system of government that is equally valid for and binding on them all, and which is defended and maintained by force. The meaning and purpose of this mutual association (that is, of the *polis*) is the safeguarding of both the external, relative and provisional freedom of the individuals and the external and relative peace of their community and to that extent the safeguarding of the external, relative and provisional humanity of their life both as individuals and as a community. The three essential forms in which this safeguarding takes place are (*a*) legislation, which has to settle the legal system which is to be binding on all; (*b*) the government and administration which has to apply the legislation; (*c*) the administration of justice which has to deal with cases of doubtful or conflicting law and decide on its applicability.

2

When we compare the Christian community with the *civil community* the first difference that strikes us is that in the civil community Christians are no longer gathered together as such but are associated with non-Christians (or doubtful Christians). The civil community embraces everyone living within its area. Its members share no common awareness of their relationship to God, and such an awareness cannot be an element in the legal system established by the civil community. No appeal can be made to the Word or Spirit of God in the running of its affairs. The civil community as such is spiritually blind and ignorant. It has neither faith nor love nor hope. It has no creed and no gospel. Prayer is not part of its life, and its members are not brothers and sisters. As members of the civil community they can only ask, as Pilate asked: What is truth? since every answer to the question abolishes the presuppositions of the very existence of the civil community. "Tolerance" is its ultimate wisdom in the "religious" sphere — "religion" being used in this context to describe the purpose of the Christian community. For this reason the civil community can only have external, relative and provisional tasks and aims, and that is why it is burdened and defaced by something which the Christian community can, characteristically, do without: physical force, the "secular arm" which it can use to enforce its authority. That is why it lacks the ecumenical breadth and freedom that are so essential to Christianity. The *polis* has walls. Up till now, at least, civil communities have always been more or less clearly marked off from one another as local, regional, national and therefore competing and colliding units of government. And that is why the state has no safeguard or corrective against the danger of either neglecting or absolutizing itself and its particular system and thus in one way or the other destroying and annulling itself. One cannot in fact compare the church with the state without realizing how much weaker, poorer and more exposed to danger the human community is in the state than in the church.

3

It would be inadvisable, however, to make too much of the comparison. According to the fifth thesis of the *Theological Declaration* of Barmen (1934), the *Christian community* also exists in "the still unredeemed world," and there is not a single problem harassing the state by which the church is not also affected in some way or other. From a distance it is impossible clearly to distinguish the Christian from the non-Christian, the real Christian from the doubtful Christian even in the church itself. Did not Judas the traitor participate in the Last Supper? Awareness of God is one thing, being in God quite another. The Word and Spirit of God are no more automatically available in the church than they are in the state. The faith of the church can become frigid and empty; its love can grow cold; its hope can fall to the ground; its message become timid and even silent; its worship and thanksgiving mere formalities; its fellowship may droop and decay.

Even the church does not simply "have" faith or love or hope. There are dead churches, and unfortunately one does not have to look far to find them anywhere. And if, normally, the church renounces the use of physical force and has not shed blood, sometimes the only reason has been lack of opportunity; struggles for power have never been entirely absent in the life of the church. Again, side by side with other and more far-reaching centrifugal factors, local, regional and national differences in the church's way of life have been and still are strong. The centripetal forces which it needs are still weak enough to make even the unity of Christian communities among themselves extremely doubtful in many places and a special "ecumenical" movement both desirable and urgently necessary. There is then no cause for the church to regard the civil community too superciliously.

4

More important still, however, is the *positive* relationship between the two communities which results from the fact that the constitutive elements of the civil community are also proper and indispensable to the Christian community. The very term *ekklesia* is borrowed from the political sphere. The Christian community also lives and acts within the framework of an order of law which is binding on all its members, of a "canon law" which it cannot regard as an end in itself but which it cannot neglect to institute as a "token of the Lordship of Christ."[69] The Christian community exists at all times and places as a *politeia* with definite authorities and offices, with patterns of community life and divisions of labour. What the legislature, the executive and the administration of the law are in the life of the state has its clear parallels in the life of the church, however freely and flexibly it may be shaped and however "spiritually" it may be established and intended. And though the Christian community does not embrace all people, but only those who profess themselves Christians and would like, more or less seriously, to be Christians — it reaches out, instituted as it is to be the "light of the world," from these few or many, to all people. The gospel, with which it is commissioned, is preached to all, applies to all. To serve all the people within range of the place, region or country where it is established, is the purpose of its existence no less than it is that of the civil community. In 1 Tim. 2.1-7 we read that the God in whose sight it is good and acceptable that Christians as such may lead a quiet and peaceable life in all godliness and honesty, will have all people to be saved and to come to the knowledge of the truth, and that Christians are therefore to pray for everybody and especially for "kings," that is, for those who bear special responsibility in the political sphere (which embraces everybody).

In this sense, therefore, the existence of the Christian community is political. Furthermore, the object of the promise and the hope in which the Christian community has its eternal goal, consists, according to the unmistakable assertion of the New Testament, not in an eternal Church but in the *polis* built by God and coming down from heaven to earth, and the nations shall walk in the light of it and the kings of the earth will bring their glory and honor into it (Rev. 21.2, 24) — it consists in a heavenly *politeuma* (Phil. 3.20) — in the *basileia* of God — in the judgment of the King Jesus on the throne of his glory (Matt. 25.31f.). Bearing all this in mind, we are entitled and compelled to regard the existence of the Christian community as of ultimate and supremely political significance.

5

The Christian community is particularly conscious of the *necessity* for the existence of the civil community. For it knows that all people (non-

Christians as well as Christians) need to have "kings," that is, need to be subject to an external, relative and provisional order of law, defended by superior authority and force. It knows that the original and final pattern of this order is the eternal Kingdom of God and the eternal righteousness of his grace. It preaches the Kingdom primarily and ultimately in this eternal form. But it also thanks God that the Kingdom has an external, relative and provisional embodiment "in the world that is not yet redeemed," in which it is valid and effective even when the temporal order is based on the most imperfect and clouded knowledge of Jesus Christ or on no such knowledge at all. This external, relative and provisional, but not on that account invalid or ineffective, form of legal order is the civil community. The Christian community is aware of the need for the civil community, and it alone takes the need absolutely seriously. For — because it knows of God's Kingdom and grace — it knows of human presumption and the plainly destructive consequences of that presumption. It knows how dangerous human beings are and how they endanger themselves. It knows human beings as sinful, as always on the point of opening the sluices through which, if not checked in time, chaos and nothingness would break in and bring human time to an end. It can only conceive the time that is still left to it as a "time of grace" in the twofold sense of being the time which it is given in order to know and lay hold of God's grace — and as the time which it is given for this very purpose by the grace of God. The Christian community itself exists in this time which is given to humanity, that is, in the space where human temporal life is still protected from chaos — and on the face of it chaos should have broken in long ago. It sees as the visible means of this protection of human life from chaos the existence of the civil community, the state's effort to achieve an external, relative and provisional humanizing of life and the political order instituted for all (for non-Christians as well as Christians — they both need it, for human arrogance is alive in both), under which the evil are punished and the good rewarded (Rom. 13.3; 1 Pet. 2.14) and which guarantees that the worst is prevented from happening. It knows that without this political order there would be no Christian order. It knows and it thanks God that — as the inner circle within the wider circle[70] — it is allowed to share the protection which the civil community affords.

6

Knowing that, it recognizes in the existence of the civil community — disregarding the Christianity or lack of Christianity of its members and officials and also disregarding the particular forms which it assumes — no less than in its own existence the operation of a *divine ordinance* (*ordinatio*, i.e. institution or foundation), an *exousia* which is and acts in accordance with the will of God (Rom. 13.1*b*). However much human error and human tyranny may be involved in it, the state is not a product of sin but one of the constants of the divine Providence and government of the world in its action against human sin: it is therefore an instrument of divine grace. The civil community shares both a common origin and a common center with the Christian community. It is an order of divine grace inasmuch as in relation to sinful people as such, in relation to the world that still needs redeeming, the grace of God is always the patience of God. It is the sign that humanity, in its total ignorance and darkness, which is still, or has again become, a prey to sin and therefore subject to the wrath of God, is yet not forsaken but preserved and sustained by God. It serves to protect people from the invasion of chaos and therefore to give them time: time for the preaching of the gospel; time for repentance; time for faith. Since "according to the measure of human insight and human capacity" and "under the threat and exercise of force" (Barmen Thesis No. 5), provision is made in the state for the establishment of human law and (in the inevitably external, relative and provisional sense) for freedom, peace and humanity, it renders a definite service to the divine Providence and plan of salvation, quite apart from the judgment and individual desires of its members. Its existence is not separate from the Kingdom of Jesus Christ; its foundations and its influence are not autonomous. It is outside the church but not outside the range of Christ's dominion — it is an exponent of his kingdom. It is, according to the New Testament, one of the "powers" created through him and in him and which subsist in him (Col. 1.16f.), which cannot separate us from the love of God (Rom. 8.37f.) because they are all given to him and are at his disposal (Matt. 28.18). The activity of the state is, as the apostle explicitly stated (Rom. 13.4, 6), a form of divine service. As such it can be perverted just as the divine service of the church itself is not exempt from the possibility of perversion. The state can assume the face and character of Pilate. Even then, however, it still acts in the power which God has given it ("Thou couldest have no power at all against me, except it were given thee from above": John 19.11). Even in its perversion it cannot escape from God; and his law is the standard by which it is judged. The Christian community therefore acknowledges "the benefaction of this ordinance of his with thankful, reverent hearts" (Barmen Thesis No. 5). The benefaction which it acknowledges consists in the external, relative and provisional sanctification of the unhallowed world which is brought about by the existence of political power and order. In what concrete attitudes to particular political patterns and realities this Christian acknowledgment will be expressed can remain a completely open question. It makes one thing quite impossible, however: a Christian decision to be indifferent; a non-political Christianity. The church can in no case be indifferent or neutral towards this manifestation of an order so clearly related to its own mission. Such indifference would be equivalent to the opposition of which it is said in Rom. 13.2 that it is a rebellion against the ordinance of God — and rebels secure their own condemnation.

7

The church must *remain the church*. It must remain the *inner* circle of the Kingdom of Christ. The Christian community has a task of which the civil community can never relieve it and which it can never pursue in the forms peculiar to the civil community. It would not redound to the welfare of the civil community if the Christian community were to be absorbed by it (as Rothe has suggested that it should) and were therefore to neglect the *special* task which it has received a categorical order to undertake. It proclaims the rule of Jesus Christ and the hope of the Kingdom of God. This is not the task of the civil community: it has no message to deliver; it is dependent on a message being delivered to it. It is not in a position to appeal to the authority and grace of God; it is dependent on this happening elsewhere. It does not pray; it depends on others praying for it. It is blind to the whence ? and whither? of human existence; its task is rather to provide for the external and provisional delimitation and protection of human life; it depends on the existence of seeing eyes elsewhere. It cannot call the human *hubris* into question fundamentally, and it knows of no final defence against the chaos which threatens it from that quarter; in this respect too it depends on ultimate words and insights existing elsewhere. The thought and speech of the civil community wavers necessarily between a much too childlike optimism and a much too peevish pessimism in regard to humanity - as a matter of course it expects the best of everybody and suspects the worst! It obvi-usly relies on its own anthropology being fundamentally superseded elsewhere. Only an act of supreme disobedience on the part of Christians could bring the special existence of the Christian community to an end. Such a cessation is also impossible because then the voice of what is ultimately the only hope and help which all people need to hear would be silent.

8

The Christian community *shares* in the task of the civil community precisely to the extent that it fulfils its *own* task. By believing in Jesus Christ and preaching Jesus Christ it believes in and preaches him who is Lord of the world as he is Lord of the Church. And since they belong to the inner circle the members of the church are also automatically members of the wider circle. They cannot halt at the boundary where the inner and outer circles meet, though the work of faith, love and hope which they are under orders to perform will assume different forms on either side of the boundary. In the sphere of the civil community the Christian community shares common interests with the world and its task is to give resolute practical expression to this community of interest. The Christian community prays for the civil community. It does so all the more since the civil community as such is not in the habit of praying. But by praying for it, it also makes itself responsible for it before God, and it would not be taking this reponsibility seriously if it did no more than pray, if it did not also work actively on behalf of the civil community. It also expresses its active support of the civil community by acknowledging that, as an operation of a divine ordinance, the civil power is also binding on Christians and significant and just from the Christian point of view. It expresses its active support of the civil community by "subordinating" itself, in the words of the apostle (Rom. 13.1) to the cause of the civil community under all circumstances (and therefore whatever the political form and reality it has to deal with *in concreto*). Luther's translation speaks of "being *subject*,"[71] which is something dangerously different from what is meant here. The last thing this instruction implies is that the Christian community and the Christian should offer the blindest possible obedience to the civil community and its officials. What is meant is (Rom. 13.6f.) that Christians should carry out what is required of them for the establishment, preservation and maintenance of the civil community and for the execution of its task, because, although they are Christians and, as such, have their home elsewhere, they also live in this outer circle. Jesus Christ is still its center: they too are therefore responsible for its stability. "Sub-ordination" means the carrying out of this *co-responsibility* in which Christians apply themselves to the same task with non-Christians and submit themselves to the same rule. The "sub-ordination" accrues to the good of the civil community however well or however badly that community is defended, because the civil cause (and not merely the Christian cause) is also the cause of the one God. In Rom. 13.5 Paul has expressly added that this "sub-ordination" is not optional but necessary, and necessary not merely "for fear of punishment," for fear of the otherwise inevitable conflict with an obscure commandment of God, but "for conscience sake": in the clear evangelical knowledge of the divine grace and patience, which is also manifested in the existence of the state and, therefore, in full responsibility towards the will of God which the Christian sees revealed in the civil community. The "sub-ordination" will be an expression of the obedience of a free heart which the Christian offers to God in the civil sphere as in the sphere of the church — although with a different purpose (rendering to Caesar what is Caesar's and to God what is God's — Matt. 22.21).

9

In making itself jointly responsible for the civil community, the Christian community has no exclusive theory of its own to advocate in face of the various forms and realities of political life. It is not in a position to establish one particular doctrine as *the* Christian doctrine of the just state. It is also not in a position to refer to any past realization of the perfect state or to hold out any prospect of one in the future. There is but one Body of Christ, born of the Word of God, which is heard in faith. There is therefore no such thing as a Christian state corresponding to the Christian church; there is no duplicate of the church in the political sphere. For if, as the effect of a divine ordinance, as the manifestation of one of the constants of divine Providence and of the historical process which it governs, the state is in the Kingdom of Christ, this does not mean that God is revealed, believed and perceived in any political community as such. The effect of the divine ordinance is that people are entrusted (whether or not they believe it to be a divine revelation) to provide "according to the measure of human insight and human capacity" for temporal law and temporal peace, for an external, relative and provisional humanization of human existence. Accordingly, the various political forms and systems are human inventions which as such do not bear the distinctive mark of revelation and are not witnessed to as such — and can therefore not lay any claim to belief. By making itself co-responsible for the civil community, the Christian community participates — on the basis of and by belief in the divine revelation — in the human search for the best form, for the most fitting system of political organization; but it is also aware of the limits of all the political forms and systems which human ingenuity can discover (even with the co-operation of the church), and it will beware of playing off one political concept — even the "democratic" concept — as *the* Christian concept, against all others. Since it proclaims the Kingdom of God it has to maintain its own hopes and questions in the face of all purely political concepts. And this applies even more to all political achievements. Though Christians will be both more lenient and more stern, more patient and more impatient towards them than non-Christians, they will not regard any such achievement as perfect or mistake it for the Kingdom of God — for it can only have been brought about by human insight and human ability. In the face of all political achievements, past, present and future, the church waits for "the city which hath foundations, whose builder and maker is God" (Heb. 11.10). It trusts and obeys no political system or reality but the power of the Word, by which God upholds all things (Heb. 1.3; Barmen Thesis No. 5), including all political things.

10

In this freedom, however, the church makes itself responsible for the shape and reality of the civil community in a quite definite sense. We have already said that it is quite impossible for the Christian to adopt an attitude of complete indifference to politics. But neither can the church be indifferent to particular political patterns and realities. The church "reminds the world of God's Kingdom, God's commandment and righteousness and thereby of the responsibility of governments and governed" (Barmen Thesis No. 5). This means that the Christian community and the individual Christian can understand and accept many things in the political sphere — and if necessary suffer and endure everything. But the fact that it can understand much and endure everything has nothing to do with the "sub-ordination" which is required of it, that is, with the co-responsibility which it is enjoined to take in the political sphere. That responsibility refers rather to the decisions which it must make before God: "must" make, because, unlike Christian understanding and suffering, Christian intentions and decisions are bound to run in a quite definite direction of their own. There will always be room and need for discussion on the details of Christian intentions and decisions, but the general line on which they are based can never be

the subject of accommodation and compromise in the church's relations with the world. The Christian community "sub-ordinates" itself
to the civil community by making its knowledge of the Lord who is Lord
of all its criterion, and *distinguishing* between the just and the unjust
state, that is, between the better and the worse political form and reality;
between order and caprice; between government and tyranny; between
freedom and anarchy; between community and collectivism; between
personal rights and individualism; between the state as described in
Rom. 13 and the state as described in Rev. 13. And it will judge all matters concerned with the establishment, preservation and enforcement
of political order in accordance with these necessary distinctions and
according to the merits of the particular case and situation to which they
refer. On the basis of the judgment which it has formed it will choose
and desire whichever seems to be the better political system in any particular situation, and in accordance with this choice and desire it will
offer its support here and its resistance there. It is in the making of such
distinctions, judgments and choices from its own center, and in the
practical decisions which necessarily flow from that center, that the
Christian community expresses its "sub-ordination" to the civil
community and fulfils its political co-responsibility.

11

The Christian decisions which have to be made in the political sphere
have no idea, system or program to refer to but a *direction* and a *line* that
must be recognized and adhered to in all circumstances. This line cannot be defined by appealing to the so-called "natural law." To base its
policy on "natural law" would mean that the Christian community was
adopting the ways of the civil community, which does not take its bear-
ings from the Christian center and is still living or again living in a state
of ignorance. The Christian community would be adopting the methods, in other words, of the pagan state. It would not be acting as a Christian community in the state at all; it would no longer be the salt and the
light of the wider circle of which Christ is the center. It would not only
be declaring its solidarity with the civil community: it would be putting
itself on a par with it and withholding from it the very things it lacks
most. It would certainly not be doing it any service in that way. For the
thing the civil community lacks (in its neutrality towards the Word and
Spirit of God) is a firmer and clearer motivation for political decisions
than the so-called natural law can provide. By "natural law" we mean

the embodiment of what humanity is alleged to regard as universally right and wrong, as necessary, permissible and forbidden "by nature," that is, on any conceivable premise. It has been connected with a natural revelation of God, that is, with a revelation known to humanity by natural means. And the civil community as such — the civil community which is not yet or is no longer illuminated from its center — undoubtedly has no other choice but to think, speak and act on the basis of this allegedly natural law, or rather of a particular conception of the court of appeal which is passed off as *the* natural law. The civil community is reduced to guessing or to accepting some powerful assertion of this or that interpretation of natural law. All it can do is to grope around and experiment with the convictions which it derives from "natural law," never certain whether it may not in the end be an illusion to rely on it as the final authority and therefore always making vigorous use, openly or secretly, of a more or less refined positivism. The results of the politics based on such considerations were and are just what might be expected. And if they were and are not clearly and generally negative, if in the political sphere the better stands alongside the worse, if there were and still are good as well as bad states — no doubt the reality is always a curious mixture of the two! — then the reason is not that the true "natural law" has been discovered, but simply the fact that even the ignorant, neutral, pagan civil community is still in the Kingdom of Christ, and that all political questions and all political efforts as such are founded on the gracious ordinance of God by which people are preserved and sin and crime confined.

What we glimpse in the "better" kind of state is the purpose, meaning and goal of this divine ordinance. It is operative in any case, even though the citizens of the particular state may lack any certain knowledge of the trustworthy standards of political decision, and the overwhelming threat of mistaking an error for the truth may be close at hand. The divine ordinance may operate with the co-operation of the men and women involved, but certainly without their having deserved it: *Dei providentia hominum confusione.* If the Christian community were to base its political responsibility on the assumption that it was also interested in the problem of natural law and that it was attempting to base its decisions on so-called natural law, this would not alter the power which God has to make good come of evil, as he is in fact always doing in the political order. But it would mean that the Christian community was sharing human illusions and confusions. It is bad enough that, when it does not risk going its own way, the Christian community is widely involved in these illusions and confusions. It should not wantonly attempt to deepen such involvement. And it would be doing no less if it were to seek the criterion of its political decisions in some form of the so-called natural law. The tasks and problems which the Christian community is called to share, in fulfilment of its political responsibility, are "natural," secular, profane tasks and problems. But the norm by which it should be guided is anything but natural: it is the only norm which it can believe in and accept as a spiritual norm, and is derived from the clear law of its own faith, not from the obscure workings of a system outside itself; it if from knowledge of this norm that it will make its decisions in the political sphere.

12

It is this reliance on a spiritual norm that makes the Christian community free to support the cause of the civil community honestly and calmly. In the political sphere the church will not be fighting *for itself* and its own concerns. Its own position, influence and power in the state are not the goal which will determine the trend of its political decisions. "My Kingdom is not of this world. If my Kingdom were of this world then would my servants fight that I should not be delivered to the Jews, but now is my Kingdom not from hence" (John 18.36). The secret contempt which a church fighting for its own interests with political weapons usually incurs even when it achieves a certain amount of success, is well deserved. And sooner or later the struggle generally ends in mortifying defeats of one sort or another. The Christian community is not an end in itself. It serves God and it thereby serves humanity. It is true that the deepest, ultimate, divine purpose of the civil community consists in creating opportunities for the preaching and hearing of the Word and, to that extent, for the existence of the church. But the only way the state can create such opportunities, according to the providence and ordinance of God, is the natural, secular and profane way of the establishment of law, the safeguarding of freedom and peace, "according to the measure of human insight and capacity." The divine purpose is therefore not at all that the state should itself gradually develop more or less into a church. And the church's political aim cannot be to turn the state into a church, that is, make it as far as possible subservient to the tasks of the church. If the state grants the church freedom, respect and special privileges in any of the ways which are open to it (guarantees of one kind or another, a share in education and broadcasting, the defence of the sabbath, financial reliefs or subsidies and the like), the church will not immediately start dreaming of a church-state. It will be thankful for the state's help, seeing in such help a result of the divine providence and ordinance: and it will show its gratitude by being a church all the more faithfully and zealously within the broader frontiers that the state's gifts make possible, thereby justifying the expectation which the state evidently reposes in it. But it will not claim such gifts as a right. If they are refused, it will look in itself for the reason, not in the state. "Resist not evil!" is an injunction that applies here. The church will ask itself whether it has already given proof to the state of the Spirit and the power of God, whether it has already defended and proclaimed Jesus Christ to the world to the extent that it can expect to be considered an important, significant and salutary factor in public life. It will ask, for example, whether it is in a position to say the tremendous things that are certainly entitled to be heard in schools. It will first and foremost do penance — when and where would it not have cause for so doing? — and it will do that best by concentrating on its own special work in the, possibly, extremely small space left to it in public life, with all the more confidence and intensity and with redoubled zeal, "with the greatest force applied at the narrowest point." Where it has first to advertise its desire to play a part in public life, where it must first establish its claim to be considered a factor of public importance, it only proves that its claim to be heard is irrelevant and it thoroughly deserves not to be heard at all, or to be heard in a way that will sooner or later afford it no pleasure. Whenever the church has entered the political arena to fight for its claim to be given public recognition, it has always been a church which has failed to understand the special purpose of the state, an impenitent, spiritually unfree church.

13

The church cannot, however, simply take the Kingdom of God itself into the political arena. The church *reminds* people of God's kingdom. This does not mean that it expects the state gradually to become the Kingdom of God. The Kingdom of God is the Kingdom where God is without shadow, without problems and contradictions, where God is all in all: it is the rule of God in the redeemed world. In the Kingdom of God the outward is annulled by the inward, the relative by the absolute, the provisional by the final. In the Kingdom of God there is no legislature, no executive, no legal administration. For in the Kingdom of God there is no sin to be reproved, no chaos to be feared and checked. The Kingdom of God is the world dominion of Jesus Christ in honor of the Father, revealed in the clear light of day. The state as such, the neutral, pagan, ignorant state knows nothing of the Kingdom of God. It knows at best of the various ideals based on natural law. The Christian community within the state does know about the Kingdom of God, however, and it calls it to mind. It reminds people of the Jesus Christ who came and is to come again. But it cannot do this by projecting, proposing and attempting to enforce a state in the likeness of the Kingdom of God. The state is quite justified if it refuses to countenance all such Christian demands. It belongs to the very nature of the state that it is not and cannot become the Kingdom of God. It is based on an ordinance of God which is intended for the "world not yet redeemed" in which sin and the danger of chaos have to be taken into account with the utmost seriousness and in which the rule of Jesus Christ, though in fact already established, is still hidden. The state would be disavowing its own purpose if it were to act as though its task was to become the Kingdom of God. And the church that tried to induce it to develop into the Kingdom of God could be rightly reproached for being much too rashly presumptuous. If its demand were to have any meaning at all, it would have to believe that its own duty was also to develop into the Kingdom of God. But, like the state, the church also stands "in the world not yet redeemed." And even at its best the church is not an image of the Kingdom of God. It would appear that when it makes this demand on the state, the church has also confused the Kingdom of God with a mere ideal of the natural law. Such a church needs to be reminded again of the real Kingdom of God, which will follow both state and church in time. A free church will not allow itself to be caught on this path.

14

The direction of Christian judgments, purposes and ideals in political affairs is based on the parabolic capacities and needs of political organizations. Political organization can be neither a repetition of the church nor an anticipation of the Kingdom of God. In relation to the church it is an independent reality; in relation to the Kingdom of God it is (like the church itself) a human reality bearing the stamp of this fleeting world. An equating of state and church on the one hand and state and Kingdom of God on the other, is therefore out of the question. On the other hand, however, since the state is based on a particular divine ordinance, since it belongs to the Kingdom of God, it has no autonomy, no independence over against the church and the Kingdom of God. A simple and absolute heterogeneity between state and church on the one hand and state and Kingdom of God on the other is therefore just as much out of the question as a simple and absolute equating. The only possibility that remains — and it suggests itself compellingly — is to regard the existence of the state as a parable, as a correspondence and an analogue to the Kingdom of God which the church preaches and believes in. Since the state forms the outer circle, within which the church, with the mystery of its faith and gospel, is the inner circle, since it shares a common center with the church, it is inevitable that, although its presuppositions and its tasks are its own and different, it is nevertheless capable of reflecting indirectly the truth and reality which constitute the Christian community. Since, however, the peculiarity and difference of its presuppositions and tasks and its existence as an outer circle must remain as they are, its justice and even its very existence as a reflected image of the Christian truth and reality cannot be given once and for all and as a matter of course but are, on the contrary, exposed to the utmost danger; it will always be questionable whether and how far it will fulfil its just purposes. To be saved from degeneration and decay it needs to be reminded of the righteousness which is a reflection of Christian truth. Again and again it needs a historical setting whose goal and content is the moulding of the state into a parable of the Kingdom of God and the fulfilment of its righteousness. Human initiative in such situations cannot proceed from the state itself. As a purely civil community the state is ignorant of the mystery of the Kingdom of God, the mystery of its own center, and it is indifferent to the faith and gospel of the Christian community. As a civil community it can only draw from the porous wells of the so-called natural law. It cannot remind itself of the true criterion of its own righteousness, it cannot move towards the fulfilment of that righteousness in its own strength. It needs the wholesomely disturbing presence, the activity that revolves directly around the common center, the political co-responsibility of the Christian community. The church is not the Kingdom of God, but it has knowledge of it; it hopes for it; it believes in it; it prays in the name of Jesus Christ, and it preaches his name as the name above all others. The church is not neutral on this ground, and it is therefore not powerless. If it only achieves the great and necessary *metabasis eis allo genos* which is the share of political responsibility which it is enjoined to assume, then it will not be able to be neutral and powerless and deny its Lord in the other *genos*. If the church takes up its political co-responsibility, it must mean that it is taking that human initiative which the state cannot take: it is giving the state the impulse which it cannot give itself; it is reminding the state of those things of which it is unable to remind itself. The distinctions, judgments and choices which it makes in the political sphere are always intended to foster the illumination of the state's connection with the order of divine salvation and grace and to discourage all the attempts to hide this connection. Among the political possibilities open at any particular moment it will choose those which most suggest a parable — a correspondence to, an analogy and a reflection of, the content of its own confession and gospel.

In the decisions of the state the church will always support the side which clarifies rather than obscures the Lordship of Jesus Christ over the whole, which includes this political sphere outside the church. The church desires that the shape and reality of the state in this fleeting world should point towards the Kingdom of God, not away from it. Its desire is not that human politics should cross the politics of God, but that they should proceed, however distantly, on parallel lines.

It desires that the active grace of God, as revealed from heaven, should be reflected in the earthly material of the external, relative and provisional actions and modes of action of the political community. It therefore makes itself responsible in the first and last place to God — the one God whose grace is revealed in Jesus Christ — by making itself responsible for the cause of the state. And so, with its political judgments and choices, it bears an implicit, indirect but nonetheless real witness to the gospel.

Even its political activity is therefore a profession of its Christian faith. By its political activity it calls the state from neutrality, ignorance and paganism into co-responsibility before God, in that it practices its own political co-responsibility. Thus it acts quite loyally to its own particular mission, in that it also acts politically. It sets in motion the historical process whose aim and content is the moulding of the state into a parable of the Kingdom of God and hence the fulfilment of the state's own righteous purposes.

15

The church is based on the knowledge of the one eternal God, who as such became *human* and thus is a human neighbor, in order to be compassionate (Luke 10.36f.). The inevitable consequence is that in the political sphere the church will always and in all circumstances be interested primarily in human beings and not in some abstract cause or other, whether it be anonymous capital or the state as such (the functioning of its departments!) or the honor of the nation or the progress of civilization or culture or the idea, however conceived, of the historical development of the human race. It will not be interested in this last idea even if "progress" is interpreted as meaning the welfare of future generations, for the attainment of which human beings, human dignity, human life in the present age are to be trampled underfoot. Right itself becomes wrong (*summum ius summa iniuria*) when it is allowed to rule as an abstract form, instead of serving the limitation and hence the preservation of human beings. The church is at all times and in all circumstances the enemy of the idol Juggernaut. Since God himself became human, real human beings are the measure of everything; they can only be risked — and in certain circumstances sacrificed — for people. Even the most wretched person must be resolutely defended — people's humanity, that is, not their egotism — against the autocracy of every mere "cause." People don't have to serve causes; causes have to serve people.

16

The church is witness of the divine justification, that is, of the act in which God in Jesus Christ established and confirmed his original claim to humanity and hence humanity's claim against sin and death. The future for which the church waits is the definitive revelation of this divine justification. This means that the church will always be found where the order of the state is based on a commonly acknowledged law, from submission to which no one is exempt, and which also provides equal protection for all. The church will be found where all political activity is in all circumstances regulated by this law. The church always stands for the constitutional state, for the maximum validity and application of that twofold rule (no exemption from and full protection by the law), and therefore it will always be against any degeneration of the constitutional state into tyranny or anarchy. The church will never be found on the side of anarchy or tyranny. In its politics it will always be urging the civil community to treat this fundamental purpose of its existence with the utmost seriousness: the limiting and the preserving of human beings by the quest for and the establishment of law.

17

The church is witness of the fact that the Son of Man came to seek and to save the *lost*. And this implies that — casting all false impartiality aside — the church must concentrate first on the lower and lowest levels of human society. The poor, the socially and economically weak and threatened, will always be the object of its primary and particular concern, and it will always insist on the state's special responsibility for these weaker members of society. That it will bestow its love on them — within the framework of its own task (as part of its service), is one thing and the most important thing; but it must not concentrate on this and neglect the other thing to which it is committed by its political responsibility: the effort to achieve such a fashioning of the law as will make it impossible for "equality before the law" to become a cloak under which strong and weak, independent and dependent, rich and poor, employers and employees, in fact receive different treatment at its hands: the weak being unduly restricted, the strong unduly protected. The church must stand for social justice in the political sphere. And in choosing between the various socialist possibilities (social-liberalism? co-operativism? syndicalism? free trade? moderate or radical Marxism?) it will always choose the movement from which it can expect the greatest measure of social justice (leaving all other considerations on one side).

18

The church is the fellowship of those who are called by the word of grace and the Spirit of the love of God to be the children of God in *freedom*. Translated into political terms, this means that the church affirms, as the basic right which every citizen must be guaranteed by the state, the freedom to carry out his decisions in the politically lawful sphere, according to his own insight and choice, and therefore independently, and the freedom to live in certain spheres (the family, culture, art, science, faith), safeguarded but not regulated by law. The church will not in all circumstances withdraw from and oppose what may be practically a dictatorship, that is, a partial and temporary limitation of these freedoms, but it will certainly withdraw from and oppose any out-and-out dictatorship such as the totalitarian state. The adult Christian can only wish to be an adult citizen, and he can only want his fellow citizens to live as adult human beings.

19

The church is the fellowship of those who, as members of the one Body of the one Head, are *bound* and *committed* to this Lord of theirs and therefore to no other. It follows that the church will never understand and interpret political freedom and the basic law which the state must guarantee to the individual citizen other than in the sense of the basic duty of responsibility which is required of him. (This was never made particularly clear in the classic proclamations of so-called "human rights" in America and France.) The citizen is responsible in the whole sphere of his freedom, political and non-political alike. And the civil community is naturally responsible in the maintenance of its freedom as a whole. Thus the Christian approach surpasses both individualism and collectivism. The church knows and recognizes the "interest" of the individual and of the whole, but it resists them both when they want to have the last word. It subordinates them to the being of the citizen, the being of the civil community before the law, over which neither the individuals nor the "whole" are to hold sway, but which they are to seek after, to find and to serve — always with a view to limiting and preserving human life.

20

As the fellowship of those who live in one faith under one Lord on the basis of a Baptism in one Spirit, the church must and will stand for the *equality* of the freedom and responsibility of all adult citizens, in spite of its sober insight into the variety of human needs, abilities and tasks. It will stand for their equality before the law that unites and binds them all, for their equality in working together to establish and carry out the law, and for their equality in the limitation and preservation of human life that it secures. If, in accordance with a specifically Christian insight, it lies in the very nature of the state that this equality must not be restricted by any differences of religious belief or unbelief, it is all the more important for the church to urge that the restriction of the political freedom and responsibility not only of certain classes and races but, supremely, of that of women, is an arbitrary convention which does not deserve to be preserved any longer. If Christians are to be consistent there can only be one possible decision in this matter.

21

Since the church is aware of the *variety* of the gifts and tasks of the one Holy Spirit in its own sphere, it will be alert and open in the political sphere to the need to *separate* the different junctions and "powers" — the legislative, executive and the judicial — inasmuch as those who carry out any one of these functions should not carry out the others simultaneously. No human being is a god able to unite in his own person the functions of the legislator and the ruler, the ruler and the judge, without endangering the sovereignty of the law. The "people" is no more such a god than the church is its own master and in sole possession of its powers. The fact is that within the community of the one people (by the people and for the people) definite and different services are to be performed by different persons, which, if they were united in one human hand, would disrupt rather than promote the unity of the common enterprise. With its awareness of the necessity that must be observed in this matter, the church will give a lead to the state.

22

The church lives from the disclosure of the true God and his revelation, from him as the *Light* that has been lit in Jesus Christ to destroy the works of darkness. It lives in the dawning of the day of the Lord and its task in relation to the world is to rouse it and tell it that this day has dawned. The inevitable political corollary of this is that the church is the sworn enemy of all secret policies and secret diplomacy. It is just as true of the political sphere as of any other that only evil can want to be kept secret. The distinguishing mark of the good is that it presses forward to the light of day. Where freedom and responsibility in the service of the state are one, whatever is said and done must be said and done before the ears and eyes of all, and the legislator, the ruler and the judge can and must be ready to answer openly for all their actions — without thereby being necessarily dependent on the public or allowing themselves to be flurried. The statecraft that wraps itself up in darkness is the craft of state which, because it is anarchic or tyrannical, is forced to hide the bad conscience of its citizens or officials. The church will not on any account lend its support to that kind of state.

23

The church sees itself established and nourished by the free *Word* of God — the Word which proves its freedom in the Holy Scriptures at all times. And in its own sphere the church believes that the human word is capable of being the free vehicle and mouthpiece of this free Word of God. By a process of analogy, it has to risk attributing a positive and constructive meaning to the free human word in the political sphere. If it trusts the human word in one sphere it cannot mistrust it on principle in the other. It will believe that human words are not bound to be empty or useless or even dangerous, but that the right words can clarify and control great decisions. At the risk of providing opportunities for empty, useless and dangerous words to be heard, it will therefore do all it can to see that there is at any rate no lack of opportunity for the *right* word to be heard. It will do all it can to see that there are opportunities for mutual discussion in the civil community as the basis of common endeavors. And it will try to see that such discussion takes place openly. With all its strength it will be on the side of those who refuse to have anything to do with the regimentation, controlling and censoring of public opinion. It knows of no pretext which would make that a good thing and no situation in which it could be necessary!

24

As disciples of Christ, the members of his church do not rule: they serve. In the political community, therefore, the church can only regard all ruling that is not primarily a form of service as a diseased and never as a normal condition. No state can exist without the sanction of power. But the power of the good state differs from that of the bad state as *potestas* differs from *potentia*. *Potestas* is the power that follows and serves the law; *potentia* is the power that precedes the law, that masters and bends and breaks the law — it is the naked power which is directly evil. Bismarck — not to mention Hitler — was (in spite of the *Daily Bible Readings* on his bedside table!) no model statesman because he wanted to establish and develop his work on naked power. The ultimate result of this all-too-consistently pursued aim was inevitable: "all that draw the sword shall perish by the sword." Christian political theory leads us in the very opposite direction.

25

Since the church is *ecumenical* (catholic) by virtue of its very origin, it resists all abstract local, regional and national interests in the political sphere. It will always seek to serve the best interests of the particular city or place where it is stationed. But it will never do this without at the same time looking out beyond the city walls. It will be conscious of the superficiality, relativity and temporariness of the immediate city boundaries, and on principle it will always stand for understanding and co-operation within the wider circle. The church will be the last to lend its support to mere parochial politics. *Pacta sunt servanda? Pacta sunt concludenda!* All cities of the realm must agree if their common cause is to enjoy stability and not fall to pieces. In the church we have tasted the air of freedom and must bring others to taste it too.

26

The church knows God's anger and judgment, but it also knows that his anger lasts but for a moment, whereas his mercy is for eternity. The political analogy of this truth is that violent solutions of conflicts in the political community — from police measures to law court decisions, from the armed rising against a régime that is no longer worthy of or equal to its task (in the sense of a revolt undertaken not to undermine but to restore the lawful authority of the state) to the defensive war against an external threat to the lawful state — must be approved, supported and if necessary even suggested by the Christian community — for how could it possibly contract out in such situations? On the other hand, it can only regard violent solutions of any conflict as an *ultima ratio regis.* It will approve and support them only when they are for the moment the ultimate and only possibility available. It will always do its utmost to postpone such moments as far as possible. It can never stand for absolute peace, for peace at any price. But it must and will do all it can to see that no price is considered too high for the preservation or restoration of peace at home and abroad except the ultimate price which would mean the abolition of the lawful state and the practical denial of the divine ordinance. May the church show her inventiveness in the search for other solutions before she joins in the call for violence! The perfection of the Father in heaven, who does not cease to be the heavenly Judge, demands the earthly perfection of a peace policy which really does extend to the limits of the humanly possible.

These are a few *examples* of Christian choices, decisions and activities in the political sphere: examples of parables, analogies and corollaries of that Kingdom of God in which the church believes and which it preaches, in the sphere of the external, relative and provisional problems of the civil community. The translation of the Kingdom of God into political terms demands Christian, spiritual and prophetic knowledge on every side. The points of comparison and the decisions we have quoted are in no sense equivalent to the paragraphs of a political constitution. They are merely intended to illustrate how the church can make decisions on a Christian basis in the political sphere. We might have taken twice or three times as many or only half as many examples or just one example to make the vital point clear. We used examples because we were concerned to illuminate the parabolic but extremely concrete relationship between the Christian gospel and certain political decisions and modes of behavior. The only more concrete way of discussing the relationship would be to refer to individual historical decisions. The reason why we mentioned many examples was that we wanted to demonstrate that the essence of Christian politics is not a system or a succession of momentary brainwaves but a constant direction, a continuous line of discoveries on both sides of the boundary which separates the political from the spiritual spheres, a correlation between explication and application. The list of such explications and applications that we have offered here is naturally incomplete. And it is of the very nature of all such points of comparison and decision as have been or could have been mentioned that the translations and transitions from the one sphere to the other will always be open to discussion as far as the details are concerned, will only be more or less obvious and never subject to absolute proof. What we have said here needs to be extended, deepened and particularised. The more one studies the problems of translation from one sphere to the other, the more one will realize that it is not possible to deal with every problem in this way. But the clarity of the message of the Bible will guarantee that all the explications and applications of the Christian approach will move in one unswerving direction and one continuous line. What we were concerned to show was the possibility and the necessity of comparisons and analogies between the two spheres and of the decisions which have to be made in the transition from one to the other.

28

Let me add a comment on the constancy and continuousness of the line of Christian political thought and action that we have indicated. We have argued not from any conception of "natural law" but from the gospel. It cannot be denied, however, that in the list of examples quoted we have more than once made assertions which have been justified elsewhere on the basis of natural law. We bear no grudge against anyone who may have been reminded of Rousseau — and who may have been pleased or angry on that account. We need not be ashamed of the affinity. We have seen that the divine ordinance of the state makes it perfectly possible for theoretical and practical insights and decisions to be reached, which are objectively right, where one would inevitably expect only errors and false steps, in view of the turbid source from which they derive. If our results really did coincide with theses based on natural law, it would merely confirm that the *polis* is in the Kingdom of Jesus Christ even when its office holders are not aware of the fact or refuse to admit it, and therefore are unable to use the insight into the nature of the *polis* which this fact suggests. Why should it be impossible that, in spite of the state's blindness, objectively correct insights have been and are being reached again and again? The pagan state lives because such leadership of the blind has repeatedly made its stability and its functions possible. All the more reason, surely, why the church cannot and must not withhold its witness to an insight based on clearly defined and consistently applicable facts.

29

A further comment on the constancy and continuity of the Christian approach in politics: it may be remarked (again, with pleasure or annoyance) that the Christian line that follows from the gospel betrays a striking tendency to the side of what is generally called the *"democratic"* state. Here again, we shall be careful not to deny an obvious fact, though "democracy" in any technical meaning of the word (Swiss, American, French, etc.), is certainly not necessarily the form of state closest to the Christian view. Such a state may equally well assume the form of a monarchy or an aristocracy, and occasionally even that of a dictatorship. Conversely, no democracy as such is protected from failing in many or all of the points we have enumerated and degenerating not only into anarchy but also into tyranny and thereby becoming a bad state. It must be admitted that the word and the concept "democracy" ("the rule of the people") is powerless to describe even approximately the kind of state which, in the Christian view, most nearly corresponds to the divine ordinance. This is no reason, however, why it should be overlooked or denied that Christian choices and purposes in politics tend on the whole towards the form of state, which, if it is not actually realized in the so-called "democracies," is at any rate more or less honestly clearly intended and desired. Taking everything into account, it must be said that the Christian view shows a stronger trend in this direction than in any other. There certainly is an *affinity* between the Christian community and the civil communities of the *free peoples*.

30

In conclusion, we propose to discuss the problem of how Christian decisions in the political sphere may be put into action.

The first method that suggests itself is the formation and activity of a special Christian party. This has long been adopted in Holland and later in Switzerland (Evangelical People's Party), and in recent times especially in France (Mouvement Républicain Populaire) and Germany (Christian Democratic Union). On the Protestant side it has been deemed possible and necessary to join forces with Roman Catholic fellow-citizens with the same political views. But parties are one of the most questionable phenomena in political life: they are in no sense its constitutive elements, and it is possible that from the very outset they have been pathological or at least no more than secondary phenomena. I wonder if the Christian community is well advised to add one more to the number of these organizations in order to fulfil its political co-responsibility? Can there be any other "Christian" party in the state but the Christian fellowship itself, with its special mission and purpose? And if what we want is a political corollary of the church in political life, can anything else be permissible and possible but — please do not be scared! — a single state party excluding all others, whose program would necessarily coincide with the tasks of the state itself, understood in the widest sense (but excluding all particularist ideas and interests)? How can there be a special Christian party alongside other political parties? — a party to which some Christians belong, whilst others do not — a party opposed by other non-Christian parties (which it must nevertheless recognize as legitimately non-Christian). To institute special Christian parties implies that the Christian community as such has no claim on the support of all its members for its own political line. It implies that it cannot help but allow the non-Christians in the state to consolidate themselves in a non-Christian bloc in order to enforce their own anti-Christian line. The church's supreme interest must be rather that Christians shall not mass together in a special party, since their task is to defend and proclaim, in decisions based on it, the Christian gospel that concerns all people. They must show that although they go their own special way, they are not in fact against anybody but unconditionally for all, for the common cause of the whole state.

In the political sphere the Christian community can draw attention to its gospel only indirectly, as reflected in its political decisions, and these decisions can be made intelligible and brought to victory not because they are based on Christian premises but only because they are politically better and more calculated to preserve and develop the common life. They can only witness to Christian truths. The claim to be witnesses to Christian truths does not necessarily make them such, however! Surely it will be inevitable that the Christian qualities for which it can have no use in the political sphere will become an embarrassment to a Christian party? And will not the aims and methods which it needs if it is to be effective as a political party (the winning of majorities and political strongholds, propaganda and the benevolent toleration and even encouragement of non-Christian or problematically Christian sympathisers and even leaders; compromises and coalitions with "non-Christian" parties and so on) compel it to deny the specifically Christian content of its policy or at any rate obscure rather than illuminate it? Will such a party not inevitably be compromising the Christian church and its message all the time? In the political sphere Christians can only bring in their Christianity anonymously. They can break through this anonymity only by waging a political battle for the church and by so doing they will inevitably bring discredit and disgrace on the Christian name. In the authentically political questions which affect the development of the civil community Christians can only reply in the form of decisions which could be the decisions of any other citizens, and they must frankly hope that they may become the decisions of all other citizens regardless of their religious profession. How can Christians mass together in a political party at all in these circumstances? The thing is only possible — and the suspicious alliance of the Protestants with the Romans in the French M.R.P. and the German C.D.U. shows that it only becomes successful, where the Kingdom of God is interpreted as a human goal founded on natural law, where an allegedly Christian law, which is in fact a mere amalgam of humanitarian philosophy and morality, is set alongside the gospel in the political sphere. When it is represented by a Christian party the Christian community cannot be the political salt which it is its duty to be in the civil community.

31

The opportunity that it is offered to fulfil this duty is simply the one that lies nearest to hand: the preaching of the whole *gospel* of God's grace, which as such is the whole justification of whole people — including politics. This gospel which proclaims the King and the Kingdom that is now hidden but will one day be revealed, is political from the very outset, and if it is preached to real (Christian and non-Christian) people on the basis of a right interpretation of the Scriptures it will necessarily be prophetically political. Explications and applications of its political content in an unmistakable direction will inevitably take place (whether in direct or indirect illumination of the political problems of the day) where the Christian community is gathered together in the service of this gospel. Whether this happens or not will depend on the preachers, but not only on them. It is a bad sign when Christians are frightened by "political" sermons — as if Christian preaching could be anything but political. And if it were not political, how would it show that it is the salt and the light of the world? The Christian church that is aware of its political responsibility will demand political preaching; and it will interpret it politically even if it contains no direct reference to politics. Let the church concentrate first, however, on seeing that the whole gospel really is preached within its own area. Then there will be no danger of the wider sphere beyond the church not being wholesomely disturbed by it.

32

The Christian community acts within the meaning and limits of its own mission and competence when it speaks, through the mouth of its presbyterial and synodal organs, in important situations in political life, by making representations to the authorities or by public *proclamations*. It will be careful to select, as wisely as possible, the particular situations in which it deems it right to speak, and it will have to choose its words very prudently and very definitely if it is to be heard. It must not give the impression that it never wakes from the sleep of an otherwise non-political existence until such matters as gambling or the abuse of alcohol or the desecration of the Sabbath or similar questions of a religious and ethical nature in the narrower sense are under discussion, as if such problems were not in fact only on the verge of real political life. The church must see that it does not make a habit of coming on the scene too late, of entering the fray only when its opinions no longer involve any particular risk and can no longer exert any particular influence. It must see above all that the idea of the church as the representative of a definitive class-conditioned outlook and morality is not allowed to gain ground, thereby confirming those who already loyally believe in this "law" and arousing the disapproval of those who are, on the contrary, unable to regard such a "law" as in any sense eternal. All this applies just as much to the Christian journalism and writing that is carried on with or even without the authority of the church. Christian publicists and writers must place themselves honestly in the service of the gospel which is intended for all people and not devote their gifts to some Christian fad or another.

33

Perhaps the most important contribution the church can make is to bear in mind in the shaping of its own life that, gathered as it is directly and consciously around the common center, it has to represent the inner within the outer circle. The real church must be the model and prototype of the real state. The church must *set an example* so that by its very existence it may be a source of renewal for the state and the power by which the state is preserved. The church's preaching of the gospel would be in vain if its own existence, constitution, order, government and administration were not a practical demonstration of the thinking and acting from the gospel which takes place in this inner circle. How can the world believe the gospel of the King and his Kingdom if by its own actions and attitudes the church shows that it has no intention of basing its own internal policy on the gospel? How can a reformation of the whole people be brought about if it is common knowledge that the church itself is bent only on self-preservation and restoration — or not even that? Of the political implications of theology which we have enumerated there are few which do not merit attention first of all in the life and development of the church itself. So far they have not received anything like enough attention within the church's own borders.

What nonsense it is, for example, that in a country like Germany which has diligently to learn the rudiments of law, freedom, responsibility, equality and so on, that is, the elements of the democratic way of life, the church considers it necessary to act more and more hierarchically and bureaucratically and becomes a refuge for nationalism in a situation in which it ought supremely to appear as the holy catholic church, and thereby help to lead German politics out of an old defile. The church must not forget that what it is rather than what it says will be best understood, not least in the state.

34

If the church is a Christian community it will not need a Christian party. If it is a true fellowship it will perform with its words and its whole existence all the functions which the disastrous enterprise of "Christian parties is evidently intended to fulfil. There will be no lack of individual Christians who will enter the political arena anonymously, that is, in the only way they can appear on the political scene, and who will act in accordance with the Christian approach and will thereby prove themselves unassuming witnesses of the gospel of Christ, which can alone bring salvation in the political sphere no less than elsewhere. Any fame that they acquire will not be founded on the fact that they are "nice, pious people" but simply that from their own distinctive point of view they will know better than others what is best for the civil community. It is not the presence and co-operation of "Christian personalities" that helps the state. One thinks of Bismarck again: assuming for the moment that he was something like the "Christian personality" that legend describes him to have been, what difference did it make to the unfortunate tendency of his politics? What help was it to poor Germany? The way Christians can help in the political sphere is by constantly giving the state an impulse in the Christian direction and freedom to develop on the Christian line. Let it not be said that there are too few of such Christians and that these few in their isolation are helpless. How much one individual can do whose heart and soul is really wrapped up in the cause! And in any case Christians are not asked to do something in their own strength, but only what they are required to do by the grace of God.

What does it matter if they are isolated and if — since there are such things as parties — they are members of different parties, that is, of one of the various "non-Christian" parties? They will take the party program, party discipline, party victories and party defeats in which they are involved, as seriously and humorously as the cause deserves. In every party they will be against narrow party policies and stand up for the interests of the whole community. By that token they will be political men and women in the primary meaning of the word. Scattered in different places, and known or unknown to one another, in touch with one another or out of touch, they will all be together — as citizens, and will make the same distinctions and judgments, choose and desire one cause, work for one cause. Let us pray that the church may supply the state with such Christians, such citizens, such political men and women in the primary meaning of the word! For in their existence the church will be fulfilling its political co-responsibility in the most direct form.

35

Let me remind you once again of the fifth thesis of the *Theological Declaration* of Barmen, which I have quoted from several times already:

The Bible tells us that, in accordance with a divine ordinance, the state has the task of providing for law and peace in the world that still awaits redemption, in which the church stands, according to the measure of human insight and human capacity, and upheld by the threat and use of force. The church acknowledges the benefaction of this divine ordinance with a thankful, reverent heart. It reminds people of God's Kingdom, God's commandment and justice, and thereby of the responsibility of governors and governed alike. It trusts and obeys the power of the Word by which God sustains all things.

I think that I have dealt with "The Christian Community and the Civil Community" within the terms of this thesis, and therefore in accordance with the mind of the Confessing Church in Germany. Some things would be different now if that church had itself given more attention to this section of the Declaration in good time. But it cannot be too late to return to it now with a new seriousness, deepened and strengthened by experience.   *(AS: 15-50)*

*

AGAINST ABSTRACT ANTI-COMMUNISM; ANSWER TO BRUNNER (1948)

Following Barth's trip to Hungary in 1948, Brunner wrote him a shrill and emotional open letter arguing that there was no fundamental difference between the "monster" of "totalitarian Communism" and the "brown mon-

ster," Nazi totalitarianism. If anything, the Nazis were "amateurs" whereas the Soviet Union was a "consistently totalitarian State" (AS, 106ff.). He criticized Barth's view that the church should not become an echo of Western cold war anti-communism. He appealed to Barth's socialism by arguing that "Socialism is engaged in a life and death struggle against 'Communism' . . . because it is fundamentally and passionately anti-totalitarian (AS, 109f.)." Further, he argued, "the totalitarian state is intrinsically atheistic" and is basically unjust in denying human rights. He concluded by asking if his Basel colleague was adopting an "attitude of passive unconcern," and — misinterpreting a famous phrase of Barth's from 1933 — doing theology "as if nothing had happened." Barth replied promptly. His answer illustrates his belief that the church of a living Lord must live in freedom for concrete witness in the changing historical conditions of political life, and cannot be imprisoned in bloc mentalities, ideologies and abstract principles.

Basel
June 6th, 1948

Dear Emil Brunner!

You do not seem to understand. At the moment I am not rousing the church to oppose communism and to witness against it, in the same way as I did between 1933 and 1945 in the case of National Socialism; you demand a "clear reply" to the question of how this is to be construed. I will come straight to the point.

Let us begin with a general statement. A certain binding spiritual and theological viewpoint in accordance with its creed is demanded of the church in the political realm in certain times of need, i.e. when it is called upon to vindicate its faith in the carrying out of its duty according to God's Word, or when it is called upon to give an explanation regarding a definite occurrence. The church must not concern itself eternally with various "isms" and systems, but with historical realities as seen in the light of the Word of God and of faith. Its obligation lie, not in the direction of any fulfilling of a natural law, but towards its living Lord. Therefore, the church never thinks, speaks or acts "on principle." Rather it judges spiritually and by individual cases. For that reason it rejects every attempt to systematize political history and its own part in that history. Therefore, it preserves the freedom to judge each new event afresh. If yesterday it travelled along one path, it is not bound to keep to the same path today. If yesterday it spoke from its position of responsibility, then today it should be silent if in this position it considers silence to be the better course. The unity and continuity of theology will best be preserved if the church does not let itself be discouraged from being up-to-date theologically.

I ask this question: Was it not true that in the years after 1933 up till the end of the war there really was this need? The Central and Western European peoples — first Germany, then the others — had succumbed to Hitler's spell. He had become a spiritual and, almost everywhere, a political source of temptation. He had English, French and American admirers. Did not even Churchill have a few friendly words to say for him? And in Switzerland there were more than two hundred sympathizers, there was a Rudolf Grob, there were innumerable people who were impressed and influenced, though also very many who were frightened and despondent. One of the most important aims of our political authorities was to preserve correct and friendly relations with our powerful neighbor. In the Swiss Zofinger Society there was a serious discussion as to whether it was not time to subject our democratic system, established in 1848 (which event we are triumphantly celebrating today) to a thorough revision. Of the state of the press one can read in the edifying book by Karl Weber, *Switzerland in the War of Nerves.* How great were the cares of our military directors can be seen from the account of our General, and from the fine book by Lt.-Col. Barbey about the five years he spent in the General's entourage. It was at that time that I made my various attempts to make the church ready for action against the temptations of National Socialism, in Germany obviously spiritual, in Switzerland obviously political. At that time it had to warn against tempters, to recall those who had strayed, to rouse the careless, to "confirm the feeble knees," to comfort sorrowing hearts.

Whether the essence of National Socialism consisted in its "totalitarianism" or, according to other views, in its "nihilism," or again in its barbarism, or anti-semitism, or whether it was a final, concluding outburst of the militarism which had taken hold on Germany like a madness since 1870 — what made it interesting from the Christian point of view was that it was a spell which notoriously revealed its power to overwhelm our souls, to persuade us to believe in its lies and to join in its evil-doings. It could and would take us captive with "strong mail of craft and power."[72] We were hypnotized by it as a rabbit by a giant snake. We were in danger of bringing, first incense, and then the complete sacrifice to it as to a false god. That ought not to have been done. We had to object with all our protestantism as though against *the* evil. It was not a matter of declaiming against some mischief, distant and easily seen through. It was a matter of life and death, of resistance against a godlessness which was in fact attacking body and soul, and was therefore effectively masked to many thousands of Christian eyes. For that very reason I spoke then and was not silent. For that very reason I could not forgive the collaborators, least of all those among them who were cultured, decent and well-meaning. In that way I consider that I acted as befits the church.

Now a second question: Is it not true that today there is again a state of emergency, this time in the shape of communism? Has history already repeated itself, in that today we only need to take the remedy (which at that time took long enough to learn) from out of our pockets and to make immediate use of it? In the last few years I have become acquainted with Western Germany and also with the non-Russian sectors of Berlin. Fear, distrust and hatred for the "Eastern monster," as you call it, I met there in abundance, but apart from the German Communists I met no people of whom I received the impression (as one did with almost everybody in 1933) that they felt that this "monster" was a vexation, a temptation, an enticement, or that they were in danger of liking it or of condoning its deeds and of co-operating with it. On the contrary, it was quite clear to everyone, and it was universally agreed that for many reasons there was nothing in it. Is the situation any different here in Switzerland? in France, England or America? Are we not all convinced, whether we have read *I Chose Freedom* or not, that we cannot consider the way of life of the people in Soviet territory and in the Soviet-controlled "peoples' democracies" to be worthy, acceptable or of advantage to us, because it does not conform to our standards of justice and freedom? Who can contradict this? A few Western European Communists! Yet are we in danger of letting ourselves be overwhelmed by this power merely on account of the existence and the activities of these latter? Who is not free — and who would not take advantage of this freedom? — to vent their anger against this "monster" to their hearts' content, and again and again to bring to light its evils as "thoroughly" and as "passionately" as they wish? Anyone who would like from me a political disclaimer of its system and its methods may have it at once. However, what is given cheaply can be had cheaply. Surely it would cost no one anything — not even a little thought — certainly nothing more, to add his bundle of faggots to the bonfire? I cannot admit that this is a repetition of the situation and of the tasks during the years 1935-45. For I cannot admit that it is the duty of Christians or of the church to give theological backing to what every citizen can, with much shaking of the head, read in the daily paper and what is so admirably expressed by Mr. Truman and by the Pope. Has the "East" or whatever we may call it, really such a hold over us that we must needs oppose it with our last breath when the last but one would suffice? No, when the church witnesses it moves in fear and trembling, not with the stream but against it. Today it certainly has no cause to move against the stream and thus to witness to communism because it could never be worthy of it, either in its Marxist or its imperialist, or let us say, in its Asiatic aspects. Must the church then move with the stream and thus side with America and the Vatican, merely because somewhere in the text-books of its professors — ever since 1934 — it has rightly been said that "totalitarianism" is a dreadful thing? Where is the spiritual danger and need which the church would meet if it witnessed to this truth, where is its commission to do so? Whom would it teach, enlighten, rouse, set on the right path, comfort and lead to repentance and a new way of life? Surely not the "Christian" peoples of the West, nor the Americans! Are they not already sure enough of the justice of their cause against Russia without this truth and our Christian support? Surely not the poor Russians and even the poor communists? For how should they be able to understand what the Western church, which in the old days and even today has accepted so much "totalitarianism" and has co-operated with it without witnessing against it, claims to have against their church? Surely not the Christian churches behind the Iron Curtain? In their struggle with the "monster" it would be no help at all to them if we were to proclaim those well-known truths as energetically as possible, since we are not asked for them anyway, nor would they cost us anything. As it is not possible to give satisfactory answers to these questions, I am of the opinion that the church today — contrary to its action between 1933 and 1945 — ought to stand quietly aloof from the present conflict and not let off all its guns before it is necessary but wait calmly to see whether and in what sense the situation will grow serious again and call for speech. If a definite spiritual crisis were again to develop as it did during the years 1933-45 — though we do not yet know from what direction it is likely to come — then a concrete answer would be demanded from us, for which we ourselves should have to pay: then it would be obvious against whom and for whom we should have to witness, and whether and how far we should be prepared for this new emergency. Then something would be at stake other than these eternal truths which you wish me to proclaim. According to my view, we shall then profit more from the first article of the Declaration of Barmen than from your knowledge of the objectionableness of "totalitarianism."

But, however that may be, with this problem in view I met responsible members of the Reformed Church in Hungary and thought that I could encourage them in their attempt to walk along the narrow path midway between Moscow and Rome. I did not take a ruler with me to draw this dividing line, so I could not leave one behind for their use. Their past history, their present situation and their task do not resemble ours, nor those of the Evangelical Church in Germany which is joining in the battle. They have come to an agreement with the new régime and are directing all their energies towards the positive tasks of their church, and this is not the same as what the central parties, which you esteem so highly, or even the "German Christians," are doing in the battle for the church in Germany. Incidentally, it is a legend without historical foundation that in 1931 I recommended "passive resistance" when I urged the Germans to fulfil their duties of Christian witness "as though nothing had happened," i.e. ignoring Adolf Hitler's alleged divine revelation. If they had consequently done so, they would have built up against National Socialism a political factor of the first order.

For Hungary, though not only for this country, everything depends on whether the church, not bound to abstract principles but to its living Lord, will seek and find its own way and also learn to choose freely the time for speech and the time for silence and all the various other times mentioned in Ecclesiastes, Chapter 3, without thereby becoming confused by any law other than that of the gospel.

Your Karl Barth

(AS: 113-118)

*

THE CHURCH BETWEEN EAST AND WEST

The year after his exchange with Brunner, Barth further explicated his views on problems of East-West relations and the Cold War. Once again he made a case for Christian freedom, and made it plain that his cry "no partisanship!" was not a call for neutrality but for a third way of "reconstruction." Indeed, by arguing that God's justice establishes human freedom and God's majestic freedom impetuously demands human justice, Barth was suggesting that the church's gospel pointed beyond the polarizations of East and West towards a true peace of God. This essay was first trans-

lated by Stanley Godman in World Review *in June-July 1949, and reprinted by Ronald Gregor Smith in 1954 in his selection of Barth's post-war writings,* Against the Stream.

1

This problem of the situation of the church between East and West is a real one; if on the surface it is merely a cloud of much wise, but even more foolish, talk and writing, in the depths it is a real difficulty and a task which concerns us all today. As it affects us so nearly, it certainly is also the concern of the God who became the brother of humanity — of all people in all ages — in his Son. And if it is his concern, then it must also be the concern of his church which is his witness on earth. The church must seek an answer to the problem. And this answer must be an honest and authentic answer.

The church is the community of Christian people, the living congregation of the living Lord Jesus Christ. In the church, therefore, no one can, as it were, stand outside and merely look at what others are doing, listen to what others are saying. In the church all are under question and all responsible. When one voice speaks in the church, that is merely an invitation and a call to all to co-operate as *Christians.* Therefore we can seek for the answer to this problem only in this community of Christians. By that I mean that we must all bring what stirs and concerns us in this problem before the judgment seat of him in whose name we are all baptized, in whom we trust that he alone will judge aright in this matter, as in all others. We must all ask for his Holy Spirit that he may illuminate us in this matter and make us to speak and to hear what is right. We cannot take it for granted that that will happen. For, besides being Christians, we are all rather a lot of other things as well — for instance, representatives of this or that economic interest, readers of this or that newspaper, perhaps members of this or that party, and in addition to all that, under the compulsion of old or new intellectual habits and traditions — and do not let us forget that we are all provided with our own greater or lesser hard-headedness and our own greater or lesser soft-heartedness. But let us approach this present problem as Christians. If we do that, we shall certainly not fail to come at least a step nearer to an answer. I say this also as a *warning* to those who may hear what I have to say merely as lookers-on, who may be passionately interested in the problem of East and West, but only slightly or not at all interested in the church. To them I should like to say: "Do not be surprised if what I shall say annoys you!" I am concerned with where we stand as *Christians* in this problem.

2

First there is a more simple form of the present conflict of East and West — and the Christian answer to that conflict can also be a more simple answer. The conflict is in its simplest terms a form of the world-political *struggle for power*. We do not wish to spend too much time on that, for the question only becomes really burning in reference to another quite different form of the conflict. But it will help us to prepare our minds for the more difficult problem if we look at it for a moment.

What do we mean by East and West? First of all certainly quite simply the two world powers: Russia and the United States of America. Whatever else one may, and must, understand by East and West, the problem acquires its present complexion and weight from the fact that it is incorporated in these two world powers: each in its natural and historical individuality, each with its special interests and aspirations, each with its special political, social, economic and also military potentialities. That the present world-political power conflict is a conflict between Russia and America is something peculiar to our time. What would a Bismarck or Gladstone, or even a Metternich and a Richelieu, have said if they had lived to see it? But the fact is that the former "great powers" of the little peninsula called Europe have almost ceased to exist as such, have ceased to compete in the struggle for world dominion, or are at any rate passing through a grave crisis in this respect — I am thinking of what we still call the "British Empire." Japan has fallen out altogether. China will perhaps become a power to be reckoned with one day, but not yet awhile. All that remains are Russia and America. They were the decisive factors in the late war. These two powers face each other today, eye to eye, ignoring their fellow-victors as well as the defeated. On the one hand, Russia asserts a claim which has been announced and prepared by her Czars since Peter the Great. And, as the incorporation of the Slavonic world, which for a thousand years was driven back to the East from the West, she is now powerfully pressing and striking back from East to West. On the other hand, America enjoys the advantage of having been able to keep her country intact during two world wars in which she did not participate at close quarters. In both wars she became rich and powerful on land and sea and in the air. And out of these she has made a completely new discovery, of which she is now making the

303

fullest use: she has discovered her own importance in the world.

Russia and America are both, though in different ways, children of old Europe. They are children who have run away from their mother or, to put it more pleasantly perhaps, children who have come of age, who, at first quietly and then very suddenly, have grown into giants. They are giant rivals who agree in this (for each says it of itself), that each, in its own way, would like to be teacher, patron, protector, benefactor — or, to put it more frankly, the master of their old mother, Europe, and with that of the rest of the world as well. Both have this, too, in common — that they are each surrounded by a safety-zone of other greater and smaller states which, though formally independent, are, to put it impolitely, vassals of one of the other, linked up more or less closely in a so-called bloc. Then between these safety-zones we have the famous Iron Curtain, through whose openings each of these two great powers proclaims its dislike of the other in abusive language and hurtful pinpricks. Both are very fond of phrases like "the free community of the nations" and "peace." It is not very clear what either of them means by "freedom," but for the present there is no reason to suppose that either of them is seeking war, and to that extent is in fact seeking peace. What they have in common is, finally, this: that they are both afraid of the other, because they both feel encircled and threatened by the other. And since the earth is spherical, both may be right in a way. One must concede to the Eastern partner, however, that its anxiety may be somewhat better founded than that of its opponent, if one observes from a map in how many places America — directly, or indirectly through her British ally — has blocked Russia's access to the open sea. That, then, is the more simple form of the present conflict between East and West.

3

The answer of the *Christian* attitude to this conflict can also be put in a comparatively *simple* form.

We must remember, above all, that, as Christians, we may be startled by an event like this, but we must under no circumstances take *fright*. Such happenings belong to a certain extent to the natural history of the world, in which the Kingdom of God, the glory of Jesus Christ, has been proclaimed but has not yet appeared, has not yet been revealed. There have been such mighty lords with their fear, one of the other, and with their quarrels; there have been such concentrations and conflicts of secular power before in history. They are probably one form of the travail in which the creature is waiting for the great Revelation, one form of that bondage of the transient life, from which the creature will one day be freed into the glorious liberty of the children of God.

They are part of the shadow of the judgments passed on humanity on the Cross of Calvary and in which God revealed himself to humanity as a God of mercy. They cannot shake the secret dominion of Jesus Christ, let alone overthrow it, and therefore they can neither shake nor overthrow the hope for the whole creation in which we, as we look up to him, look towards the end of the ways of God. They can put the belief in his promise to the test, but they cannot endanger it. One thinks instinctively of the situation of Israel between Egypt on the one hand, and Assyria on the other. One thinks of those great wild animals which are spoken of in the Book of Daniel. There is no reason why one should not take that as a starting point and think of all the great movements and crises of world history from the appearance of Jesus Christ right up to our own day. They came and they went. There was always a community of Christian people there in the midst of them, suffering and enduring, but surviving them. At least, their Christian witness joyfully outlasted the roaring of the animals again and again. The extent of the contemporary conflict does not make it any more difficult for us than smaller conflicts of this kind have been for the men of other ages. So far as the conflict between Russia and America is concerned, one single hymn by Paul Gerhardt is stronger than the worst that we have read in the papers or will ever read or experience ourselves. It would be a great gain for the whole discussion of the East-West problem if we were to become quite clear as Christians, at any rate, that fear must not be allowed to be our counsellor in this matter. That is one thing which we have to tell ourselves and our companions today.

The other is: *not to take part* in the conflict. As Christians it is not our concern at all. It is not a genuine, not a necessary, not an interesting conflict. It is a mere power-conflict. We can only warn against the still greater crime of wanting to decide the issue in a third world war. We can only speak in favor and support of every relaxation of the tension, and do what we can to increase the remaining fund of reason which may still be at the disposal of notoriously unreasonable humanity. With the gospel in our hearts and on our lips, we can only go through the midst of these two quarrelling giants with the prayer: "Deliver us from evil! . . ." What we can do in the midst of the conflict can only consist in the wholehearted, sincere and helpful sympathy which we are in duty bound to extend to all its victims as far as lies within our power. What we

Swiss would have to defend if it came to the worst could never be anything but our Swiss neutrality and our Christian freedom: only the forgotten cause of God and humanity in international life and never the cause of Russian or American imperialism.

The third thing that has to be mentioned is what I have called the Christian *disillusionment,* which we can gain from this first aspect of the matter. We shall have to look at that under a different aspect shortly. We shall see that the antithesis of East and West does not consist only in a world-political power conflict. But we must not forget the first aspect of the matter for a single moment. We shall have to look at the ostensibly higher conflict with which we now have to deal very closely to see whether it is not, in fact, so closely related to the very unholy battle between the two giants which we have been discussing as to make it impossible to see good on the one side, and evil on the other, here an Angel of Light, there the incarnation of Satan. Whatever we now have to consider, the first aspect of the matter should have been a warning to us, forcing us to ask ourselves whether it can be Christian from any point of view to *take sides,* as the conflict between East and West is primarily simply this quarrel between two giants. Will not the way of the community of Jesus Christ have to be another, a *third* way, its *own* way?

4

What is the meaning of "East and West"? It is true that it is, among other things — and it is already becoming more difficult to describe it — the conflict which has become so acute today between two different anthropologies, and especially of the social and politico-economic ordering of life, between two powerful intellectual *principles* and *systems,* two *"ideologies,"* to use the term of which the Russians are particularly fond. This conflict is, moreover, not merely a quite interesting but harmless "academic" quarrel between the adherents of two different schools of thought, but a conflict between two modes of living, applied quite consistently to all the details of daily life, a conflict between two sets of facts, two textures of life, in which not merely America and Russia, but under their leadership a great part of the world is involved, co-responsibly and as co-sufferers. What are the issues? As it is a quarrel, let us simply listen to the accusations which East and West hold out against each other.

This is what the West says, what it complains of: what you want and what you are putting into practice in the East is based on a completely wrong, one-sidedly materialistic anthropology. You act as if people were merely economic beings, as if production and consumption were the only problem in life, and their organization the task to which all others must be subordinated. You have the absurd belief that human beings will be good once this organization is properly established. You have the absurd belief that humanity is already at any rate good enough to create the perfect organization for which you imagine, absurdly, that you have the recipe in your pocket, the recipe of radical socialism. And precisely in order to bring about this perfect organization of economic relationships of yours, you allow the individual only enough freedom to produce and consume, enough freedom to take part in the fight for this perfect order — and woe to any one who claims for himself any other freedom in his actions and words or even in his thoughts in so far as they can be guessed from outside! Thus you make people mere components of a collective whole, of a machine; you make them into *Massenmenschen*. And in carrying through the struggle for this socialism of yours, you know and respect no higher law and make use of any available means: whether it is the most transparent propaganda, or the most reckless agitation or, even worse, the most calculatingly cruel and brutal police methods imaginable. In fighting this struggle, you sacrifice ruthlessly not merely thousands, but millions, of human lives. We charge you with *inhumanity*. But this is not surprising, for it is obvious and you even say so yourselves, that you have either never known Christian civilization or you have cast it wantonly away. You live by a faith in which the barren demon of your idea of social progress has taken the place of God. This *false faith* is the other charge we bring against you. This is how the West speaks to, and about, the East. But as Christians it is right that we should hear what the other side has to say as well.

This is what the East says; this is the burden of its complaint against the West: what you in the West want and what you put into practice is based on a completely wrong, because hypocritical, spiritual and moral anthropology. You know as well as we do that people are economic beings and that, in fact, life really revolves around production and consumption in the West just as much as it does with us in the East. But you will simply not admit it because things are not what they should be with you. You criticize our materialism and you talk so much about spiritual things and morality because you have something to hide: namely, the fact that you are ruled by money, by blind, anonymous capital, and the yield of interest; some few of you are the wheels, but most of you, the overwhelming majority, whether you know it or not, are under the wheels of the cart on which your real god sits enthroned. *You* are breeding the real *Massenmenschen,* not *we!* Do not come along to us with your merely formal democracy as if that made you free, because you pay an occasional visit to the polling-station, are allowed to have and express your own opinions and have independent papers and parties and all the rest of the bag of tricks. To whom do they all owe allegiance in the last resort — your papers and parties and unions from which you get your supposedly free opinions, and your democratically elected councils, and even your courts of law? Where else but in the great banks are the wires pulled on which you dance in your imagined freedom; who else but the banks decide in the last resort whether you are able to work or not, to earn or not to earn, and therefore to live or not to live? Is not any means good enough for you when you are carrying on your partly wilful, partly deluded fight for the dominion of this god of yours; any kind of war, and in peacetime any civilized brutality and fraud, any machination and profiteering, any lying about inconvenient facts and persons? Your whole so-called democracy is dust thrown in the eyes of the masses to which, above all, your so-called intellectuals belong as well. Your pretended esteem for spiritual things and morality and, above all, your pretended Christianity in which you speak of *God,* so that real human life shall not be discussed and revealed, in which you refer people to *heaven* so that everything shall remain as it is on earth, in which you talk about cultivating the *inner life* as if there could be any inner life worth speaking of when the outer life is so corrupt — all this is dust thrown in the eyes of the people, a deliberate deception. What charges do we bring against you? *Inhumanity* in the first place and a *false,* because absolutely hypocritical, *faith* in the second!

So there we have the two choruses to whose alternating song we have to listen today.

5

And now what about the *church?* What about us *Christians?* If we speak of ourselves, of our church and of ourselves as Christians, then it will be as well to be quite clear in the first place that we are not disinterested, nor impartial in this matter. Geographical and natural circumstances inevitably lead us to take sides with America and the Western hemisphere. And therefore we are influenced in our judgment of the issue. We hear the voice of the Western chorus; we hear its battle-hymn against the East much more strongly, much more clearly than that of the East against the West. Furthermore, something inside us instinctively joins in the battle-hymn of the West, whilst it goes against the grain for us to listen to the chorus of the East at all. Now, it has pleased God to bring us into the world as people of the West. But it does not follow by any means that it pleases him that we should simply give way to Western prejudices and especially to the pressure of our Western environment. It follows rather that we must be all the more on our guard against regarding our *Western judgment* as the right and *Christian judgment.* We have, precisely because we are here in the midst of the Western world, every reason to remember our *duty* and our *freedom* as Christians.

Now it is certainly merely a Western opinion, and by no means simply on that account a Christian opinion, that the political attitude which it is incumbent on the church to take up today should consist in a choice between the two opposing and quarrelling world systems. Your money or your life! Clearly defined words! Clear decision! Open partisanship! Such are the cries that go up today from every street in the West, and it is taken for granted which party it is intended the church should support. How the Amsterdam Church Conference was criticized for not coming to the clear-cut partisan decision on this issue that was expected of it! Curiously enough, the West has not always cried thus to the church. In other cases it has not always showed the same interest in being confronted by the church with a clear-cut either-or. The same West has, in fact, blamed us, either in certain or uncertain language, for taking sides, when we regarded it as our duty to do so, and has spared no effort in reminding us that the church should stand above all conflicts and parties. Why this eagerness today? We are not going to pursue the question, but simply want, first of all, to state quite clearly that the church is *not* identical with the West, that the Western conscience and judgment is not necessarily the Christian judgment. Just as the Christian judgment and the Christian conscience are not necessarily the Eastern conscience and judgment either. That is precisely what they are trying to ram into the Eastern church today with the same eagerness, that the conscience and judgment of the Eastern church must be identical with that of the East. And how can we see exactly from this distance whether the Christians in Prague and Budapest would prefer to remain "firm" rather than tread the path of collaboration? Would *we* be remaining firm, would we not rather already be treading the path of collaboration with the West if we were to succumb to that cry "Your money or your life!"? We have *no* Christian reason to meddle with that at all. We have rather every Christian reason, simply to say quite clearly and decisively: *neither* money nor life! — no partisanship! That is the first element in our Christian *political* attitude: our refusal to fight one way or the other in this conflict. We are not saying that merely as an edifying truth in the quietness of the study; we are saying it to the West, to all of you: The cause of the West may be our cause because we happen to live in the West, happen to inherit Western traditions, but it is not therefore necessarily God's cause — just as the cause of the East is certainly not God's cause either. Therefore, as far as we are concerned, what we have to say is, first of all: Away with the knives! No more oil on this fire! For, if we simply go on cursing each other until there is nothing left to do but have another war, then nothing will improve in any case, no one will be helped and no problem solved. The only possible way is a third way. Let the church in the East see to it that it says the same thing there! It is all we have to say, we of the church in the West.

6

Ten years ago one single and absolutely clear-cut political and spiritual menace stood on the horizon, and to turn against the wild boar then was not to commit the folly of exposing one's rear to the wolf. Ten years ago it was a question of National Socialism, and that was not a movement which had a single serious question to put to us, but it was quite simply a mixture of madness and crime in which there was no trace of reason. At that time it was still impossible for anyone to realize the full depth and extent of its madness and criminality. But, with a bit of instinct, it was not difficult to make a fairly accurate guess! The whole business was complicated by the fact that National Socialism tried to represent and recommend itself in the guise of a falsified Christianity. Ten years ago it was one's simple duty to call the world to *order*. And ten years ago, and during the first years of the war, it was necessary to warn people to keep *alert* and *watchful*, because, in spite of everything, there was a certain magical quality in Nazism, and it was a long time before the enemy was recognized as such, and he had stupid supporters and advocates even in the very church itself. There was a curious softness and adaptability in the whole European attitude towards the Nazi movement and above all, even at that time, a great and trembling *fear* of it. Incidentally, ten years ago it *cost* something to say the one-sided, unequivocal "No" that it was necessary and imperative to say at that time. For anyone who said that "No" was not able to whistle it with all the sparrows from the rooftops. At that time he saw himself surrounded by the careful silence of most of the fine people who are so excited today, saw himself criticized, by the same papers that shout so loudly today, as a prejudiced fanatic, saw himself accused of infringing the law of Christian love with his speeches, and of endangering Swiss neutrality. The situation ten years ago was wonderfully simple: with a good conscience and clear understanding one could *only* say "No" and it only needed a bit of intrepidity really to say "No." It was good that the church, or at any rate one or two voices in the church, really did say this simple "No" at that time.

And so everybody is rushing about today crying that the same "No" must be said again, with the same intonation, by the church, or at least by those in the church who spoke out ten years ago, against the East, against Soviet Russia and the satellite "peoples' democracies." As if such simple repetitions ever occurred in history! And as if the church were an automatic machine producing the same goods today as yesterday as soon as you put your penny in the slot! It may be remembered, however, that people became receptive to these same goods at that time only very hesitantly, slowly and after much resistance! In all friendliness I must say that the whole campaign really is a feverish agitation. Ten years ago we said that the church *is*, and *remains*, the church, and must not therefore keep an un-Christian silence. Today we say that the church is, and *remains*, the church, and must not therefore speak an un-Christian word. We have reason to say precisely that today and for the same reason as ten years ago.

Red is just as bad as brown; one totalitarianism is as bad as another — so what! this is what people are crying out at us today. Now at least none of the many contemporaries and fellow-Christians are justified in joining in this cry who were rather glad to see brown at one time because brown was so much against red: none of those, that is, who thought the good thing about National Socialism was that it seemed to form such a strong dam against communism. Neither are those entitled to join in — and certain circles in the Allied Military Governments in Germany seem to belong to them — who consider it right to play off the newly awakened nationalistic instincts of the Germans against the Russians. Neither are any of those entitled to join in who do not find anything amiss in the fact that the West has so far not hurt a hair of the head of the Spanish dictator Franco, but that it is by no means averse to including this totalitarianism, of which the Spanish Protestants can tell us a good deal, in the planning of its future eastern front. And why was so remarkably little said here when shortly before Christmas last the Dutch with whom, generally speaking, we have so much in common, attacked their

Indonesians with a *Blitzkrieg* which inevitably reminded one to a quite remarkable degree of certain proceedings in May 1940? This is what we want to ask: is it *really* totalitarianism and its methods which we are being called upon to fight? For if that is really a *Christian* call to battle, then it ought to be directed against every totalitarian system. The battle-cry which we are being asked to join today is, in fact, not a Christian battle-cry because it is only directed against the East. It is, in a word, not quite honest. Therefore we must refuse to make it our own.

If we compare Russian communism with the National Socialism of ten years ago, quite calmly, we shall see that at any rate the Christian church has no cause to repeat itself quite so simply as is so much desired, in its attitude to the Russian communist East. One can have much on one's heart and say much too against the East on account of its totalitarianism and its methods. All that Asiatic despotism, cunning and ruthlessness in the Near and Far East, and especially in Russia, has been and has meant from time immemorial, has certainly become abominably and horrifyingly aggressive today in the guise of Russian communism, and we are terribly conscious of it. In the past we have probably not taken sufficient notice of the fact that that kind of thing has always been active — even eithout communism — in that part of the world. Our memory of the atrocities of the French Revolution (on the "achievements" of which, incidentally, our whole Western system is based) and of the atrocities of the preceding allegedly Christian era in Europe (including certain outrages committed by the old Swiss!) is also not as lively as it might be. Those atrocities are no excuse for the disgusting methods of the East today. We are right to be indignant. But if we have learned to discriminate by taking a glance at the French Revolution and at our so-called "Christian era," if, as I hope, we do not condemn the Asiatic world outright simply because some form or other of despotism has always been, and very largely still is, the accepted form of public life, then it is pertinent not to omit to *discriminate* in our view of contemporary communism between its totalitarian atrocities as such and the positive intention behind them. And if one tries to do that, one cannot say of communism what one was forced to say of Nazism ten years ago — that what it means and intends is pure unreason, the product of madness and crime. It would be quite absurd to mention in the same breath the philosophy of Marxism and the "ideology" of the Third Reich, to mention a man of the stature of Joseph Stalin in the same breath as such charlatans as Hitler, Göring, Hess, Goebbels, Himmler, Ribbentrop, Rosenberg, Streicher, etc. What has been tackled in Soviet

Russia — albeit with very dirty and bloody hands and in a way that rightly shocks us — is, after all, a constructive idea, the solution of a problem which is a serious and burning problem for us as well, and which we with our clean hands have not yet tackled anything like energetically enough: the *social* problem.

Our Western "No" to the solution of this question in Russia could only be a *Christian* "No" if we had a better conscience with regard to what we mean and intend with our Western freedom, if we, too, were attempting a more humane but no less energetic solution to this problem. As long as one cannot say that of that West — with all due recognition of the good intentions of the British Labour Party for example — as long as there is still a "freedom" in the West to organize economic crises, a "freedom" to dump our corn into the sea here whilst people are starving there, so long as these things can happen, we Christians, at any rate, must refuse to hurl an absolute "No" at the East. We are not wrong to accuse the East of inhumanity in its methods. But do not let us forget that the East, as we have already heard, also accuses us of inhumanity, the inhumanity of our intentions, and charges us with a mode of thinking and feeling basically corrupted by our appalling respect for material values; charges us not only with hard deeds, but also with hard-heartedness. So long as the East can do that even with the slightest semblance of truth — and there is indeed more than a semblance of truth in these charges — we have, at any rate seeing and judging the matter as Christians, reason to regard and to treat the very existence of the charges as a thorn in our flesh, of which no noisy declamations against the wrongs of the East can rid us.

The other important difference as compared with the situation ten years ago is this: the cause of the Russian communist East is doubtless a decidedly *godless* business: the cause of a false belief in accordance with which Christianity is seen and treated as an inconvenience from a pedagogical-tactical standpoint: tolerated for the moment, but in the expectation that in the process of development, that is, with the dawn of the great kingdom of socialist justice, it will vanish of its own accord, which does not, of course, exclude the possibility of a little coaxing if necessary. But please note that, in its relationship to Christianity, communism, as distinguished from Nazism, has not done, and by its very nature cannot do, one thing: it has never made the slightest attempt to reinterpret or to falsify Christianity, or to shroud itself in a Christian garment. It has never committed the basic crime of the Nazis, the removal and replacement of the real Christ by a national Jesus, and it has never committed the crime of *anti-Semitism*. There is nothing of the false prophet about it. It is not anti-Christian. It is coldly non-Christian. It does not seem to have encountered the gospel as yet. It is brutally, but at least honestly, godless. What should the church do? Protest? Join in a general Eastern front as the representative of the special interests of the Divine? This is the first I have heard of its being the duty of Christendom to react against the oppressions and persecutions perpetrated by the godless with protests and a summons to political warfare. Something quite different is required here, namely the "patience and faith of the saints," joyful perseverance and fearless profession. If the church achieves that, it stands on a rock; it can laugh at the whole godless movement, and whether they hear it or not — one day they will hear it — it has something positive to say to the godless. In fact, if it has the gospel to confess, it has not merely the philosophy and morality of the West, not a religious disguise in the place of real life, not a mere injunction to escape into the inner life of the spirit or into heaven, no imaginary, but the living God and his Kingdom, the crucified and risen Jesus Christ as the Lord and Savior of the whole human being. Therefore, not that which the East, in returning the accusations of the West, can call a false belief! Is there no truth at all in the East's counter-accusation? We shall not dismiss it merely by reproaching those in the East for their false belief. We are being asked about our own faith: where, then, is the Christian West that could look straight into the eyes of the obviously un-Christian East even with a modicum of good conscience? Whence has the East derived its godlessness if not from the West, from our philosophy? Is its cold non-Christianity something so completely different from the wisdom that is allowed to swagger about even here in the West in every street and in every newspaper and (naturally toned down a little) even in our churches to a very large extent? *Whence* does it draw its sustenance, this non-Christianity, if not from the offence that has been given to it by the fragility of Orthodox, of Roman and of Protestant Christianity? And are we Christians in the West being asked not to notice that, or to act as though we had not noticed it? Where is our justification for talking about a "Christian West" and all of a sudden wanting to come to the aid of this "Christian West" with a summons to an intellectual, political and one day even a military crusade? What fools or hypocrites we should have to be to stoop to that!

Against the false belief of the East, only the true, the clear, Christian faith can hold its ground. If we fail to participate in it completely afresh, then we shall also lack its steadfastness. But it is precisely this Christian steadfastness which will have nothing to do with a partisan attitude to the East, with the agitation, the propaganda and other machinations which such partisanship involves, with any kind of crusade in fact. Not a crusade but the Word of the Cross is what the church in the West owes to the godless East, but above all to the West itself, the Word through which the church itself must allow itself to be rebuilt completely afresh.

The third important difference between today and the situation ten years ago is this: so far no one has told us in what the desired Christian attitude against the East is really to consist. In a kind of new *confession*, like that of Barmen in 1934? But the church declares confessions when it has to defend itself against a temptation. But for which of us is communism a temptation? Or should it consist in a call to *prayer* for the destruction of the bulwarks of the false prophet, such as we made in 1938? But communism is not even a false prophecy, and if it were, then we should have to pray in the same breath for the destruction of the bulwarks of the Western Anti-Christ as well. No, in actual practice, what is demanded of the church in the way of a partisan attitude to the East-West conflict could consist, in great contrast to the earlier episode of the Nazi period, merely in cheap, idle and useless talk: *cheap* because it needs no kind of intellectual effort and demands no self-sacrifice today, to keep on repeating here in the security of the West what we all have it in our hearts to say against Eastern communism — *idle*, because the profoundly unsatisfactory nature of the whole Eastern set-up is so obvious that it is really not worth while repeating again in Christian terms what is being said *ad nauseam* in every newspaper in secular terms — and *useless*, because with such protests we definitely make not the slightest impression on the wild man of the East and would be helping no single man or woman suffering out there under the wild man, and because such partisanship is the last thing that the Christian churches in the East expect of us. If the worst were to come to the worst again, as happened ten years ago, then we should see who would then be standing in the front ranks: those who are calling for some kind of "definite" word from the church or those who are of the opinion that our only political strength now lies in quietness and hope. Let me sum up: the partisanship of ten years ago was a matter of a good Christian-political *confession*. Today, if we were to become guilty of the kind of partisanship which is desired of us, it could only be a matter of merely dabbling in politics and expressing badly certain completely unclarified and imperfectly grounded *Western feelings*. The Christian-political confession today must consist precisely in the *renunciation* of such partisanship.

Only therein? No, not only therein! Just as Swiss neutrality is not merely something negative, not merely renunciation, but in so far as it is a genuine neutrality, a positive contribution to the life of the European community of nations: a contribution which, for all its modesty, has proved itself more solid and more valuable than the old League of Nations and the new U.N.O. put together. The church is freer in this matter than Switzerland, in that it is not pledged to any "eternal neutrality." It can, if need be, *take sides.* If, in contrast to the situation of ten years ago, it has reasons for not doing so, then this *"No"* is also a quite definite "Yes," just as Swiss neutrality is positive and affirmative and not merely negative.

This does not mean that the church is *uninterested* in political events today. It does not mean that its responsibility in the state and for a good state, the responsibility of the Christian community for the civil community, the connection between the justification which God alone can give and the law which we honor, love and should continuously confirm and protect, that all these things are suspended or should to a certain extent be allowed to rest. Everything that had to be said about this connection between the church and politics ten years ago is still absolutely valid today — and especially today.

But today it is not a question of struggle, but of *reconstruction.* That is the basic idea for which we Christians have to be responsible in the political world today. It is not easy to judge from here in what measure and to what purpose, serious, solid and promising reconstruction work is being carried on in the East. But let us see to it that all our thoughts are based on reconstruction in the West, at any rate! If we are concerned with reconstruction in the West, then we need have no fear of the East. If we are not concerned with that, then there may well be cause for anxiety! All these choruses of hate and anger, the Western just as much as the Eastern, are going to lead to further destruction — as if enough had not been destroyed already! The result is that the more important thing which should be happening on both sides — to remove the mutual fear — is being neglected. That is why we cannot join in these choruses of hate and anger. But we do not ignore the fact that something like reconstruction seems to be intended on both sides of the quarrel.

Both sides seem to be concerned with *"humanity,"* since each side accuses the other so violently of "inhumanity." In any case, it is striking that both sides make enormous use of the same words: democracy, freedom, justice and peace. Only the *justice* of which the East speaks still seems to be a long way from finding a right relationship to *freedom*. And the *freedom* of which the West speaks still seems to be a long way from finding a right relationship to *justice*. And the *peace* of which both sides speak, in all sincerity no doubt, is full of secret threats and the danger of war. The Christian church stands for reconstruction. It cannot therefore agree with one side and disagree with the other. It can only take both sides at their word. It believes in, and it proclaims, the justice of *God* which does not cancel out *human freedom* but establishes it in its inviolable dignity and sacredness. But it also believes in, and proclaims, the *freedom* of God, namely the majestic freedom of his grace which does not make *human justice* superfluous, but which in fact impetuously demands the rule of human justice. It believes in, and proclaims, the peace of *God*, which is beyond all understanding and therefore comprehends all human understanding, and keeps it intact, and which sees to it that we do not fall upon one another on the pretext of unreasonable reasonings, and which therefore cares for *human peace*. The Christian church can therefore stand neither against the West nor the East. It can only walk between the two — which only means that here in the West — may our brothers in the East do their share too — we must stand all the more *emphatically* for those things which might be overlooked and forgotten in the West, for those things, therefore, which it is necessary to say and to hear in the West. Its task must be to call people back to humanity, and that is its contribution to reconstruction. The church can only be the church in this particular time if it remains *free* to fulfil that task. It can only stand for *Europe*: not for a Europe controlled by the West or the East, but for a *free* Europe going its own way, a third way. A free church is perhaps the last chance for such a free Europe today.

Now both East and West seem to be concerned with something else besides, with faith. Both sides accuse each other of a false belief. Our beliefs seem hypocritical to the East and theirs seem demonic and godless to us in the West. Very well, we hear what both sides have to say, and as Christians we shall hardly be able to deny that there is something in what both of them say about each other.

What can be done about it? May I tell you a little story: in the summer of 1947 I sat in Berlin for a whole afternoon with a group of real, flesh-and-blood German communists: please believe me when I say I did sometimes contradict what they had to say! Towards the end of the discussion they complained vigorously enough in their own way about the attitude of the Western church. "Allow me to inform you of something in the Bible!" I said to them at the end, and recited to them these words from Ecclesiastes: "Be not righteous over much; neither make thyself over wise; why shouldst thou destroy thyself?" (adding that that could be truly said to the Western church as well!), and then continuing: "Be not over much wicked, neither be thou foolish; why shouldst thou die before thy time?" (adding that that might well be said against or rather for you men of the Eastern persuasion!). Curiously enough, these communists put up with this without a murmur and allowed it to be the final word in our discussion, and presumably to be recorded in the minutes too. I think that is precisely what the church must say to both sides today. It can only stand for the *right* faith, which has just as little to do with the hypocrisy, which might well be hidden behind our all too boastful Western justice and wisdom, as it has to do with the admittedly all too great godlessness of the Eastern persuasion. It stands for reconstruction. It can only take both sides at their word: both sides are, in fact, aiming at something like a right faith, if one disregards their mutual invective. What shall the church do? It must exercise itself in the *true faith* in order to be able to proclaim it to both sides with a good conscience. Here in the West — and may our brothers in the East do their part in this respect as well — it must say the more *urgently* that the truth of the faith which comes from the Lord in whom we believe cannot be sufficiently thoroughly cleansed of the Western hypocrisy and alienation from life which creep into our faith all too easily. Let the church in the West see to it that it keeps itself in and through the Word of God so that it may proclaim it first to the West and then to the East with a joyful conscience. If it stands and lives and speaks in *faith*, then it will be serving the cause of *reconstruction*.

So the church looks out over the conflict between East and West in which it now stands and suffers with the whole of humanity, but in which it can participate only believing, loving and hoping and thinking of the word of promise, the Word of God through the prophet Isaiah:

"In that day shall Israel be the third with Egypt and with Assyria, even a blessing in the midst of the land: whom the lord of Hosts shall bless, saying, Blessed be Egypt, my people, and Assyria the work of my hands, and Israel mine inheritance."[73]   *(AS: 127-146)*

*

ATOMIC WAR AS *STATUS CONFESSIONIS*

Those members of the Confessing Church like Martin Niemöller who opposed the re-arming of the Federal Republic of Germany as part of NATO protested particularly strongly against atomic weapons. The informal groups of this protest movement were called "kirchliche Bruderschaften" (church brotherhoods), and in March, 1958 they sent a petition with several hundred signatures to the Synod of the Evangelical Church in Germany. They challenged the Synod to declare that atomic war was a status confessionis[74] issue for the church, that the church's position was a categorical No to nuclear war, and that Christians may not participate in any way in preparations for atomic war. The petition produced a great debate in the church and the public press. A deeply divided Synod passed a general resolution against weapons of mass destruction and requested the end of atomic weapon research; but it did not adopt the position of the petition. Barth was invited to an autumn meeting of the Bruderschaften in Frankfurt. Unable to attend, he wrote a letter of support, dismissing the rumor that he disagreed theologically with the ten theses of the petition: "You may say to all and everyone that I am in agreement with these Theses (including the 10th![75]), as if I had written them myself. . . ." In fact, Barth himself was the author of the theses (KB, 431).

The text of the petition was printed in Junge Kirche *of March 10, 1958 and Barth's letter in its October 10, 1958 issue. The translations were published by John Howard Yoder in his* Karl Barth and the Problem of War;[76] *Yoder calls the conflict about nuclear weapons in Germany in the 1950's "the second German church struggle."[77]*

PETITION OF THE *BRUDERSCHAFTEN* ON ATOMIC WEAPONS (1958)

I. The Evangelical Church confesses that in Jesus Christ she finds "joyous liberation from the godless bonds of the world unto free, thankful service to his creatures" (Barmen Thesis 2). This *forbids* to her not only any approval of or collaboration in an atomic war and its preparation, but also her tacitly letting it happen. This awareness demands that in the obedience of faith . . . here as in every issue . . . we ourselves must take the first step to hold back the threatening destruction and to trust more in the reality of the Word of God than in the "realism" of political calculation. The first step is the act of *diakonia* which we, as Christians, owe to the menaced and anxious world of today. Let the faithless hesitate . . .; we as Christians may and must dare it in trust in God, who created this world and every living creature in East and West for the sake of the suffering and victorious Jesus Christ, and will preserve the same through Christ and the preaching of his Gospel until his day.

II. If the Synod finds itself unable to assent to this confession, we must ask how the Synod can refute it on the grounds of Scripture, the Confessions, and reason.

For the sake of the men and women for whom we are responsible, and for our own sakes, we must insist upon receiving an answer to this question. We owe it to the Synod to remind it of its spiritual responsibility, since it is in the shouldering of this responsibility that it shows itself to be the legitimate authority in the church. It is our conviction that in the face of this issue the church finds herself in the *status confessionis*.

If the Synod agrees with us, that an unreserved *No* is demanded of Christians facing the problem of the new weapons, must she not also say promptly and clearly to the state, that the true proclamation of the Gospel, also in the military chaplaincy, includes the testimony that the Christian may not and cannot participate in the design, testing, manufacture, stocking and use of atomic weapons, nor in training with these weapons?

III. We, therefore, ask the Synod whether she can affirm together with us the following ten propositions, for the instruction of consciences concerning Christian behavior with regard to atomic weapons:

1. War is the ultimate means, but always, in every form a questionable means, of resolving political tensions between nations.
2. For various reasons, good and less good, churches in all lands and all ages have hitherto not considered the preparation and the application of this ultimate means to be impossible.
3. The prospect of a future war to be waged with the use of modern means of annihilation has created a new situation, in the face of which the church *cannot* remain *neutral*.
4. War, in the form of *atomic war*, means the mutual annihilation of the participating peoples as well as of countless human beings of other peoples, which are not involved in the combat between the two adversaries.
5. War, in the form of atomic war, is therefore seen to be *an instrument incapable of being used* for the resolution of political conflicts, because it destroys every presupposition of political resolution.
6. Therefore, the church and the individual Christian can say nothing but an *a priori No* to a war with atomic weapons.

7. Even preparation for such a war is under all circumstances *sin against God and the neighbor,* for which no church and no Christian can accept responsibility.

8. We therefore demand in the name of the Gospel that an *immediate end be made* to preparations for such a war within our land and nation regardless of all other considerations.

9. We challenge all those who seriously want to be Christians to *renounce,* without reserve and under all circumstances, any participation in preparations for atomic war.

10. In the face of this question, the opposing point of view, or neutrality, *cannot be advocated* Christianly. Both mean the denial of all three articles of the Christian faith.

*

. . . It is perhaps also good if I am not there in person — among other reasons because the younger generation must learn to push more and more into the front lines and to fight the battles which must be waged on the practical-theological front, on the basis of their own insight and responsibility. . . . This, however, does not mean that I in any way withdraw from my preoccupation with the problems to be dealt with in Frankfurt. These problems have also become significant here in Switzerland in a very special way, and demand my daily attention. The West German *Bruderschaften,* having their origin in, and belonging together with, what happened 25 years ago, should be assured that I am with them wholeheartedly and stand behind them, always, but especially in the concern which disturbs them now, and that I shall continue to do so in the future all the more joyously, the more they continue the pathway upon which they have entered, free of all profundity and despair, clear and decided, uncompromisingly and consistently. What was the rumor spread about in Germany's newspapers, "that Professor Barth is not theologically in agreement with the Ten Theses of the Petition"? You may say to all and to everyone, that I am in agreement with these Theses (including the 10th!), as if I had written them myself, and that I desire nothing more earnestly than that they should be maintained and interpreted worthily, convincingly, and joyfully, but in principle unbendingly, in Frankfurt and thereafter in all the Evangelical Church in Germany.

5

"SOUNDING GOD'S GLORY"

MOZART

Mozart was Barth's favorite composer. He began each day with the music of Mozart, then read the daily newspaper, and only then worked on his Dogmatics. *"If I ever get to heaven," Barth wrote, "I would first of all seek out Mozart and only then inquire after Augustine, St. Thomas, Luther, Calvin and Schleiermacher" (M, 16). Barth loved Mozart because he could play, not merely frivolously, but as one who knows the center and essence of things. Barth loved Mozart because his music contained pain and joy, storm clouds and sunshine, tears and laughter. He "translated into music . . . real life in all its discord. But in defiance of that, and on the sure foundation of God's good creation, and because of that, he moves always from left to right, never the reverse" (M, 33f.). Barth loved Mozart because of his freedom, freedom from making his music serve some cause, whether didactic or confessional, and freedom from the composer's own subjectivity. Barth once said that Mozart's music was a parable of the kingdom of heaven; his understanding of Mozart is certainly a parable of his own theology. "It may be," Barth once wrote in a letter to Mozart in heaven, "that when the angels go about their task of praising God, they play only Bach. I am sure, however, that when they are together* en famille, *they play Mozart and that then too our dear Lord listens with special pleasure" (M, 23).*

The first text is from the Doctrine of Creation in Church Dogmatics *III/3, and the second is from the commemorative address on "Mozart's Freedom" in the collection of Barth's essays on Mozart,* Wolfgang Amadeus Mozart *(Foreword by John Updike[78]) published in 1986 in celebration of the 100th anniversary of the birth of Karl Barth.*

ON MOZART AND CREATION (1950)

I must again revert to Wolfgang Amadeus Mozart. Why is it that this man is so incomparable? Why is it that for the receptive, he has produced in almost every bar he conceived and composed a type of music for which "beautiful" is not a fitting epithet: music which for the righteous [*Gerechten*] is not mere entertainment, enjoyment or edification but food and drink; music full of comfort and counsel for their needs;

music which is never a slave to its technique nor sentimental but always "moving," free and liberating because wise, strong and sovereign? Why is it possible to hold that Mozart has a place in theology, especially in the doctrine of creation and also in eschatology, although he was not a father of the church, does not seem to have been a particularly active Christian, and was a Roman Catholic, apparently leading what might appear to us a rather frivolous existence when not occupied in his work? It is possible to give him this position because he knew something about creation in its total goodness that neither the real fathers of the church nor our Reformers, neither the orthodox nor liberals, neither the exponents of natural theology nor those heavily armed with the "Word of God," and certainly not the existentialists, nor indeed any other great musicians before and after him, either know or can express and maintain as he did. In this respect he was pure in heart, far transcending both optimists and pessimists. 1756-1791! This was the time when God was under attack for the Lisbon earthquake, and theologians and other well-meaning folk were hard put to it to defend him. In face of the problem of theodicy, Mozart had the peace of God which far transcends all the critical or speculative reason that praises and reproves. This problem lay behind him. Why then concern himself with it? He had heard, and causes those who have ears to hear, even today, what we shall not see until the end of time — the whole context of providence. As though in the light of this end, he heard the harmony of creation to which the shadow also belongs but in which the shadow is not darkness, deficiency is not defeat, sadness cannot become despair, trouble cannot degenerate into tragedy and infinite melancholy is not ultimately forced to claim undisputed sway. Thus the cheerfulness in this harmony is not without its limits. But the light shines all the more brightly because it breaks forth from the shadow. The sweetness is also bitter and cannot therefore cloy. Life does not fear death but knows it well. *Et lux perpetua lucet* (sic!) *eis* — even the dead of Lisbon. Mozart saw this light no more than we do, but he heard the whole world of creation enveloped by this light. Hence it was fundamentally in order that he should not hear a middle or neutral note, but the positive far more strongly than the negative. He heard the negative only in and with the positive. Yet in their inequality he heard them both together, as, for example, in the Symphony in G-minor of 1788. He never heard only the one in abstraction. He heard concretely, and therefore his compositions were and are total music. Hearing creation unresentfully and impartially, he did not produce merely his own music but that of creation, its twofold and yet harmonious praise of God. He neither needed nor desired to express or represent himself, his vitality, sorrow, piety, or any program. He was remarkably free from the mania for self-expression. He simply offered himself as the agent by which little bits of horn, metal and catgut could serve as the voices of creation, sometimes leading, sometimes accompanying and sometimes in harmony. He made use of instruments ranging from the piano and violin, through the horn and the clarinet, down to the venerable bassoon, with the human voice somewhere among them, having no special claim to distinction yet distinguished for this very reason. He drew music from them all, expressing even human emotions in the service of this music, and not *vice versa*. He himself was only an ear for this music, and its mediator to other ears. He died when according to the worldly wise his life-work was only ripening to its true fulfilment. But who shall say that after "The Magic Flute," the Clarinet Concerto of October 1791 and the Requiem, it was not already fulfilled? Was not the whole of his achievement implicit in his works at the age of 16 or 18? Is it not heard in what has come down to us from the very young Mozart? He died in misery like an "unknown soldier," and in company with Calvin, and Moses in the Bible, he has no known grave. But what does this matter? What does a grave matter when a life is permitted simply and unpretentiously, and therefore serenely, authentically and impressively, to express the good creation of God, which also includes the limitation and end of humanity. *(CD: III/3, 297-299)*

*

FROM "MOZART'S FREEDOM"

One more thing must be noted and said. The Mozartean "center" is not like that of the great theologian Schleiermacher — a matter of balance, neutrality, and, finally, indifference. What occurs in Mozart is rather a glorious upsetting of the balance, a *turning* in which the light rises and the shadows fall, though without disappearing, in which joy overtakes sorrow without extinguishing it, in which the Yea rings louder than the ever-present Nay. Note the *reversal* of the great dark and the small light episodes in Mozart's life! At the conclusion of *The Magic Flute* we hear, "The rays of the sun *drive out* the night." The play can and must go on, or begin all over again. At some level, high or low, it is a contest to be won; actually it is already won. This fact gives it its direction and character. We will never hear in Mozart an equilibrium of forces and a consequent uncertainty and doubt. This is as true of his operas as of his instrumental music and especially so of his sacred works. In the latter, does not every *Kyrie*, every *Miserere*, no matter how darkly foreboding its beginning, sound as if borne upward by the trust that the plea for mercy was granted long ago? *Benedictus qui venit in nomine Domine!* In Mozart's version he evidently has already come. *Dona nobis pacem!* — a prayer, but a prayer already answered. This feature is enough to mark Mozart's church music as truly sacred, all objections notwithstanding. Mozart never lamented, never quarrelled, though he certainly was entitled to. Instead, he always achieved this consoling turn, which for everyone who hears it is priceless. And that seems to me, insofar as one can say it at all, to be the secret of his *freedom* and with it the essence of Mozart's *special quality* which engaged our attention at the beginning.   *(M: 55-56)*

325

SELECT BIBLIOGRAPHY

BIBLIOGRAPHIES

Kwiran, Manfred. *Index to Literature on Barth, Bonhoeffer and Bultmann.* Basel: Friedrich Reinhardt Verlag, 1977 (*Theologische Zeitschrift,* Sonderband VII). An index by author and subject to 2823 items of secondary literature on Barth including books, articles, dissertations and book reviews.

Wildi, Hans Markus. *Bibliographie Karl Barth.* Zürich: Theologischer Verlag, 1984. (This publisher plans a parallel volume on secondary literature which will supersede the Kwiran above.)

PRIMARY SOURCES

Ad Limina Apostolorum. An Appraisal of Vatican II. Richmond, Virginia: John Knox, 1968

Against the Stream. Shorter Post-War Writings 1946-52 (ed. Ronald Gregor Smith). London: SCM; New York: Philosophical Library, 1954

Anselm: Fides Quaerens Intellectum. London: SCM; Richmond, Virginia: John Knox, 1960 (reprinted by Pickwick Press, Pittsburgh, 1975); Cleveland: World, 1962

Church Dogmatics. Edinburgh: T. & T. Clark. Vols. I/1 (1936) -IV/3.ii (1962); see also IV/4, The Doctrine of Reconciliation (Fragment) published by Clark in 1969, and *The Christian Life. Church Dogmatics IV/4, Lecture Fragments* published by Eerdmans in 1981; see also *Church Dogmatics. Index Volume.* Edinburgh: T. & T. Clark, 1977

Community, State and Church. Garden City, New York: Doubleday, 1960. Reprinted by Peter Smith, Gloucester, Massachusetts, 1968

Deliverance to the Captives. New York: Harper & Brothers, 1961

Ethics. New York: Seabury, 1981

Evangelical Theology. An Introduction. New York: Holt, Rinehart and Winston; London: Weidenfeld & Nicholson, 1963

Final Testimonies. Grand Rapids, Michigan: Eerdmans, 1977

How to Serve God in a Marxist Land (with Johannes Hamel). New York: Association, 1959

Letters 1961-1968 (ed. Jürgen Fangmeier and Hinrich Stoevesandt). Grand Rapids, Michigan: Eerdmans, 1981

"No! Answer to Emil Brunner" in Emil Brunner and Karl Barth, *Natural Theology*. London: Centenary, 1946; reprinted by University Microfilms International, Ann Arbor, Michigan and London, 1979

Protestant Theology in the Nineteenth Century. London: SCM, 1972; Valley Forge: Judson, 1973. (Eleven chapters of this complete edn. were published as *From Rousseau to Ritschl* (London: SCM, 1959) and as *Protestant Thought from Rousseau to Ritschl* (New York: Harper & Brothers, 1959; reprinted by Ayer Publishing Co. 1971, 1987)

"Rudolf Bultmann: An Attempt to Understand Him" in *Kerygma and Myth* II, ed. H. W. Bartsch. London: SPCK, 1962

The Epistle to the Romans. London: Oxford, 1933

The German Church Conflict. London: Lutterworth; Richmond, Virginia: John Knox, 1965

The Humanity of God. London: Collins, 1961. Title essay also in *God, Grace and Gospel.* Edinburgh: Oliver and Boyd, 1959

The Teaching of the Church regarding Baptism. London: SCM, 1948

The Word of God and the Word of Man. London: Hodder and Stoughton, 1928; New York: Harper and Row, 1957

Theological Existence Today. London: Hodder & Stoughton, 1933. Reprinted by American Theological Library Association, 1962

Theology and Church. Shorter Writings 1920-1928. London: SCM; New York: Harper & Row, 1962

Wolfgang Amadeus Mozart. Foreword by John Updike. Grand Rapids, Michigan: Eerdmans, 1986

SECONDARY SOURCES

Berkouwer, G. C. *The Triumph of Grace in the Theology of Karl Barth.* London: Paternoster, 1956

Bromiley, Geoffrey W. *An Introduction to the Theology of Karl Barth.* Grand Rapids, Michigan: Eerdmans, 1979

Busch, Eberhard. *Karl Barth. His life from letters and autobiographical texts.* Philadelphia: Fortress, 1976

Casalis, Georges. *Portrait of Karl Barth.* Garden City, New York: Doubleday, 1963

Frei, Hans. W. *The Doctrine of Revelation in the Thought of Karl Barth, 1909 to 1922.* Ph.D. dissertation, Yale University, 1956

Frei, Hans W. "Niebuhr's Theological Background" in Paul Ramsey ed., *Faith and Ethics: The Theology of H. Richard Niebuhr.* New York: Harper & Row, 1957

Gollwitzer, Helmut ed. *Karl Barth: Church Dogmatics. A Selection.* Edinburgh: T. & T. Clark, 1961; New York: Harper & Row, 1962

Hunsinger, George ed. *Karl Barth and Radical Politics.* Philadelphia: Westminster, 1976

Jüngel, Eberhard. *Karl Barth, a Theological Legacy.* Philadelphia: Westminster, 1986

Küng, Hans. *Justification. The Doctrine of Karl Barth and a Catholic Reflection.* (Includes response by Karl Barth.) Philadelphia: Westminster, 2nd edn., 1981

Rumscheidt, H. Martin ed. *Karl Barth in Re-view. Posthumous Works Reviewed and Assessed.* Pittsburgh: Pickwick Press, 1981

Villa-Vincencio, Charles ed. *On Reading Karl Barth in South Africa.* Grand Rapids, Michigan: Eerdmans, 1988

Sykes, Stephen W. ed. *Karl Barth. Studies of his Theological Method.* Oxford: Clarendon; New York: Oxford, 1979

von Balthasar, Hans Urs. *The Theology of Karl Barth.* New York: Holt, Rinehart and Winston, 1971; Garden City, New York: Doubleday, 1972

Weber, Otto. *Karl Barth's Church Dogmatics. An Introductory Report.* Philadelphia: Westminster, 1953

NOTES TO THE INTRODUCTION

[1] Typical of Barth, this Mozart essay was entitled "Mozart's Freedom"; cf. M, 43ff.

[2] Barth, *How I Changed My Mind* (Richmond: John Knox, 1966), 79.

[3] See, for example, "The Gift of Freedom" in HG, esp. 76ff.

[4] GS I, 19 translated in Bethge, *Dietrich Bonhoeffer*, (New York: Harper, 1970), 132; translation revised by H. M. Rumscheidt in *Karl Barth in Re-View* (Pittsburgh: Pickwick Press, 1981), xxviii.

[5] Eberhard Busch, "Introduction" to *Karl Barth in Re-View*, ed. H. Martin Rumscheidt, xxiii.

[6] In his Foreword to Barth, *Wolfgang Amadeus Mozart* (Grand Rapids: William B. Eerdmans, 1986), 7.

[7] The biographical material which follows is heavily indebted to Eberhard Busch, *Karl Barth. His life from letters and autobiographical texts* (Philadelphia: Fortress Press, 1976).

[8] Cf. Hunsinger's discussion of this article: RP, 198f.

[9] It is important to note that for Barth "the *essence* or the content of socialism must be identified as justice for humanity, and not merely as improvement of the lot of the working class"; summarized by Eberhard Jüngel, from an unpublished 1915 manuscript in the Barth archive, in *Karl Barth. A Theological Legacy* (Philadelphia: Westminster, 1986), 89.

[10] *The Word of God and the Word of Man* (London: Hodder and Stoughton, 1928), 18.

[11] Cited by Gollwitzer in RP, 119 n. 39; see the discussion of the context of this remark in Jüngel, *Karl Barth. A Theological Legacy*, 96ff., esp. 100.

[12] As Hunsinger points out, this was the party of Lenin during his Swiss exile, and was "the most radical organized political movement of the day" (RP, 194). Barth joined to show his solidarity, notwithstanding his sharp public criticisms of the party.

[13] See the dispute between Hüssy and Barth in RP 37-45, and between Barth and Hochuli in KB 88, 104, 107.

[14] Jüngel, *Karl Barth. A Theological Legacy* (Philadelphia: Westminster, 1986), 89.

[15] KB, 79; translation altered. For Barth's relation to and break from Religious Socialism, see Busch, KB, and George Hunsinger, "Toward a Radical Barth," RP, esp. 209ff.

[16] I use "*neo*-Protestant" to differentiate from the Reformation tradition the form of modern Protestantism of which Barth was so critical, as in this passage. Note also that Barth's term "evangelical," as used in this passage, is roughly equivalent to the common English use of "protestant"; it does not refer to the conservative wing of Protestantism, as frequently in America.

[17] Barth's biographer quotes Friedrich Naumann: "All religion is right for us . . . whether it is called the Salvation Army or Islam, provided that it helps us to hold out through the war" (KB, 84).

329

[18] See Hunsinger's "Toward a Radical Barth" (1976) RP, 181-227 and Jüngel's "Barth's Theological Beginnings" (1982) in his *Karl Barth. A Theological Legacy* (Philadelphia: Westminster, 1986). Frei's 1956 Yale Ph.D. dissertation is entitled *The Doctrine of Revelation in the Thought of Karl Barth, 1909 to 1922: The Nature of Barth's Break with Liberalism.* Marquardt's work is *Theologie und Sozialismus: Das Beispeil Karl Barths* (Munich: Chr. Kaiser, 1972); Barth's socialism is discussed below.

[19] See the essay with this title in the collection of Barth's early writings, *The Word of God and the Word of Man* (London: Hodder and Stoughton, 1928).

[20] Comparisons of the two editions can be found in KB 92ff., 117ff., and RP 207ff.

[21] Cf. Donald K. McKim ed., *How Karl Barth Changed My Mind* (Grand Rapids: William B. Eerdmans, 1986), ix, n. 1.

[22] The Bultmann volume of this series, *Rudolf Bultmann. Interpreting Faith for the Modern Era,* by Roger A. Johnson, contains his review of the second edition of Barth's *Romans.*

[23] See the critical article on Barth which Tillich wrote shortly after he came to the United States: "What is Wrong with the 'Dialectic' Theology?" *Journal of Religion* XV.2 (April, 1935), 127-45. It is reprinted in the Tillich volume of this series, ed. Mark K. Taylor. While Tillich said that Barth's greatest quality was his freedom not to be his own disciple, Barth said in 1960 "that Tillich (like Niebuhr) still thought of him 'as though I had been asleep since 1920' " (KB, 437). The article documents this point, still quoting *Romans* in 1935 and ignoring *Church Dogmatics* I/1 which had been published for three years; further, ignoring the Anselm book and the importance of analogy in the *Dogmatics,* Tillich read Barth as a "supernaturalist."

[24] *Prolegomena zur Christlichen Dogmatik. Die Lehre vom Worte Gottes* (Munich: Christian Kaiser, 1927); the work has not been translated into English.

[25] Barth, *Ethics,* ed. Dietrich Braun (New York: Seabury Press, 1981).

[26] CD III/4, 116ff. In fact, Busch definitely asserts her influence, and reports several of her own lectures on the subject (KB, 363). See also Clifford Green, "Liberation Theology? Karl Barth on Women and Men", *Union Seminary Quarterly Review* XXIX.3 & 4 (Spring & Summer, 1974), 221-31.

[27] Barth, *How I Changed My Mind* (Richmond: John Knox Press, 1966; Edinburgh: St. Andrews Press, 1969), 42f.

[28] See George Hunsinger's excellent commentary on the contribution of Barth's Anselm book to his theological development (RP, 220ff.) and its conceptual connection to Barth's socialism.

[29] Barth, *How I Changed My Mind,* 43.

[30] "The Ant and the Emperor," in Donald K. McKim ed., *How Karl Barth Changed My Mind* (Grand Rapids: Eerdmans, 1986), 44.

[31] Two important contemporaneous pieces are *Theological Existence Today,* subtitled "A Plea for Theological Freedom" (London: Hodder and Stoughton, 1933; reprinted 1962 by the American Theological Library Association) and "The First Commandment as a Theological Axiom" in H. Martin Rumscheidt ed., *The Way of Theology in Karl Barth* (Allison Park, PA: Pickwick Publications, 1986).

[32] See the two volumes of sermons: *Deliverance to the Captives* (London: SCM; New York: Harper & Row, 1961) and *Call for God* (same publishers, 1967).

[33] Barth felt that the role of the Bultmann school (as distinct from Bultmann himself) in theology was part of a general reactionary movement in politics (Adenauer), the church and church politics in the Federal Republic (KB, 448f.).

[34] The English translation appeared in 1936; a second edition with a revised translation was published in 1975.

[35] Cf. CD I/2, par. 17, sec. 2, "Religion as Unbelief." The translation of this paragraph heading, "The Revelation of God as the Abolition [*Aufhebung*] of Religion," while it catches the point of unbelief, is nevertheless misleading; it could more accurately be paraphrased as "the revelation of God as the death and resurrection of religion."

[36] From "The Guiding Principles of the Faith Movement of the 'German Christians'," June 6, 1932; cited in Arthur C. Cochrane, *The Church's Confession under Hitler* (Philadelphia: Westminster, 1962), 222.

[37] Pastor Leutheuser, August 30, 1933; cited in J. S. Conway, *The Nazi Persecution of the Churches* (New York: Basic Books, 1968), 48.

[38] Reich Bishop Müller, cited in Conway, *loc. cit.*

[39] A clear allusion to Hitler's *Mein Kampf.*

[40] Cited in G. L. Mosse, *Nazi Culture* (New York: Grosset & Dunlap, 1966), 241f.

[41] The crucial difference is that the humanity of Jesus is true humanity, whereas in the Bible and the church humanity is marred by sin; hence the priority and sequence mentioned in the next paragraph.

[42] *Die Lehre vom Worte Gottes. Prolegomena zur christlichen Dogmatik* (Munich: Christian Kaiser, 1927), 63. This volume was a start at a dogmatics, *Die Christliche Dogmatik im Entwurf,* but only this first volume was written and the project was superseded by the *Kirchliche Dogmatik* in 1932.

[43] See also Barth's introduction to Arthur Frey, *Cross and Swastika* (London: SCM, 1938), esp. 19f. "Where would the confessing Christians . . . have been, where would the Confessing Church have been if God's Word had not entered the field in the Germany of these years, if it had not itself carried out its gracious work among men?" See also KB, 235ff.

[44] Cf. Rolf Ahlers, *The Barmen Theological Declaration of 1934* (Lewiston, NY: Edwin Mellen Press, 1986), 40, 184 n. 21, 225 n. 22.

[45] Barth's paradigm for the relation of divine and human in these "signs" is the doctrine of the two natures of Christ as classically expressed in the Chalcedonian Decree (451).

[46] See George Hunsinger's translation of Barth's essay, "Fate and Idea in Theology," in H. Martin Rumscheidt ed., *The Way of Theology in Karl Barth* (Allison Park, PA: Pickwick Publications, 1986), 32, 38f.

[47] The important study, *The Theology of Karl Barth,* by the Catholic theologian Hans Urs von Balthasar (New York: Holt, Rinehart and Winston, 1971) focuses on the concept of analogy, and criticizes Barth's interpretation of the doctrine of analogy in Thomas Aquinas.

[48] This alone ought to give pause to those who charge Barth with "christo-monism."

[49] See Barth, *God, Grace and Gospel* (Edinburgh: Oliver & Boyd, 1959), 10; another translation is found in Barth, *Community, State and Church* (Garden City, NY: Doubleday, 1960).

[50] Cf. E. R. Hardy ed., *Christology of the Later Fathers* (Philadelphia: Westminster, 1954), 372.

[51] See his *Creation and Fall* (New York: Macmillan, 1965), esp. 37f. where Bonhoeffer writes that the analogy to God in the *imago* is not *analogia entis* but *analogia relationis*.

[52] These sentences are a brief version of the two theses of Pars. 58 and 59 at the beginning of the Doctrine of Reconciliation, CD IV/1.

[53] See CD I/2, Par. 15, "The Mystery of Revelation." See also the distinction in Bonhoeffer, *Christology* (London: Collins, San Francisco: Harper & Row, 1978, as *Christ the Center*) between the proper "who question" and the improper "how question."

[54] Paragraphs 60, 65 and 70; see Outline (above, 169).

[55] CD IV/2, 721, cited Gollwitzer RP, 89f.

[56] Deschner, "Karl Barth as Political Activist," *Union Seminary Quarterly Review* 28 (Fall, 1972), 55; cited by Hunsinger, RP, 227.

[57] Published in *God, Grace and Gospel* (Edinburgh: Oliver & Boyd, 1959) and in *Community, State and Church* (Garden City, New York: Doubleday, 1960).

[58] The title of Barth's 1953 lecture on "the foundation of evangelical ethics" published in *The Humanity of God* (London: Collins, 1961).

[59] See the essay "Justification and Justice," in *Community, State and Church*.

[60] Mark 10.32-35.

[61] It is typical of Barth to root tyrannicide and "just defense" in God's judgment enclosed by God's mercy, rather than in a theory of natural rights; among other things, this is his way of protecting against the practical abuses of "just war" teaching.

[62] Munich: Christian Kaiser; 3rd edn., 1980.

[63] The best place to enter the debate is George Hunsinger, *Karl Barth and Radical Politics* (Philadelphia: Westminster, 1976), which hopefully will be reprinted. it contains a summary essay by Marquardt, "Socialism in the Theology of Karl Barth," and a very judicious assessment of Marquardt, both appreciative and critical, by Hunsinger.

[64] Barth had been critical of Bolshevist socialism ever since the Russian revolution and its aftermath, as was evident in the treatment of Romans 13 in the second edition of his commentary, the version translated into English.

[65] Cited by Hunsinger (RP, 231, n. 84) from John Deschner (quoting interview of Margareta Deschner with Barth), "Karl Barth as Political Activist," *Union Seminary Quarterly Review* 28 (Fall, 1972), 56; see also Hunsinger's statement that Barth's "theoretical grounding for his socialist praxis was strictly theological" (RP, 202).

[66] Compare Barth's treatment of God's revolution in his *Romans*, where Rom. 12.21-13.7 is discussed under "The Great Negative Possibility."

[67] Cited by Gollwitzer in RP, 99f. Cf. Karl Barth, *Letters 1961-1968* (Grand Rapids: William B. Eerdmans, 1981), 251. This is a more comprehensive summary by Barth than the remark about his "very limited interest in

socialism," the point of which was to stress the *practical* nature of his early work with trade unions rather than a theoretical interest in "socialist principles and ideology" (KB, 104).

[68] See Gollwitzer, RP 79f., 85.

[69] The essays in *Wolfgang Amadeus Mozart* translated to celebrate the 100th anniversary of Barth's birth were previously translated by Walter Mosse and contributed by Barth to the Tillich Festschrift, *Religion and Culture*, edited by Walter Leibrecht (London: SCM, 1959).

[70] Jüngel, *Karl Barth, a Theological Legacy* (Philadelphia: Westminster, 1986), 20f.

NOTES TO THE SELECTED TEXTS

[1] Barth has in mind Augustine's *Retractationes.*

[2] Here Barth is appropriating and interpreting the formula of the Council of Chalcedon (451) about the relation of the divine and human natures in Jesus Christ, and actually quotes key terms from the Council's decree; cf. 53.

[3] In his important essay "Gospel and Law," Barth was already speaking in 1935 of "God's own humanity" in Jesus Christ; cf. *God, Grace and Gospel*, Scottish Journal of Theology Occasional Papers No. 8 (Edinburgh: Oliver & Boyd, 1959), 5.

[4] Ed. note, CG: Hans Urs von Balthasar; see his *The Theology of Karl Barth* (New York: Holt, Rinehart & Winston, 1971).

[5] Ed. note, CG: The English words "superordination" and "subordination" do not convey Barth's meaning well. He is thinking of sequence in an order, of initiative and response; the model is dialogue in partnership, not dominance. Cf. also "The Christian Community and the Civil Community," above, 273f.

[6] See Barth's explanation in his Feuerbach essay, above, 95.

[7] Ed. note, CG: Psalm 8.4.

[8] Ed. note, CG: A method of studying biblical texts by examining their literary form and life situation as found in oral tradition.

[9] Ed. note, CG: In this paragraph Barth alludes to some famous phrases of Bonhoeffer in his letters beginning April 30, 1944, published in his *Letters and Papers from Prison.*

[10] Cf. CD I/1, 51.

[11] See Barth's "Rudolf Bultmann — An Attempt to Understand Him" in *Kerygma and Myth II*, ed. H. W. Bartsch (London: SPCK, 1962). Barth mentions below Bultmann's review of the second edition of his *Romans*; this is printed in Roger Johnson's volume in this series, *Rudolf Bultmann. Interpreting Faith for the Modern Era* (London: Collins, 1987).

[12] Translated by Louise Pettibone Smith, with an Introduction by T. F. Torrance (London: SCM; New York: Harper & Row), 1962.

[13] *From Rousseau to Ritschl* (London: SCM; New York: Harper & Brothers, 1959). *Protestant Theology in the Nineteenth Century* (London: SCM, 1972; Valley Forge: Judson Press, 1973).

[14] Ed. Dietrich Ritschl (Edinburgh: T. & T. Clark; Grand Rapids: William B. Eerdmans, 1982). An independent assessment of Barth's interpretation is found in Richard R. Niebuhr, "Karl Barth's 'Schleiermacher': a review essay," *Union Seminary Quarterly Review* 39.1-2 (1984), 129-36.

[15] Ed. note, GH: *Anfänge der dialektischen Theologie*, 2 vols., ed. by J. Moltmann (Munich: Chr. Kaiser Verlag, 1962; ET *The Beginnings of Dialectical Theology*, ed. James M. Robinson (Richmond, VA: John Knox Press, 1968). *"Dialektische Theologie" in Scheidung und Bewährung, 1933-1936* ed. by W. Fürst (Munich: Chr. Kaiser Verlag, 1966).

[16] Paul Seifert, *Die Theologie des jungen Schleiermacher* (Gütersloh: G. Mohn Verlag, 1960), 11.

[17] Ed. note, CG: God is not a member of a class (*genus*), i.e. God is singular, incomparable — the thought is related to Anselm's formula (see below, 144), that God is "that than which nothing greater can be conceived."

[18] Ed. note, CG: see note 9 above.

[19] Ed. note, CG: Rudolf Bultmann, "Karl Barth's *Epistle to the Romans* in its Second Edition," in James Robinson ed., *The Beginnings of Dialectical Theology*, 100 (translation slightly revised by GH); reprinted in Roger A. Johnson, *Rudolf Bultmann. Interpreting Faith for the Modern Era* (London: Collins, 1987).

[20] Barth, *Theology and Church*, trans. Louise Pettibone Smith (London: SCM; New York: Harper & Row), 1962, 217-37.

[21] See Barth's introductory essay to Ludwig Feuerbach, *The Essence of Christianity* (New York: Harper & Brothers, 1957), xxvi.

[22] New York: Harper, 1957.

[23] Ed. note, CG: Isaiah 9.2.

[24] See the Schleiermacher essay above, 71f.

[25] See Barth's complaints about being a victim of "hoary summations" and "hasty theological journalism" in his Foreword to the English edition of Otto Weber, *Karl Barth's Church Dogmatics* (Philadelphia: Westminster, 1953).

[26] KB, 121.

[27] Ed. note, CG: The hidden God, which Luther understood especially in the sense of I Cor. 1.18ff.

[28] Ed. note, CG: cf. Genesis 3.5.

[29] Ed. note, CG: Psalm 111.10.

[30] Ed. note, CG: Cf. Job 38.1, 40.6.

[31] Ed. note, CG: I Timothy 6.16.

[32] Here and elsewhere Hoskyns translates with "dissolution" Barth's *Aufhebung*. Hegel used this term, with its opposite popular meanings of destroy and preserve, in his dialectic. In Barth it means not only negation, dissolution, but also overcoming and transcending. Theologically Barth thinks of the logic of justification by grace, of the negation and affirmation in the gospel of cross and resurrection; cp. his discussion in CD I/2, Par. 16, "The Revelation of God as the *Aufhebung* of religion," where the German word is misleading if translated simply as "abolition."

[33] Ed. note, CG: cf. Matthew 27.51ff., Joshua 10.12.

[34] Ed. note, CG: Revelation 21.1.

[35] Here Barth quotes the well-known phrase of the 19th century German historian, Leopold von Ranke.

[36] Ed. note, CG: Mark 15.34.

[37] Perhaps the most famous quotation from the whole book has previously been mistranslated by omission of the word "infinite"!

[38] Ed. note, CG: John 20.29.

[39] Ed. note, CG: Mark 1.22, 3.21, John 7.12, Matthew 11.19.

[40] Ed. note, CG: Luke 2.14.

[41] Ed. note, CG: Luke 10.18.

[42] Matthew 11.5f.

[43] *Anselm* (Cleveland: World, 1962), "Preface to the second edition" [1958], 11.

[44] Barth, *How I Changed My Mind*, ed. John Godsey (Richmond: John Knox, 1966), 42f.; originally published in *The Christian Century*, (September, 1939).

[45] Ed. note, CG: translation follows M.J. Charlesworth, *St. Anselm's Proslogion* (London: Oxford University Press, 1965), 169.

[46] Ed. note, CG: translation follows Charlesworth, *op. cit.*, 103.

[47] The slogan of the German Christians was: "The Swastika on our breasts, and the Cross in our hearts."

[48] (Philadelphia: Westminster, 1962); see also John Conway, *The Nazi Persecution of the Churches, 1933-45* (New York: Basic Books, 1968) and Rolf Ahlers, *The Barmen Theological Declaration of 1934* (Lewiston, NY: Edwin Mellen Press, 1986).

[49] Ed. note, CG: The four allusions are to Hitler's seizure of power in 1933, the exalting of "blood and soil," Hitler himself, and the ideology of the *Volk*.

[50] Ed. note, DB: *Anordnung* (to be understood in the sense of the Latin *ordinatio*) as distinct from *Ordnung* (Lat. *ordo*, Eng. "order"), a critically important word in the orthodox German Lutheran theology of church and state.

[51] Barth, *Natural Theology* (London: Centenary Press, 1946), 101.

[52] Emanuel Hirsch was a German theologian, contemporary with Barth, described as a "Nazi intellectual" in Robert P. Ericksen's *Theologians Under Hitler* (New Haven: Yale University Press, 1985).

[53] *Catholica*, 1934, No. 3, 113ff.

[54] Edinburgh: T. & T. Clark, 1977. Edited by G. W. Bromiley and T. F. Torrance, this volume also contains almost 300 pages of excerpts from Barth commenting on particular Biblical texts set out as "Aids for the Preacher."

[55] Edinburgh: Oliver & Boyd; Richmond, VA: John Knox Press, 1963.

[56] *The Christian Life (Fragment). Baptism as the Foundation of the Christian Life*, (Edinburgh: T. & T. Clark, 1969).

[57] *The Christian Life. Church Dogmatics IV/4. Lecture Fragments.* Translated by G. W. Bromiley. Grand Rapids: Eerdmans, 1981.

[58] *Final Testimonies* (Grand Rapids: Eerdmans, 1977), 35f.

[59] Ed. note, CG: Cf. Luke 14.10.

[60] *Das Nichtige*, that which God has not willed or created or chosen; it has connotations of nothingness, non-being, evil; see III/3, "God and Nothingness."

[61] Here Barth rehearses the perfections of divine freedom (omnipresence, omnipotence, eternity) and divine love (wisdom, righteousness, holiness) which he has discussed in the Doctrine of God, II/1, pars. 30 and 31.

[62] CD III/2, Par. 44.

[63] Ed. note, CG: Derived from the Greek δοκέιν, to seem, docetism in Christology is the heresy that Jesus only seemed to be truly human, that his human, physical nature was apparent rather than real and not essential to his true being.

[64] Cf. on this point CD IV/1, Par. 62, 3.

[65] Cf. on this concept CD IV/1, 662-68.

[66] CD I/1, 3.

[67] This volume should not be confused with the part of IV/4 published by T. & T. Clark, Edinburgh, in 1969 containing the paragraph (75) on "Baptism as the Foundation of the Christian Life." Though a second title page is headed

"The Christian Life," the official title of the Clark volume is *Church Dogmatics* Volume IV, The Doctrine of Reconciliation, Part Four (Fragment).

[68] Karl Barth, *Community, State and Church*, edited and introduced by Will Herberg (Garden City, NY: Doubleday, 1960). This also contains "Church and State," a translation originally published by SCM Press in 1939 of Barth's *"Rechtfertigung und Recht"* [Justification and Justice, 1938], and "Gospel and Law"; another translation of *"Evangelium und Gesetz"* (1935; second, unaltered edition 1956) is found in Karl Barth, *God, Grace and Gospel* (Edinburgh: Oliver & Boyd; Richmond: John Knox, 1959), Scottish Journal of Theology Occasional Papers No. 8.

[69] A. de Quervain, *Kirche, Volk und Staat*, 1945, 158.

[70] Cf. O. Cullmann, *Königherrschaft Christi und Kirche im Neuen Testament*, 1941.

[71] Ed. note, CG: The AV and RSV translate "be subject" and the NEB uses "submit." Here, and elsewhere, Barth makes a basic distinction between *unterordnen*, in the sense of being responsible to an *order*, and *untertan*, with its connotation of subservience.

[72] Ed. note, CG: From Luther's hymn, "Ein feste Burg ist unser Gott."

[73] Ed. note, CG: Isaiah 19.24.

[74] *Status confessionis*, a situation requiring a confession of faith by the church, is one where the central affirmations of the gospel and thus the very existence of the church are at stake. Use of this phrase in 1958 deliberately recalled the situation of the Barmen Declaration in 1934. (Since World War II the two issues which have often been designated matters of *status confessionis* are nuclear weapons and apartheid.)

[75] This reportedly included in an earlier draft the sharp, explicit statement of excommunication, now only implied, that opposition to or neutrality about the theological-ethical position in the articles "excludes one from the communion of the Church Universal."

[76] Nashville: Abingdon, 1970.

[77] *Op. cit.*, p. 123.

[78] "Sounding God's Glory" is the title under which Updike's Foreword was republished in *Books and Religion* 14.3 (March, 1986).

BIBLICAL INDEX

SUBJECT INDEX

Abraham 194
Act 207ff., 216
Adam 163, 165
Africa 11
Analogia entis 27, 332
Analogia fidei 27
Analogia gratiae 27
Analogy 19, 26ff., 39, 51, 57, 63, 138, 141, 265, 281f., 289, 331
Anarchy 276, 283
Angels 20
Anthropocentrism (cf. religion) 21, 27, 48, 51, 60, 77, 79
Anthropology 91ff.
AntiChrist 27
Antinomianism 64
Anti-Semitism 25, 298, 314
Apologetics 93
Apostles 17, 182
Apostles' Creed 75
Asia 11
Atheism 101
Atomic weapons 20, 41, 319
Atonement 94, 138

Baptism 93, 160
Barmen Declaration 20, 24-26, 148ff., 172, 177, 268, 275, 296, 301, 315, 319, 331, 337
Barth,
  life 13-21
  pastor 13ff., 113
  personality 12f.
  professor 18-21
Basel 13, 20f., 72
Benefit 192ff.
Berlin 13, 68f., 82
Bible (see also Old Testament, New Testament, Scripture) 15f., 19, 23, 25f., 37, 48ff., 53, 59, 64, 77, 148, 176, 179
Bodiliness 90f.

Calling 88
Calvinism 95, 178
Capitalism 14, 42f., 98, 107ff., 307
Catholic theology 19
Chalcedon, Council of 22, 29f., 33f., 334
Chance 196, 211
Christian unity 39

Christliche Welt 13, 69, 71
Christocentrism 18, 20, 24, 28, 35, 46, 218, 254
Christological paradigm 29f., 33f., 200ff., 220, 250f.
Christology 29ff., 52, 54f., 88, 93ff., 200ff.
Church 30, 36ff., 60, 64, 82, 88, 104, 159f., 195, 197, 205ff., 234-54, 266-96, 302
Church Dogmatics 11, 16, 19ff., 28, 30, 35, 38, 46, 88, 115, 140, 170, 186, 252, 255
Church law 38
Church Struggle 172f., 177, 321
Class 37
Co-humanity 29f., 33, 66
Cold war 20, 37, 40, 297, 301-18
Collectivism 41, 276, 285
Commandment 61, 162, 193
Communism 11, 23, 40, 42, 300, 311f., 315
Communist Manifesto 110
Community 33, 36, 43, 54f., 59, 114, 195, 197, 205ff., 234ff., 265ff.
Confessing Church 26, 41, 148, 151, 178ff., 296, 319, 331
Confession of faith 65, 195, 202, 205f., 217, 266, 315
Congregation 65
Conscience 39
Covenant 36f., 53, 57, 59, 61f., 123, 182, 187ff., 205f., 225f., 235, 254
Covenant, internal basis of creation 32, 187ff.
Covenant-partner 57, 184, 189
Creation 28, 32f., 129, 135, 154, 159f., 205, 210, 322ff.
Creation as benefit 33, 191ff.
Creation, external basis of covenant 32, 187ff.
Creature 30, 32, 186ff., 194, 197, 231f.

Dahlem, Synod of 177
David 194
Death 97, 204, 217, 226, 244, 283
Democracy 275, 290f., 295, 308, 316
Demythologizing 75
Dialectical materialism 90
Dialectical theology 16, 17, 19, 44, 73, 78, 83, 115, 152

341

INDEX OF NAMES